Further praise for *A Re istory of the United States*

"Thaddeus Russell's *A Renegade History of The United States* is a work of history like no other—a bold, controversial, original view of American history that will amuse, inspire, outrage, and most of all instruct readers. Russell strips away conventional wisdom and explodes many myths. In the process, he sheds new light on ideas, institutions, and people." – Alan Brinkley, Allan Nevins Professor of History, Columbia University, and author of *The Publisher: Henry Luce and His American Century and American History: A Survey*

"Thaddeus Russell has broken free of the ideological prisons of Left and Right to give us a real, flesh-and-blood history of America, filled with untold stories and unlikely heroes . . . This wonderful book follows the best American traditions of iconoclasm and—what is the same thing—truth-telling." – Thomas E. Woods, Jr., author of *The Politically Incorrect Guide to American History*

"The book tells good stories, all in the cause of illuminating larger historical struggles between social control and freedom, repression and letting go . . . This is a controversial book, but certainly not a dull one." –Elliott Gorn, Brown University, Department of History

"This lively, contrarian work [is] . . . A sharp, lucid, entertaining view of the 'bad' American past." – *Kirkus Reviews*, starred review

"Howard Zinn wrote the 'People's History' of the United States. But Thaddeus Russell has written the history of the American People Whom Historians Would Rather Forget . . . There is no understanding of American feminism, sexual liberation, civil rights, or dancing in the streets without this careful analysis that Russell has put before us." –Susie Bright, syndicated columnist, author of *The Sexual State of the Union*

'A bracing read; equal parts revelation and provocation' –Phil Harrison, Book of the Week, *Time Out*

"Thaddeus Russell is a trouble-maker for sure. Whether you call his book courageous or outrageous, his helter-skelter tour through the American past will make you gasp and make you question—as he does—the writing of 'history as usual.'" – Nancy Cott, Jonathan Trumbull Professor of American History, Harvard University, and author of *Public Vows: A History of Marriage and the Nation and The Grounding of Modern Feminism*

"Raucous, profane, and thrillingly original, Thaddeus Russell's A Renegade History of the United States tu of the "American character" on their heads with a rare mix Johnson, author of *Everything I*

A **Renegade**
History of
the United States

Also by Thaddeus Russell

OUT OF THE JUNGLE: JIMMY HOFFA AND
THE REMAKING OF THE AMERICAN WORKING CLASS

A **RENEGADE**
HISTORY OF
THE UNITED STATES

Thaddeus Russell

SIMON &
SCHUSTER

London · New York · Sydney · Toronto

A CBS COMPANY

First published in Great Britain in 2010 by Simon & Schuster UK Ltd
This edition published in Great Britain in 2011 by Simon & Schuster UK Ltd
A CBS COMPANY

1 3 5 7 9 10 8 6 4 2

Simon & Schuster UK Ltd
1st Floor
222 Gray's Inn Road
London
WC1X 8HB

www.simonandschuster.co.uk

Simon & Schuster Australia
Sydney

A CIP catalogue copy for this book
is available from the British Library.

ISBN: 978-1-84739-864-2

Designed by Julie Schroeder
Printed in the UK by CPI Cox & Wyman, Reading, Berkshire RG1 8EX

For Toby
and his freedom

Contents

—Part Three—
FIGHTING FOR BAD FREEDOM

—Part Four—
WHICH SIDE ARE YOU ON?

Introduction

This is a new story.

When American history was first written, it featured and often cel-ebrated politicians, military leaders, inventors, explorers, and other "great men." Textbooks in high school and college credited those goliaths with creating all the distinctive cultural and institutional characteristics of the United States. In this history from the top down, women, Indians, Afri-can Americans, immigrants, and ordinary workers—in other words, most Americans—seldom appeared. In the 1960s and 1970s, a new generation of scholars began to place labor leaders, feminists, civil rights activists, and others who spoke on behalf of the people at the center of the story. This became known as history "from the bottom up." Yet more often than not, it seemed to me, the new stars of American history shared many of the cul-tural values and assumptions of the great men. They not only behaved like "good" Americans but also worked to "correct" the people they claimed to represent. They were not ordinary.

A Renegade History goes deeper. It goes beneath what the new "social history" portrayed as the bottom. It tells the story of "bad" Americans—drunkards, prostitutes, "shiftless" slaves and white slackers, criminals, ju-venile delinquents, brazen homosexuals, and others who operated beneath American society—and shows how they shaped our world, created new pleasures, and expanded our freedoms. This is history from the gutter up.

A Renegade History also offers a different way of conceiving historical progress than is found in textbooks. The story of this country is not just one of struggles between rich and poor, white and black, men and women. American history was also driven by clashes between those interested in preserving community and those more interested in pursuing their own desires—the "respectable" versus the "degenerate," the moral versus the immoral, "good citizens" versus the "bad." This is the story of American civilization and its discontents.

On one side of this struggle, *A Renegade History* groups together people we normally think of as fundamentally different. The founding fathers, abolitionists, great capitalists, socialist revolutionaries, suffragists, the Ku Klux Klan, New Dealers, civil rights activists, and conservative leaders all held or sought power, which meant they also sought social control and therefore worked to limit the personal liberties of their constituents. Every one of these groups of "good" Americans strongly promoted the work ethic, condemned sexual freedom, and decried the decadence of consumerism. So there has always been a conflict between these power-seeking moral reformers and the "lowbrow" culture of saloons, immigrant and black resistance to work, shopping, dance halls, rock-and-roll, and the ever-advancing sexual revolution.

Because this book is a renegade history, it spends as much time in the street, the bedroom, the movie theater, and the saloon as it does listening to speeches. You will see inside brothels and gay nightclubs. You will see the secret parties held by slaves and understand why so many refused to leave the plantation when they were freed. You will see people avoiding work, fighting cops, and fornicating shamelessly. You will see prostitutes ruling over men. You will see Irish, Jewish, and Italian immigrants dancing like blacks before they became white. And in every instance, you will see American freedom expanding.

At the most basic level, this book is about the fight that political philosophers have always identified as the central conflict in human history: that between the individual and society. Thus far, scholars have shown little interest in finding this conflict in American history, and even less interest in the kinds of individualists who are at the center of this book.

The leading historians of early America brilliantly narrate the dynamic tensions between settler and Indian, democrat and monarchist, slave and master, merchant and craftsman. But often not a single prostitute, ruffian, drunken laborer, bawdy pirate, slacking laborer, or shiftless slave makes an appearance in their books, even though such people filled the streets of American cities. The great historians of the colonial and revolutionary periods have given us masterful analyses of the transatlantic economy, the class basis of the revolutionaries, and the ideological origins of American democracy. But too often they are uninterested in the ways in which individual freedoms were constrained in the service of democracy, and how, despite its place as the "capital of liberty," America developed a national culture that was more sexually restrained and work obsessed than Victorian England.

The pivotal events of the nineteenth century have been similarly whitewashed, especially (and ironically) in the telling of black history. Unfortunately, because the historians who came of age during the 1960s and 1970s were so eager to make the masses into heroes, they did not see that it was precisely the nonheroic and unseemly characteristics of ordinary folks that changed American culture for the better. Historians of slavery rarely acknowledge that slaves and their descendants were the vanguard in the struggle against Victorian repression. Instead textbooks show African Americans of the era as the hardest-working, thriftiest, most sober, and family oriented of all Americans.

In the telling of the history of the West, "bottom-up" scholars replaced the silly romanticism of older historians with a far more intelligent and hardheaded narrative of American expansion. But now we have scores of books in which the story of the West is an unrelenting litany of oppression, exploitation, and genocide, in which ghost towns, bleak Indian reservations, depressed barrios, and strip mines dominate the scene. None of this is "wrong," but it surely reduces human experience to its most unpleasant aspects. More importantly, it neglects the remarkable freedoms and pleasures that miners, lumberjacks, railroad workers, prostitutes, Indians, blacks, Mexicans, and Chinese enjoyed—often together, in the same rooms—in the lawless, wide-open towns of the American frontier.

The historians who created women's history were especially egregious in the silencing of "bad" behavior. Following the first and second waves of feminists who inspired them to write the history of women, the women's historians of the 1970s and 1980s seldom mentioned sex and fun, and they were loathe to credit lower-class women for leading the consumer revolution that brought a new world of pleasure to America.

Of course, there are now many historians who study popular culture, lowbrow entertainment, and the people of the streets, but I am always dismayed to find that they treat every saloon, high-heel shoe, or rock song as something *else*. If they are sympathetic to the people who consumed them, such things are remade into "resistance" against oppression or "collective alternatives" to capitalist individualism. God forbid they could be simply and only "fun." Historians hostile to popular culture—who are far more numerous—dismiss it as part of the "culture of consumption" that was forced on the masses by advertisers, who were labeled by one historian as "the captains of consciousness." Though billions of Americans have gained real pleasure, radically improved their lives, and determined the production of goods by what economists call "voting with one's feet," nearly all histories of consumerism are negative. Allegedly "progressive" scholars write as if they are unaware that bourgeois moralists of the nineteenth century were the first to criticize the "base" desires and "unseemly" spending habits of the masses.

Sex—the act, not the biological category—was *never* discussed during my training as a historian and in only a tiny few of the hundreds of books, ostensibly devoted to the history of the human experience, that I read for my PhD. It always struck me as curious that psychologists had been saying for a century that sexuality informs all of our social activities and that people are obsessed with sex, but historians rarely mentioned it. Mammoth textbooks covering the entire span of American history ignore what people apparently were doing and thinking every day. Similarly, in standard histories, violence is carried out only by armies, police, strikebreakers, and racists—not by "the people" for their own good. And crime, in particular the small-time street crime that was always part of the fabric of ordinary people's lives, and which enlarged so many of our freedoms, rarely makes the cut as "important" history.

But let me make one thing absolutely clear. This book does not advocate a renegade revolution. Were the heroes of this book to take control of society, it would be a living hell. No one would be safe on the streets, chaos would reign, and garbage would never be collected. The social guardians are enemies of freedom, but there is no claim here that they are morally wrong. They chose to take the role they believed was best for them, a decision I would like to treat as autonomous of moral claims. More importantly, they provide essential functions that nearly all of us value: safety, security, and clean streets. The argument here is not that "bad" people should replace the disciplinarians but that in American history the struggles between the two have determined the breadth of personal liberty. I make no claims for other parts of the world, where at times renegades have overwhelmed the guardians of order, but in this country the more "bad" people existed, resisted, and won, the more freedom was expanded.

As you read this book, you might count the number of previously illicit pleasures and freedoms pushed forward by renegades that you now either cherish in your own life or desire to have. Let their struggle with civilizers be eternal. But let us all see how they have made the land of the free, free.

Part One

MAKING RENEGADES
INTO AMERICANS

★ 1 ★

DRUNKARDS, LAGGARDS, PROSTITUTES, PIRATES, AND OTHER HEROES OF THE AMERICAN REVOLUTION

In the spring of 1777, the great men of America came to Philadelphia for the fourth meeting of the Continental Congress, the de facto government of the rebel republic. When they stepped from their carriages onto the cobblestone streets, they could see that they were in for a very long war. New York had already been lost to the British, armies of redcoats and Hessian mercenaries were poised to cut off New England, and British plans were afoot to conquer Philadelphia and crush the rebellion. Thousands of troops in the Continental army had been lost to typhus, dysentery, smallpox, starvation, and desertion. They were outnumbered and outgunned. But it was not just the military power of the kingdom that worried the leaders of the American War of Independence. There was a far more sinister and enduring enemy on the streets they walked. "Indeed, there is one enemy, who is more formidable than famine, pestilence, and the sword," John Adams wrote to a friend from Philadelphia in April. "I mean the corruption which is prevalent in so many American hearts, a depravity that is more inconsistent with our republican governments than light is with darkness."

Adams was right. Many, and probably most, inhabitants of early American cities were corrupt and depraved, and the Founding Fathers knew it. Alexander Hamilton called the behaviors of Americans "vicious" and "vile." Samuel Adams saw a "torrent of vice" running through the new country. John Jay wrote of his fear that "our conduct should confirm the tory maxim 'that men are incapable of governing themselves.'" James Warren, the president of the Provincial Congress of Massachusetts and a Paymaster General of the Continental army, declared during the Revolution that Americans lived "degenerate days." As the war with the British thundered on, John

Adams grew so disgusted at what he saw on the streets that at times he believed Americans deserved death more than freedom. Their dissolute character "is enough to induce every Man of Sense and Virtue to abandon such an execrable Race, to their own Perdition, and if they could be ruined alone it would be just." Adams feared that after winning independence, Americans "will become a Spectacle of Contempt and Derision to the foolish and wicked, and of Grief and shame to the wise among Mankind, and all this in the Space of a few Years." In September of 1777, with the British army under the command of General William Howe on the verge of conquering Philadelphia, Adams told his wife of his secret wish for America to be conquered. "[I]f it should be the Will of Heaven that our Army should be defeated, our Artillery lost, our best Generals kill'd, and Philadelphia fall into Mr. Howes Hands, . . . It may be for what I know be the Design of Providence that this should be the Case. Because it would only lay the Foundations of American Independence deeper, and cement them stronger. It would cure Americans of their vicious and luxurious and effeminate Appetites, Passions and Habits, a more dangerous Army to American Liberty than Mr. Howes."

But what the Founding Fathers called corruption, depravity, viciousness, and vice, many of us would call freedom. During the War of Independence, deference to authority was shattered, a new urban culture offered previously forbidden pleasures, and sexuality was loosened from its Puritan restraints. Nonmarital sex, including adultery and relations between whites and blacks, was rampant and unpunished. Divorces were frequent and easily obtained. Prostitutes plied their trade free of legal or moral proscriptions. Black slaves, Irish indentured servants, Native Americans, and free whites of all classes danced together in the streets. Pirates who frequented the port cities brought with them a way of life that embraced wild dances, nightlong parties, racial integration, and homosexuality. European visitors frequently commented on the "astonishing libertinism" of early American cities. Renegades held the upper hand in Philadelphia, Boston, New York, and Charleston, and made them into the first centers of the American pleasure culture. Rarely have Americans had more fun. And never have America's leaders been less pleased by it.

But the Founding Fathers invented a way to make Americans think fun was bad. We call it *democracy*.

NURSERIES OF VICE AND DEBAUCHERY

On nearly every block in every eighteenth-century American city, there was a public place where one could drink, sing, dance, have sex, argue politics, gamble, play games, or generally carouse with men, women, children, whites, blacks, Indians, the rich, the poor, and the middling. The Founding Fathers were keenly, painfully aware of this.

Each morning during the meetings of the Continental Congress in 1777, John Adams squeezed his round body into breeches, waistcoat, wood-sole shoes, and powdered wig, and walked stiffly from his residence on Walnut and Third streets to the Pennsylvania State House (now Independence Hall) four blocks away on Chestnut between Fifth and Sixth streets. Along the way, he passed by at least a dozen of the more than 160 licensed taverns in Philadelphia that serviced the city's population of 24,000. There were also scores of unlicensed taverns, which means that there was at least one tavern for every 100 residents. (By contrast, in 2007 there was one alcohol-serving business for every 1,071 residents in Philadelphia.) Other early American cities contained even greater tavern densities during the time of the Revolution. In New York in the 1770s, there were enough taverns to allow every resident of the city to drink in a bar at the same time. In Boston in the middle of the century, it was estimated that liquor was sold at one of every eight residential houses. "The cities," writes Sharon V. Salinger, the author of *Taverns and Drinking in Early America,* "were packed with taverns."

And what would Adams have found if one morning he had clopped into one of the taverns along his way to creating the American republic? If it was one of the lower-class establishments on Walnut Street, the kind of place where most Philadelphians went, before he reached the front door, Adams would have heard white men fiddling Irish reels and black men pounding out driving African rhythms on hand drums, rattles, and wooden blocks. He would have heard a hybrid, flagrantly sexual sound that was the first American urban party music. As he opened the front door, Adams would have felt the vibrations of dancing feet on loose wooden floors. Once inside, the statesman's ears would have been assaulted by chants, responding chants, glasses clinking and breaking, laughing, and hollering of "fuck," "shit," "bastard," and "cunt." He would have inhaled the stink of old beer and the sweet aroma of warm, rum-laden grog.

Though Adams was short of stature, he would have felt uncomfortably large inside the narrow, smoky, sweaty room that amplified the noise and made everyone very, very close. But the intimacy of the room would not have been the first thing to strike the Founding Father. If he was in a typical lower-class eighteenth-century American urban tavern, he would have seen white men and black men sitting together and drumming their fingers to the music on long wooden tables. He would have seen white women dancing with black men and black women dancing with white men. He would have seen prostitutes openly and shamelessly selling their services. And, quite possibly, he would have seen a woman behind the bar who not only served the drinks but also owned the place. John Adams would have seen renegade America in all its early glory. And he would have known the enemy.

A line drawing of a typical lower-class tavern in an early American city. Flamboyant dancing, the mixing of whites and blacks, and the presence of women were commonly described in such establishments. *From Hawser Martingale, Tales of the Ocean (1840).*

During the War of Independence, Americans drank an estimated 6.6 gallons of absolute alcohol per year—equivalent to 5.8 shot glasses of 80-proof liquor a day—for each adult fifteen or over. This is a staggering statistic, to be sure, though it likely understates beer consumption. The historian W. J. Rorabaugh has called the period of the Revolution the beginning of America's "great alcoholic binge."

There was virtually no moral or legal proscription against drinking until after the War of Independence. Historians have found only a handful of prosecutions for drunkenness or unlawful behavior in taverns in colonial county records. In New York, not a single defendant was brought before the court on such charges in all of the eighteenth century. Salinger concludes that this was likely because "magistrates did not place drunkenness high on their list of offenses warranting prosecution." Indeed, drunkenness was often encouraged.

On his morning walks to the meetings, Adams would have seen and smelled men and women drinking before or instead of working. When he walked by the shops where craftsmen built furniture, shoes, wagons, tools, and other staples of the early American economy, he would have witnessed workers seated in front of tables on which sat their wares alongside their mugs. It was not only accepted but also expected to mix drinking with work. Laborers of all sorts drank beer throughout the workday and took frequent breaks for liquor and lounging. Construction workers and shipbuilders expected employers to provide them with beer at breaks. According to the historian Peter Thompson, even highly skilled artisans, the managers of early American manufacturing, "jealously defended heavy drinking as a right and a privilege."

In the early American economy, workers, not bosses, decided when they would show up and when they would go home. Long afternoon periods of eating, drinking, and sleeping were taken for granted. On the eighteenth-century worker's schedule, Sunday was followed by another day of rest known as "Saint Monday," which, Benjamin Franklin was irritated to see, "is as duly kept by our working people as Sunday; the only difference is that instead of employing their time cheaply in church, they are wasting it expensively in the alehouse." The *New Haven Gazette* reported that no matter how much an employer wished for sober workers, "a laboring man must have his half pint or pint every day, and at night half his wages in rum." Even in New England, where the Puritan influence remained strong through the eighteenth century, taverns were often located next door to churches so that congregants could have a drink before and after worshipping.

Tavern culture repelled authority and discipline. Typical was the scene at a Boston "public house" in 1714, when a judge was summoned from his home to expel a group of tipplers who refused to leave at closing time. The magistrate "Found much Company. They refus'd to go away. Said were there to drink the Queen's Health, and they had many other Health's to drink. Call'd for more Drink: drank to me, I took notice of the Affront to them . . . I threaten'd to send some of them to prison; that did not move them . . . I told them if they had not a care, they would be guilty of a Riot." Only then did the revelers exit the premises. Alexander Graydon, an officer in the Continental army and a frequent visitor to Philadelphia's taverns, found in them a "high-minded contempt for the industrious and the plod-ding." This kind of irreverence was typical in all the colonies. In Virginia, a clergyman complained in 1751 that taverns had become "the common Re-ceptacle and Rendezvous of the very Dreggs of the People; even of the most lazy and dissolute that are to be found in their respective Neighbourhoods, where not only Time and Money are, vainly and unprofitably, squandered away, but (what is worse) where prohibited and unlawful Games, Sports, and Pastimes are used, followed, and practiced, almost without any In-termission; namely cards, dice, Horse-Racing, and cock-fighting, together with Vices and Enormities of every other kind."

This was a shameless and public culture. The prominent Virginia planter and political leader William Byrd II noted in his diary that on a single day in the spring of 1710 in Williamsburg, "some people came to court and got drunk in defiance of the sickness and bad weather," and he "saw several drunk people in the churchyard." Later that year, on a warm summer night, Byrd walked to the courthouse to get his mail, "where the people were most of them drunk." He also explained his sleeplessness as due to "a great noise of people drunk in the street a good part of the night." Far from condemning the practice, Byrd did his part to contribute to it. While participating in a militia muster, he supplied an entire hogshead—sixty-three gallons—of rum punch, which "entertained all the people and made them drunk and fighting all the evening, but without mischief." Such mixing of formal activity with heavy drinking was the norm. "Most occa-sions in Virginia," writes the historian Salinger, "could not be celebrated without enormous amounts of alcohol."

This culture enlarged the freedom of everyone, but of blacks especial-ly. In 1732 Philadelphia's common council noted with alarm "the frequent and tumultuous Meetings of the Negro Slaves, especially on Sundays." The lawmakers called for an ordinance to restrain them but never passed one. In the 1740s, the city's governors heard several complaints about "great numbers of Negroes" drinking and carousing in public, but, according to the historian Jessica Kross, "In the end the common council seems to have taken no action about slave drinking." A 1744 grand jury chaired by Benjamin Franklin estimated that one out of ten houses in Philadelphia "sell strong drink," that most were "nurseries of vice and debauchery," and because of the intense competition for customers, were in general "under greater temptation to entertain apprentices, servants, and even Negroes."

Lower-class taverns were the first racially integrated public spaces in America. Black, white, and brown Americans came together through mutual desire centuries before the federal government brought them together by force. Although the law in all the colonies barred blacks from public houses, the law was often ignored by tavern keepers, white patrons, and by free blacks and even slaves. Early court records tell of drinking establishments across the colonies that disregarded the color line. Typical was a Burlington, New Jersey, grand jury's charge in 1707 that a laborer named William Cale kept a "common house of drinking . . . and there received harbored and supported diverse vagabond and other idle and suspected persons of evil conversation as well as diverse servants and Negroes of the inhabitants of the town." Occasional attacks by law enforcers did little to stem the inflow of various colors into American taverns. Again, the less "respectable" a public house was, the more likely it was to facilitate the mixing of races. This was most notable inside the dark drinking houses of New York City. Here, as throughout American history, the lowest "scum" were interracial pioneers. "All colonies prosecuted those who kept disorderly houses, but the infraction included a range of activities from selling liquor without a license to operating a brothel," writes Salinger. "New York's version of the practice was unique; it was synonymous with multiracialness." The freedom in such places at times spilled into the streets and terrified the guardians of social order.

John Hughson was an illiterate, thieving piece of trash and one of the unknown heroes of American liberty. Hughson's tavern, near the site of what became the World Trade Center, was filthy, ramshackle, and nightly filled with the bottom of human life in colonial New York City. Like almost all such places, it was a place where freedom and desire brought together "whorish" women, "brutish" immigrants, and shiftless, sensual slaves. Neighbors complained about the lowlifes the tavern brought to their street, as well as the noise from raucous singing, shouting, cursing, jesting, drumming, fiddling, and dancing. According to court records, Hughson's tavern was one of many businesses that gave free and enslaved blacks a place "to resort, and be entertained privately (in defiance of the law) at all hours." According to one judge, the greatest crime committed by these slingers of drink and purveyors of commercial sex "was not only of making Negro slaves their equals, but even their superiors, by waiting upon, keeping with, and entertaining them with meat, drink, and lodging." On holidays and Sundays, Hughson served feasts where the rabble acted like kings. "They sat all round the table, and had a goose, a quarter of mutton, a fowl, and two loaves of bread," said a witness. "Hughson took a flask of rum out of a case and set it on the table, and two bowls of punch were made; some drink drams; a cloth was laid."

A group of slaves also regularly bought and sold stolen goods with Hughson, including a great deal of Dutch Geneva gin, after which they named their social group the Geneva Club. The second floor of the tavern contained rooms to rent, including one inhabited by "Margaret Sorubiro, alias Salingburgh, alias Kerry, commonly called Peggy, or the Newfoundland Irish beauty." Peggy was a prostitute known to prefer black customers, and the rent for the room she kept was paid by Caesar, a leader of the Geneva Club, with whom she had a child.

On March 18, 1741, the roof of the New York governor's house burst into flames. The fire swept through surrounding Fort George on the Battery. Many of the soldiers and civil servants who lived there, fearing that the stores of gunpowder would explode, fled from the fort. The fire raced from one building to the next, consuming the chapel, the secretary's office, and the barracks. By the end of the day, everything inside the walls of the fort was ashes. One week later, the home of Captain Peter Warren of the British navy caught fire. Over the next month, it seemed as if all of New York was burning. Houses, stables, and warehouses went up in flames across the city, as did shouts of "The Negroes! The Negroes!" Magistrates ordered slaves newly arrived in the city to be rounded up and thrown in jail. Then two women reported that they had seen three slaves dancing as they sang "Fire, Fire, Scorch, Scorch, A Little, damn it, By and By!" The three black men were arrested, tortured, and burned to death. Mary Burton, a sixteen-year-old indentured servant of John Hughson, told the authorities that her master, Peggy, along with Caesar and the Geneva Club, had conspired "to burn this city, and to kill and destroy us all." All the alleged plotters were hanged or burned at the stake, but the culture they helped to create lived on. It proved to be far more menacing to repressive self-rule in the American republic than it was to social order under the king.

BASTARDS, WHORES, AND THE AMERICAN (SEXUAL) REVOLUTION

In Philadelphia, on Walnut Street between Second and Third, just around the corner from where Adams laid his head during the Second Continental Congress, were three of the dozens of "bawdy houses" that operated—openly and legally—in the revolutionary capital. When Adams walked to the State House, he was almost certainly propositioned by prostitutes advertising their trade. They would have shown him their breasts and asked if he cared for a "nice romp" or a "quick fuck." Some of the whores would have been black, some Indian, a few Jewish, and many Irish. Prostitutes, even white ones, were widely regarded as the most willing members of American society to cross the color line. "If 'tis but a Negroe, they do not much Care," as one 1765 poem put it, referring to a white streetwalker's criterion for clientele. "For as long he had money to spend he may Stay." According to historian Clare Lyons, "Members of all classes and both races frequented taverns, bawdy houses, and 'Negro' houses for sexual adventure." At these places, according to the *Pennsylvania Gazette,* "all the loose and idle characters of the city, whether whites, blacks, or mulattoes . . . indulge in riotous mirth and dancing till the dawn." They were also where couples copulated with impunity. Many such establishments were run by African Americans, such as John York, a free black man who operated one of the most popular bawdy houses in Philadelphia and hosted many white patrons.

In the era of the American Revolution, writes Lyons, "individuals moved in and out of sexual relationships with ease, and the broader society accommodated them." Prostitution was rarely punished, either legally or culturally. Whores frequently appeared in almanac stories, stage plays, songs, and poems—as heroines as often as villainesses—but they seldom turned up in court records or in newspaper reports of crime in the city. In fact, only three women were prosecuted for prostitution in Philadelphia in the 1760s and 1770s. According to Lyons, prostitution "thrived" in early Philadelphia and became "the most common nonmarital sexual behavior of Philadelphians during the late eighteenth century." In the years after the Revolution, prosecution of prostitutes increased but only gradually. In the 1790s, when streetwalkers "flooded the streets and bawdy houses appeared in every neighborhood," on average fewer than two women were arrested for prostitution per month. Several foreign visitors to Philadelphia commented on the ubiquity of whores in the revolutionary capital. A young Brazilian wrote in his diary in 1798 that "prostitutes in Philadelphia are so many that they flood the streets at night, in such a way that even looking at them in the streets without men you can recognize them." A French traveler reported in the 1790s that "a great many husbands" patronized whorehouses as "a means to libertinism." Sex was bought and sold not just in bawdy houses but also in the back rooms of taverns, in theaters, alleys, in the prison, and often right on the street. Much of this activity took place in public, often in full view to any passersby. Sexuality in revolutionary America was gloriously shameless.

Women in particular enjoyed the freedom from sexual shame. When men did not satisfy their wives, the wives felt free to leave them. In 1797 Louisa Lovinger not only committed adultery but also justified it in a way that would have been punishable by death earlier in the Puritan era and by imprisonment or ostracism later in the Victorian period. When a neighbor asked if she was ashamed of her actions, Lovinger replied "that she [was] not, that her husband was away the whole week at the store and she had not good of him, and that she will not stay with him much longer." Eleanor Lightwood deserted her husband in 1788 because he was "an ugly little fellow," and "she saw a number of faces that she liked abundances better." While Eliza McDougall's husband was away at sea, she took another lover and bore a child with him. When her husband returned, he told her, according to a friend who overheard the conversation, "Betty I will forgive you all that has happened if you will tell me who was the father of the child." To this she replied, "It was a better fellow than you." And while women who worked even briefly as prostitutes in later periods were branded with infamy forever, in the early new nation, one's participation in the profession was not a bar to respectability or marriage. Some prostitutes during this era even married into high society. In 1809 William Penn, the great-grandson of the founder of Pennsylvania, married a woman known in Philadelphia as "a common Prostitute of this city" and did not lose his standing among the local elite.

The sexual terrain in other early American cities was not much different. In 1774 one British visitor to New York, Patrick M'Roberts, was astonished to find in the neighborhood around St. Paul's Chapel, where George Washington attended services during the two years that New York City was the nation's capital, that public sex was entirely normal. There were "above 500 ladies of pleasure [who] keep lodgings contiguous within the consecrated liberties of St. Paul's. This part of the city belongs to the church, and has thence obtained the name of the *Holy Ground*. Here all the prostitutes reside, among whom are many fine well-dressed women, and it is remarkable that they live in much greater cordiality one with another than any nests of that kind do in Britain or Ireland." King's College (later Columbia University), also situated on the Holy Ground at Park Place and Broadway, was a great source of customers for the many prostitutes who provided "a temptation to the youth that have occasion to pass so often that way." An aristocratic lieutenant of the British army named Isaac Bangs inspected the Holy Ground in 1776 to find out why half of his soldiers had sought out "an intimate Connexion with these worse than Brutal Creatures." When he first saw them, "I thought nothing could exceed them for impudence and immodesty; but I found the more I was acquainted with them, the more they excelled in their Brutality." After visiting New York in 1794, the Frenchman Moreau de St. Mery wrote, "Whole sections of streets are given over to streetwalkers for the plying of their profession." Women "of every color can be found in the streets, particularly after ten o'clock at night, soliciting men and proudly flaunting their licentiousness in the most shameless manner." Similar scenes were witnessed at Fell's Point in Baltimore and on Ann Street on Boston's North End.

Evidence that American cities were libertine havens literally played in the streets—thousands of children born out of wedlock. Never in American history have more "illegitimate" children been born, per capita, than during the era of independence. Lyons estimates that in Philadelphia alone, in the years 1767 to 1776, one in roughly thirty-eight adults was parent to an illegitimate child. After the war, nonmarital sex appears to have grown increasingly popular. From 1790 to 1799 there was one parent of a bastard in roughly twenty adults. Between 1805 and 1814, the next documented ten-year period, there was one illegitimate parent in roughly ten adults in the cradle of American liberty. During this period, the population of Philadelphia almost tripled, but "bastardy" increased tenfold.

Promiscuity was rampant in early American cities. Of the more than one thousand women who bore bastard children in Philadelphia in the second half of the eighteenth century, only five had more than one child with the same man. Upper-class moralists blamed the rise in bastardy on irresponsible fornication among the lower classes. They were right. Of the bastardy cases in which economic class could be ascertained, 25 percent of the fathers were so poor that they paid no taxes; 34 percent were taxed at the lowest level of one or two pounds; and 30 percent paid three to eight pounds but worked as butchers, bakers, carpenters, carvers, metalsmiths, joiners, hatters, bricklayers, upholsterers, weavers, and schoolteachers. When John Adams went to a local shop or bookseller in Philadelphia, Boston, or New York, he would have seen evidence that the rabble were having more fun than he was: shelves full of sheep-gut condoms, pornographic almanacs, and various pills and potions to cure venereal disease. According to many accounts, such items were standard in early American retail businesses.

Does all of this mean that many women in early American cities—especially poor women—were sluts and whores, and that poor men were more animalistic than upper-class men? Well, yes. But if you value your personal freedom, these people should be your heroes.

Like laws against prostitution, laws against fornication and adultery were largely ignored in the revolutionary period. In Philadelphia, between 1790 and 1799, only one couple was arrested for cross-racial fornication; only two couples were brought before the courts for fornicating in public; and not one person was charged for simple fornication between two consenting single white adults, despite overwhelming evidence that most Philadelphians were breaking these laws. Seventy percent of adultery cases that were mentioned in divorce proceedings were not criminally prosecuted.

Even in the Puritan stronghold of New England, premarital sex increased markedly in the late eighteenth century. European visitors to the region were frequently shocked at the liberties taken by young and old alike. "I have entered several bedchambers," wrote Alexandre Berthier, a member of the French military who toured Massachusetts in 1780, "where I have found bundling couples, who are not disturbed and continue to give each other all the honest tokens of their love." Observers were most amazed at the permissiveness of parents and older adults toward the intimacies of young people. The German traveler Johann Schoepf saw during his stay in New England in 1783–84 that when parents knew of late-night bed sharing, "the young woman's good name [was] no ways impaired." Indeed, young people rarely felt the need to hide such couplings and did not need to be formally courting to spend the night with someone. "[O]n the contrary, the parents are advised, and these meetings happen when the pair is enamored and merely wish to know each other better." The growing practice of "bundling" was not always just innocent cuddling. Historians estimate that between 30 percent and 40 percent of pregnancies in late-eighteenth-century New England were premarital.

Women were extraordinarily free during this period, most strikingly in their ability and willingness to leave their husbands. The monarchy and colonial governments declined to regulate marriage, and so there were virtually no divorce laws in America until after independence. Perhaps because of this lack of formal consequences, in the late colonial period—when the cities had grown large enough to offer many choices of mates and work and social networks—women fled their husbands in great numbers. Between 1726 and 1786, when Pennsylvania passed its first divorce law, 801 husbands in the colony placed advertisements in newspapers announcing that their wives had left them and their marriages were null and void. And again, it was the bottom classes who drove this part of the first American sexual revolution: 62 percent of the men who advertised the dissolution of their marriage were from the city's lowest laboring classes. What is most striking, and most liberated, about the runaway wives is that most of them showed no shame: only 5 percent of the advertised runaways offered a public explanation for their actions. The prevalence of the self-divorce advertisements demonstrates, as Lyons puts it, "that for many segments of eighteenth-century society, marriage did not have to be permanent. For these couples and the community that countenanced their behavior, marriage was not tightly bound for life; marital bonds could be broken."

Far more women chose not to marry at all during this period than at any time in the first two hundred years of the United States. Researchers estimate that at least one-quarter of women living in late colonial American cities were not married. Nowhere were women more free from the expectations that they be wives and mothers than in revolutionary Philadelphia, where more than one-third of the adult female population was not only unmarried but also living with nonrelatives.

Many generations before feminists made women's work in the "public sphere" acceptable, female inhabitants of the early, freewheeling American cities worked in every imaginable profession. They were blacksmiths, butchers, distillers, dockworkers, hucksters, innkeepers, manual laborers, mariners, pawnbrokers, peddlers, plasterers, printers, skinners, and wine-makers. Many women in the eighteenth century not only worked in what later became exclusively male occupations but also owned a great number of businesses that would soon be deemed grossly unfeminine. Hannah Breintnall was typical of a class of female entrepreneurs who benefited from the looseness of gender norms in early America. When her husband died, Breintnall opened the Hen and Chickens Tavern on Chestnut Street in Philadelphia, not far from the residences of many of the Founding Fathers and the State House where the United States was made. The fact that a woman owned the bar did not stop the sheriff from holding public auctions at the Hen and Chickens, nor did it stop patrons from making Breintnall, by the time she died in 1770, one of the wealthiest inhabitants of the city. In Philadelphia alone, in the two decades before the drafting of the Declaration of Independence, at least 110 women worked as tavern keepers, and more than 75 operated retail shops of various sorts. Historians have estimated that as many as half of all shops in early American cities were owned and operated by women. Moral judgments appear to have had little effect on these renegade women. Many operated houses of prostitution inside their taverns. Margaret Cook, one of these shameless tavern owners, should be celebrated by every American woman who values her freedom. In 1741 Cook was brought into court on charges that she welcomed as patrons "Whores, Vagabonds, and divers Idle Men of a suspected bad conversation" and that she "continually did keep bad order and Government." Twenty years later, apparently unchastened, Cook returned to court to face the very same charges.

Women owned and operated a large percentage of American taverns before and during the Revolution, especially in the rough-and-tumble port cities. Roughly 40 percent of the taverns in Boston during the 1760s were owned by women. In Charleston in the fifteen years before the Revolution, a *majority* of the tavern keepers were women. The less respectable the tavern, the more likely it was to be owned by a woman.

Public houses that aimed for a refined clientele almost invariably barred women from serving or drinking on the premises. According to Salinger, "Women only rarely operated taverns described as genteel places with good entertainment." But in most of American society, through most of the eighteenth century, women not only served alcohol in public but also drank it. Most upper-class "society" taverns barred women, and respectable women rarely drank in taverns, but fortunately, most taverns were low class and most women were not respectable. In fact, the modern dating scene was predated in many colonial taverns that were known as places where men and women could meet one another. Historians estimate that women consumed from one-eighth to one-quarter of the spirituous liquor in early America, and early temperance organizations claimed that one hundred thousand women were bona fide "drunkards."

SODOM AND THE SEA

One day during his stay in Philadelphia, John Adams walked to the docks and, with his back turned to the pleasure-filled streets of the city and his eyes to the Delaware River, felt his spirit rise as he looked upon the newly built USS *Delaware* launching into the river. Adams "stood upon the Wharf to see the fine figure and Show she made." To his son Charles, he wrote that from such a sight "Thus you see, that a Foundation is laying, in Arts, and Manufactures, of a rising State." He then toured the foundries on Front Street along the river, where war ships and cannons were manufactured for the patriots. He could see that so long as hunks of iron and brass continued to be melted down, molded, and hammered into weapons, the rebels had a chance. In March 1777, he wrote excitedly to Charles of the foundries where he had seen "Howitzers" and "several brass six Pounders newly cast." But right behind him, the wharf was filled with the bawdiest, most depraved, and most pleasurable houses of ill repute in America.

In the early eighteenth century, pirates made the wharves of port cities around the world the wildest scenes of freedom and pleasure in the early modern age. Pirates brought to shore an antiwork, libertine ethos that was eloquently stated by Bartholomew Roberts, better known as Black Bart, a famed buccaneer who prowled the Atlantic coast from the West Indies to Newfoundland. Comparing legitimate employment with piracy, Roberts quipped, "In an honest Service there is thin Commons, low Wages, and hard Labour; in this, Plenty and Satiety, Pleasure and Ease, Liberty and Power." After retiring from their lives on the high seas, many pirates stayed on the wharves or fathered children who built ships or became stevedores, sailors, or other sorts of maritime workers. And so on Ann Street (now North Street) on Boston's North End, Water Street at the southern tip of Manhattan, Fell's Point on the Baltimore Harbor, and all along Front Street in Philadelphia, where John Adams admired the shipworks, sailors on leave spent their money freely on drink, women, and flamboyant clothes, impromptu dances spilled out of taverns, and people of all colors tangled together.

Pirates and other rowdy seafarers also helped create something that, were we to see it now, we would call gay liberation. When John Adams explored the streets, he might have walked past men exposing their penises, the eighteenth-century transatlantic code for men seeking partners of the same sex. Adams might have brushed past Ann Alweye or Mary Hamilton, tall women with large hands and protruding Adam's apples, who slept with men and were themselves males—males who dressed as women. Daniel Sweeny was another male who enjoyed bending his gender in early Philadelphia. He was arrested for "being a Nuisance" by "dressing in woman's clothes" but, further suggesting a looseness of sexual mores, was released after four days. These were the transvestites who appear in the public record. There were many more. In 1784 the newspaper the *Philadelphiad* described effeminate "fops" filling the city's public spaces:

> At ev'ry corner and in ev'ry street / Some gaudy useless animal we meet, / Resembling men in nothing but their shape, / . . . / Observe the thing its gaudy pinions spread, / Pride in its eye with sense inverted head. / . . . / Come, lend a hand, we'll learn him how to dance. / . . . / His green silk breeches grafted blue behind, / With all his trapings of a piece with these, / Behind a fright, before designed to please.

Significantly, two of the fops mentioned in the newspaper, "Tom Tug" and "Jack Tinsel," were both seafarers. If John Adams had visited one of the city's four libraries, a source of great pride among the Founding Fathers, he might have noticed that one of the most frequently borrowed books was *The Adventures of Roderick Random,* a novel featuring Lord Strutwell and Captain Whiffle, effeminate dandies festooned in pink and red satin, ornate jewelry, powder, and perfume, who seduce young men with discussion of sodomy among the ancients and claims of "the exquisite pleasure" of "this inclination." According to Lyons, such men by and large lived "unmolested by Philadelphia society at the end of the eighteenth century."

Before the pirates brought their ways ashore, acts of "sodomy" (homosexuality was invented as a term and a concept much later) were condemned and punished in various and spectacular ways. John Winthrop, the founder of the Massachusetts Bay Colony, explained that it was necessary to execute sodomites because their activities "tended to the frustrating of the ordinance of marriage and the hindering [of] the generation of mankind." Men who were caught "spending their seed upon one another" were hanged, whipped, and branded across the colonies in the seventeenth century. But as piracy flourished in the Atlantic from the late seventeenth century into the mid–seventeen hundreds, a great number of men spent their seed upon one another unpunished. The historian B. R. Burg claims that during the so-called golden age of piracy, most if not all of the buccaneers had sex with one another. Pirates were primarily devoted to pleasure, and they cared little how they got it. Thus, "[t]he male engaging in homosexual activity aboard a pirate ship in the West Indies three centuries past was simply an ordinary member of his community, completely socialized and acculturated." Prosecutions for sodomy declined sharply in the colonies in the eighteenth century, even as the population increased geometrically, and in the port cities during the American Revolution, little or no misspent seed was punished. In Philadelphia, where at least 20 percent of the adult male population spent time at sea, there was not a single prosecution for sodomy from 1750 to 1800.

Same-sex intimacy was not exclusive to men. Moreau de St. Mery was shocked by the number of women in Philadelphia who "give themselves up at an early age to the enjoyment of themselves." Even more shocking, something "almost unbelievable," was that "they are not at all strangers to being willing to seek unnatural pleasures with persons of their own sex. Among common people, at a tavern keeper's, for example, or at a small shopkeeper's, the daughter of the house, when no longer a child, sleeps with the [female] servant."

A MOTLEY RABBLE

The culture of pleasure and freedom was dangerous not just to American revolutionaries but also to anyone interested in maintaining social order. The British army learned this lesson in Boston on March 5, 1770, the night the American Revolution began.

When the drunkards in the taverns heard the church bells ringing, they put down their cups and rushed into the streets. The mob grabbed sticks, rocks, and chunks of ice and ran atop the cobblestones to King Street. There they saw young boys cursing and hurling snowballs and horse manure at a column of British soldiers who were standing guard with muskets and bayonets in front of the customshouse. The troops had been in Boston for nearly two years to protect customs officers who were being harassed, beaten, and tarred and feathered for bringing British goods into the colonies. Many of the seven hundred soldiers stationed in the city were being quartered in the homes and taverns of Bostonians, and fights broke out nearly every day over their presence in the city. But on March 5, the rowdy libertines who made up much of the city's population were ready for a bigger fight. They called the soldiers "sons of bitches," "bastards," and "cunts." The air that night on King Street, according to the historian Edmund S. Morgan, "was thick with epithets." The heckling and pelting increased as more and more of the taverngoers arrived. When the crowd became a seething, intoxicated mob of several hundred, one man stepped forward, swung his club, and leveled one of the soldiers. Shots exploded into the crowd. Eleven men fell. Five died.

No one will ever know what the men who became known as the martyrs of the Boston Massacre were thinking or why they confronted armed soldiers. But we do know that they came from taverns, they were white and black, and they were not gentlemen. They had been drinking, gambling, and, if they were like most taverngoers in early Boston, cavorting with prostitutes. They were unruly, foulmouthed, and thuggish. One of them, a former slave named Crispus Attucks, who had been quaffing drinks at the Royal Exchange, is widely thought to have been the one who clobbered the hapless British soldier. Textbooks like to make Attucks and the mob on King Street into allies of the Founding Fathers, and indeed, their actions led not only to the removal of the troops from Boston but also to increased militancy against the British that most historians agree was the beginning of the American Revolution. Moreover, the Boston Massacre provided much of the rationale for the Third and Fourth Amendments of the Constitution, which protect us from soldiers being quartered in our homes and from "unreasonable searches and seizures." But the greatest concern of the Founding Fathers was not the restrictions on the personal freedom of citizens—it was that such restrictions, especially in a renegade town like colonial Boston, inevitably cause social disorder. As John Adams put it shortly after the Boston Massacre, "soldiers quartered in a populous town will always occasion two mobs, where they prevent one. They are wretched conservators of the peace!"

The Founding Fathers knew better than our textbooks. They knew that the drunks swinging clubs and slinging horseshit at the authorities that night were a problem as much for them as for the British Empire. It is little known that the lawyer who defended the British soldiers in the ensuing trial was none other than John Adams. During the trial, Adams correctly described the victims as "a motley rabble of saucy boys, Negroes and molattoes, Irish teagues, and outlandish jack tarrs." He also accurately characterized their actions as "shouting and hazing and threatening life . . . whistling, screaming, and rending an Indian yell . . . throwing every species of rubbish they could pick up in the street." Adams, like the Founding Fathers generally, was greatly interested in perfecting and maintaining social order. As he later explained to a friend, "I had a good Policy, as well as sound Law on my side, when I ventured to lay open before our People the Laws against Riots, Routs, and unlawful assemblies. Mobs will never do—to govern States or command armies . . . To talk of Liberty in such a state of things—!"

Most important, Adams understood that such disorder was virtually inevitable among people controlled by a standing army and external force. All the kings and queens of Europe, with all their soldiers and ships and dungeons, could not put an end to the kind of freedom that flowed through the streets of colonial America. In fact, such freedom was even greater among the European peasantry, who had flooded into London, Paris, and Amsterdam and transformed them into raging carnivals.

Much better, the Founding Fathers learned, that the people be trained to control themselves.

COUNTERREVOLUTION

The men who created the United States were truly revolutionaries: they revolutionized the concept of freedom.

The Founding Fathers were part of a transatlantic movement in the eighteenth and nineteenth centuries to replace the external controls over subjects in absolutist regimes with the internal restraints of citizens in republics. This movement began what is now called the Modern Age. The modernist movement required not just the overthrow of monarchs but also the repression of what was called "man's animal passions." The problem with the discipline of the gallows, the lash, and the sword, according to these revolutionaries, was that it was far less effective than individual self-discipline in keeping social order. Even though peasants, slaves, and the colonial subjects we have seen in taverns and bawdy houses held no formal political power, they were, according to this view, actually *too free* because they had no reason to control themselves. So the Founding Fathers redefined freedom as self-control and built a political system around it called democracy.

To solve the lack of order they saw all around them, the fathers seized on one of the great—and often missed—ironies in world history: the only thing that could make men forsake their own freedom and still believe they were free was self-rule. A government of the people, John Adams argued, would make the people disciplined, stern, hard working, and joyless—the qualities he most admired. It would "produce Strength, Hardiness Activity, Courage, Fortitude, and Enterprise; the manly noble and Sublime Qualities in human Nature, in Abundance." A monarchy, on the other hand, would let them have too much fun and, paradoxically, allow them too much liberty. It "would produce so much Taste and Politeness, so much Elegance in Dress, Furniture, Equipage, so much Musick and Dancing, so much Fencing and Skaiting, so much Cards and Backgammon, so much Horse Racing and Cockfighting, so many Balls and Assemblies, so many Plays and Concerts that the very imagination of them makes me feel vain, light, frivolous, and insignificant." Adams understood that democracy forced the people to shed their pleasures and surrender their personal freedom, because they alone would shoulder the responsibility of managing society. "Under a well-regulated Commonwealth, the People must be wise virtuous and cannot be otherwise. Under a Monarchy they may be as vicious and foolish as they please, nay, they cannot but be vicious and foolish . . . [T]here is one Difficulty which I know not how to get over. Virtue and Simplicity of Manners are indispensably necessary in a Republic among all orders and Degrees of Men. But there is so much Rascallity, so much Venality and Corruption, so much Avarice and Ambition such a Rage for Profit and Commerce among all Ranks and Degrees of Men even in America, that I sometimes doubt whether there is public Virtue enough to Support a Republic." The Founding Fathers understood what we now choose to ignore: democracy is the enemy of personal freedom.

Adams was well-acquainted with the liberty spawned by monarchy. One night in 1760, at the beginning of his political career, the young lawyer met with friends at Thayer's Tavern in Braintree, Massachusetts, where he found persons of all sorts enjoying uninhibited, integrated fun: "Negroes with a fiddle, young fellows and girls dancing in the chamber as if they would kick the floor thru . . . fiddling and dancing of both sexes and ages, in the lower room, singing, dancing, fiddling, drinking flip and toddy, and drams." Adams saw this frivolity as evidence that public houses had "become the eternal Haunt, of loose disorderly People of the same Town, which renders them offensive and unfit for the Entertainment of a Traveller of the least delicacy." The people he found at Thayer's were "the trifling, nasty vicious Crew, that most frequent them." Adams promptly asked the Braintree town meeting to reduce the number of taverns in order to correct "the present prevailing Depravity of Manners, through the Land in General, and in this Town in particular, and shameful neglect of Religious and Civil Duties." Though Adams was unsuccessful in 1760, the culture turned in his favor during the War of Independence. As the historians Mark Edward Lender and James Kirby Martin put it, "The bitterest denunciation of distilled spirits came in the immediate aftermath, and as part of the zeitgeist, of the Revolution."

During what we call the American Revolution, a second American revolution took place: a counterrevolution against the pleasure culture of the cities. Personal freedom and sensual pleasure came under attack during the democratic revolution not because the revolutionaries were puritans but because democracy is puritanical.

We normally think of democracy as a system of rights and freedoms: voting, speaking freely, equal treatment under the law, and so forth. But true democracy, the kind of democracy that the Founding Fathers wanted, is much more than that. John Locke, the man who, in the English world, helped invent the notion that the people should rule and who inspired all of the American democratic revolutionaries, made this brutally clear. "It seems plain to me," he wrote in *Some Thoughts Concerning Education* (1693), "that the principle of all virtue and excellency lies in a power of denying ourselves the satisfaction of our own desires, where reason does not authorize them." Locke knew that managing society is a big job requiring enormous discipline. If the people were to do it, then the people would have to renounce their personal freedom. Most importantly, they would have to be taught to feel shame for their selfish desires. "Esteem and disgrace are, of all others, the most powerful incentives to the mind, when once it is brought to relish them," Locke wrote. "If you can once get into children a love of credit, and an apprehension of shame and disgrace, you have put into 'em the true principle, which will constantly work and incline them to the right." The kind of punishment used by monarchs and slave owners to keep the people orderly and productive—whipping, flogging, executions, and the like—only "patches up for the present, and skins it over, but reaches not to the bottom of the sore; ingenuous shame, and the apprehensions of displeasure, are the only true restraint. These alone ought to hold the reins, and keep the child in order."

With these ideas in mind, the Founding Fathers fought simultaneous wars against the British and the renegade impulses of Americans.

The precipitating event of the Revolution, the Sugar Act of 1764, which effectively increased import duties on sugar, molasses, wine, coffee, and cloth and indigo used for fine clothing, was passed by Parliament in order to finance the maintenance of Britain's many colonies around the world. It virtually halted the rum industry in the colonies and sharply limited Americans' access to fancy garments. In response, some American colonists protested "taxation without representation," and merchants in Boston launched a boycott of British goods. But many of the men who would lead the American Revolution were actually happy about the new taxes and the boycotts that followed. Richard Henry Lee said of the Sugar Act, "Possibly this step of the mother country, though intended to oppress and keep us low, in order to secure our dependence, may be subversive of this end. Poverty and oppression, among those whose minds are filled with ideas of British liberty, may introduce a virtuous industry, with a train of generous and manly sentiments."

During the Sugar Act crisis, Benjamin Franklin and other prominent Pennsylvanians repeatedly and fruitlessly petitioned the colonial government to take action against taverns and drinking. Franklin charged that "Many bills have been presented to late Governors to lessen the number, and to regulate those nurseries of idleness and debauchery, but without success, from whence it seems evident, that so long as the Proprietaries [of the Pennsylvania colony] are interested in our ruin, ruined we must be." Charles Thomson, a Philadelphia merchant and later a secretary of the Continental Congress, backed Franklin's campaign to reduce the number of taverns and reinforced his argument that drinking in America was tantamount to British subversion. Thomson recalled the way in which Cyrus the Great of ancient Persia, in conquering the Lydian Empire, "took to break the spirit and soften the warlike disposition of the Lydians and render them the most abject slaves by erecting bagnios [brothels] and public inns . . . I will not say [that this] is the design of our Great Ones. But it is true that in almost every tavern keeper, the Proprietors [of the colony] have a warm advocate, and the more effeminate and debauched the people are, the more they are fitted for an absolute and tyrannical government."

In 1765 Parliament passed the Stamp Act, imposing taxes on colonists for printed materials including newspapers, pamphlets, bills, legal documents, licenses, almanacs, dice, and playing cards. This was followed by the Quartering Act, requiring colonists to house British troops and supply them with food. Several of the men who would become known as the Founding Fathers petitioned Parliament and King George III, asserting that no taxes should be imposed on the colonists "but with their own consent, given personally, or by their representatives." By the end of the year, more than two hundred merchants joined the boycott against British goods. After Benjamin Franklin warned Parliament that military enforcement of the Stamp Act might cause a revolution in the American colonies, in 1766 King George III signed a bill repealing the law. But on the same day, Parliament passed the Declaratory Act, affirming the "full power and authority" of the British government "to make laws and statutes of sufficient force and validity to bind the colonies and people of America . . . in all cases whatsoever." The following year, Parliament adopted the Townshend Revenue Acts, imposing new taxes on the colonists to help pay for the administration and military protection of the American colonies. The act also established a board of customs commissioners in Boston to oversee tax collecting. In October 1767, Boston merchants renewed the boycott of British luxury goods.

Boycotts against British goods became a favorite tactic among the colonial rebels, in part because of the austerity they required. The pro-independence *Boston Evening-Post* scolded Americans for having been "of late years insensibly drawn into too great a degree of luxury and dissipation." But thanks to boycotts, "by consuming less of what we are not really in want of, and by industriously cultivating and improving the natural advantages of our own country, we might save our substance, even our lands, from becoming the property of others, and we might effectually preserve our virtue and our liberty, to the latest posterity."

Tensions increased considerably in 1768, when several colonial assemblies endorsed Samuel Adams's circular letter calling for no taxation without representation. Customs officers were harassed and attacked on the streets of Boston. British warships sailed into Boston Harbor, and two regiments of the British army were deployed into the city to keep order. By the following year, resolutions opposing taxation without representation and boycotts of British goods had spread across the colonies. But one pro-independence newspaper, the *Virginia Gazette,* actually welcomed taxation without representation for its disciplining effect. "Luxury," Americans were told, "has taken deep root among us, and to cure a people of luxury were an Herculean task indeed; what perhaps no power on earth but a British Parliament, in the very method they are taking with us, could possibly execute."

As we already know, the first violence in the conflict occurred in Boston in 1770, when drunkards, ruffians, and gamblers tumbled out of taverns to curse, throw rubbish and horse manure, and assault British soldiers. Uproar over the ensuing massacre forced the British to withdraw troops from the city, repeal the Townshend Acts, eliminate all duties on imports into the colonies except for tea, and allow the Quartering Act to be discontinued. Yet a few months later, Samuel Adams still saw much more work to be done. He told a friend that "the Conspirators against our Liberties are employing all their Influence to divide the people, . . . introducing Levity Luxury and Indolence . . ." In 1772, he organized a "committee of correspondence" that proclaimed the right of the colonies to self-rule. By the end of 1773, committees of correspondence were established in Virginia,

New Hampshire, Rhode Island, Connecticut, and South Carolina. That year Parliament passed the Tea Act, maintaining tax on tea brought into the colonies and granting a monopoly on tea sales to the British East India Company. A group of pro-independence activists boarded cargo ships in Boston Harbor and dumped crates of tea into the water. But another pro-independence newspaper hailed taxation without representation as good for the soul. "The Americans have plentifully enjoyed the delights and comforts, as well as the necessaries of life," said the *Newport Mercury*, "and it is well known that an increase of wealth and affluence paves the way to an increase of luxury, immorality and profaneness, and here kind providence interposes; and as it were, obliges them to forsake the use of one of their delights, to preserve their liberty."

In response to the Boston Tea Party, in 1774 Parliament passed a series of Coercive Acts that closed the port of Boston, eliminated most forms of self-rule in Massachusetts, and allowed British soldiers to be housed in colonial buildings. Shortly thereafter, Massachusetts was placed under military rule. In response, the First Continental Congress convened in Philadelphia with fifty-six delegates, representing every colony except Georgia. Members of the Congress included John Adams, Patrick Henry, George Washington, Samuel Adams, and John Hancock. The Congress declared that the Coercive Acts were "not to be obeyed," called for the formation of local militia units, and established a boycott of all British imports and an embargo on all exports to Britain. The boycott was aimed not only against British goods but also against British pleasures, the delegates declared, as "We will, in our several stations, encourage frugality, economy, and industry, . . . and will discountenance and discourage every species of extravagance and dissipation, especially all horse racing, and all kinds of gaming, cock fighting, exhibitions of shews, plays, and other expensive diversions and entertainments." That year, a letter to the *Newport Mercury*, authored by "Frugality," continued the redefinition of American freedom as self-denial: "We may talk and boast of liberty; but after all, the industrious and frugal only will be free." And Abigail Adams wrote to her husband, John, while he attended the Continental Congress, "If we expect to inherit the blessings of our Fathers, we should return a little more to their primitive Simplicity of Manners, and not sink into inglorious ease . . . [I]n the Country you must look for that virtue, of which you find but small Glimerings in the Metropolis . . . As for me I will seek wool and flax and work willingly with my Hands, and indeed there is occasion for all our industry and economy."

The simultaneous wars for independence and virtue then reached the point of no return. In 1775 the British military and colonial militias began firing at each other in the battles of Concord and Lexington and at Bunker Hill, and the Second Continental Congress convened in Philadelphia, where it elected John Hancock as its president and appointed George Washington general and commander in chief of the new Continental Army.

The following year, one day after Congress endorsed the Declaration of Independence, John Adams wrote hopefully that greater hardships—for Americans—would ensue: "It may be the Will of Heaven that America shall suffer Calamities still more wasting and Distresses yet more dreadfull. If this is to be the Case, it will have this good Effect, at least: it will inspire Us with many Virtues, which We have not, and correct many Errors, Follies, and Vices, which threaten to disturb, dishonour, and destroy Us. The Furnace of Affliction produces Refinement, in States as well as individuals." A few months later, Adams lamented that Americans had not yet suffered enough. "There is too much Corruption, even in this infant Age of our Republic," he said. "Virtue is not in Fashion. Vice is not infamous." In 1777 Benjamin Rush, a signer of the Declaration of Independence, participant in the Continental Congress, and surgeon general of the Continental Army, worried that the war would end before Americans had been forced to control themselves: "I hope the war will last until it introduces among us the same temperance in pleasure, the same modesty in dress, the same justice in business, and the same veneration for the name of the Deity which distinguished our ancestors." And in the fall of that year, when British forces under General Howe appeared poised to invade Philadelphia, John Adams told his wife of his secret wish for the revolutionary capital to be captured by the British, for it "would cure Americans of their vicious and luxurious and effeminate Appetites, Passions and Habits." One month later, British forces under General Howe did occupy Philadelphia, forcing Congress to relocate to York, Pennsylvania. But as we have seen, it did not "cure" Americans.

In 1778 welcome news came from France, which entered the war on the side of the Americans. Yet troubling news came from the streets, where vast indulgences in pleasure continued to plague the revolutionaries. When Samuel Adams heard that Bostonians were dressing flamboyantly, he thought that such behavior alone could doom independence. "Luxury and Extravagance are in my opinion totally destructive of those Virtues," he declared, "which are necessary for the Preservation of the Liberty and Happiness of the People." Yet the shame initiated by the revolutionaries began to circulate among ordinary Americans and penetrate into their own identities.

Many early American convicts applauded their own punishment as necessary for the control of "vice" and the preservation of the republic. In 1778 convicted murderers James Buchanan, Ezra Ross, and William Brooks hailed their impending hangings as a warning to Americans of the dangers of freedom and pleasure. They coauthored a statement "that we are indeed guilty . . . and that hereby we have forfeited our lives into the hands of public justice." To avoid such a fate, American youth should avoid "bad company, excessive drinking, profane cursing and swearing, shameful debaucheries, disobedience to parents, [and] profanation of the Lord's day."

The tide in the military conflict seemed to turn in favor of the British in 1779 and 1780, with the British capture of Savannah, Georgia, and Charleston, while the tide of commerce seemed to turn against virtue. Henry Laurens, a South Carolina delegate and president of the Second Continental Congress, seemed at times to be more concerned about the materialism of his countrymen than the loss of his native land to the British. "Reduce us all to poverty and cut off or wisely restrict that bane of patriotism, Commerce, and we shall soon become Patriots," he wrote in 1779, "but how hard is it for a rich or covetous Man to enter heartily into the Kingdom of Patriotism?" Laurens particularly hated festive celebrations and believed that the Olympic Games "and other fooleries brought on the desolation of Greece."

THE SOBER HOUSE

The Americans reversed the momentum of the military war in 1781 with decisive victories in North Carolina and at Yorktown, Virginia. A preliminary peace treaty was signed in Paris the following year, and in 1783 Britain officially ended hostilities. The Treaty of Paris, ratified in 1784, gave the Americans independence but precipitated a catastrophic economic depression in the former colonies. George Washington called for the "proper regulation" of trade, "freed, as much as possible, from those vices which luxury, the consequences of wealth and power, naturally introduce." Many of the founders welcomed the economic crisis because it would force Americans to abandon the luxuries that Thomas Jefferson called a "more baneful evil than toryism was during the war." At that time Jefferson and his compatriots also welcomed a comprehensive attack on drinking.

In 1784, Benjamin Rush, America's founding doctor, published *An Inquiry into the Effects of Spiritous Liquors,* which became one of the most important of the Founding Fathers' many antipleasure manifestoes during the early national period. Over the subsequent decades, more than 170,000 copies were distributed. Rush, the new nation's foremost medical authority, argued that drink and democracy could not mix. He also developed the idea that chronic drunkenness is a biological disease. "It belongs to the history of drunkenness to remark, that its paroxysms occur, like the paroxysms of many diseases, at certain periods, and after longer or shorter intervals." Though in such cases "The use of strong drink is at first the effect of free agency," it becomes a "necessity" and a "disease of the will." Because it seizes and overwhelms its victims, only one remedy was available. "My observations authorize me to say that persons who have been addicted to them should abstain from them suddenly and entirely," Rush declared. " 'Taste not, handle not, touch not' should be inscribed upon every vessel that contains spirits in the house of a man who wishes to be cured by habits of intemperance." These claims, though impossible to prove scientifically, became the basis not only for the temperance movement in the nineteenth century but also for the Prohibition movement in the early twentieth century, the "science" of addiction treatment in the late twentieth century, and, perhaps most significantly, the widely held belief that abstinence is the only cure for problem drinking. The idea of the modern-day rehabilitation center was also invented by Rush, who called for drunkards to be taken off the streets and locked up in a special asylum in Philadelphia called the Sober House. Interestingly, temperance reformers who followed Rush could not find a single medical or legal record of any loss of control due to drinking before Rush's writings appeared.

The Founding Fathers, who had done a substantial share of the drinking in America, nonetheless unanimously agreed that the bodily pleasures brought to the fore by alcohol had to be attacked and contained. David Ramsay, a South Carolina delegate to the Continental Congress, warned that "the temptations to drunkenness are so great and so common, as partly resulting from the climate, that great self-command, prudence and fortitude, and a strict discipline of the passions and appetites, are absolutely necessary to maintain the empire of reason over sense." Just before delegates arrived at the Constitutional Convention in Philadelphia in 1787, Rush wrote that the conflict between the republic and the body was nothing less than war:

> The American war is over; but this is far from being the case with the American Revolution. On the contrary, nothing but the first act of the great drama is closed ... The temple of tyranny has two doors. We bolted one of them by proper restraints; but we left the other open, by neglecting to guard against the effects of our own ignorance and licentiousness.

Soon after the delegates drafted a constitution for the new nation, Alexander Hamilton circulated *Federalist 12*, one of the Federalist Papers encouraging ratification, in which he argued that a tax on liquor, "if it should tend to diminish the consumption of it ... would be equally favorable to the agriculture, to the economy, to the morals and to the health of the society. There is perhaps nothing so much a subject of national extravagance as these spirits."

Hamilton's friend Tench Coxe expressed the hopes of many of the delegates to the Constitutional Convention that the encouragement of manufacturing would force Americans to restrain their desires for the pleasures of the body. Coxe, who served in the administrations of the first four presidents, stated that American industries would "lead us once more into the paths of virtue by restoring frugality and industry, those potent antidotes to the vices of mankind, and will give us real independence by rescuing us from the tyranny of foreign fashions and the destructive torrent of luxury." And while the Constitution was being drafted, Thomas Jefferson, who railed against drink and luxury with as much vitriol as any of his compatriots, wrote to his daughter a paean to work that could have been penned by the most stringent of Puritans:

It is your future happiness which interests me, and nothing can contribute more to it (moral rectitude always excepted) than the contracting a habit of industry and activity. Of all the cankers of human happiness, none corrodes it with so silent, yet so baneful a tooth, as indolence. Determine never to be idle. No person will have occasion to complain of the want of time, who never loses any. It is wonderful how much may be done, if we are always doing.

In 1788, while the states were ratifying the Constitution, Benjamin Rush recommended the elimination of fairs, horse racing, cockfighting, and Sunday amusements, which led to "gaming—drunkenness—and uncleanness" as well as "habits of idleness and a love of pleasure." Moreover, taverns and "Clubs of all kinds, where the only business of the company, is feeding (for that is the true name of a gratification that is simply animal) are hurtful to morals." The following year, Congress completed the establishment of an independent republic with the election of Washington as president and Adams as vice president, but most of the states had already formalized the conflict between the republic and bodily pleasures by declaring in their constitutions that the life of the nation depended upon "a firm adherence to justice, moderation, temperance, frugality, and virtue."

In 1790, when more than one hundred thousand Americans were living in tavern-filled cities, Secretary of the Treasury Alexander Hamilton succeeded in winning passage of an excise tax on the production of whiskey. Hamilton argued before Congress that it would serve the twin purposes of strengthening the federal government by opening a source of revenue for it while tightening the morals of the people:

The consumption of ardent spirits particularly, no doubt very much on account of their cheapness, is carried to an extreme, which is truly to be regretted, as well in regard to the health and the morals, as to the economy of the community. Should the increase of duties tend to a decrease of the consumption of those articles, the effect would be, in every respect, desirable. The saving which it would occasion would leave individuals more at their ease, and promote a more favorable balance of trade.

In the following year, the Bill of Rights was ratified and added to the Constitution, and Benjamin Rush published *The Drunkard's Emblem,* a condemnation of heavy drinking. Rush also wrote to Thomas Jefferson that whiskey and rum were "antifederal" and "the companions of all those vices that are calculated to dishonor and enslave our country."

Though lower-class Americans continued to fill taverns, the class of men who led the Revolution were undergoing a radical self-reformation. Upper-class colonists had drunk just as heartily as their social inferiors before the War of Independence, but in the new nation, foreign visitors often commented that it was much more difficult to get a drink at an upper-class dinner party than it had been during the colonial era. American elites gave up drinking and flocked to coffeehouses. But the people did not follow. George Washington, James Madison, and Robert Morris were among many of the Founding Fathers who supported excise taxes on alcohol after the Revolution as a means to curb drinking. Virtually all of these attempts, however, were voted down or went unenforced. The government's attempt in 1794 to enforce the national whiskey tax in western Pennsylvania resulted in what came to be called the Whiskey Rebellion, when renegades all over the region not only refused to pay up but also tarred and feathered tax collectors.

For a time, it appeared as if the antidrinking campaign had failed. Average annual consumption of absolute alcohol for adults rose from 5.8 gallons in 1790 to 7.1 gallons by 1810. But the fight had begun in an enduring civil war over pleasure.

A PURE NATION

Revolutionary leaders believed—rightly—that sexual desire was an even greater threat than drunkenness to the new nation of self-regulating men. This was why, according to Jefferson, any American should be discouraged from visiting Europe, where "he is led by the strongest of all the human passions, into a spirit for female intrigue, destructive of his own and others' happiness, or a passion for whores, destructive of his health, and, in both cases, learns to consider fidelity to the marriage bed as an ungentlemanly practice, and inconsistent with happiness." Benjamin Rush best explained why America had to attack sensual pleasure. For much of his career, Rush wrote and spoke about the inherent conflict between sexuality and a republic of "free" men. In 1788 he wrote that the pleasure culture in the cities had a "pernicious influence upon morals, and thereby prepare our country for misery and slavery."

What followed was what historian Clare Lyons calls "the assault on nonmarital sexuality."

First came increased prosecution of illicit sex. The number of arrests for prostitution in Philadelphia grew by more than 60 percent over the first twenty years of independence. Then came "reform." In Philadelphia in 1790, the Association of the District of Southwark for the Suppression of Vice and Immorality was the first of many antivice organizations to be established in the early years of the republic. These groups targeted gambling houses, brothels, dance halls, and lower-class taverns.

The movement against renegades gained institutional teeth in the second decade of the United States with the rapid growth of reformatory asylums. The Magdalen Society was founded in Philadelphia and New York with the mission of "relieving and reclaiming unhappy females who have Swerv'd from the paths of virtue." Members of the society visited not only prostitutes but also women who were simply promiscuous in prisons and almshouses and attempted to persuade them to enter the society's asylum, where in exchange for free room, board, and medical care, they would give up a life of sexual license for a program of chastity, domestic labor, regimentation, and moral instruction. The objective of these asylums was to make the "fallen women" into wives and mothers. Many women took the deal as the only means to obtain treatment for venereal disease. Once inside the asylum, however, inmates found that they could not leave: the doors remained locked, and the grounds were enclosed by a fence. Only the managers decided who could be discharged. Some women escaped by climbing the fence, but most stayed until they were told they were properly "respectable" and ready to enter society as "pure" women. This process of purification took from several months up to a year.

On the streets after the Revolution, arrests increased for cross-racial sexuality. Whereas for most of the eighteenth-century copulation across the color line flourished largely unpunished, in the early national period, many women were arrested simply for having sex with men of another race. Barbara Clifford was arrested in Philadelphia in 1801 for "being caught in Bed with a Black man." Elizabeth Flanagan was charged in 1802 with "frequently going to Bed with different black men." Margaret Fisher

committed a grave crime in 1803, that of "being found in bed with a Negro man and with a white man at another [time]." Managers of brothels
were suddenly charged with the specific crime of sexual race mixing. In
1802 Rachel White was arrested for "keeping a bawdy house by letting
black men and white women go to bed together." Rosanna Grovis, a black
madam, also committed the crime of "keeping Girls of Different Colours"
in her brothel.

Most tellingly, in the decades after the Revolution, a raft of medical
literature appeared that counseled against all forms of nonmarital—and
even many forms of marital—sex. Various behaviors were described in
great detail and labeled as "deviant." Men were advised to redirect their
sexual energies into work, and women were told that females were naturally nonsexual and that "good" women were pure and chaste. In the
1810s and 1820s, Benjamin Rush authored a series of sexual manuals
for the new nation in which he declared that indulgence in bodily pleasures, "when excessive, becomes a disease of both the body and mind."
Too much sex could cause not only vertigo and epilepsy but also "seminal
weakness, impotence . . . pulmonary consumption, hypochondriasis, loss
of memory . . . and death." Even self-pleasure was suddenly dangerous,
as a number of doctors claimed. One of the most prolific fields of invention in the young United States was anti-masturbation. By the middle of
the nineteenth century, one could purchase a wide variety of devices and
medication to control the desire to play with oneself, including penis cases
and sleeping mitts. More than twenty patents were awarded for devices to
keep women from spreading their legs.

As for the principal regulator of sexuality—marriage—colonial governments for the most part had treated divorce as a matter between husband and wife and perhaps involving the local community, not as a matter
of interest to the government. But spurred on by the Founding Fathers,
during the early national period the states replaced the few and vague divorce laws of the colonies with laws tightly and specifically regulating
divorce. This ended the massive eighteenth-century trend of self-divorce.
As the historian Nancy Cott puts it, "Post-Revolutionary legislators wanted
to reassert their authority over what (some) people had done under the
aegis of local tolerance." Granting divorce rights has often been seen as
a move toward individual freedom, but the state of Georgia knew better.
The state's legislators understood that it was actually a move toward greater

control of intimate life. Acknowledging its inability to control "circumstances" that "may require a dissolution of contracts founded on the most binding and sacred obligations," in 1802 the state enacted a law regulating divorce because "dissolution [of a marriage] ought not to be dependent on private will, but should require legislative interference; inasmuch as the republic is deeply interested in the private business of its citizens." After independence, a marriage remained legally binding until, according to Cott, a plaintiff for divorce proved to the court that he or she had upheld "ideal spousal behavior" and that the spouse was adulterous, sexually dysfunctional, or chronically absent. No longer could an unhappy wife or husband simply walk away from a marriage. "A wife petitioning for divorce had to show how attentive, obedient, and long-suffering she had been (and, of course, sexually faithful) while she was being victimized. A husband's adequacy rested in economic support."

"True crime" pamphlets became enormously popular in the early nineteenth century, and among the common true crimes recounted in them were sexual crimes, including prostitution, sodomy, adultery, and fornication. Women who bore illegitimate children in true crime stories were depicted as immoral and their children as unhealthy. In the early national period, public relief (welfare) for unmarried mothers was discontinued and replaced by asylums for illegitimate children. Women who bore children out of wedlock were forced to turn them over to the state, which officially labeled them as "illegimate." Children were not allowed to be taken out of the asylums until the cost of caring for them had been reimbursed by a parent. If a debt was not paid, the asylums would typically put the child "out to service" until he or she worked off what was owed. Many illegitimate "bastards" became permanent orphans.

A NEW WAR

John Adams rose to the heights of American politics, but his life ended in disappointment. After his term as vice president under Washington, he ran for president in 1796 on the Federalist Party ticket and narrowly defeated his rival, Thomas Jefferson of the Democratic-Republicans. Four years later, however, Jefferson reversed the results in another close vote. Following his 1800 defeat, Adams retired from politics and returned to farming at his home in Quincy, Massachusetts. He eventually reconciled with Jefferson and in 1812 began a lengthy epistolary friendship with the Virginian. By then many Americans had subscribed to the philosophies of the Founding Fathers and had devoted themselves to the rigors of democratic life. But despite the best efforts of the nation's founders to train the people for self-governance, "decadence" and "vice" did not disappear in the early years of the republic. Drinking increased. The cities, with their saloons and prostitutes and illicit couplings, grew exponentially. New, mass-produced goods introduced luxuries to common people. Poor folk, even slaves, began to dress ostentatiously. And many of the newly rich resembled the aristocracies of Europe. Facilitating all of this vice was a new economic order that Adams, Jefferson, and most of the Founding Fathers feared.

Today, many on the conservative side of the political spectrum like to make the founders into champions of a free-market economy, while many on the left claim that they were simply the tools of the rising merchant class. Neither of these sides understands that the market economy has always been a friend of renegades and an enemy of moral guardians. When Americans lived on farms in isolated towns where they grew, made, and bartered for everything they used, they could not purchase beer at a saloon, sex from a prostitute, contraceptives and pornography from a corner shop, or flashy clothes from British importers. They had nowhere to go to dance, gamble, or search for paramours in public. And they had to work, pulling their livelihoods from the soil, from before dawn until after dusk. This is why so many of the founders wished that Americans would stay on farms and away from cities and commerce. It is why Jefferson declared that "those who labor in the earth are the chosen people of God if ever He had a chosen people" and that "the mobs of great cities add just so much to the support of pure government as sores do to the strength of the human body." It is why John Adams warned that "commerce, luxury, and avarice have destroyed every republican government." It is why he denounced credit, which allowed ordinary people to purchase extraordinary things, as being responsible for "most of the Luxury & Folly which has yet infected our People." And it is why most of the Founding Fathers insisted that the states allow only landowners to vote and hold public office, which insured that farmers, and not merchants, bankers, manufacturers, or consumers, would control the government. But what Adams called the "universal gangrene of avarice" continued to spread in the streets underneath the government.

In the last years of his life, Adams wrote to his friend Jefferson a set of plaintive questions: "Will you tell me how to prevent riches from becoming the effects of temperance and industry? Will you tell me how to prevent riches from producing luxury? Will you tell me how to prevent luxury from producing effeminacy, intoxication, extravagance, vice, and folly?" Jefferson had no answer. And there would be no winner in the war between pleasure and discipline. During the Revolution, Americans began what would be a long resistance to the obligations and sacrifices required by the dark side of democracy. The fight was on between disciplinarians and renegades, but neither would win. The founding of the United States simply began the war that continues today.

★ 2 ★

THE FREEDOM OF SLAVERY

When he rubbed burnt cork onto his white face, Dan Emmett knew the secret of slavery. When he let his body move on stage the way he never would off stage, he knew what the abolitionists would not say. When he sang songs of easy work and lazy days, told jokes about sex in black dialect, and heard his audience roar its approval, he knew what our history textbooks still keep secret. Emmett, one of the creators of the blackface minstrel show, knew that slaves enjoyed pleasures that were forbidden for white people. He knew that slaves were often the envy of America.

Whites imitating blacks is America's oldest pastime. It began on the decks of ships that brought the first slaves to the New World, where European crewmen gleefully joined the dances of their African hostages, and it continued on the plantations in the southern colonies, where masters and overseers were known to partake in the revelries in the slave quarters. But this curious phenomenon became a national obsession with the advent of steamboats and railroads in the early 1800s, when, for the first time, isolated white Americans from all over the country could easily travel south to see large numbers of black people in person.

In the 1810s, soon after giant paddlewheel boats began carting passengers along the rivers that ran from Pittsburgh and Cincinnati to St. Louis, Memphis, through the Mississippi Delta, and all the way down to New Orleans, white entertainers imitating black songs and dances became a common sight on the streets of major cities. By the 1840s, when the curious could ride a train from New York City to Pittsburgh, then take steamboats to the cotton fields of Mississippi, whites all over America were acting black. The ethnomusicologist Dale Cockrell has estimated that by

1843, characters in blackface had appeared in more than twenty thousand American stage performances. "The facts are that blackface theater was extremely common, and Americans had ample opportunities to see it, often had to choose between competing performances on the same night, and attended blackface performances with enthusiasm."

On the night of February 6, 1843, at the shabby, raucous Amphitheatre of the Republic in the Bowery district of New York City, Emmett and three other white men, calling themselves the Virginia Minstrels, made it into a form of art. That night they put on the first theatrical performance devoted entirely to a blackface minstrel act. The quartet, dressed as slaves, sang songs and told jokes in black dialect and did their best to perform the dances that Emmett had seen on the streets of Cincinnati, on Kentucky plantations, and on the steamboats that plied the Ohio River. The performance was so popular that the theater in which it was staged soon began booking minstrel shows exclusively. By the middle of the decade, the *Spirit of the Times,* one of the leading theater journals in New York, reported that theaters staging minstrel shows "are among the best frequented and most profitable places of amusement in New York," and that while an attempt to put on an Italian opera house "has resulted in bankruptcy, the Ethiopian Opera has flourished like a green bay tree." Dozens of minstrel troupes performed on New York's biggest stages and toured the country. Theaters devoted to the genre appeared in every major American city by the 1860s, and by the end of the century, blackface performance was a common, accepted, and respectable amusement. According to virtually all historians of American popular culture, it was the preeminent form of entertainment in the nineteenth century.

Blackface minstrelsy is now often considered to be antiblack parody, and some of it certainly was, but scholars have recently begun to see the songs of Dan Emmett and many other performers in the genre as expressions of desire for the freedoms they saw in the culture of the slaves. "Just as the minstrel stage held out the possibility that whites could be 'black' for a while but nonetheless white," David Roediger, the leading historian of "whiteness," has written, "it offered the possibilities that, via blackface, preindustrial joys could survive amidst industrial discipline." One of Emmett's first songs was "De Boatman's Dance," a tribute to the slaves and free blacks who worked on the steamboats of the Old South. Emmett admired what he saw as their embrace of pleasure, the freedom of their bodies, and their attitude that work was simply a means to fun:

> Hi ho, de boatmen row,
> Floatin' down de river de Ohio.
>
> De boatmen dance, de boatmen sing,
> de boatmen up to ebry ting,
> An when de boatmen gets on shore,
> he spends his cash and works for more,
>
> Den dance de boatman dance,
> O dance de boatman dance,
> O dance all night till broad daylight,
> an go home wid de gals in de morning.

The tragedy of Dan Emmett's song about these black men—the tragedy of all minstrelsy and of being a free white man—was that this kind of freedom could only be visited:

> I wen on board de odder day
> To see what de boatman had to say;
> Dar I let my passions loose
> An dey cram me in de callaboose.
>
> I've come dis time, I'll come no more,
> Let me loose I'll go on shore.

If we dismiss the men who painted their faces black as deluded racists, we miss what they were telling us, even if subconsciously, about what free Americans were missing from their lives. As we will see, much of what they missed could be found in the lives of real slaves. Yet those who wished to be considered good American citizens knew that distancing oneself from all that African American culture represented was a principal qualification. So they allowed themselves to enjoy the pleasures of blackness only vicariously.

This is not an endorsement of slavery. But it is an argument that many freedoms we now cherish were available only to slaves in early America, and that citizenship in the young republic was a terribly constrained thing. It also reveals why slaves and their descendents were able to create a culture that has been so envied—and resented—not just by white Americans but also by the world.

Emmett began writing songs of longing for plantation life soon after he saw slaves for the first time. In 1834, when he arrived in Cincinnati from his home in central Ohio, Emmett encountered a city that was uniquely situated at the crossroads of slavery and freedom. Set among hills that looked across the Ohio River and onto plantations in Kentucky, there was no better place in America from which to compare the two cultures. Because it was the only major northern city located on the border between the two societies, in Cincinnati one could see in a single day great numbers of fugitive slaves, free blacks, and whites of every class and immigrant group who worked, fought, danced, and slept together. It is certainly no accident that most of the creators of blackface minstrelsy spent time in the city known as "the Queen of the West."

Thomas Dartmouth "Daddy" Rice, the "father of American minstrelsy," made his way from New York City down the Ohio River to Cincinnati, where he found inspiration for one of the classic characters of the American theater in a song about "Jim Crow," sung by a black stage driver. Stephen Foster began writing songs soon after he moved to Cincinnati to work for his brother's riverboat company. He produced a large portion of the minstrel genre, including "Camptown Races," "Swanee River," and "My Old Kentucky Home." Dan Rice, perhaps the most famous blackface performer of the nineteenth century—and Abraham Lincoln's favorite— imitated the slaves and ex-slaves he encountered as a horse jockey and riverboat gambler along the Ohio River. Other minstrel performers traveled deeper in the South and sought company with slaves. Billy Whitlock, who gained fame as the banjo player in Emmett's troupe, toured plantations where he would "quietly steal off to some Negro hut to hear the darkeys sing and see them dance, taking with him a jug of whiskey to make them all the merrier."

Soon after arriving in Cincinnati, Emmett enlisted in the army and was stationed at a base just over the river in Newport, Kentucky. According to his diary, he joined the marching band and "practiced the drum incessantly." A year later Emmett was transferred to a base in Missouri, a state where slaves made up more than 15 percent of the population. Discharged in the summer of 1835, the young musician returned to Cincinnati, but the songs he began writing showed that he'd left much of his heart with the slaves. When he looked across the Ohio River from the free North, he saw the promised land:

> I just arrived in town, for to pass de time away,
> And I settled all my bisness accordin',
> But I found it so cold when up de street,
> Dat I wish'd I was on de oder side ob Jordan.

> So take off your coat, boys,
> And roll up your sleeves,
> For Jordan is a hard road to trabel.

In the late 1830s, Emmett joined a traveling circus, where he began performing in blackface and imitating the slaves and ex-slaves he had encountered. Emmett performed with both the Virginia Minstrels and as a solo act. A common theme in his music was a lament for having been born free. One of his troupe's most popular acts was a skit called "Hard Times," a portrayal of life in freedom in which Emmett played a character named Showman, "a chap that won't work." During the Civil War, Emmett wrote "Road to Richmond," in which he imagined the regret of a slave who joined the Union army:

> When I was young and in my prime,
> Labor nebber done.
> I used to work, but took my time.

It was during the war that Emmett gained national prominence for his most famous song, which today is known as the anthem of Southern racism, but for Emmett was actually a wish to be a slave:

> I wish I was in Dixie,
> Hooray! Hooray!
> In Dixie Land, I'll take my stand,

> *To lib and die in Dixie,*
> *Away, away,*
> *Away down south in Dixie . . .*
> *Freedom to me will never pay!*

Writing from Pittsburgh in 1851, a few years after leaving Cincinnati, Stephen Foster expressed similar regrets in "Farewell, My Lilly Dear":

> *Old massa sends me roaming,*
> *So Lilly, fare-you-well!*
> *Oh! Fare-you-well, my true love,*
> *Farewell, old Tennessee.*

Dan Emmett was just one of many songwriters who saw black men as objects of desire, as in "Dandy Jim from Caroline":

> *For my ole massa tole me,*
> *I'm de best looking nigga in de county oh,*
> *I look in de glass, as I found it so,*
> *Just as massa tell me, oh . . .*

> *Oh, beauty is but skin deep,*
> *But wid Miss Dinah none compete;*
> *She changed her name from lubly Dine,*
> *To Mrs. Dandy Jim of Caroline.*

Much has been made of the occasional references to grotesque Negro facial features, but minstrel songs, particularly those written during slavery, more frequently referred to longings for beautiful slave women on the plantation. Benjamin Hanby's "Darling Nelly Gray," a popular song in the 1850s, told of love amid the pastoral splendor of Kentucky: "When the moon had climb'd the mountain, and the stars were shining too, / Then I'd take my darling Nelly Gray, / And we'd float down the river in my little red canoe, / While my banjo sweetly I would play." The beauty of the land was often compared to the loveliness and grace of slave women, as in Stephen Foster's "Melinda May":

Lubly Melinda is bright as de beam,
No snow-drop was ebber more fair,
She smiles like de roses dat bloom round de stream,
And sings like de birds in de air.

And John P. Ordway's "Twinkling Stars Are Laughing, Love":

While your bright eyes look in mine,
Peeping stars they seem to be.
Golden beams are shining, love,
Shining on you to bless;
Like the queen of night you fill
Darkest space with loveliness.

To the twenty-first-century ear, these lyrics sound conventionally romantic. But to Victorian America, any such expression of physical desire—no
matter how sweetly phrased—was disreputable, lowbrow, and black.

Blackface minstrelsy was widely popular but not "respectable." It was
criticized on moral grounds not because it was seen as racist but because
it was seen as wild, erotic, and free. There was no greater evidence of the
freedoms experienced in blackface than the attacks on it by the keepers
of American morality. Newspapers catering to a genteel readership called
minstrels "demons of disorder" who "made night hideous." In one of its
many outraged reviews, the *Spirit of the Times* declared,

> But we scarcely believe a respectable audience would not patronize
> or encourage Negro buffo songs here. We hope they would not. It
> is a duty society owes to itself to discountenance everything which
> tends to vitiate public taste.

The *New York Mirror* called on audiences to give blackface performers
"all the success they deserve—which is a sound and glorious pelting from
the stage." A group of moral reformers in New York City was so alarmed
by the first performed impersonations of slaves that in 1832 it purchased
the theater that staged them and converted it to an evangelical chapel.
White America was at war with itself. "The two most popular charac-

ters in the world at the present time," the *Boston Post* reported in 1838, "are Victoria," the queen who symbolized bourgeois repression, "and Jim Crow."

But the creator of Jim Crow, T. D. Rice, claimed to know in his most famous song what was really in the hearts of the Victorians:

> *I'm so glad dat I'm a niggar,*
> *An don't you wish you was too*
> *For den you'd gain popularity*
> *By jumping Jim Crow.*
>
> *Now my brother niggars,*
> *I do not think it right,*
> *Dat you should laugh at dem*
> *Who happen to be white.*
>
> *Kase it dar misfortune,*
> *And dey'd spend ebery dollar,*
> *If dey only could be*
> *Gentlemen ob colour.*
>
> *It almost break my heart,*
> *To see dem envy me.*

The literary critic W. T. Lhamon Jr., who has authored several pathbreaking books on race in American culture, grants that depictions of blacks in minstrel songs were stereotypes but reminds us that there is no such thing as an "accurate" or "authentic" portrayal of black culture, either. More important, Lhamon argues that slave culture represented pleasure and freedom to blackface performers and fans, and danger to good citizens. In early minstrel shows, whites "were identifying with blacks as representations of all that the YMCAs [which taught industrial discipline to urban youth] and evangelical organizers were working to suppress." The renegades who rubbed burnt cork onto their faces in the antebellum period "unmistakably expressed fondness for black wit and gestures."

Dan Emmett and the first generation of blackface minstrel performers were pioneers of what is now a global phenomenon. Blues, jazz, and rhythm and blues became more popular among whites than among African Americans, and there are now more fans of what is often called "the music of freedom" in Europe and Japan than in the United States. The same is true of hip-hop, whose white and non-American listeners outnumber the entire African American population. Radio stations from Orange County to Stockholm, Johannesburg, and Jakarta fill their playlists with sounds from the Bronx, Atlanta, and Compton. But to find the original source of this envy, we must return first to the lives of free white people in early America, and then to the plantation.

INFINITE LABOR

Dan Emmett knew well what it meant to be a free American. Born in 1815 in Ohio—a state where slavery was banned—he came of age during a time when the meaning of freedom was being hammered out. As Emmett learned, American freedom was curiously burdensome and restrictive. His father and mother knew this before he was born. Sometime in the early eighteen hundreds, they trekked to the flat plain between the Ohio River and Lake Erie and settled in Mount Vernon, which was then a few small buildings in a forest of tall trees. Like other Americans who headed west in search of the physical foundation of American freedom—land—Abraham and Sarah Emmett found that to be free was to work hard and constantly. Abraham felled trees and then shaped them into logs, from which he built their home by hand. To make a living, he pounded hot metal into tools and weapons as the town's only blacksmith, while Sarah undoubtedly worked even harder as the housekeeper and mother of four children.

Life in frontier towns like Mount Vernon was nearly constant toil. From colonial times through the nineteenth century, observers frequently reported on the enormity of the workload for American settlers. A Virginia official in the 1620s reported back to England that for settlers in the colony, "[t]he labor is infynite." John Winthrop Jr., the son of the governor of the Massachusetts Bay Colony, detailed the tasks necessary to make a civilization in the wilderness. "Plantations in their beginnings have [more than] worke [e]nough, and find difficulties sufficient to settle a comfortable way of subsistence, thee beinge buildings, fencings, clearinge, and breakinge up of ground, lands to be attended, orchards to be planted, highways and bridges and fortifications to be made, and all thinges to doe, as in the beginning of the world." The prospect of owning land whipped many American colonists to outwork everyone else on the planet.

Governor William Bradford of the Plymouth Colony recalled that once private land ownership was made available to his settlers, "The women now went willingly into the field and took their little ones with them to set corn; which before would allege weakness and inability; whom to have compelled would have been thought great tyranny and oppression." Partly out of necessity, partly for independence, and partly from their devotion to the Protestant work ethic, the first American colonists eliminated many forms of leisure enjoyed by those who remained in England, including various folk dances, singing festivals, communal feasts and games, and scores of holidays. Work only grew more intense in the eighteenth century, when patterns of labor moved from seasonal to continuous schedules in every part of the colonial economy. By the start of the nineteenth century, most households had added manufacturing to their grueling agricultural production.

The English writer Frances Trollope, who lived for several years on the Ohio frontier in the 1820s and 1830s, wrote with astonishment about the life of women who held Sarah Emmett's position. In addition to cooking and cleaning and minding the children, they spun and wove all the clothes for the family, manufactured all the soap and candles, and made butter to use and to sell for sundries in town. "The life she leads," Trollope wrote, "is one of hardship, privation, and labour." Whether a farm produced only enough for subsistence, produced a surplus for sale, or both, those who lived on it typically spent nearly every waking hour at work. Unlike slaves, these "freeholders" were entirely responsible for their livelihood, and so, even when all the work was done, their thoughts remained occupied by it. Diaries of farmers in the eighteenth and nineteenth centuries are filled with detailed records of labor done and labor in need of doing, as well as motivational sayings on the virtues of diligence, frugality, and discipline.

Of course, hard work was necessary for a decent life in a preindustrial land, but in American culture it was celebrated as a good thing in itself. No people worked harder, scorned leisure more fervently, or expressed more pride in these traits than did the free Americans of the new republic.

"There is, probably, no people on earth with whom business constitutes pleasure, and industry amusement, in an equal degree with the inhabitants of the United States of America," said the Viennese immigrant and author Francis Grund, who, like many European visitors to the early-nineteenth-century United States, commented with pity on what was often called the American "disease of work." Grund noted that, for Americans, work was "the principal source of their happiness" and they were "absolutely wretched without it."

From the time of the Puritan settlers through Dan Emmett's lifetime, children's books, school primers, newspaper editorials, poems, pamphlets, sermons, and political speeches told Americans that to work was to be godly and to be idle was to be wretched. Cotton Mather instructed parents to keep their children in "continual Employment" so as to "deliver them from the Temptations of Idleness," and Thomas Shepard spoke for all Puritans when he told his son to "abhor . . . one hour of idleness as you would be ashamed of one hour of drunkenness." In the eighteenth century, Benjamin Franklin adapted the Puritan work ethic to the age of capitalism with his enormously popular aphorisms that counseled Americans to work all hours of the day in order to achieve dignity and respect. "It is the working man who is the happy man," he wrote in *Poor Richard's Almanack*. "It is the idle man who is the miserable man." With the beginning of mass industrial production in the nineteenth century, pride in work and shame in leisure became the defining characteristics of good citizens of the young nation.

A textbook in Dan Emmett's school might have been *A New Picture-Book*, a standard primer in the 1830s, whose first words are this poem:

How doth the little busy bee
Improve each shining hour;
And gather honey all the day,
From every opening flower;

In works of labor or of skill,
I would be busy too;
For Satan finds some mischief still,
For idle hands to do.

His Sunday school book might have been *Little Verses for Good Children,* which includes a similar injunction:

> *Work with your might,*
> *'Tis God's command:*
> *Let work and prayer*
> *Go hand in hand.*
>
> *All honest labor*
> *God will bless;*
> *Let me not live*
> *In idleness.*

American schools in the early nineteenth century taught children to avoid the "frivolities" of play and to make themselves "useful" through the exercise of self-denial. "Love not the world, nor the things that are in the world," was one lesson in *The United States Spelling Book,* a commonly used textbook in early-nineteenth-century schools. "For all that is in the world, the lust of the flesh, and the lust of the eye; is not of him that made us; but is of the world." And Dan Emmett almost certainly read Noah Webster's *American Spelling Book,* the best-selling primer of the nineteenth century, which instructed its young readers that "[a] wise child loves to learn his books, but the fool would choose to play with toys."

THE SECRET

White minstrels were not the only people who knew the secret of slavery. Junius Quattlebaum knew it, too. In 1937 a young white man named Henry Grant brought a tape recorder to Quattlebaum's little wooden shack on a dirt patch near a brick factory on the outskirts of Columbia, South Carolina. Grant was one of hundreds of writers hired by the Federal Writers' Project, an agency of Franklin Roosevelt's New Deal government, to record the memories of former slaves. "Well, sir, you want to talk to me 'bout them good old days back yonder in slavery time, does you?" Quattlebaum asked. "I call them good old days, 'cause I has never had as much since." Quattlebaum was typical of the 2,300 ex-slaves who were interviewed. Many did tell of whippings, sadistic overseers, loved ones being sold away, and of wishing to be free. But we must come to terms with the fact that a *majority* of ex-slaves who offered an evaluation of slavery—field hands and house slaves, men and women—had a positive view of the institution, and many unabashedly wished to return to their slave days.

Racists point to such statements as evidence of black inferiority. Our textbooks ignore them. But we can look squarely at the longing for slavery and turn racism on its head.

Junius Quattlebaum expressed the experience of many when he re-called, "I has worked harder since de war betwixt de North and de South than I ever worked under my marster and missus." The plantation was cer-tainly no paradise, but to many people who had experienced both slavery and freedom, the former was clearly preferable. "All de slaves worked pretty hard sometimes but never too hard," said Quattlebaum. "They worked wid light and happy heart 'cause they knowed dat marster would take good care of them; give them a plenty of good vittles, warm clothes, and warm houses to sleep in, when de cold weather come." Quattlebaum concluded his com-parison of slavery with freedom in virtually the same language used by the minstrels. "Easy livin' is 'bout half of life to white folks but it is all of life to most niggers," he said. "It sho' is."

Mary Frances Brown, who was born a slave in Marlboro County, South Carolina, insisted, "Dey were happy time back dere." As for the food on the plantation, "I ain't nebber see de lak no time" in freedom. "Dem were de times to lib." Brown sang a song for her interviewer that she said was popu-lar among ex-slaves. It is remarkably similar to dozens of minstrel songs:

> We got a home ober dere,
> Come an' let us go,
> Come an' let us go,
> Where pleasure neber die
>
> Oh! Let us go where pleasure neber die,
> Neber die,
> Come and let us go,
> Where pleasure neber die, neber die.

Again and again, the ex-slaves told of regret when freedom came. "Course, after the war, nothing was right no more," remembered William Curtis, who had been a slave in what is now Oklahoma. "Yes, we was free, but we didn't know what to do. We didn't want to leave our old Master and our old home." Most of the interviewees feared and hated the Union troops who freed them, and many, like Gabe Emanuel of Mississippi, sabotaged their liberators. "Dey'd eat up all de marster's vit'als an' drink up all his good lik-ker," Emanuel remembered. "One time us sot fire to a bridge de Yankees had to cross to git to de plantation. Dey had to camp on de other side, 'cause dey was too lazy to put out de fire. Dat's ju' lak I figgered it . . . Lawdy! I sho' was happy when I was a slave."

Henri Necaise, who was a slave in Pass Christian, Mississippi, until his early thirties, expressed the preference of most of the interviewees. "I was better off when I was a slave dan I is now, 'cause I had ever'thing furnished me den," he said. "Now I got to do it all myse'f." Many of the ex-slaves who remembered being sold or whipped still wished to return to the "good old days." As Dave Harper of Danville, Missouri, bluntly put it, "I was sold for $715. When de freedom come, I said, 'Give me $715 and I'll go back.'" Likewise, Clara Young of Alabama, who was in her twenties when she was emancipated, remembered being sold and whipped but when asked what she thought about slavery declared, "Well, leetle Miss, I tell you, I wish it was back. Us was a lot better off in dem days dan we is now. If dem Yankees had lef' us 'lone we'd been a lot happier." Many of the interviewees were aware that their feelings and recollections contradicted the dominant view of slavery in the twentieth century. James Lucas, who was owned by Jefferson Davis, remarked, "I guess slav'ry was wrong, but I 'members us had some mighty good times . . . One thing I does know is dat a heap of slaves was worse off after de War . . . Now dey is got to work or die. In dem days you worked an' rested an' knowed you'd be fed. In middle of de day us rested an' waited for de horn to blow to go back to de fiel'.'"

Many of the interviewees remembered the following as the most popu-lar song among slaves during the Civil War:

Jeff Davis is President
Abe Lincoln is a fool
Come here, see Jeff ride the gray horse
And Abe Lincoln the mule.

Contrary to what popular images of emancipation tell us, when given the opportunity to leave the plantation, most slaves stayed. Lina Hunter's memory of the moment of freedom was similar to that of most of the interviewees. After the Yankees came, "Freedom didn't make so many changes on our place right at fust, 'cause most of de slaves stayed right on dar, and things went on jus' lak dey had 'fore dere was any war," she recalled. "Marse Jack had done told 'em dey was free, but dat dem what wanted to stay would be tuk keer of same as 'fore de war. Dere warn't many what left neither, 'cause Marse Jack had been so good to evvy one of 'em dey didn't want to go 'way." The quantitative historian Paul D. Escott tabulated all of the ex-slave interviews and found that 9.6 percent stayed with their master after freedom but were uncertain as to how long, 18.8 percent stayed for one to twelve months, 14.9 percent stayed for one to five years, and 22.1 percent stayed for more than five years. By contrast, only 9 percent left immediately after emancipation.

What these statistics and the wistful recollections of hundreds of ex-slaves point to is that slaves were able to create the culture so envied by whites not despite slavery, but *because* of it. In fact, slaves held enormous advantages over those considered free—especially over those who wished to be good American citizens—and they participated in a broader range of activities and self-expression than any other group in early America.

LIFE OVER WORK

When Dan Emmett moved to Cincinnati, he might have crossed paths with a young seminary student and abolitionist named Theodore Dwight Weld. Like most abolitionists, Weld believed, contrary to what we now assume, that one of slavery's evils was its promotion of sloth. He argued that because slavery denied the incentive to work, it produced not only "ignorance and stupidity" but also "the petty thefts of the slaves, the necessity of constant watching," and, rather than the willful exertion of free labor, "reluctant service."

Opponents of slavery disagreed over many issues—whether it should be abolished immediately or gradually, whether slavery was a moral or political problem, whether blacks were naturally inferior—but all agreed that "the peculiar institution" made people less industrious. The Republican

Party members who drove the North to war believed that the laziness of slaves and masters threatened the hard-working culture of the free states. "Free labor languishes and becomes degrading when put in competition with slave labor," said a leading member of the party in 1860, "and idleness, poverty, and vice, among large classes of non-slaveholders take the place of industry and thrift and virtue." Party leaders produced reams of statistics to support their view that slave labor was less productive than free labor and publicized observations on the work habits of the slaves made by northern visitors to the South.

In the 1850s, Frederick Law Olmsted spent a year's time touring the South and wrote three volumes describing what he saw. Nothing was more striking to Olmsted than the inefficiency of slaves, who appeared "to move very slowly and awkwardly." The slaves he saw avoided work every chance they got, as he observed on one plantation near Charleston: "The overseer rode about among them, on a horse, carrying in his hand a raw-hide whip, constantly directing and encouraging them; but, as my companion and I, both, several times noticed, as often as he visited one end of the line of operations, the hands at the other end would discontinue their labor, until he turned to ride towards them again." Typical tasks for slaves, wrote Olmsted, "certainly would not be considered excessively hard by a Northern laborer; and, in point of fact, the more industrious and active hands finish them often by two o'clock."

Slave owners publicly denied the charges made by their anti-slavery opponents that their laborers were unproductive, but privately they admitted it. One planter in North Carolina wrote with great insight on how the nature of slavery limited its productivity. The slaves, he said, "are not stimulated to care and industry as white people are, who labor for themselves. They do not feel themselves *interested* in what they do, for arbitrary masters and mistresses, and their education is not such as can be expected to inspire them with sentiments of honor and gratitude." A planter in eighteenth-century Virginia frequently complained in his diary about the "poor work" of his slaves. They were "quite indifferent both as to the time they go about it, and indeed the care they ought to use," he wrote. "I find it almost impossible to make a Negro do his work well. No orders can engage it, no encouragement persuade it, nor no Punishment oblige it." Most slave owners refused to acknowledge that they had less power than the employer of free labor, and they chalked up their slaves' shiftlessness to what they believed to be the natural inferiority of blacks.

The slaves were indeed shiftless, but given the quality of their lives compared to the lives of free laborers, we might ask whether they were in fact the superior group.

There is now wide agreement among historians of the Old South that slaves did not share the American devotion to work. And here was the key to understanding Dan Emmett's envy. The beautiful irony of slavery was that it guaranteed food, shelter, clothing, health care, and child care for the enslaved—and even allowed for the acquisition of luxuries and money—without requiring the self-denial of "free" labor.

On every plantation he visited, Olmsted found at least one slave not working "on account of some illness, strain, bruise or wound, of which he or she was complaining." According to Olmsted, "[t]he slave, if he is indisposed to work, and especially if he is not treated well, or does not like the master who has hired him, will sham sickness—even make himself sick or lame—that he need not work." We have substantial quantitative evidence of this from three Mississippi plantations in the early nineteenth century. On the Wheeles plantation, one out of seven working days was lost to slaves claiming they were too sick to work. On the Bowles plantation, of the 159 days missed due to illness in one year, only five were Sundays, when there was the least work to do. The Leigh plantation, where only thirty slaves worked, reported 398 sick days in one year. At these plantations, the rates of sickness peaked on Saturdays and during the planting and harvest seasons, when there was the most work to be done. This kind of resistance to work was simply unavailable to free whites dependent on their own labor for survival. If they were like most Americans, such resistance would have carried the heavy price of shame. Slaves rarely, if ever, paid that price.

The concept of a "vacation," and certainly the belief that one was entitled to leave the duties of work and home for extended periods, did not exist among free Americans until well after the Civil War. Slaves, on the other hand, while not employing the concept of a vacation, pioneered the practice. "Sometimes," an ex-slave named Lorenzo L. Ivy remembered, "slaves jes' run' 'way to de woods fo' a week or two to git a res' fum de fiel', an' den dey come on back." Sallie Smith took frequent breaks from work, and unlike most free laborers, she felt no shame in it. "Sometimes I'd go so far off from the plantation I could not hear the cows low or the roosters crow," she said. Vacating the workplace in this way was called "truancy" by slave owners, and it was rampant. Virtually all the plantations whose records are available show that disappearances lasting days, weeks, months, and even years were common. Olmsted noted that masters were limited in their ability to increase workloads by the "danger of a general stampede to the 'swamp'—a danger the slave can always hold before his master's cupidity." Further suggesting the power of slaves over their masters, historians have found as many reports of masters declining to punish truants upon their return as of those who levied a penalty. Often a slave would stay in the woods, on a neighboring plantation, or in a nearby town until receiving a promise of amnesty. Remaining away from the plantation for an extended period was often made possible by the assistance of other slaves, who provided runaways with food and other provisions, news from home, and warnings of patrols. As a judge in South Carolina lamented, "[t]he strictest watching could not at times prevent them from visiting their acquaintances." Some truants simply moved their residency to the quarters of a neighboring plantation. The number of slaves who regularly ran away was so great that Dr. Samuel Cartwright, one of the South's leading medical authorities, concluded that blacks were uniquely susceptible to a disease he called "drapetomania," whose main symptom was "the absconding from service."

Even the slaves themselves agreed that they were averse to work. A stunning number of slaves agreed with their masters that they were biologically disinclined to work. "De black man is natchally lazy, you knows dat," said James Johnson, voicing a commonly expressed sentiment in interviews with ex-slaves. "De reason he talks lak he does, is 'cause he don't want to go to de trouble to 'nounce his words lak they ought to be." Many believed that only physical coercion could make a slave work. "When he come here, de white man made him work, and he didn't like that," said Jane Johnson, "[h]e is natchally lazy . . . Ever since the first time de nigger found out he had to work, he has silently despised the white man."

The belief that this reluctance to work was "natural" was discounted by the eminent black social scientist W. E. B. DuBois, who explained it as the inevitable consequence of forced labor: "All observers spoke of the fact that the slaves were slow and churlish; that they wasted material and malingered at their work. Of course they did. This was not racial but economic. It was the answer of any group of laborers forced down to the last ditch.

They might be made to work continuously but no power could make them work well." DuBois went even further, arguing that this was the slaves' inherent advantage over whites who worked for themselves. The slave "was not as easily reduced to be the mechanical draft-horse which the northern European laborer became. He was not easily brought to recognize any ethical sanctions in work as such but tended to work as the results pleased him and refused to work or sought to refuse when he did not find the spiritual returns adequate; thus he was easily accused of laziness and driven as a slave when in truth he brought to modern manual labor a renewed valuation of life." Yes, DuBois seemed to say to his white readers, slaves did not believe that work is better than life, and why do you?

Truancy and malingering were also effective means of getting rid of one's boss. Many shiftless slaves were sold by masters who could no longer afford their inefficiency. Indeed, in an era when the vast majority of free Americans lived on family farms, were born to their employers—their fathers—and were morally prohibited from leaving their jobs, it is entirely reasonable to argue that slaves possessed more occupational mobility than the average free American.

For all these reasons, slaves not only worked with less intensity than free Americans, they also worked much less often. Economic historians have determined that on average, Northern farmers worked four hundred more hours per year than did slaves. And no group in world history worked more than industrial workers in the nineteenth-century United States. For the unlucky souls who found themselves in the first American factories, the typical workday was fourteen hours, the typical workweek was six days, and putting in more than one hundred hours in a week was not at all uncommon.*

LIMITS OF THE LASH

Even the reader who concedes that slaves labored less than free workers and enjoyed many liberties that American citizens denied themselves

---

* The economist Robert Fogel has claimed that slaves produced more than free farmers but acknowledges that this may have been the result of the division of labor and specialization that gang labor on large plantations allowed, as well as the fact that southern plantations monopolized the most fertile soil in North America. Robert Fogel, *Without Consent or Contract: The Rise and Fall of American Slavery* (New York: W. W. Norton, 1989), chapters 2–4.

might at this point raise the objection that, in the final analysis, the physical punishment suffered by slaves unquestionably made their lives worse. The life of Horace Lane provides one easy answer to this. Born in 1788, Lane was whipped repeatedly before he reached seven years old. At seven he was forced to work in the fields, and he was frequently beaten by his overseer. As an adult, he suffered "many severe floggings" for neglecting his work and for stealing. Very few slaves suffered as much physical punishment as this, and Horace Lane was a free white man from New York State. Lane's memoir, *The Wandering Boy,* is one of many accounts of severe and frequent physical punishment experienced by free people during the age of slavery.

Corporal punishment was promoted and frequently practiced in free American homes and schools until the middle of the nineteenth century. Parents and teachers used the birch, rod, and whip, as well as the open hand, to keep children in line. Because Dan Emmett was fond of dancing and other amusements, he almost certainly suffered physical applications of one of the sternest lessons in Webster's *American Spelling Book*: "As for those boys and girls that mind not their books, they will come to some bad end, and must be whipt till they mend their ways." Early American schools "resounded with strokes of the rod," as one historian has put it. Schoolmasters beat their pupils not only with wooden rods but also with cat-o'-nine-tails and leather whips. Children caught talking in class were gagged and then had their necks clamped together between wooden blocks called "whispering sticks." Because Quakers were barred by their religion from using violence, their schools in Pennsylvania instead disciplined students by locking their necks and hands in pillories, shackling their legs, or hanging them in sacks. Six out of nine child-rearing books published in the United States in the early nineteenth century advocated the use of corporal punishment, and government authorities rarely took action against it. Typical was one Massachusetts judge's ruling that corporal punishment was an "imperative duty" of schools and necessary "to maintain good government . . . and secure proper subordination in all."

Several of America's greatest heroes who were born during the age of slavery were whipped far more often than most slaves. Davy Crockett's father continually beat him with a hickory stick. Robert E. Lee was raised by an aunt who believed that the best way to instruct children was to "whip and pray and pray and whip." John D. Rockefeller was frequently tied to a tree and whipped by his mother. Abraham Lincoln's father beat him with fists and a horsewhip. Most significantly, none of these men believed that their treatment was abnormal. The historian Elizabeth Pleck has found fifty-eight diaries and autobiographies of free white people who were born before 1850 that recount instances of physical punishment. These were the children of merchants, plantation owners, ministers, farmers, lawyers, craftsmen, and schoolteachers, in the North and South. All of the children in this group, born between 1750 and 1799, were hit with an object, usually a whip, and among those born between 1800 and 1850, 80 percent were struck with an instrument at least once. It was also common and considered appropriate as a means of training for craftsmen to beat the children and young adults who served them as apprentices.

Among free whites, severe physical punishment, including death, at the hands of authorities was a common occurrence. During the colonial period, not only murder and rape but also arson, adultery, buggery, and witchcraft were punishable by death. In eighteenth-century Virginia, a first conviction for hog stealing brought twenty-five lashes; the second offense was punished by two hours in the pillory, nailed by the ears. The third offense sent one to the gallows. In Massachusetts, first-time burglars were branded on the forehead with the letter *B*; second offenders were branded and whipped; a third offense made one "incorrigible" and, therefore, subject to death. All of the colonies ordered whipping, branding, and other forms of bodily mutilation for crimes such as breaking the Sabbath, petty larceny, and sedition. Laws in several colonies called for children over the age of sixteen who struck or cursed their parents to be punished with death, whipping, or imprisonment. Debtors and drunkards, and those simply suspected of criminal activity or moral degeneracy, were placed in stocks and public cages, where they were spit on, pelted with rocks, punched, and kicked by passersby. In the military, flogging was the standard punishment for drunkenness, swearing, and insubordination until the late nineteenth century.

After the founding of the United States, a new, modern form of punishment became increasingly popular. It was more brutal, more dehumanizing, and more comprehensive than anything experienced by slaves, and it was designed exclusively for free people. In the first American prisons, inmates were confined in crowded, dark, unventilated, filthy, windowless rooms. Some prisons were built in old mine shafts, so that the convicts would live and die entirely underground. Disease, rape, beatings, murder, and riots were so common that reformers in the nineteenth century developed a new kind of correctional system that reflected the American ideal of self-discipline and was in many ways more severe than the original dungeons.

There were two types of prison in nineteenth-century America. Luckier convicts were sent to prisons based on Auburn State Prison in New York. There they slept alone, one to a cell. Communication among prisoners—even the exchange of glances—was prohibited. While visiting the Auburn prison in 1831, Alexis de Tocqueville was struck by its absence of life. "Everything passes in the most profound silence, and nothing is heard in the whole prison but the steps of those who march, or sounds proceeding from the workshops." When the inmates were in their cells, "the silence within these vast walls" was "that of death." Tocqueville and his traveling partner "felt as if we had traversed catacombs; there were a thousand living beings, and yet it was a desert solitude." In this total silence and isolation, the inmates performed repetitive manual labor eight to ten hours a day, six days a week. Less fortunate convicts were sent to prisons based on the Eastern State Penitentiary in Philadelphia, where the isolation was so complete that newcomers wore hoods over their heads on the way to their cells so they would neither see nor be seen by anyone. In a "Pennsylvania plan" prison, inmates worked alone in their cells and were allowed nothing to read but the Bible. As in the Auburn prisons, communication among prisoners was forbidden. The purpose of both prison systems was to force, through external coercion, the discipline of American life onto free citizens who had not internalized it. It was not intended or used for slaves. As Sylvia Canon, an ex-slave from South Carolina, remembered many years after black people became eligible for incarceration, "Times was sho better long time ago den dey be now . . . Never hear tell bout no colored people been put in jail 'fore freedom."

As for the physical punishment of slaves, the records of the Bennet Barrow plantation in Louisiana provide the most reliable source of quantitative evidence. During a two-year period in the early 1840s, there were, according to which historian you believe, either 0.7 or 1.03 whippings per slave per year. Whichever number is more accurate—and to the twenty-first-century mind a single whipping in a lifetime is an unspeakable horror—it is quite likely that free whites, especially children, received physical punishments more frequently than this. Historians now widely agree that slave masters were forced to limit the amount of punishment given to slaves, since they were likely, after a certain point, to receive diminishing returns from the pain they administered. Said one owner about the inherent limitations of the lash, "[i]n working niggers, we always calculate that they will not labor at all except to avoid punishment, and they will never do more than just enough to save themselves from being punished, and no amount of punishment will prevent their working carelessly or indifferently." Overuse of punishment worked against the master because it pushed the slave away from obligation to work and toward rebellion: "It always seems on the plantations as if they took pains to break all the tools and spoil all the cattle that they possibly can, even when they know they'll be directly punished for it." A northern journalist assigned to cover southern agriculture in the 1840s observed that "all the whips in Christendom cannot drive them to perform more than they think they ought to do, or have been in the habit of doing." George Washington, who knew quite a bit about the problems of managing slaves, understood this well: "When an overlooker's back is turned, the most of them will slight their work, or be idle altogether, in which case correction cannot retrieve either but often produces evils which are worse than the disease," he wrote in a farming instruction manual.

One consequence of whipping was the loss of untold numbers of man-hours. Thousands of notices advertising for the capture of fugitive slaves were distributed every year, and they frequently stated that the escapee had been recently punished. One slaveholder advised a friend that slaves would not accept being "dealt harshly with—otherwise they will run off—and if once the habit of absconding is fixed, it is difficult to conquer it." Other slaves made their masters pay for abuse in other ways, as did Andy Anderson of Texas after his first whipping: "After dat whippin' I doesn't have de heart to work for de massa. If I seed de cattle in de cornfield, I turns de back, 'stead of chasin' 'em out."

Those who whipped slaves often paid even more dearly. One day in 1846, James Ward, an overseer on a plantation in Mississippi, delivered one blow too many to a slave named David, who killed him instantly with an axe to the back of the head. A similar fate befell Matthew Lassley, another particularly brutal overseer in Mississippi, who had an axe blade driven three inches into his skull by a slave named Bill. Sometimes retaliation was carried out in secret. The ex-slave Anthony Abercrombie remembered that one of his overseers was killed on the bank of a creek one night. "Dey never did find out who killed him, but Marse Jim always b'lieved de field han's done it." Even slave women retaliated against overseers. Silvia DuBois struck one with "a hell of a blow with my fist." Often in these cases, the humiliation was so great that the owner refused to intervene. As one master told an overseer who had been beaten by a slave woman, "[W]ell, if that is the best you could do with her, damned if you won't just have to take it." We do not have precise numbers for such incidents, but we do know that every district in the South reported at least one violent act of resistance by a slave to a whipping. Even more remarkably, in many cases, the resistant slave was allowed to live, and sometimes no punishment was meted out at all. What the slaves had to their advantage that free whites did not was their status as the most valuable property in their society. Masters were therefore often reluctant to kill slaves, even those who struck back against whites.

TOO FREE

Perhaps the best-kept secret of slavery is that its opponents were also opponents of freedom. Abolitionists continued the movement of the Founding Fathers to replace external controls over the people with strict self-discipline. Accordingly, many opponents of slavery also led a campaign against the use of corporal punishment. Theodore Dwight authored a child-rearing manual in which he argued that "the child must be made his own disciplinarian." School reformers in Massachusetts wrote that "If internal and moral restraints be not substituted for the external and arbitrary ones that are removed, the people, instead of being conquerors and sovereigns over their passions, will be their victims and their slaves." Theodore Dwight Weld (no relation to Theodore Dwight), a leader of both the antislavery and school reform movements, aptly declared that inner restraints "are the web of civilized society, warp and woof."

William Ellery Channing, an intellectual founder of abolitionism, made plain the ugly irony of his movement. The problem with slavery was that slaves were *too* free:

> That the slave should yield himself to intemperance, licentiousness, and, in general, to sensual excess, we must also expect. Doomed to

live for the physical indulgences of others, unused to any pleasures but those of sense, stripped of self-respect, and having nothing to gain in life, how can he be expected to govern himself? . . . What aid does the future give him in withstanding desire? That better condition, for which other men postpone the cravings of appetite, never opens before him. The sense of character, the power of opinion, another restraint on the free, can do little or nothing to rescue so abject a class from excess and debasement.

Of particular concern to the abolitionists was the sexual freedom of slaves. "The state of morals among slaves, especially in regard to licentiousness," wrote Henry Stanton from Lane Seminary, "is sickening!" James Thome, the son of a Kentucky planter who joined the antislavery cause at Lane, declared that what he had seen growing up was "one great Sodom." According to Thome, one of very few abolitionists with firsthand knowledge of plantation life, the slaves were having entirely too much fun. They "roam over the village streets, shocking the ear with their vulgar jestings, and voluptuous songs, or opening their kitchens to the reception of the neighbouring blacks, they pass the evening in gambling, dancing, drinking, and the most obscene conversation, kept up until the night is far spent, then crown the scene with indiscriminate debauchery." What caused this unspeakable freedom? Not biology, said Thome, but the exclusion of slaves from the culture of self-restraint. "This pollution is the offspring of slavery; it springs not from the *character* of the *Negro,* but from the *condition* of the *slave.*" The *Genius of Universal Emancipation,* one of the first abolitionist journals, lamented in 1826 that Southern law "takes no notice of Fornication, Adultery, Incest, Polygamy, &c. among slaves," and that, therefore, "The sensual appetite is left to be gratified by promiscuous indulgence, without any restraint, except what the Negroes impose on themselves."

The *Philanthropist,* a leading abolitionist journal published in Cincinnati, explained that because slaves knew "not the laws of God nor comprehend the institutions of men," they were "enslaved by carnal lusts and licentious practices." William Lloyd Garrison's *Liberator,* the most militant voice of the abolitionist movement, amplified the argument that the master's reliance on external coercion let loose the slaves' passions. A correspondent reported from Georgia that "without moral observance, except when urged by fear to conform to rules of moral conduct," the slaves were "apt to disregard chastity—lewd in the last degree—lovers of obscene language and obscene jests—unthinking starers at every passing object . . . Hoggish! His bent of genius is vicious, his inclination funny, with starts of mischief, prognostic of greater mischief, *if the cow-hide does not operate on his fears.* Their lewdness is extreme and appalling."

Slaves probably didn't have quite the party imagined by abolitionists, but they certainly enjoyed far greater sexual freedom than did free white Americans, who during the late eighteenth and nineteenth centuries were waging war against their bodily desires.

After the American Revolution, as we have seen, doctors and political leaders believed that for the new nation to flourish, its citizens needed to exert strict control over their bodies. Benjamin Rush argued for the abolition of both slavery and masturbation. He penned several tracts opposing the slave trade and many more against the evils posed to the republic by self-pleasuring. Rush spoke for virtually the entire American medical profession when he declared that this "state of degeneracy" must be avoided by "close application of the mind to business, or study of any kind." If the patient still succumbed to temptation, Rush prescribed "a vegetable diet, temperance, bodily labor, cold baths, avoidance of obscenity, music, a close study of mathematics, military glory, and, if all else failed, castor oil."

Sex of any kind was considered dangerous at best, and, accordingly, it was hunted down and caged. According to Estelle B. Freedman and John D'Emilio, authors of *Intimate Matters,* the leading history of American sexuality, a "prolific sexual advice literature" in the early nineteenth century "inundated Americans with the message that bodily well-being required that individuals exercise some measure of control over their sexual desires." To be sure, many free white Americans violated the norm of sexual control—especially among the new urban working class—but those who did were considered to be not only unworthy of citizenship but also, as we have seen during the early national period, threats to the nation itself.

But how powerful were these admonitions against sex? Fornicators and other "persons of infamous character and conduct," as they were called in a Pennsylvania law, were arrested and prosecuted. A Philadelphia couple was convicted in 1797 of leading a "debauched mode of living that tends to corrupt the morals of the Citizens." We have seen that thousands of "fallen women"—not just prostitutes but also those who had engaged in any non-marital sex—were placed in asylums where they were trained to repress their desires and become either servants for respectable families or wives of upstanding men. And historians have attributed at least part of the sharp decline in births in the nineteenth century to a culture that proscribed even marital sex if it was not for reproduction.

As for the sex lives of slaves, recent scholars have overthrown attempts made by liberal historians of the 1960s and 1970s to portray slaves as being just as "respectable" as whites and therefore equally repressed. Some slaves certainly did adopt the sexual norms of whites, upholding monogamous marriage and the patriarchal nuclear family as the best forms of intimate relations, but most, according to the historian Brenda Stevenson, "exhibited a diversity of form and relationship, that marked them [as] substantially different from those of European Americans." While some slaves established informal marriages that, while not legally recognized, imitated the culture of white marriage, others "sweethearted" and "took up" in nonmarital relationships. "Sweethearting" and "taking up" were usually nonmonogamous relationships, which according to historian Anthony Kaye, were "a temporary tie that entailed more prerogatives than obligations and many new feelings and pleasures." Many sweethearts had children together, but rather than the "bastards" of white culture who bore the shame of their parents' illicit coupling throughout their lives, these children carried no stigma and were often described as "sweetheart children." Slaves were also much less willing to subject their relationships to the rules and scrutiny of the broader community. Couples who sweethearted or took up, according to Kaye, preferred to "keep their relationship entirely their own affair. Whereas couples took some pains to enlist both their fellow slaves and their owners to participate in marriage ceremonies or recognize husbands and wives who were living together, sweethearts and couples who were taking up went to great lengths to be left to their own devices."

Ironically, the definition of slaves as subhuman gave them many advantages, not the least of which was that in regard to sex among themselves, they were exempt from many of the repressive laws that governed whites in the South, including those against fornication, adultery, and promiscuity. As one Maryland lawyer explained:

[S]laves are bound by our criminal laws generally, yet we do not consider them as the objects of such laws as relate to the commerce between the sexes . . . Their propensions in their different sexes, are as ardent and irresistible as those of others, and they need not be more. There is no danger that the consideration of their progeny's condition will stop propagation, and as the laws do not regulate, neither do they punish, the gratification of them, when the rights of others are not hurt.

Slaves chose to exempt themselves from many of the whites' unwritten laws as well. Slave women, unlike free women, were not expected to be virgins before marriage, nor were they scorned for having extramarital sex. Once married, slaves did not lock themselves into the relationship, regardless of its quality. As Eugene Genovese, the preeminent historian of slavery, put it, "they saw no reason to live forever with their mistakes." Divorce rates, therefore, were much higher among slaves than among "free" people. Fertility rates were also much higher among slaves than among free whites, which is proof to many that blacks were less ashamed of sex and therefore inferior. The evidence seems clear that the former assumption is true; it is up to the reader to decide whether a lack of shame about sex is the sign of an inferior or a superior culture.

Even the reader who grants that slaves enjoyed greater sexual freedom than whites might insist that the control slave owners exerted over the bodies of the women they owned made the lives of slave women worse than those of free women. Again, though, the structure of slavery, the repressive logic of American freedom, and the available evidence say otherwise. According to the economic historians Robert Fogel and Stanley Engerman, "the main thrust of the economic incentives generated by the American slave system operated against eugenic manipulation and against sexual abuse. Those who engaged in such acts did so, not because of their economic interests, but despite them." Plantation archives contain many instructions given by slave owners to overseers warning against "undue familiarity" with slaves. One Louisiana planter tolerated no sexual interaction between overseers and slaves: "Having connection with any of my female servants will most certainly be visited with a dismissal from my employment, and no excuse can or will be taken." An overseer who was known to have crossed the line would not have had an easy time finding employment. "Never employ an overseer who will equalize himself with the Negro women," the Texas planter Charles Tait counseled his sons. "Besides the morality of it, there are evils too numerous to be now mentioned." A journal for slaveholders admonished: "Every effort should be used to prevent that sexual intercourse, which degrades the master and is the cause of discontent to the slave. As far as is practical, it would be advisable to have elderly servants only in families, and the young should be employed wholly in agrestic and other manual labours."

Statistics further suggest that rapes were rare on plantations. Most people of "mixed race" in the South were either slaves who lived in cities, where opportunities for interracial liaisons were far greater, or free. According to the 1860 census, 20 percent of urban slaves and 39 percent of free blacks in southern cities were mulattoes. But among rural slaves, who made up 95 percent of the slave population, only 9.9 percent were mulatto. Of the slave population as a whole, mulattoes made up only 7.7 percent in 1850 and 10.4 percent in 1860. Moreover, only 1.2 percent of the former slaves interviewed by the Works Progress Administration in the 1930s reported being raped by a master, only 5.8 percent reported hearing about the rape of another slave, and only 4.5 said that one of their parents had been white. According to Fogel and Engerman, all of the available evidence taken together indicates that "the share of Negro children fathered by whites on slave plantations probably averaged between 1 and 2 percent." Even Fogel and Engerman's most hostile critics concede that it was no more than 8 percent. There is also evidence of significant numbers of consensual relations between white men and slave women, which would make the percentage of children produced by rape even smaller.

While no laws protected the slave from a rapist, masters and overseers had many reasons not to force themselves on enslaved women. For one, such attacks almost inevitably brought reprisals from the victims, their mates, the attacker's wife, or the surrounding community. The rape of a slave woman disrupted the workings of the plantation, since angry slaves were not hard-working slaves. As Haller Nutt, one of the most prominent planters in Mississippi, counseled in his "General Rules to Govern Time of an Overseer":

> Above all things avoid all intercourse with Negro women. It breeds
> more trouble, more neglect, more idleness, more rascality, more
> stealing, & more lieing up in the quarters & more everything that
> is wrong on a plantation than all else put together . . . In fact such
> intercourse is out of the question—it must not be tolerated.

Many slave women also physically attacked pursuers, though a more common response was to run away—usually not forever, but quite frequently for days, weeks, or months at a time. The historian Stephanie Camp has found records from plantations showing that female slaves constituted from 19 percent to 41 percent of truants and that their absences averaged six days. Angry slaves were also dangerous slaves, and in addition to the documented cases of slaves' lethal vengeance, there were many stories of poison or ground glass mixed in with the master's food and white children under the care of slave women who died unexpectedly.

Slave mistresses were also a potent force operating against the free exercise of a masters' sexual desires. Liaisons with slave women were sometimes tolerated, but they were always considered to be shameful and required to be kept hidden. According to historian Catherine Clinton, who was the first to write on this issue, white men "were required in their public lives to obey the plantation culture's rigid dictates concerning race and sex." Many prominent members of the Southern gentry lost their place in "decent society" when their encounters with slaves were revealed. Thomas Foster Jr., the son of a wealthy Mississippi planter, was given an ultimatum by his family to either discontinue his love affair with a slave woman or exile himself from his home and Southern society. He chose the latter. Richard Johnson, who served as vice president under Martin Van Buren, may very well have won the presidency were it not for the scandal concerning his mulatto mistress, with whom he had two children. Because he refused to deny the "monstrous rumor," Johnson was widely attacked for his "scorn of secrecy" and for threatening to bring "amalgamation" to the White House.

And how many free white women were forced to have sex against their will? One advantage that slave women had over free women was that a rapist who attacked a woman he owned would have to live, face-to-face and every day, with the shame, resentment, disruption, and threats of violence that his act produced. Many if not most rapes of free white women, on the other hand, went unreported or unsolved, and the attacker remained anonymous. For these reasons, according to the historian Sharon Block, "rape in early America was both pervasive and invisible." In fact, coerced sex was commonplace among free women. Nearly all free women in the nineteenth century were married at some point, and husbands held legal dominion over their bodies. Until the twentieth century, American laws and customs regarding marriage were derived from the English *Lawes Resolutions of Women's Rights* of 1632, which declared that it was "a locking together," that a wife's identity became her husband's, and that "[h]er new self is her superior; her companion, her master." The American publication in 1806 of the British legal manual *A Treatise of the Pleas of the Crown,* declared that "a husband cannot by law be guilty of ravishing his wife, on account of the matrimonial consent which she cannot retract." A popular advice book in the 1830s told young American women, "[I]n whatever situation of life a woman is placed from her cradle to her grave, a spirit of obedience and submission, pliability of temper, and humility of mind, are required from her." This concept of "coverture" meant that a husband not only legally owned every piece of property in his family but also was, according to law and American culture, incapable of raping his wife.

Without doubt, the sale of a slave that broke apart a family was one of the most brutal aspects of being enslaved. There is disagreement over exactly what percentage of families were disrupted this way, but during the lifetime of slavery in America, at least tens of thousands of people were forcibly removed from their loved ones. Whatever the exact number, however, it is certainly smaller than the number of free people who were forced from their homes by compulsion or obligation. More than five million free Americans, a large percentage of whom were conscripted, participated in the War of Independence, the War of 1812, the Mexican-American War, and the Civil War. More than six hundred thousand never returned from the battlefield. Economic transformations forced millions more to leave their families. The rise of large-scale commercial farming and the growth of manufacturing before the Civil War dissolved family farms and compelled not just fathers and sons but also mothers and daughters to relocate to support themselves or their families. Sometimes families would shut down their farms and move together to a city, but more often the children able to work were sent off on their own.

"Thousands of illustrious families," a newspaper lamented in 1834, "are compelled to take the situation of tenants, or are scattered into factories, and into the kitchens of the rich—or, more happily for them, driven in exile to the remoter West." Beginning in the 1830s, teenage girls and young women from all over New England left their families and took jobs in the textile mills that were America's first factories. Untold numbers of men—many of them fathers—left their homesteads to find a better life in the West. The vast majority did not take their families with them.

Perhaps the greatest advantage that slaves had over free Americans was their exemption from the ultimate obligation of citizenship. In addition to the more than six hundred thousand free Americans who died fighting in the country's wars before 1865, a roughly equal number were wounded. Among the wounded were those who were blinded or crippled, lost limbs, or were otherwise maimed. Except for the very few slaves who were forced to fight, and the even smaller number who volunteered, this suffering was reserved entirely for the free.

GOING DOWN

A common, seemingly fantastical theme in early minstrelsy was the flamboyant dress of the slave characters. Dan Emmett's boatman wore a "[s]ky blue jacket and tarpaulin hat," and "Dandy Jim" sported pantaloons. Sheet music for many songs, such as the famous "Zip Coon," showed black "dandies" in top hats and tuxedos and "dandizettes" in elaborate gowns. The dandy, dressed in tails, top hat, ruffles, watch chain, and white gloves, was a stock figure in minstrel shows. But this was based more on observation than imagination. In their study of thousands of advertisements of runaway slaves—which often included detailed descriptions of the fugitives' appearances—as well as accounts of white observers and slaves themselves, Shane White and Graham White, authors of the most comprehensive history of African American expressive culture, found evidence of "an almost bewildering variety in slave apparel." They also found that slaves quite often dressed better than free whites. The fugitive notices comprise a virtual catalog of the finest clothing available in early America. According to the masters who wrote the notices—and who had every reason to be accurate in their descriptions—the runaways' wardrobes included imported waistcoats and petticoats, velvet capes, fur hats, silk bonnets and hats trimmed with gauze and feathers, ball gowns, high-heeled shoes, linen shirts, ruffles, silver cufflinks and buckles, gold lace, stockings, and various items made of "superfine Cloth."

How was all this finery obtained? According to White and White, there is ample evidence that many blacks stole clothes but also many admissions by slave owners that they gave away their clothes to their bondmen. A great many slaves also purchased clothes with their own money, which they earned from jobs they took outside their masters' domain. Historians widely agree that this kind of hiring out was common in the slave South, and that slaves were usually allowed to keep some or all of the wages they earned. Best of all, unlike legally free workers, when their jobs ended, they were ensured of having room, board, medical care, and child care provided for them. They were also, unlike "good" citizens, not ashamed to enjoy the fruits of their labor.

The men who created the ideal American citizen dressed him in homely clothing. "He appear'd in the plainest Country Garb," said Benjamin Franklin. "His Great Coat was coarse and looked old and thread-bare; his Linnen was homespun; his Beard perhaps of Seven Days Growth, his Shoes thick and heavy, and every Part of his Dress corresponding." As we have seen, leaders of the new nation were universally adamant that Americans must acquire wealth but not please themselves with it. The revolutionary scribe Joel Barlow warned in 1787 that "[w]henever democratic states degenerate from those noble republican virtues which constitute the chief excellency, spring, and even basis of their government, and instead of industry, frugality, and economy, encourage luxury, dissipation and extravagence, we may justly conclude that ruin is near at hand . . . No virtue, no Commonwealth." Hezekiah Niles, a journalist and leading spokesman for American independence, understood well the connections between pleasure and slavery, between discipline and what he called freedom: "[B]efore a nation is completely deprived of freedom, she must be fitted for slavery by her vices."

The attacks on ostentation continued in the early national period. In 1843 Cornelius Mathews, the poet of "Young America," described the "Man in the Republic" as living "With plainness in thy daily pathway walk / And disencumbered of excess." Women were instructed to wear dresses of "surpassing neatness and simplicity," and respectable urban men were expected to become what a business directory in the 1850s called "the unknown knight, with his plain unostentatious black armor." In 1853 William Marcy, the secretary of state in Franklin Pierce's new administration, ordered diplomats to wear "the simple dress of an American citizen," which would best demonstrate their "devotion to republican institutions."

Slaves were happily free of such obligations to the nation. In 1744, less than a decade after South Carolina issued restrictions on clothing that black people could wear, a grand jury expressed concern that slaves didn't seem to care: "[I]t is apparent, that Negro Women in particular do not restrain themselves in the Cloathing as the Law requires, but dress in Apparel quite gay and beyond their Condition." Twenty-five years later, the slaves still didn't care. A letter to the *South Carolina Gazette* complained that "many of the *Female* Slaves [are] by far more *elegantly* dressed, than the Generality of *White Women* below Affluence." A Canadian visitor to Charleston in 1845 was amazed at the attire of slaves: "[S]uch exquisite dandies, such gorgeously dressed women, I never saw before—howling swells, all of them! All slaves!" Similarly, Frederick Law Olmsted noted that many blacks in Richmond, Virginia, on a Sunday were "dressed with foppish extravagence, and many in the latest style of fashion." In wealthier neighborhoods, "there were many more well-dressed and highly-dressed coloured people than white; and among this dark gentry the finest French cloths, embroidered waistcoats, patent-leather shoes, resplendent brooches, silk hats, kid gloves, and *eau de mille-fleurs*, were quite common." Olmsted also remarked that slaves took "a real pleasure, for instance, such as it is a rare thing for a white man to be able to feel, in bright and strongly contrasting colours, and in music, in which nearly all are proficient to some extent." During the Civil War, a northerner in Houston saw "innumerable Negroes and Negresses parading about the streets in the most outrageously grand costumes," clothes that greatly surpassed the "simple dresses" of their mistresses.

The greatest object of white envy was the musical felicity of slaves, and on this score many black people actually expressed pity for their imitators. One of them, Solomon Northup, saw how white people danced when he played the violin at his master's balls. He couldn't help but feel sorry for them: "Oh, ye pleasure-seeking sons and daughters of idleness, who move with measured step, listless and snail-like, through the slow winding cotillon, if ye wish to look upon the celerity, if not the 'poetry of motion'—upon genuine happiness, rampant and unrestrained—go down to Louisiana and see the slaves dancing in the starlight of a Christmas night." In fact, many whites did "go down" to see the slaves dancing. They came from the North. They came from Europe. And they came down from the big house. What they all saw was a joy that was alien to them. Laura Towne traveled from her home in Philadelphia to South Carolina to educate and "civilize" freed slaves during the Civil War. She was appalled by slave culture, but especially by the fun she witnessed:

> Tonight I have been to a "shout" which seems to me certainly the remains of some old idol worship. The Negroes sing a kind of chorus—three standing apart to lead and clap—and then all the others go shuffling round in a circle following one another with not much regularity, turning round occasionally and bending the knees, and stamping so that the whole floor swings. I never saw anything so savage. They call it a religious ceremony, but it seems more like a regular frolic to me.

The British painter Eyre Crowe, who toured the South with the author William Thackeray, wrote of his amazement at a slave ball in Charleston:

> We had the privilege of being invited to one of these amusements . . . The minstrels were embowered in greenery as they played waltzes and quadrilles, which were danced with great zest, and the hall rang with good-humored laughter . . . The striking features of Negro evening dress consisted in astonishing turbans with marabou feathers, into which add accessories of squib shape and other forms were inserted.

The *South Carolina Gazette* could barely contain its envy in its description of a "Country Dance, Rout or Cabal of Negroes":

> It consisted of about 60 people, 5–6th from Town, every one of whom carried something, in the manner just described; as bottled liquors of all sorts. Rum, Tongues, Hams, Beef, Geese, Turkes and

> Fowls both drest and raw, with many luxuries of the table as sweet-
> meats, pickles & . . .
>
> Then they *danced, betted, gamed, swore, quarreled, fought,* and
> did everything that the most modern accomplished gentlemen are
> not ashamed of.

Many white observers commented that slaves danced with bent knees and elbows, which according to the historian Peter Wood, was probably an expression of the West African belief that "straightened knees, hips, and elbows"—which characterized European styles of dance—epitomized death and rigidity, "while flexed joints embodied energy and life." Slaves were aware of this difference as well. At one plantation, "[t]hey did a takeoff on the high manners of the white folks in the 'big house,' but their masters, who gathered around to watch the fun, missed the point."

Such derision did not stop planters from building platforms from where they viewed the dances. Many paintings of plantation scenes show whites on these platforms or, closer to the action, on the ground watching slaves enjoying themselves. Elen Campbell, a former slave from Georgia, recalled in a WPA interview that white men who attended such festivities were attracted to more than just the music and dancing: "Den sometimes on Saddy night we have a big frolic. De nigger frum Hammond's place and Phinizy place, Eve place, Clayton place, D'Laigle place all git togedder fer big dance and frolic. A lot o de young white sports used to come derre and push de nigger bucks aside and dance wid de wenches." Frank Adamson of South Carolina, like many slaves who complained of the presence of whites at their dances, recalled that the sons of his master would "mix in wid de 'fairs of slave 'musements."

Slaves on most plantations held dances every Saturday night, but they also enjoyed themselves at impromptu weeknight gatherings and even on the day when fun was sacrilege. In colonial Maryland, whites complained to judicial authorities that slaves were "drunke on the Lords Day beating their Negro drums by which they call considerable Number of Negroes together in some Certaine places." A visitor to New Orleans reported in 1799 that on a Sunday he saw "vast numbers of Negro slaves, men, women, and children, assembled together on the levee, dancing in large rings." In 1804, another white voyeur in the city saw dancing Negroes "in great masses on the levee on Sundays." In early-nineteenth-century St. Louis, Sunday frolics of slaves and free blacks were so large and boisterous that the military was brought out to suppress them. The unauthorized recreational activities of slaves in the Edgefield and Barnwell districts of South Carolina were so rampant that slaveholders formed the Savannah River Anti-Slave Traffick Association in the mid-1840s to stop the drinking and sneaking "abroad to night meetings" by the people they owned. "Hundreds of Negroes it may be said without exaggeration are every night, and at all hours of the night, prowling about the country." Worse still, the slaves were doing this at the expense of their work: "The Negroes themselves are seriously impaired in physical qualities," and "their nightly expeditions are followed by days of languor."

The white people who loved the "frolics" are often accused of romanticizing slave culture, but minstrels' imaginings of slave parties are quite similar to descriptions made by the participants themselves. Betty Jones, who had been a slave on the Alvis plantation in Hendersonville, Kentucky, remembered the parties around the quarters:

> Every gal with her beau and such music! Had two fiddles, two tambourines, two banjos, and two sets of bones. Was a boy named Joe who used to whistle, too. Them devilish boys would get out in the middle of the flo' and me, jenny and the devil right with 'em.

Fanny Berry of Virginia offered a similar description of the dancing of couples: "Dey come up an' bend over toward each other at de waist, an' de woman put her hands on her hips an' de man roll his eyes all roun' an' grin an' dey pat de flo' wid dey feet just like dey was puttin' it in place." One ex-slave no doubt shocked his white interviewers in the 1930s when he recalled the celebrations on his plantation after the master and mistress gave out presents to the slaves. "After all dis, everybody was happy, singin' and laughin' all over de place. Go 'way from here, white man! Don't tell me dat wasn't de next step to heaven to de slaves on our plantation. I sees and dreams 'bout them good old times, back yonder, to dis day."

Though Dan Emmett never lived those times, he dreamt about them all his life. After the Civil War, he moved from New York to Chicago, where he continued to sing and play fiddle in minstrel shows. By the 1880s, minstrelsy had shed some of its lowbrow reputation and attained a degree of mainstream respectability. Emmett became a folk hero in the North, with performances in his honor at the Academy of Music and Grand Opera House in Chicago, and, more problematically, in the South. During the war, "Dixie" had been sung by both Union and Confederate soldiers, who were apparently untroubled by Emmett's intention to make the song's narrator a black slave. When the Confederacy became a memory and a symbol of whiteness, the song was captured and remade by the leaders of the Lost Cause. Just before Emmett died in 1904, the United Daughters of the Confederacy, the United Confederate Veterans, and the United Sons of Confederate Veterans declared "Dixie" to be the "official song of the Confederacy" but replaced the original lyrics with "more appropriate words" that made the narrator a white soldier. When told that his song had been adopted by the white South, Emmett replied, "if I had known to what use they were going to put my song, I will be damned if I'd have written it."

"Dixie" and hundreds of songs like it gave voice not to a hatred of black people but to a love of *blackness*. And, as paradoxical as it seems, if we free our minds from modern morality, we can see that such a life-loving and infectious culture could only have been created by slaves. Free from the bondage of citizenship, is it any wonder that the slaves were able to enjoy themselves? Liberated from the responsibility of sustaining themselves and their offspring, should we be surprised that they sang and danced with a joy that was unknown to whites? Living outside the confines of American norms, was it a miracle that their descendants created America's most important contribution to world culture—a music that operated outside and against Western musical structures with its celebration of improvisation and its rhythms that moved the body? Never fully a part of America, slaves were America's original renegades.

★ 3 ★

THE SLAVERY OF FREEDOM

Every day, seven days a week, John Freeman woke before dawn, washed himself, then immediately headed off to work. He worked as hard as he was physically able—regardless of the kind of labor he was doing or how much he was paid for it—all day long. The only breaks he took were those necessary to keep his body functioning and for church on Sundays. After twelve or fourteen or even sixteen hours of labor, John Freeman put his head down and returned immediately to his home. He did not drink alcohol or smoke tobacco. He did not dance. He wore plain and simple clothes and ate plain and simple food. He spent not a single cent on anything for his own enjoyment and did not go anyplace for fun. He had sex only with his wife and only to make children, never for pleasure. Clarissa Freeman, John's wife, rose from bed with her husband before dawn. She then cooked and cleaned and straightened until she went to bed at night, shortly after supper. She never left the house. She never did anything for her personal pleasure. She covered her body from chin to toe in plain, drab, and formless clothing. She lived entirely for her husband and eight children. And she most certainly never had sex for fun.

Our textbooks tell us that Reconstruction, an attempt by the federal government and its allies during and after the Civil War to make the former slaves into American citizens, was a tragedy because it was abandoned. In the leading college textbook of the 1990s and 2000s, Reconstruction was "a small but important first step in the effort by former slaves to secure civil rights and economic power."* But "when it came to an end, finally in

---

* This has been the dominant interpretation of Reconstruction among scholars since the

the late 1870s . . . the freed slaves found themselves abandoned by the federal government to face a system of economic peonage and legal subordination alone." The current definitive scholarly history of Reconstruction, Eric Foner's *Reconstruction: America's Unfinished Revolution 1863–1877,* proclaims that "for blacks its failure was a disaster whose magnitude cannot be obscured by the accomplishments that endured. For the nation as a whole, the collapse of Reconstruction was a tragedy that deeply affected the course of its development." What these historians either willfully ignore or cannot see is that the promise of Reconstruction was to make all Americans—ex-slaves *and* whites—unfree. That is, unless you think the Freemans were free.

John and Clarissa Freeman were fictional ex-slaves who were the main characters in a textbook used in government-run schools to teach the former slaves how to think and behave as "free men." They were the promise— and the *demand*—of Reconstruction. And they were no different, except for skin color, than the heroes of schoolbooks that white children all over the United States were forced to read.

Reconstruction began in the early months of the Civil War, in the fall of 1861, when the Union army first captured plantations in the South. Some political leaders in the North believed the newly freed slaves should remain permanently on the plantations, under the management of white landowners. Others thought that they should be allowed to compete with whites for jobs anywhere, North or South, in the country or in the cities. And the boldest of the Reconstructionists—so-called "Radical Republicans"— advocated that the government assist the ex-slaves in acquiring their own farms. But virtually all leaders of the Union cause agreed that the freed slaves had to be trained to become good citizens. This became more and more urgent with Abraham Lincoln's Emancipation Proclamation in 1863, the Union army's conquest of large parts of the South during the war, and the states' ratification in 1865 of the Thirteenth Amendment to the Con-

1970s, when an older, explicitly racist interpretation was overthrown. The older view was established by John Burgess's 1902 book, *Reconstruction and the Constitution,* and then popularized by William Dunning's *Reconstruction, Political and Economic, 1865–1877,* which was first published in 1907 but remained the leading college textbook on the subject for most of the twentieth century. To Burgess and Dunning, the crime of Reconstruction was that it gave power to animalistic and childlike blacks.

stitution, which outlawed slavery and involuntary servitude. By the end of the Civil War, four million slaves, carrying a culture that was in many respects antithetical to American citizenship, had been let loose upon the land.

So when conquering Union officers rode onto plantations and were suddenly faced with a group of newly emancipated slaves, they often spoke to them of their new status as free people. They explained that freedom meant giving up all the pleasures they had created for themselves on the plantations. They would work harder as citizens than as slaves, and they would surrender their own desires to national obligations. Some slaves welcomed this odd kind of freedom. They became soldiers in the Union army, civil servants, diligent farmers, and devoted family men and women. But others ignored what their liberators had to say, wandering across the land, refusing to work, refusing to marry, and refusing to sacrifice for the government that now claimed them as its people. So at the war's end in 1865, Congress created the Freedmen's Bureau, an agency of the army that would provide food and housing for the ex-slaves, and most important, train them to become citizens in a democratic republic. The ex-slaves soon learned that democratic citizenship is as much about responsibilities as it is about rights, and that protection of those rights by the government always comes with a steep price. Many slaves willingly and eagerly paid the price. Others, like many white renegades who had resisted and ignored the calls for obligation and sacrifice since the War of Independence, decided it was too high to pay. They took the vote but turned down the rest of democracy.

FREE TO WORK

Slaves generally considered work to be only a means to wealth, but after emancipation, Americans told them that work—even thankless, nonremunerative work—was a virtue in itself. "You must be industrious and frugal," Freedmen's Bureau agents instructed newly freed slaves. "It is feared that some will act from the mistaken notion that Freedom means liberty to be idle. This class of persons, known to the law as vagrants, must at once correct this mistake." One bureau agent named Charles Soule greeted a group of newly freed slaves in Orangeburg, South Carolina, with a new kind of whipping:

You must remember that your children, your old people, and the cripples, belong to you to support now, and all that is given to them is so much pay to you for your work. If you ask for anything more; if you ask for a half of the crop, or even a third, you ask too much; you wish to get more than you could get if you had been free all your lives. Do not ask for Saturday either: free people everywhere else work Saturday, and you have no more right to the day than they have. If your employer is willing to give you part of the day, or to set a task that you can finish early, be thankful for the kindness, but do not think it is something you must have. When you work, work hard. Begin early—at sunrise, and do not take more than two hours at noon . . .

Remember that all your working time belongs to the man who hires you: therefore you must not leave work without his leave not even to nurse a child, or to go and visit a wife or husband . . . If you leave work for a day, or if you are sick, you cannot expect to be paid for what you do not do; and the man who hires you must pay less at the end of the year . . .

When ex-slaves flooded into the Freedmen's Bureau schools, they were probably expecting to learn how to read, write, and do arithmetic. The schools did teach those things, but when the illiterate ex-slaves listened to their teachers read from storybooks like *John Freeman and His Family*, they heard a very different kind of lesson. In the opening scene of *John Freeman*, the master and missus run away from the plantation, and the slaves greet their freedom with a "jubilee shout" and "the greatest excitement, crying, laughing, leaping, and dancing." But John quiets his fellow freedmen with sober counsel that freedom is not fun. "'Now we are free,'" he tells them, "'we must work.'"

"Now, children, we've blessed the Lord for that, the next thing is to inquire what we are going to do; what it is to be free. It is not to be let loose like the wild hogs in the woods, to root along in the bogs and just pick up a living as we can. No; we are men now, and we're free men, too; and we've got to do just what free men do. You look round and you see every freeman, black and white, works for a living; works, I say, not grubs and roots."

Then there is Prince, "a lazy and careless fellow" who resents the new work discipline and misses his less strenuous days as a slave. John and the other freedmen scorn him, and a white teacher singles him out for a special lesson:

> "[E]very body must work, Prince. God has made us to work. Adam and Eve, the first man and woman who were made, were placed in a garden to dress and keep it. God knew they would be happier to have something to do, and he knows that we shall be, and so he has made it a duty to labor."

All the other freedmen happily agree with this new idea that work in itself is good. But "Prince said nothing."

Unlike the writers of our textbooks today, the authors of freedmen's textbooks and the leaders of Reconstruction understood the dark side of democracy. At the turning point in *John Freeman,* a Yankee lieutenant addresses the ex-slaves: "'You have come out from your bondage, my friends, to enjoy the blessings of freedom, and have put yourselves under the protection of the United States government. . . . But, if you come to this flag for protection, you must be willing to do service for the flag.'" When a man in the crowd pledges to "'work for you,'" the lieutenant concludes, "'That's it; we'll help each other. We will be brothers, as God made us to be. All we want is for you to be industrious and orderly, and we will take care of you.'" There was no racial double standard here. The lesson that the government secures our rights only if we abide by democracy's demand to sacrifice and restrain ourselves had been broadcast to white citizens since the Revolution. All citizens and potential citizens were told that the more they worked and the less they lived for themselves, the more they were entitled to protection.

Other freedmen's textbooks hammered home the work ethic as a necessary component of citizenship. Clinton B. Fisk, a former abolitionist and Union army colonel and a senior officer in the Freedmen's Bureau, wrote *Plain Counsels for Freedmen* as a manual for citizenship. "I was myself brought up to hard work from my very childhood, and I am not speaking to you upon a matter that I know nothing about," Fisk wrote, correctly offering himself as a model American. "No, my friends, I love work, and nothing would be a greater punishment to me than enforced idleness.

I would rather work ten days than to be idle one day." His devotion to work was ruthless and complete: "I would rather every one of my children should die and be buried thus, than that they should be raised in idleness, and thus be exposed to dishonesty." Fisk and the Reconstruction project replaced the master's whip with a new, internal lash.

> Good and great men are all hard workers. And do you know what it is that makes a free state so rich and strong? It is, above all things save God's blessing, *patient, honest work*. . . . Now free labor does not imply that you may perform your work irregularly, carelessly, and dishonestly; and that your employer must put up with it, and say nothing about it. When you were a slave, it may have been your habit to do just as little as you could to avoid the lash. But now that you are free, you should be actuated by a more noble principle than fear.

The whip of leather that fell upon their skin could not make them work well. But a whip of shame that fell upon their conscience could make them work like mules. For the first time in their lives, the ex-slaves were "bad" for not working.

Some ex-slaves adopted the work ethic. The *Southern Workman,* a magazine published with assistance by agents of the Freedmen's Bureau, featured letters from ex-slaves preaching the gospel of labor to their brethren. The most famous black proponent of the work ethic was the ex-slave Booker T. Washington, who spent decades after the Civil War extolling "the dignity of labor" and discouraging agitation for equal rights. But early civil rights leaders were also powerful transmitters of the lessons taught in the Freedmen's schools. Frederick Douglass, now regarded as one of America's greatest freedom fighters, revered the regimented labor he saw among northern workers:

> I saw industry without bustle, labor without noise, and heavy toil without the whip. There was no loud singing, as in southern ports, where ships are loading or unloading—no loud cursing or swearing—but everything went on as smoothly as the works of a well adjusted machine . . . Men talked here of going whaling on a

four *years'* voyage with more coolness than sailors where I came from talked of going on a four *months'* voyage.

Ida B. Wells, another member of the early civil rights pantheon and upholder of the work ethic, considered her education in Freedmen's Bureau schools to be a gift from God: "All my teachers had been the consecrated white men and women from the North who came into the South to teach immediately after the end of the war. It was they who brought us the light of knowledge and their splendid example of Christian courage." Some employers of freedmen happily reported that their workers had learned the new lesson of labor. A planter in Mississippi was delighted to find that "the Negroes on our plantation were industrious and efficient, and we had little reason to complain of them in this regard." Two ex-Union officers who owned a plantation in Alabama exclaimed that they had "never employed so docile, industrious, and good humored a set of people in all our experience." It appears, however, that far more ex-slaves had little use for the work ethic.

After the war, a great many northerners bought plantations in the South, taking advantage of cheap prices for land and labor and assuming that the ex-slaves would be as industrious as northern workers. Nearly all of these men challenged the racist notion that blacks would not work as hard as whites. They argued that their "Negro brethren" were fully human and that it was therefore perfectly natural for them to absorb the work ethic. What they did not understand was that there was nothing natural about a life devoted to labor.

Only a few months after the Freedmen's Bureau started placing ex-slaves in jobs on plantations owned by northerners, where time and work practices were regulated, stories began to circulate about "an unaccountable prejudice among the colored people [against hiring] themselves to Northern people." One ex-slave working on a plantation in Georgia had a good question for his northern employer: What was the use of a man being free "if he had to work harder than when he was a slave?" One freedman, Frank Smith, moved from Alabama to Illinois but didn't like the kind of freedom he saw there: "I didn't lak de Yankees. Dey wanted you to wuk *all de time,* and dat's sump'n I hadn't been brung up to do." The white abolitionist Charles Stearns moved with his wife from Massachusetts to a Georgia plantation after the war to help civilize the freedmen. But he found constant resistance to demands for regularity and discipline among his black employees. His hands insisted that they be allowed to take their guns into the field and stop their work whenever a game animal happened by. To Stearns's consternation, this considerably limited productivity, but when he instructed his employees that free men do not take such breaks, they informed him that to change the practice "was a great encroachment upon their rights as freemen." Even Margaret, Stearns's cook, who had worked for years in "big houses" as a slave, required constant supervision to perform her duties in a timely and efficient manner. But Margaret was having none of it. She threatened to quit and declared, "Dem Yankees is a darn sight meaner than de old rebs; it's no use to try to suit 'em." Other northern employers were shocked that ex-slaves refused to work in conditions that would not daunt a farmer in the North. When one asked his employees to work in inclement weather to clear some cotton out of clogged ditches, they replied that "dey was free, and dey wouldn't work in de mud and de water for nobody."

Organized strikes of freedmen broke out all over the South over issues of wages, working conditions, hours, and treatment from managers. But many employers also reported frequent, spontaneous, and informal work stoppages when their black workers felt as if they were working too much or paid too little. Stearns noted with great irritation that whenever his employees "deemed it necessary for their physical welfare that they should enjoy a holiday, they *took* that holiday however different might be our opinion on the subject." A great number of freedmen also supplemented their wages by another entirely un-American means. Meat, corn, livestock, clothes, jewelry, bales of cotton, and vegetables planted in gardens disappeared from free-labor plantations all over the South. Employers put their pantries, smokehouses, barns, and homes under lock and key, but to little avail. "The truth is," one plantation owner admitted, "that with all our vigilance, the niggers will steal, & we may congratulate ourselves if they do not get the Lion's share."

Historians assume that the freedmen universally desired land, and there is certainly evidence that many did want to become independent farmers. Some leaders of Reconstruction wanted to give land to the freedmen, in part because they knew that nothing disciplines a person faster or more thoroughly than handing them a portion of uncultivated earth from which they must produce all of their livelihood. The life of someone who must grow all of his own means of support is a life of constant toil. Thaddeus Stevens, a leader of the Radical Republicans, argued that giving the ex-slaves "a small tract of land to cultivate for themselves" would "elevate the character of the freedman."

> Nothing is so likely to make a man a good citizen as to make him a freeholder. Nothing will so multiply the productions of the South as to divide it into small farms. Nothing will make men so industrious and moral as to let them feel that they are above want and are the owners of the soil which they till. It will also be of service to the white inhabitants. They will have constantly among them industrious laborers, anxious to work for fair wages.

Some slaves saw such a life as freedom, but many others seemed more interested in something that could be gotten and enjoyed immediately: *money*. Employers of ex-slaves reported relentless demands for higher pay. The planter Edward Philbrick found it difficult to attract workers, since most would work for him only if they were paid "a great deal more than they were last year." Whitelaw Reid complained that "nothing seemed more characteristic of the Negroes than their constant desire to screw a little higher wages" out of him. James Waters, a Louisiana planter, suffered constant demands from his black employees for more: "Always several of them grumble and complain & are impudent and sometimes even have cried (the women only) because they thought they had not been paid enough." According to historian Lawrence N. Powell, ex-slaves "seldom received their wages without challenging the planter's accounts." They were also quick to demand overtime payment when they were asked to work past their contracted hours. On the South Carolina Sea Islands, some expected overtime pay even if the workday lasted only fifteen minutes longer than what they had agreed to. Freedmen's demands for land were sporadic, according to Powell, "but the demand for money was constantly heard throughout the region in these years." It appears that in the minds of most ex-slaves, work remained a means to an end, not a good in itself.

Further evidence of the ex-slaves' resistance to the demands of American culture is the great number who were arrested for "loitering" and "vagrancy," which were euphemisms for willful unemployment. All the new state legislatures established after the war enacted sets of laws known as the Black Codes, which gave power to local officials to arrest any black person who appeared to be unemployed and to fine them for vagrancy. Thousands of black men were rounded up for refusing to work. Any arrestee who could not afford to pay the fine, which was nearly all, would be hired out to private employers to satisfy the fine. Many in the North thought this to be an attack on the humanity of the freedmen, who they believed would "naturally" desire to work if allowed to do so on their own volition. In response to what it considered to be outrages committed by the Southern states with the help of the Tennessee-born president Andrew Johnson, in December 1865, the Radical Republicans, who controlled the Congress and who led the Reconstruction project, refused to seat the representatives from the Southern states that had been "restored" by Johnson and which did not allow blacks the vote. The Radicals then showed that they were deadly serious about making ex-slaves into citizens.

In April 1866, Congress passed the Civil Rights Act, which declared African Americans to be citizens of the United States and gave the federal government the power to intervene on their behalf against the states if state officials abridged their rights. In July 1866, Congress passed the Freedmen's Bureau Bill, which extended the life of the bureau and gave it the power to nullify any work agreements forced on ex-slaves under the Black Codes. Both bills were passed over Johnson's vetoes. But local officers of the Freedmen's Bureau complained that a great many ex-slaves still had not acted on their natural inclination to work. Frustrated with the freedmen's misunderstanding of freedom, the bureau encouraged state governments to round up shiftless black men and force them to sign labor contracts on plantations.

There is no evidence to suggest that the refusal by so many ex-slaves to work was "racial" in the biological sense. Indeed, we will never know for sure why they chose a different kind of freedom than the one offered them by America. But what we can say is that, were it not for renegades like them, we would all be as "free" as John Freeman and his family.

THE BRAND OF SHAME

The leaders of Reconstruction were as united against sex as they were in favor of work. During the war, Congress established the American Freed-

men's Inquiry Commission to recommend what to do with the emancipated slaves. In its hearings, the commission heard from administrators of
the "contraband" camps that were set up to house black refugees. Colonel
William Pile, who oversaw the camp in Vicksburg, Mississippi, testified
that

> one great defect in the management of the Negroes down there
> was, as I judged, the ignoring of the family relationship. . . . My
> judgement is that one of the first things to be done with these peo-
> ple, to qualify them for citizenship, for self-protection and self-
> support, is to impress upon them the family obligations.

In its reports to the secretary of war, the commission upheld the dominant
view among whites that blacks were uncivilized, but it also overturned the
assumption that they could not *become* civilized. Just as it had done for
whites during and after the American Revolution, the government and its
allies would teach blacks to whip themselves. For the newly freed slave,
"the law, in the shape of military rule, takes for him the place of his master,
with this difference—that he submits to it more heartily and cheerfully,
without any sense of degradation." There was no more effective mecha-
nism for this transformation than marriage, "the great lever by which [the
freed men and women] are to be lifted up and prepared for a state of civilization."

Met with near unanimous endorsement among Union leaders, the
commission's recommendations were put into practice. Federal officials
running the contraband camps were instructed, "Among the things to be
done, to fit the freed people for a life of happiness and usefulness, it was obvious that the inculcation of right principles and practices in regard to the
social relations ought to find a place." For ex-slaves under the care of the
Union government, nonmarital sexual relations were outlawed. In April
1863, John Eaton, the federal director of the camps, reported that "all entering our camps who have been living or desire to live together as husband
and wife are required to be married in the proper manner. . . . This regulation has done much to promote the good order of the camp." Thereafter,
superintendents of the contraband camps reported that "the introduction
of the rite of Christian marriage and requiring its strict observance, exerted a most wholesome influence upon the order of the camps and the

conduct of the people." Secretary of War Edwin Stanton formally endorsed Eaton's rule and ordered Freedmen's Bureau agents to "solemnize the rite of marriage among Freedmen." Local administrators were ordered to coerce ex-slaves into marriage so as to bring them into civilization:

> The past marriages of freedmen, although often formally solemnized, have not been so authenticated that misconduct can be legally punished, or inheritance rightly determined. It is most urgently and plainly needful that this out growth of a by gone system should now cease. A general re-marriage (for the sake of the record) of all persons married without license, or living together without marriage should be insisted upon by employers and urged by all who have any connection with, or knowledge of such persons. They should know that, if after ample facilities have been for some time afforded, they have not conformed to this necessity of social life, they will be prosecuted and punished.

After its establishment at the end of the war, one of the first missions of the Freedmen's Bureau was to eliminate the sexual freedom of slaves. Just a few months after it began operations, in the summer of 1865 the bureau issued "Marriage Rules" to "aid the freedmen in properly appreciating and religiously observing the sacred obligations of the marriage state." The rules not only granted the legal right to marry to ex-slaves but also established the rules of marriage for them (including eligibility for marriage and for divorce) and, most significantly, made marriage, like it was already for free whites, an *obligation*: "No Parties . . . will be allowed to live together as husband and wife until their marriage has been legally solemnized."

Ex-slaves were warned by bureau officials that "the loose ideas which have prevailed among you on this subject must cease," and that "no race of mankind can be expected to become exalted in the scale of humanity, whose sexes, without any binding obligation, cohabit promiscuously together." The books that were read aloud by Freedmen's Bureau teachers to the ex-slaves were filled with attacks on nonmarital sex. "When you were slaves you 'took up' with each other, and were not taught what a bad thing it was to break God's law of marriage," intoned *Plain Counsels for Freedmen*. "But now you can only be sorry for the past, and begin life anew, and on a pure foundation. . . . God will not wink at adultery and fornication among you now." Black women, who as slaves were not punished or shamed for nonmarital sex, received fiery warnings:

> Let it be your first aim to make of yourself a true woman. Allow no man, under any pretense, to despoil you of your virtue. The brand of shame rests upon the brow of the unchaste woman. She is hated, even by those who are as bad as she is. No man can ever love her. . . . If in your slave life you have been careless of your morals, now that you are free, live as becomes a free Christian woman. Stamp a lie upon the common remark, that colored women are all bad . . .
>
> Avoid the company of bad men and women. Do not go with a man who does not care for the virtue of a woman. Keep away from gamblers. Never be found in the company of a woman who cares nothing about a good name. Lewd women will lead you down quick into hell.
>
> Now if you wish to build upon the solid rock, to be on good terms with yourself, to be able to look every man in the face, and to have peace with your God, keep yourselves pure. Avoid all vice, and especially all those things which are forbidden by the wholesome laws of society.

The ending of an unsatisfactory relationship among slaves did not bear the stigma that was attached to divorce among Americans, but the ex-slaves were told to never leave their spouses. As John Freeman told Clarissa on their day of liberation, "White folks always gets married with the book and the minister and a heap of ceremony like, and the man says yes, and the woman says yes, and they vows it before the Lord, and then they live together, and nothing can ever separate them. Now, let's you and I do that way, and begin all over new, like free folks."

As with the work ethic, many ex-slaves willfully—even eagerly—adopted the new sexual ethic. Thousands of freed men and women rushed to get married after the war, and countless, perfectly respectable black families emerged across the nation. Black political leaders and ministers uniformly endorsed the new rules. One minister counseled his people, "[l]et us do nothing to rekindle the slumbering fires of prejudice between the two races. Remember, we are on trial before the tribunal of the nation and of the world, that it may be known . . . whether we are worthy to be a free, self-governing people."

But despite the incessant moralizing by their leaders and protectors, many of the freedmen maintained their own ideas about marriage, relationships, and sex. Agent reports flooded into bureau offices complaining that the freed men and women persisted in "the disgusting practice of living together as man and wife without proper marriage," "living together and calling themselves man and wife as long as it conveniently suits them," and maintaining bigamous or adulterous relationships. In "many instances," wrote one agent, "where after being legally and lawfully married they live together but a short time. Separate and marry again or live together without any obligation at all." Time and again, the agents complained that blacks continued to "act as they did in time of slavery," clinging to "old habits of an immoral character." They could barely contain their frustration with the continued practice of "taking up" with a person without a lifetime commitment. "It would appear to be more difficult to change their ideas in this matter than on any other affecting their welfare," wrote Alvan Gillem, who headed the bureau in Mississippi, in 1868.

Freedmen's Bureau agents frequently reported their dismay with the manner in which freed people ignored the requirements of the law, even when they were fully aware of its technical demands. A local agent in Mississippi wrote in 1867 that he would

> hear of men leaving their wives and running away with other women to parts unknown and some women leaving their husbands, taking up with other men. I feel confident these acts are not done through ignorance of the law in such cases, but more from the want of a will to comply with the law. I have explained the law to them with reference to adultery etc. but without much avail.

Another bureau officer could scarcely believe that many freedmen considered having more than one sexual partner to be "a right which no one has a right to interfere with." Chaplain C. W. Buckley, the assistant superintendent of freedmen in Montgomery, Alabama, reported that he was "pained daily" by the sexual relations among ex-slaves: "Husbands & wifes [sic] are separating at a fearful rate and 'taking up' with other persons. Not infrequently a man is living with two or three wifes. Though this has been the custom of the race and habit of the country for years, yet it cannot be looked upon in any light than a huge system of prostitution by sane persons." But coercion had only a limited effect on people who did not want to live like the Freemans. The Virginia assistant commissioner reported, despite the bureau's massive efforts to domesticate the freedmen, "indifference and repugnance of the Negro to registering in reference to marriage, for both men and women still have an aptitude for change of their marriage relations, and their animal propensities are so strong that they heed not the consequences of the change." To be sure, many freed people searched for spouses who had been taken from them by sale, but "many Freedmen," as one bureau official observed, "now take advantage of their freedom to get rid of their Old Wives, and allege as a reason that they were not 'married by the Book.'" One Virginia officer said it all when he reported that many ex-slaves were displeased with legal marriage, "think[ing] their liberties very much curtailed by their freedom."

Frustrated bureau agents successfully lobbied Southern state legislators to legally mandate marriage for black couples. Many of the states' "civil rights" laws passed during Reconstruction included what legal historian Katherine Franke has called "the automatic marriage statute." The Mississippi civil rights law, passed in 1865, contained the standard language: "All freedmen, free Negroes and mulattoes, who do now and have heretofore lived and cohabited together as husband and wife shall be taken and held in law as legally married." Freedmen's Bureau agents monitored the living and sexual arrangements of ex-slaves and turned in alleged adulterers, bigamists, and fornicators to local authorities for prosecution under local criminal laws. Gillem asked law enforcement officials in Mississippi to jail ex-slaves who engaged in "deplorable" activities. He explained to the Washington bureau office in September 1868 that "I have caused the proper steps to be taken to bring this matter before the Civil Courts and shall urge that offenders be brought to trial and punished." After all, Gillem maintained, the purpose of the bureau's marriage rules was "to enforce matrimony between tens of thousands of freedpeople." One woman, when asked why she had legally married a man she already considered to be her husband when they were slaves, explained, "they were arresting people that did not have a ceremony between them."

As with white citizens in the early republic, new black citizens after the

Civil War were suddenly punished for producing children out of wedlock. Thousands of black unmarried mothers and fathers were arrested, fined, imprisoned, or suspended by their thumbs. Countless black children were labeled "bastards," placed in orphanages, and made wards of the state. This was an entirely new punishment for people who, when they were in a state of what was called bondage, thought nothing was shameful or "illegitimate" about unmarried parents.

WHITE RECONSTRUCTION

Moral rules for white Americans during Reconstruction were no less severe. White children were pummeled by moral injunctions to work. The most widely used schoolbook in the mid-nineteenth century, *McGuffey's Reader,* taught children to read with stories and poems such as "Lazy Ned," about a boy who "would never take the pains / To seek the prize that labor gains, / Until the time had passed; / For, all his life, he dreaded still / The silly bugbear of *up hill*, / And died a dunce at last." *McGuffey's* stories also warned its young readers to shun the choices of the "idle school boy" who "was indolent about every thing" and now "goes about the streets, begging his bread" and the laggard who ended up "despised by everyone . . . a poor wanderer, without money and without friends." Such tales were intended to instruct American children "how sinful and ruinous it is to be idle" and to create a culture in which work was a constant, haunting presence:

> The idle boy is almost invariably poor and miserable; the industrious boy is happy and prosperous. But perhaps some child who reads this, asks, 'Does God notice little children in school?' He certainly does. And if you are not diligent in the improvement of your time, it is one of the surest evidences that your heart is not right with God. You are placed in this world to improve your time. In youth, you must be preparing for future usefulness. And if you do not improve the advantages you enjoy, you sin against your Maker.

A poem featured in a popular school reader for girls, "Exhortation to Diligence," was typically morbid: "Toil, and be glad! Let Industry inspire / Into your quickened limbs her buoyant breath! / Who does not act, is dead;

absorbed entire / In miry sloth, no pride, no joy he hath; O leaden-hearted men, to be in love with death!"

Moral commands to labor continued to rain down on Americans in adulthood. Abraham Lincoln, like virtually all political leaders in the period, demonstrated the effects of this. On the eve of the Civil War, he wrote to a friend, "Work, work, work, is the main thing." In 1876, as Reconstruction neared its end and a depression crippled much of Northern industry, Washington Gladden, who was both a leader of the Freedmen's education movement and a leading proponent of labor reform in the North, authored a book of friendly advice to the (white) working man that was virtually identical to the freedmen's textbooks. "Shovel dirt, saw wood, do any kind of reputable work, rather than abide in idleness," Gladden counseled. "The only relief for our present distresses will come through industry and frugality; through a chastening of our ambitious notions of life, and the cultivation of simpler tastes and a more contented spirit." In 1878 an employer of shoemakers in Massachusetts voiced the general view when he defended the maintenance of ten- and eleven-hour work days by claiming, "Nothing saves men from debauchery and crime so much as labor, and that, till one is tired and ready to return to the domestic joys and duties of home." Leaders of government widely agreed with this assessment, as did the Ohio Bureau of Labor in 1879: "Labor is *not* a curse; it is not the hours per day that a person works that breaks him down, but the hours spent in dissipation." Give men "plenty to do, and a long while to do it in, and you will find them physically and morally better."

QUITTING TIME

Black people weren't the only Americans who violated the rules of Reconstruction. For one thing, they did not have a monopoly on shiftlessness. Though many white Americans had made themselves into the hardest workers in the world, fortunately, great numbers had been ignoring and resisting the work ethic since the Revolution. When the first factories were built, with their regimented work rules and long hours, many of the white people employed in them proved to be terrible workers. Among the very first factories built in the United States were the Hamilton Company mills in Lowell, Massachusetts, which employed only women. Within two years of the company's founding in 1825, more than half its work force had been fired for the following reasons:

6 were discharged for misconduct
5 were discharged for mutiny
3 were discharged for disobedience to orders
1 was discharged for impudence to the overseer
1 was discharged for levity
1 would not do her duty
5 were discharged for lying, misrepresentation, or circulating false stories
1 was discharged for captiousness
1 ran away
1 was hysterical
1 had written after her name emphatically "regularly discharged *forever*"

Cobblers in the first shoe factories in Lynn, Massachusetts stopped work for games, political debates, to hear one another read from a newspaper, and to shuffle off to the grog shop. A factory superintendent in Chicopee, Massachusetts, complained of "[t]he general indisposition" of his employees "to work steady."

Informal renegade behaviors often created enormous margins of freedom in people's lives. The men who built barrels—one of the major industries of the early American economy—were normally paid for six days of work, but on Saturday they began drinking beer in the morning, then would "sit around upturned barrels playing poker," and generally "lounged about" until they received their weekly pay. According to a historian of the industry, the partying continued into the evening as "Saturday night was a big night for the old-time cooper. . . . Usually the good time continued over into Sunday, so that on the following day he usually was not in the best of condition to settle down to the regular day's work." Therefore, "Blue Monday" was spent doing very little and was "more or less lost as far as production was concerned." Simply by being lazy, the coopers made for themselves a three-day weekend.

Employers regularly complained of such behavior in the nineteenth century. During Reconstruction, the complaints mounted, as workers from premodern cultures in Europe began to come in masses to the United States. Immigrant workers in New York City shipyards infuriated their bosses by taking breaks for cake, candy, trips to saloons for whiskey, and leisurely lunches. British-born workers in New Jersey pottery factories were known to work in "great bursts of activity" and then disappear for "several days at a time." Immigrants also continued the early American tradition of informal three-day weekends. "Monday," said one employer, "was given up to debauchery." A cigar manufacturer complained in 1877 that his employees spent more time slacking than working: "The difficulty with many cigarmakers is this. They come down to the shop in the morning; roll a few cigars and then go to a beer saloon and play pinnocio or some other game, . . . working probably only two or three hours a day."

GOING OUT

Abolitionists and the leaders of Reconstruction relaunched another of their projects after the Civil War, and as with the reformation of the slaves, achieved only mixed results. The temperance movement, stalled momentarily by the exigencies of the war, took flight again after the Confederate surrender. Leaders of the new movement coalesced as the Women's Christian Temperance Union in 1874. Activists in the campaign to purge America of "demon rum" not only continued to lobby for legal prohibition but also began invading saloons and demanding that the patrons put down their cups forever. Some barmen threw fruits, vegetables, eggs, and handfuls of sawdust from the floor at the reformers. Others cursed at them, threatened them with violence, loosed dogs on them, or "baptized" them with buckets of beer. In brew-loving Cincinnati, when the local WCTU threatened to protest against the existence of a beer garden, the owner "mounted an old cannon at the entrance to his place and threatened to blow the ladies to kingdom come."

American consumption of alcohol did decline after the Civil War from its previous stratospheric levels, but the nation remained very much an "alcoholic republic." In the ten years between the founding of the Freedmen's Bureau in 1865 and the founding of the WCTU in 1874, when citizens and those being trained for citizenship were told to avoid public places of sin and renounce personal pleasure, sixty-two million gallons of liquor were consumed in the United States. And in the first ten years of the WCTU's existence, the figure rose to seventy-six million gallons.

Another postwar moral reform institution with many former abolitionists and supporters of Reconstruction was the Young Men's Christian Association, whose mission was to protect the new urban masses from the sins of the city. It had its work cut out for it. In 1866 the YMCA counted in New York City alone eight thousand saloons, seven hundred brothels, four thousand prostitutes, and numerous sellers of pornography. The American pleasure culture experienced a renaissance after the war. Rather than heed the demands of citizenship, millions of Americans instead supported with their cash a vast proliferation of beer halls, brothels, dance halls, billiard rooms, pleasure gardens, concert saloons, and variety theaters. The last two have been described by one historian as "barrooms with free or cheap entertainment offered in adjacent backrooms, halls, or theaters." The major source of revenue in the concert saloons was the sale of alcohol, "with prostitution an important side line." The typical establishment, with "the floor filled with peanut shells and spilt beer; the air saturated with tobacco smoke," was correctly described by moral reformers as a gateway to sexual misbehavior. Not only were prostitutes staple attractions, but the staged performances nearly always included "bawdy" or "purple" acts featuring America's first professional strippers. The historian Timothy J. Gilfoyle has called the years between 1836 and 1871 "the halcyon years of commercialized sex."

THE PROMISE

The leaders of Reconstruction demonstrated that they were deadly serious about making the ex-slaves into citizens with a series of truly radical policies. Just before nullifying the Black Codes, the Republican-controlled Congress proposed a Fourteenth Amendment to the Constitution that defined American citizenship as belonging to anyone born in the United States or to anyone naturalized. The proposed amendment also stated that all citizens were entitled to all the "privileges and immunities" guaranteed by the Constitution, including, most importantly, equal protection of the laws by both the state and national governments. The Fourteenth Amendment moved four million people from slavery to full citizenship virtually overnight. In the winter and spring of 1867, Congress passed three breathtakingly aggressive "Reconstruction Acts" over Johnson's vetoes. The bills divided the South (except for Tennessee, which was readmitted into the Union only because it had agreed to ratify the Fourteenth Amendment) into five military districts and gave supreme authority over those districts to officers of the United States Army. Even more radical, the Reconstruction Acts limited suffrage to all *black* men and to white men who had not participated in the rebellion. At first, about one-fourth of all white men in the South were excluded from suffrage. This created black voting *majorities* in several states. Congress mandated that a state could be readmitted into the Union only if its constitution included provisions for black suffrage and if its legislature ratified not only the Fourteenth Amendment but also a new Fifteenth Amendment, which made illegal the denial of suffrage to any citizen on account of "race, color, or previous condition of servitude." By 1870, all the states of the former Confederacy had submitted to the demands of Reconstruction. The immediate result was that in every former slave state, black men held public office during Reconstruction, including twenty in the U.S. House of Representatives, two in the U.S. Senate, and hundreds in state legislatures. This was a remarkable transformation in Southern politics.

Other accomplishments were stunning in their scope and ambition. The Freedmen's Bureau established nearly four thousand schools, in which approximately two hundred thousand ex-slaves received the first formal education of their lives. Spending by Republican-controlled state governments increased geometrically, as roads, hospitals, prisons, asylums for orphans and the insane, and public schools were built all over the South. Though most state governments distributed very little land to the ex-slaves, South Carolina gave land to fourteen thousand black families in an effort to fulfill Thaddeus Stevens's hope that independent farming would "elevate the character of the freedman." Republicans fiercely protected ex-slaves from vigilante violence. In 1871 President Ulysses S. Grant signed the Ku Klux Klan Act, which empowered federal troops to arrest Klansmen and gave jurisdiction in such cases to federal courts, where juries were often predominantly black. The subsequent prosecution and imprisonment of hundreds of Klan members effectively destroyed the KKK as an organization.

But support for the Reconstruction project began to fade in the 1870s. Many Republicans complained that the ex-slaves were not taking on the responsibilities of citizenship. The journalist and former abolitionist James S. Pike toured South Carolina and reported with dismay that, despite the injunctions of Freedmen's Bureau teachers and agents to work at least six full days per week, ex-slaves in Charleston "average about four days labor in the week." Other freedmen showed that they were "habitually guilty of thieving and of concubinage." Granting the rights of citizenship to people who did not adopt the cultural restraints of citizenship had resulted in the "rule of ignorance, barbarism, and vice." Pike's report, which was widely read by Republican politicians, caused many to abandon hope of remaking the black renegades. Carl Schurz, a leading Republican senator and an early supporter of Reconstruction, stated in 1872 that "the inevitable consequence of the admission of so large an uneducated and inexperienced class to political power" was "the probable mismanagement of the material interests of the social body" as well as "political corruption and demoralization" and "financial ruin."

By 1872, there was so much frustration with making the ex-slaves into citizens that the Freedmen's Bureau was abolished. Over the next five years, the Democrats steadily regained power as, one by one, the Republicans lost their will to transform the Southern states. By 1876, the demoralized Republicans agreed to withdraw federal troops from the South in exchange for giving the presidency to Republican Rutherford B. Hayes in an election that had gone to Congress because of a dispute over which party had won the most electoral votes. By the end of 1877, all of the military power that had kept the Reconstruction state governments in power were removed from the South.

The turn against Reconstruction has been interpreted as the Republicans' submerged racism coming to the surface and as evidence that they were never fully committed to making ex-slaves into citizens. This interpretation implies that the ex-slaves complied with the rules of citizenship and were therefore cheated of their place in American society. But even if they were motivated by racism—and some of them surely were—Schurz and the Republicans who complained of the freedmen's behavior were *correct*: many and possibly most of the ex-slaves did not take on the responsibilities of citizenship, did not restrain their personal freedoms, did not devote their lives to work, monogamy, frugality, and discipline. Their attitudes and behaviors delayed the project begun by the Founding Fathers, continued by abolitionists, and made comprehensive by the leaders of Reconstruction: of making us into the enemies of our own freedom. And for this, I suggest, we should celebrate them.

THE GIFT

Something was let loose with the slaves, something described by W. E. B. DuBois in *Black Reconstruction in America* as a magical gift:

> A great song arose, the loveliest thing born this side the seas. It was a new song. It did not come from Africa, though the dark throb and beat of that Ancient of Days was in it and through it. It did not come from white America—never from so pale and hard and thin a thing, however deep these vulgar and surrounding tones had driven. Not the Indies nor the hot South, the cold East or heavy West made that music. It was a new song and its deep and plaintive beauty, its great cadences and wild appeal wailed, throbbed and thundered on the world's ears with a message seldom voiced by man. . . .
>
> They sneered at it—those white Southerners who heard it and never understood. They raped and defiled it—those white Northerners who listened without ears. Yet it lived and grew; always it grew and swelled and lived, and it sits today at the right hand of God, as America's one real gift to beauty; as slavery's one redemption, distilled from the dross of its dung.

To DuBois, slavery kept African Americans out of the culture of repression that whites had created, and because of this, slaves created a uniquely liberated culture that valued pleasure over work and freedom over conformity. DuBois argued that there were some ex-slaves who behaved like John Freeman. But many did not, and to DuBois, the culture of the slaves that was let loose by emancipation was a gift to America and the world. In fact, during Reconstruction many ex-slaves fled the fields for cities, where they found horns and formed "jubilee" bands. Many discovered pianos and invented a music called ragtime that set millions of white feet dancing. And others picked up guitars and began to play a music we call the blues.

Out of that alchemy emerged a gift to all those who hated work, loved pleasure, and yearned to be as free as a child. The great tragedy of Reconstruction, according to DuBois, was that so many whites turned down the gift, "sneered" at black culture and mocked it, and chose to consider it inferior. But DuBois, like most historians today, nonetheless wished that the ex-slaves had been made into full American citizens. What he did not understand was that John Freeman and all the ex-slaves who chose citizenship turned down the gift as well. If Reconstruction had been fully realized, many of the freedoms and joys given to us by the slaves would have been taken away. If the freedmen had been made into citizens, there would be no jazz.

★ 4 ★

WHORES AND THE ORIGINS OF WOMEN'S LIBERATION

In the nineteenth century, a woman who owned property, made high wages, had sex outside of marriage, performed or received oral sex, used birth control, consorted with men of other races, danced, drank, or walked alone in public, wore makeup, perfume, or stylish clothes—and was not ashamed—was probably a whore. In fact, prostitutes won virtually all the freedoms that were denied to women but are now taken for granted.

Prostitutes were especially successful in the wild, lawless, thoroughly renegade boomtowns of the West. When women were barred from most jobs and wives had no legal right to own property, madams in the West owned large tracts of land and prized real estate. Prostitutes made, by far, the highest wages of all American women. Several madams were so wealthy that they funded irrigation and road-building projects that laid the foundation for the New West. Decades before American employers offered health insurance to their workers, madams across the West provided their employees with free health care. While women were told that they could not and should not protect themselves from violence, and wives had no legal recourse against being raped by their husbands, police officers were employed by madams to protect the women who worked for them, and many madams owned and knew how to use guns.

While feminists were seeking to free women from the "slavery" of patriarchal marriage, prostitutes married later in life and divorced more frequently than other American women. At a time when birth control was effectively banned, prostitutes provided a market for contraceptives that made possible their production and distribution. While women were taught that they belonged in the "private sphere," prostitutes traveled extensively, often by themselves, and were brazenly "public women." Long before social dancing in public was considered acceptable for women, prostitutes invented many of the steps that would become all the rage during the dance craze of the 1910s and 1920s. When gambling and public drinking were forbidden for most women, prostitutes were fixtures in western saloons, and they became some of the most successful gamblers in the nation. Most ironically, the makeup, clothing, and hairstyles of prostitutes, which were maligned for their overt sexuality (lipstick was "the scarlet shame of streetwalkers"), became widely fashionable among American women and are now so respectable that even First Ladies wear them.

Women who wished to escape the restrictions of Victorian America had no better place to go than the so-called frontier, where a particular combination of economic and demographic forces gave renegade women many unusual advantages.

BOOM

Between 1870 and 1900, the number of farms in the United States doubled, and more land was brought under cultivation than in the previous two and half centuries. Most of this newly cultivated land was in the Great Plains and the Southwest. In addition to all of this farming, other industries developed rapidly in the West during the second half of the nineteenth century. The largest of these were metal and coal mining in California, the Rockies, and parts of the Southwest; cattle ranching on the Plains; lumber in the Pacific Northwest; large-scale fruit and vegetable agriculture in the inland valleys of California; and oil in Texas, Oklahoma, and Southern California. Connecting these industries to one another and to eastern U.S. and European markets were railroads, which crisscrossed the West by the end of the nineteenth century. The federal government contributed to this explosive growth with massive expenditures for the building of the Transcontinental Railroad, which ran from the Pacific Ocean to the Missouri River, but also to the building of roads, dams, and vast irrigation systems without which the West as we know it could never have been created.

Towns were created virtually overnight in mountains where precious metal was discovered, in deserts near oil strikes, along cattle trails and around railroad stations, and in forests next to lumber mills and logging stands. Some boomtowns grew into the major urban hubs of San Francisco, Los Angeles, Denver, and Seattle. The people who filled those towns were overwhelmingly male, since the labor that brought them there was brutal, physically onerous, and almost universally considered to be men's work. The non-Indian population of California in 1850 was 93 percent male. In the mining towns along the Comstock Silver Lode in Nevada, a census taker in 1860 counted 2,306 men and 30 women. These were men without families, without land, without property, and without a stake in any one community. They moved from town to town in search of money. And, since most of the towns they lived and worked in were brand new, the legal apparatus was usually very weak. These were exactly the conditions that bred bad people.

THE WHOREARCHY

With good reason, the keepers of American morality in the nineteenth century were terribly worried about all the single men in the West. One Protestant minister wrote, "Left by themselves, men degenerate rapidly and become rough, harsh, slovenly—almost brutish." He was correct. Ironically, most of these men were white and full American citizens. But they cared little for the restrictions and responsibilities of citizenship. One moral reformer in Montana reported this about life in a mining town: "Men without the restraint of law, indifferent to public opinion, and unburdened by families, drink whenever they feel like it, whenever they have the money to pay for it, and whenever there is nothing else to do. . . . Bad manners follow, profanity becomes a matter of course. . . . Excitability and nervousness brought on by rum help these tendencies along, and then to correct this state of things the pistol comes into play." In the silver mining boomtown of Leadville, Colorado, in 1879 there were 120 saloons, 19 beer halls, 188 gambling houses, and only 4 churches.

Into this world stepped legions of women who understood something about supply and demand. A U.S. Department of Labor study in 1916 found that in the major legitimate occupations for women—department store clerking and light manufacturing—the average weekly wage was $6.67, which at the time represented a subsistence standard of living. In such industries, jobs were few, and due to the ban on women's labor in most of the economy, the number of available workers in the industries that allowed women was great. This oversupply of labor pushed wages down to the minimum. By contrast, women who chose prostitution enjoyed a highly favorable market for their labor. Demand was enormous and constant, especially in the West, and the pool of available labor was kept relatively small by the great number of women who internalized or feared the stigma attached to prostitution. According to historian Ruth Rosen, who pioneered the social history of prostitution in the United States, "The average brothel inmate or streetwalker"—the lowest positions in the trade—"received from one to five dollars a 'trick,' earning in one evening what other working women made in a week." Prostitutes in a 1916 study reported earnings between $30 to $50 per week, at a time when skilled male trade union members averaged roughly $20 per week. In their study of Virginia City, Nevada, George M. Blackburn and Sherman L. Ricards found that prostitutes in that 1860s boomtown, unlike the stereotype of the innocent, young "white slave," were actually considerably older on average than women of the western mining states Colorado, Idaho, and Nevada. "From the age data on prostitutes, it is clear that they were old enough to realize the nature of their behavior and also old enough to have married had they so desired, for this was an area with many unattached men. Thus we conclude that these were professional women intent on economic success." After working as a domestic in El Paso, Texas, for $3 per week, a Mexican-born woman quit her job and "decided to become a *puta*" for the extra money. She later recalled, "It took me a long time to get used to having men intimately explore my body. . . . Of course, I had guilt feelings at the beginning, but they soon disappeared when I saw my savings begin mounting up."

Even in the tighter markets of the East, prostitutes were extraordinarily well paid. In New York City, according to historian Timothy Gilfoyle, "an affluent, but migratory, class of prostitutes flourished." Low wages "in the factory and the household made prostitutes the best-paid women workers in the nineteenth-century city." In studies conducted in New York during the 1900s and 1910s, 11 percent of prostitutes listed coercion as the reason for entering the trade, but almost 28 percent named the money they could earn. Members of the Vice Commission of Chicago, like many anti-prostitution reformers, faced the hard truth of the wealth being accrued by prostitutes with a bitter question: "Is it any wonder that a tempted girl who receives only six dollars per week working with her hands sells her body for twenty-five dollars per week when she learns there is a demand for it and men are willing to pay the price?" One Chicago prostitute who supported her family with her wages had an answer. She told an interviewer, "Do you suppose I am going back to earn five or six dollars a week in a factory, and at that, never have a cent of it to spend for myself, when I can earn that amount any night, and often much more?" Historian Ruth Rosen was "struck again and again by most prostitutes' view of their work as 'easier' and less oppressive than other survival strategies they might have chosen."

Prostitutes were the first women to break free of what early American feminists described as a system of female servitude. Charlotte Perkins Gilman, one of the leading feminist intellectuals at the turn of the twentieth century, noted that human beings were the only species in which "an entire sex lives in a relation of economic dependence upon the other sex." Since wages in respectable occupations were so low, the only culturally sanctioned means for a woman to attain wealth was through a rich husband. And since states in the nineteenth century granted few or no property rights to married women, even women who "married well" owned little or nothing of their own. But women who chose to be bad could live well on their own.

Prostitutes who rose to the top of the industry to become "madams" owned more wealth than any other women in the United States. Indeed, they were among the wealthiest people in the country, and especially in the West. "Diamond Jessie" Hayman began work as a prostitute in the gold country of the Sierra Nevada foothills in the 1880s, then moved to San Francisco to become one of the most successful prostitutes in the city's history. Hayman's three-story brothel in the Tenderloin district of San Francisco included three fireplaces, a saloon, a champagne cellar, and fifteen suites filled with imported furniture. She provided each of her employees with a $6,000 wardrobe that included a fox fur coat, four tailored suits, eight hats, two dress coats, twelve pairs of shoes, twelve pairs of gloves, seven evening gowns, and seven negligees. Hayman earned enough money from her business to buy several parcels of land in the city. After the 1906 earthquake that destroyed much of San Francisco, Hayman and other madams provided food and clothing to the thousands left homeless. She died in 1923 with an estate worth $116,000.

Jennie Rogers, the "Queen of the Colorado Underworld," owned several opulent brothels in Denver that featured ceiling-to-floor mirrors, crystal chandeliers, oriental rugs, marble tables, and grand pianos. Rogers provided her prostitutes with personal hairstylists and dressmakers, ensuring that they were among the most stylish women in the world. Her profits were so great that she was able to purchase large tracts of Denver's most valuable land as well as several shares of an irrigation and reservoir project that not only provided the city with much of its water but also paid Rogers sizable dividends. Rogers's major competitor was Mattie Silks, who had risen from the ranks of streetwalkers in Abilene, Texas, and Dodge City, Kansas, to become a brothel owner by the age of nineteen. Soon after moving to Denver in 1876, she purchased a three-story mansion with twenty-seven rooms, then outfitted it with the finest furnishings available. Visitors to the Silks brothel were greeted by a symphony orchestra in the main parlor. Silks eventually opened three other brothels and purchased a stable of race horses. After her retirement from the trade, she told a newspaper, "I went into the sporting life for business reasons and for no other. It was a way for a woman in those days to make money, and I made it. I considered myself then and I do now—as a businesswoman." Her employees, who were among the highest paid women in the United States, "came to me for the same reasons that I hired them. Because there was money in it for all of us."

Other madams ruled major portions of the West. Eleanora Dumont purchased real estate in gold and silver boomtowns all over the Rockies and Sierra Nevada, where she established lucrative brothels, saloons, and gambling houses. Josephine "Chicago Joe" Airey used the proceeds from her brothels to purchase a sizable portion of Helena, Montana's, real estate in the 1870s and 1880s. Lou Graham was not only early Seattle's most prominent madam, she was also one of its wealthiest residents. Graham arrived in Seattle in 1888 and soon opened an immaculately appointed brothel in the Pioneer Square area. To advertise her business, she paraded with her employees on carriages through the city streets. Graham invested heavily in the stock market and in real estate, becoming, according to one historian, "one of the largest landholders in the Pacific Northwest." The "Queen of the Lava Beds" also contributed enormous sums to help establish the Seattle public school system and saved many of the city's elite families from bankruptcy after the panic of 1893. Anna Wilson, the "Queen of the Omaha Underworld," owned a substantial portion of the city's real estate. Toward the end of her life she bequeathed to the city her twenty-five-room mansion, which became Omaha's first modern emergency hospital and a communicable-disease treatment center.

It is unlikely that there were more wealthy or powerful black women in nineteenth-century America than Mary Ellen "Mammy" Pleasant and Sarah B. "Babe" Connors. Pleasant was born a slave but became one of the most influential women in early San Francisco. She operated boarding-houses in which wealthy businessmen were paired with prostitutes. With the revenue from her primary business, she invested in mining stock and made high-interest loans to the San Francisco elite. Pleasant also filed suit to desegregate the city's streetcars, making her "the mother of the civil rights movement" in California. Connors's brothels in St. Louis were among the most popular in the Midwest. Known as "the Castle" and "the Palace," they featured luxurious rugs, tapestries, art work, and crystal chandeliers. The parlor of the Palace was famous for its floor, which was made entirely of mirrored glass. Connors herself was always elegantly appointed with drapes of jewelry on her body and gold and diamonds embedded in her teeth. Many of the most famous songs of the ragtime genre—the principal precursor to jazz—were invented by Letitia Lulu Agatha "Mama Lou" Fontaine, who performed as the house act at Connors's brothels.

High-end madams were not the only prostitutes who acquired substantial wealth. A middle-class reformer in Virginia City, Nevada, noted with disdain that local prostitutes were "always dressed the richest." The historians Blackburn and Ricards concluded that while prostitutes in Virginia City were not the richest people in town, they "did amass more wealth than most of their customers. In addition, compared with other women of the city, the white prostitutes were well-to-do. This was because virtually none of the married women and very few unmarried women had any money at all. If the prostitutes came West to compete economically with others of their sex, they were successful."

Similarly, historian Paula Petrik found that approximately 60 percent of the prostitutes who worked in Helena, Montana, between 1865 and 1870 "reported either personal wealth or property or both." The town's "fancy ladies" also made 44 percent of the property transactions undertaken by women and acquired all twenty mortgages that were given to women during the period. Most impressive of all were Helena prostitutes' wages compared to male workers in the town. Petrik estimates that the average monthly income of "a fancy lady plying her trade along Wood Street" was $233. By contrast, bricklayers, stone masons, and carpenters earned between $90 and $100, and even bank clerks made only $125 per month. Moreover, "[c]ompared with the $65 monthly wage the highest paid saleswomen received, prostitutes' compensation was royal." At a time when leading feminists were demanding an end to women's economic dependence, the red-light district in Helena was, in Petrik's words, "women's business grounded in women's property and capital."

Today's women attorneys might also find their earliest ancestors among western madams, who regularly appeared in court on their own behalf and won quite frequently. Petrik found a large number of court cases in Helena in which prostitutes brought suit against one another to "settle petty squabbles among them that could not be resolved by the Tenderloin's leaders" or to "challenge men who assaulted, robbed, or threatened them." In half of the cases involving a prostitute's complaint against a man, "the judge or jury found for the female complainants." Petrik discovered in Helena "a singular lack of legal and judicial concern with sexual commerce" before the influx of moral reformers. "[O]fficers of the law arrested no women for prostitution or keeping a disorderly house before 1886, even though the police court was located in the red-light district" and prostitution had been a central part of the town's economy for two decades. The era of legal tolerance coincided with a period in which Helena's prostitutes suffered very little of the self-destructiveness assumed to be common among sex workers. "Not one whore in Helena died by her own hand before 1883," and though the town's prostitutes were "rampant users of alcohol and drugs," there were "no reports of prostitutes dying of alcoholism or drug overdose between 1865 and 1883 in Helena."

Some madams abused their employees or placed them in peonage, but these tended to be the less successful brothel keepers. To attract women in the highly competitive markets of western boomtowns, where red-light districts nearly always included several brothels, most madams not only paid their employees far higher wages than they would find in any other employment, they also provided free birth control, health care, legal assistance, housing, and meals for their employees. Few American workers of either sex in the nineteenth century enjoyed such benefits.

By the middle of the nineteenth century, the wealth, power, and ubiquity of prostitutes caused several urban reformers to warn of a "whore-archy" that threatened to undermine the virtues of the nation. Madams led an "under-ground universe" with "a regularly organized community of thieves, who have their laws and regulations," as George Foster put it in his 1850 novel *Celio: or, New York Above-ground and Under-ground*. In George Ellington's 1869 journalistic account, *The Women of New York: or, the Underworld of the Great City*, madams were "female fiends of the worst kind, who seem to have lost all the better qualities of human nature." Worse still, they had "entrée to the good society of the metropolis" with "the friends and chosen companions of some of the wealthiest and most intellectual men of the city."

SHAMELESS

The sexual repression that was so central to Victorian ideology, particularly regarding women, was often stunningly absent from prostitutes' minds. When the Denver city council attempted to humiliate local prostitutes by passing an ordinance requiring all "women of ill repute" to wear yellow ribbons, the city's madams dressed themselves and their employees in yellow from head to toe. This drew even more attention to the city's streetwalkers and embarrassed the city council into rescinding its order. Denver's madams also demonstrated their immunity from bourgeois norms by taking out ads for their businesses in a widely-distributed publication called the *Denver Red Book: A Reliable Directory of the Pleasure Resorts of Denver*. A guide covering the entire state was published in 1895 as the *Travelers' Night Guide of Colorado*. Prostitutes in San Francisco were so shameless that they held weekly parades down Market Street, dressed in the finest clothes in the world, to advertise their services. When the census was taken in Sweetwater, Texas, the town's best-known prostitute, Libby "Squirrel Tooth Alice" Thompson, unabashedly listed her occupation as "one who diddles and squirms in the dark."

It is commonplace to assume that prostitution is inherently degrading and that no mentally healthy or economically secure woman would choose it. Underneath this assumption is another assumption that selling the function of one's body for sex causes greater physical and psychological harm than selling the function of one's body for other, legitimate kinds of work. Yet many of the prostitutes in the nineteenth century who were asked about it contradict these assumptions.

In an 1859 poll of 2,000 New York City women who sold sex, Dr. William Sanger asked, "What was the cause of your becoming a prostitute?" About 1,100 gave him answers he expected to hear, such as "destitution," "seduced and abandoned," "ill-treatment of parents, relatives, or husbands," and "bad company." But to Sanger's great surprise, 513 prostitutes—more than one-quarter of those he interviewed—said they chose their profession out of "inclination." The doctor called this response "incredible." A large number of the women did not even see their profession as work: 181 stated as their main reason for choosing it "drink, and the desire to drink," while 124 saw prostitution "as an easy life." Twenty-nine women—who might be the baddest renegades in American history—said they became prostitutes because they were "too idle to work." Says Gilfoyle, "these women did not view prostitution as deviance or sin; rather, they considered it a better alternative to the factory or domestic servitude." Prior to the legal crackdown on prostitution in New York after the Civil War, prostitutes in the city "did not see themselves as 'fallen women.'" In court and in the press, "They publicly defended their personal integrity and private property instead of succumbing to violent intimidation, and they refused to act as fugitives from justice."

Prostitutes undermined virtually every sexual taboo that limited the freedom of women. The birth control devices that had circulated among the rabble of early American cities came under attack by the middle of the nineteenth century, when contraceptives were used widely and shamelessly. A visitor to Boston noted in 1872 that there was "hardly a newspaper that does not contain their open and printed advertisements, or a drug store whose shelves are not crowded with nostrums publicly and unblushingly displayed." The production and distribution of devices that made sex purely recreational was, according to the historian Andrea Tone, "a robust and increasingly visible commerce in illicit products and pleasures that seemed to encourage sexual license by freeing sex from marriage and childbearing." The growing numbers of prostitutes in the mid-nineteenth century greatly supported this market, then kept it alive when moral reformers threatened to kill it. In the 1860s and 1870s, several books with titles such as *Serpents in the Doves' Nest* and *Satan in Society* condemned birth control as a violation of "the laws of heaven," "the invention of hell," and a "hydra-headed monster" bent on killing the American family. These complaints became law in 1873 with the passage by the U.S. Congress of an Act of the Suppression of Trade in, and Circulation of, Obscene Literature and Articles of Immoral Use, commonly called the Comstock Law. The law, named after the anti-obscenity crusader Anthony Comstock, made it illegal to distribute through the U.S. Postal Service any "obscene, lewd, or lascivious" materials "or any article or thing designed or intended for the prevention of conception or producing of abortion."

An underground army of renegades made up of what Comstock called "bad" men, "sly" Jews, "moral-cancer-planters," and "old she-villains" continued to produce, distribute, and purchase contraceptives and keep sexual freedom alive. But the steadiest and largest pool of consumers was prostitutes, who by the 1870s made up an estimated 5 percent to 10 percent of women in American cities, or several million purchasers of birth control. These she-villains kept afloat underground birth control businesses between 1873 and the legalization of contraceptive production and distribution in the 1920s. During this time, according to Tone, "the American condom trade was fiercely competitive, crowded, and replete with bootleggers." A typical contraceptive business was Joseph Backrach's secret factory—run inside the Brooklyn home he shared with his wife and seven children—which by the 1880s was annually producing several thousand condoms, "male caps," and "womb veils."

One of Backrach's chief competitors was Julius Schmid, like Backrach a German-Jewish immigrant, who saw an opportunity at his job cleaning animal intestines at a sausage factory. In 1883 he took home hundreds of intestines and founded what would become Julius Schmid Inc., the manufacturer of Fourex, Ramses, and Sheik condoms. In 1890 Comstock's New York vice squad arrested Schmid at his home on Forty-sixth Street in Manhattan, which was ideally located amid what was then New York's largest red-light district, and found 696 prophylactic "skins" and "one form for manufacturing same." Schmid was jailed and fined for "selling articles to prevent conception" but was encouraged by the enormous market of bad people and continued his trade. This was twenty-six years before Margaret Sanger more famously opened her first birth control clinic. Using a technique invented in Germany, Schmid became the first American to mass-produce rubber condoms and the leading condom manufacturer in the United States. During World War I, he provided condoms to the British, French, Russian, and Italian armies, but not to the American army, which, following the ban on contraceptives, instructed its soldiers to use "moral prophylaxis" in their encounters with prostitutes. As a result, roughly 10 percent of American GIs contracted venereal disease during the war. By World War II, the ban had been lifted, allowing the U.S. armed forces to make Schmid its official condom supplier.

In the nineteenth century, when oral sex was universally condemned as a sin, brothels were known to be the only place a man could receive it without coercion. Until well into the twentieth century, medical sexual manuals and marriage advice books either ignored oral sex or condemned it as pathological and perverted. As of 1950, fellatio—even when practiced by a married couple—was a felony in all forty-eight states, and cunnilingus was a felony in forty-one. No doubt many Americans practiced oral sex anyway, but prostitutes were practically the only ones to do so publicly and with no apparent shame. In a 1934 survey of Chicago prostitutes, only five solicited what investigators called "the 'normal' coitus," while more than one hundred offered fellatio. The report noted that 90 percent of the solicitations observed by investigators "consisted of offers of gross perversion." Prostitutes were the vanguard of the sexual revolution that broke open the erotic lives of Americans. Until the 1970s, when many observers declared that "everyone" was doing it, oral sex among heterosexuals was considered to be the exclusive practice of whores.

Even the dance craze of the 1910s and 1920s originated in brothels. Until then, respectable social dancing was limited to upper-class balls where, according to historian Lewis A. Erenberg, the dancing "exhibited control, regularity, and patterned movement." The waltz, the most popular of the respectable dances in the nineteenth century, demanded "a certain unity in the steps, creating a standardized form of motion." Erenberg's description of the waltz—which required a distance between the partners of three to four inches at the shoulders, "increasing downward"—shows just how revolutionary were slaves, minstrels, prostitutes, and the renegade Americans who emulated them on the dance floor:

The waltz perhaps expressed the emphasis on disembodied love in the nineteenth century. It was a more companionate dance to be sure, but the movement of the dance, much like the mobility enshrined in the society, kept the man and woman apart.

Any overtly sexual dancing was considered the practice of only blacks and prostitutes. Moreover, dancing was consigned to private, well-regulated spaces. Jesse Lasky, a vaudeville performer who created Hollywood's first film studio, said that in 1911 "it was still scandalous to dance in a public place." But in the second decade of the twentieth century, renegade pleasures and freedoms bubbled up from the gutter.

While good Americans were dancing the waltz, bad people were enjoying dirty dancing in houses of ill repute all over the country. Places called "concert saloons" appeared in cities during the 1840s and 1850s and gained popularity through the nineteenth century. By 1910, San Francisco's red-light district, known as the Barbary Coast, contained more than 300 concert saloons within a six-block radius, and the South Side of Chicago had more than 285. New York's Bowery and Tenderloin (Julius Schmid's neighborhood) and the French Quarter in New Orleans contained several hundred similar establishments.

Concert saloons were known to offer four things: liquor, music, dancing, and sex for sale. According to the historian Russel B. Nye, "the girls who frequented them were nearly always prostitutes, amateur and professional." They were also, like the brothels of the Wild West, frequently integrated. Many of the concert saloons in the big cities were owned by African Americans, and most were known to host mixed clientele. Even perfectly genteel establishments began to offer the freedoms and pleasures that were previously found only in brothels. In 1912, cafes on Broadway in New York started afternoon dances, often called "tango teas," for unescorted women, single men, and even gigolos hired by management to dance with the female patrons. They became all the rage. Moral reformers rightly pointed to the scum of society as the source of the phenomenon. "It is simply an evil condition working upward into other strata of society," said Belle Moskowitz, who led a campaign to ban all forms of sensual and public dancing in New York. As the New York *World* quite accurately noted, "From the slum to the state, from the state to the restaurant, from restaurant to home, the dive dances have clutched and taken hold upon the young who know no better and the old who should."

Historians have estimated that in the 1910s more than one hundred new dances became fashionable in perfectly respectable public spaces. These dances overturned Victorian conventions against overt sexuality. According to Erenberg, they "fostered an unheard-of casualness between partners, permitted greater options in holds and distances, and symbolized the high value placed on mutual heterosexual intimacy and attraction." Most shocking to the keepers of social order, "couples often held each other very close, grasping each other firmly about the waist or about the neck as in a hug . . . the one-step, the bunny hug, and the other new dances allowed a lingering close contact." The most influential of the new dances, which scholars cite as the sources of both swing dance and the gyrations at early rock-and-roll dances, were the turkey trot, the fox-trot, the Charleston, and the Texas Tommy. According to the leading historians of American vernacular dance, all of these dances were invented by ex-slaves and their descendants in the South, then popularized among whites by prostitutes in the Barbary Coast district of San Francisco. "By turning to the animal world, black culture, and the red-light district for the sources of their cultural regeneration," writes Erenberg, "well-to-do urbanites were searching for a way to liberate some of the repressed wilder elements, the more natural elements, that had been contained by gentility."

PISTOLS AND PAINT

American prostitutes gave the lie not only to the Victorian belief that women were innately asexual but also to the common assumption that women were incapable of defending themselves from physical violence. Biographies of virtually all the major madams include at least one story of armed self-defense against a male assailant. Jessie Hayman always kept a pistol in her pocket. "I keep my customers close and my gun closer," she often said. "It's helped me settle many an argument." Caroline "Cad" Thompson, the queen of the silver mining town Virginia City, Nevada, responded to her husband's threat to kill her by pointing a pistol at his head and holding him at bay until the police arrived. When "Big Nose Kate" Horony was fifteen years old, she stopped a man from raping her by knocking him unconscious with an ax handle. Later, as a prostitute in St. Louis, Horony gained fame by shooting to death a man who had killed the madam who was her mentor. Eleanora Dumont was known to have shot many men in her days roaming the West, and on one occasion she saved not only herself but an entire town on the Missouri River in Montana. When a steamboat known to be carrying smallpox attempted to unload its passengers, Dumont aimed her derringer pistol at the captain and fired two shots into the deck just inches from his feet. "The second shot was to prove the first was no accident," she said. "If you don't turn this boat around, the next bullet goes through your head." With that, the captain turned his wheel and sped off down the river.

It is common now for feminists and others critical of our "beauty culture" to think of women's use of fashion and cosmetics as submission to male desire, the promotion of superficiality over substance, a means to conformity, narcissistic, and a form of self-oppression. These criticisms are not new, nor were they launched by women. Moralistic Englishmen first raised the cry against cosmetics in the seventeenth century. Puritan clergyman Thomas Tuke's 1616 *A Discourse Against Painting and Tincturing* warned that cosmetics were "brought into use by the devil" to make women worship themselves. By allowing women to remake themselves, cosmetics violated the natural order: "And though she bee the creature of God, as she is a woman, yet is she her owne creatrisse, as a picture." Tuke counseled women who wished to be respectable to "leave these base arts to the commo[n] strumpets, of whom they are fittest to be used, that by that filthiness they may be known and noted." In early modern England, as later in the young United States, makeup was the tool of whores. "To most Americans," writes historian Kathy Peiss, "the painted woman was simply a prostitute who brazenly advertised her immoral profession through rouge and kohl." In the nineteenth century, "[n]ewspapers, tracts, and songs associated paint and prostitution so closely as to be a generic figure of speech." Makeup represented "the aesthetic side of vice."

Prostitutes were the first women in America to wear brightly colored clothes, and red was the color of the sex trade. The protagonist in Nathaniel Hawthorne's "My Kinsman, Major Molineux," recognizes the lady on the street with a "saucy eye" as a prostitute by her "scarlet petticoat." George G. Foster's 1850 account of street life in *New York by Gas-Light* tells of "two ladies" who were immediately identifiable as prostitutes by their extravagant jewelry, dresses of "an ultra fashionable make," and shawls "of that gorgeous scarlet whose beamy hue intoxicates the eye." In Nella Larsen's 1928 novel *Quicksand,* a woman wearing a red dress at a church revival meeting is singled out as a fallen woman:

> At the sight of the bare arms and neck growing out of the cling-ing red dress, a shudder shook the swaying man at her right. On the face of the dancing woman before her a disapproving frown gathered. She shrieked: "A scarlet 'oman. Come to Jesus, you pore los' Jezebel!"

By the early twentieth century, as more and more women left the country-side and entered the expanding world of the city and all its freedoms, Peiss notes, "they made elements of this racy public style their own."

Peiss found that between 1909 and 1929 "the number of American per-fume and cosmetics manufacturers nearly doubled, and the factory value of their products rose tenfold, from $14.2 million to nearly $141 million." The first respectable women to adopt the styles of prostitutes were women at the high and low ends of the economic scale: saleswomen in depart-ment stores, factory workers, and upper-class socialites. At the new urban dance halls, where "working girls" predominated, the liberal use of rouge, powder, and lipstick was an "almost universal custom." Many newspapers noted that the wealthiest women had also adopted the look of the street. In 1890 the New York *World* reported that "society women now paint," even those in "very select circles." Having moved past the taboo of making up, "it is the very best upper-crustdom that puts aside tradition and author-ity and bedizens itself as much as it pleases." By the 1910s, according to Peiss, "it was often difficult to distinguish the dress and style of respectable women from prostitutes at dances." In 1917 vice investigators at a New York dance hall were told by a waiter, "The way women dress today, they all look like prostitutes."

The movement begun by prostitutes did not go unchallenged. A woman protested to the *Baltimore Sun* in 1912 that in the past "the painted face was the bold, brazen sign of the woman's character and call-ing" but "now women and young girls of a respectable society are seen on our streets and fashionable promenade with painted faces." The social reformer and feminist Lillian D. Wald complained in her 1915 memoir of working-class girls on the Lower East Side adopting the customs of prostitutes, including a "pronounced lack of modesty in dress," which, along with "their dancing, their talk, their freedom of manner, all combined to render them conspicuous." In 1920 a juvenile court judge in Los Angeles restricted a delinquent teenage girl "from any use of make-up, such as rouge and pencil which she has been using against the mother's desires for some time in the past." And more than half of the girls in a 1937 study reported fighting with their parents over lipstick. The use of makeup was, according to Peiss, seen by many young women as a means to freedom, pleasure, and control over their own lives: "The sudden appearance of rouge and lipstick on a teenage girl's face often accompanied a demand to keep more of her wages, to choose her boyfriends, and to enjoy greater autonomy in leisure activities."

Before smoking and wearing skirts above the ankles were considered respectable for women, this early-twentieth century photograph of a prostitute in the Alaska and Yukon territories shows her casually blowing smoke rings and revealing her legs. *From the MacBride Museum of Yukon History.*

Despite the efforts of sexual conservatives, by the middle of the twentieth century, the looks pioneered by prostitutes were not only respectable but also normal. Massive adoption of whore style began in the 1910s, when, for the first time, respectable women unabashedly revealed the skin below their necks. "An unprecedented public display of the female figure characterized the period," writes the historian James R. McGovern. Hems became shorter, hosiery was rolled down to reveal parts of the leg, and dresses were deeply cut to expose cleavage. In 1917 *Ladies' Home Journal* offered fashion advice that just a few years earlier could have been the words only of a madam: "Fashion says—Evening gowns must be sleeveless . . . afternoon gowns are made with semitransparent yokes and sleeves." Women smoking and drinking in public, which had been the exclusive practice of prostitutes and unassimilated German immigrants, "were becoming fashionable for married women of the upper class and were making headway at other class levels."

The famous short, cropped, often wavy hairstyle of the flappers of the 1920s was seen by many as a rebellion against the maternal femininity of the Victorian era, when women were expected to wear long hair elaborately arranged on top of the head. To many flappers, the weight and the work of the Victorian style literally and symbolically kept women from moving freely. But historians of prostitution have found evidence that short hairstyles were first adopted in brothels. Photos taken of New Orleans prostitutes in 1912 by E. J. Bellocq show many wearing what would become the dominant hairstyle of the 1920s and 1930s. Similarly, a 1913 vice report in Philadelphia noted that a black prostitute wore "black bobbed hair." Within two decades, the style pioneered by prostitutes was so popular that the First Ladies Lou Henry Hoover and Eleanor Roosevelt wore it in their official portraits.

In 1933 *Vogue* magazine declared wearing lipstick one of the "gestures of the twentieth century." Peiss found evidence of many mothers in the 1930s adopting their daughter's beauty regimens and a few mothers "who seem to have gone beyond their daughters in embracing the modern style of 'flaming youth,' despite traditional proscriptions." The sociologist Walter Reckless said it best in his 1933 study of prostitution in Chicago. Until the 1910s, prostitutes "were in fact an outcast group with distinctive manner, dress, style." They lived in "the 'half-world,'" where they were "free to do what was tabu [*sic*] for the respectable woman." The "painted lady" of the street had "an uncontested monopoly of rouge, the bleaching of hair, and strong perfumes, all of which have been means of sexual attraction." But by the 1920s, "women of ill-fame no longer form[ed] a distinct caste readily distinguished from other women by dress, manners, and place of residence. . . . The activities of modern women—slumming, night life, exaggerations in dress, an unchaperoned life outside the home, entrance into business and sports—have erased the outward distinction between the painted sport and the paler protected lady."

Even "the scarlet shame" of whores became the symbol of American female respectability. At the unveiling of the First Ladies Red Dress Collection, a charity for heart disease begun in 2005, Laura Bush spoke on behalf of her six predecessors:

> Mrs. Reagan's love of the color red is well known. Maybe her passion started when a dashing Ronald Reagan proposed to her in a red upholstered booth at a bistro in Los Angeles. America's First Ladies have found many occasions to wear red. Lady Bird Johnson celebrated her eightieth birthday in her red evening gown. Betty Ford's and Rosalynn Carter's red dresses were reliable favorites. Barbara Bush wore red to a state dinner—accompanied, of course, by her pearls. Hillary Clinton's red dress set just the right tone on Valentine's Day. And I wore my red dress to the Bolshoi Ballet in Moscow. We've all made good use of our red dresses, and now we're using them to promote our common interest in women's health.

BLACK AND TAN

During the height of Jim Crow, the period in the late nineteenth and early twentieth centuries when lynchings were weekly events in the South and not uncommon in the North, countless thousands of black men had sex with white women with impunity in the brothels of the wild towns of the West. In fact, no place on the planet was more integrated than the nineteenth-century western whorehouse, saloon, or dance hall. This is all the more remarkable considering that the heyday of the Wild West coincided with the advent of segregation. In nearly every Western boomtown, one could find blacks and whites living next to Asians and Native

Americans, and immigrants of dozens of nationalities working alongside native-born Americans. Many residents and travelers in the West reported on the "kaleidoscopic" social makeup of saloons and dance halls. They also reported on the high incidence of interracial sex—in particular but not exclusively in brothels. "Black and tans"—brothels employing white and black prostitutes—were common. Even the brothels that were segregated stood side by side in red-light districts. In big western cities like Denver, San Francisco, and Los Angeles, the typical brothel contained not just black and white prostitutes but also women from China, Japan, Mexico, and all parts of Europe. There were Jewish madams and Italian madams and Cherokee madams. Chinese and Mexican madams controlled much of the commerce in early San Francisco and Los Angeles. There were many wealthy, powerful, and famous madams who had been born into slavery.

Bad women pioneered racial integration. Mollie Johnson, the "Queen of the Blondes" in roughneck Deadwood, South Dakota, broke through just about every barrier for white women in Victorian America. She celebrated the success of her brothel by parading through the streets in carriages, dressed in the highest fashions of the time. She and her "ladies" frequently appeared in press reports of their wild and public debaucheries. And in 1878 she married the local stage performer Lew Spencer, also known as "Dutch Nigger" Lew Spencer. Johnson continued her profession through her marriage and, as one historian puts it, "didn't 'act' much like any other married woman."

Archivists at the Montana Historical Society found from studying nineteenth-century censuses that black Montanans were not segregated into separate neighborhoods as they were in most of the United States. Rather, they lived side by side—sometimes even in the same domicile—as peers with white Montanans. The red-light districts in early Los Angeles were notorious not just for their dens of vice but also for their multihued populations. City ordinances created in 1876 confined prostitution to poor and mixed-ethnic neighborhoods. For many decades, Los Angeles police rarely interfered in the red-light districts, contributing to their renegade character. This, according to historian Mark Wild, "encouraged participants in the sex trade (both workers and customers) to converge on those neighborhoods regardless of their ethnoracial background." Whites in Los Angeles, "who might have segregated themselves in other social contexts, therefore came much closer to other Angelenos when they bought or sold sexual favors." The integration of desire was not just black and white. When Protestant ministers launched a campaign to eliminate the city's red-light districts in 1903, they distributed fliers offering to "rescue" prostitutes, written in English, Chinese, Spanish, Portuguese, German, and French. In 1917 the California Commission of Immigration and Housing named the major red-light district "the most cosmopolitan district of Los Angeles." One year later, the Church of All Nations, a Methodist missionary organization in the district, counted forty-two nationalities in its vicinity.

This is not to suggest that prostitutes were morally committed to racial justice, but that like all good renegades they were committed to no morality. When asked by a university researcher in the early 1930s why they serviced customers of other races, a white prostitute and a black prostitute gave similarly self-interested answers. "It ain't that I'm so crazy about Colored men," the white woman explained, "but I can make more money here among them." The black woman was motivated as well by only one thing: "I like to have white trade because they will pay more."

The "Great Migration" of African Americans from the rural South to cities, which began in great numbers during World War I, when large numbers of industrial jobs opened up as white men left for military service, and peaked in the 1920s, also produced an exodus across the sexual color line. In Chicago and New York, moral reformers reported on the proliferation of brothels that sold the violation of America's greatest taboo. Some brothels in the cities during this period "were for whites, some for blacks," according to the historian Kevin J. Mumford, "but the majority were probably black-white clubs, the institutional descendants of Black and Tans." Many of these establishments "catered to a particular black-white dyad, whether black men seeking white prostitutes or white men seeking black." In 1928, one year before Martin Luther King Jr. was born and decades before the civil rights movement began, undercover investigators of "Speak-easy Houses of Prostitution" found racial integration nearly everywhere they looked. One particularly thriving New York establishment called Spann's advertised itself as a club of "white inmates for colored men." Another speakeasy was described by investigators as employing "white inmates, operated for colored men only." When a Chicago reformer visited a black-white club, he found "nine white women, eight of whom were there in the company of black men." The moral reformers surveilling this underground scene were particularly appalled when they saw white women enticing black men with dancing that was "very sexual and indecent," "degenerate," and "obscene." A Chicago vice investigator reported on a club in which "black men were seen dancing with white girls and vice versa." The "actions of these people," of course, "were absolutely disgusting." Worst of all were the white prostitutes who liked servicing black customers, such as the woman in a New York speakeasy who worked part-time as a "hostess in a Broadway nightclub" but also "consorted with black men" in Harlem and declared that she preferred "the colored man's technique."

Like their counterparts in the western boomtowns, the proprietors of black-white brothels in the northern cities were pure renegades who cared little for morality, social conventions, or the wishes of the community. As one put it, "We take anybody that has the money." And like all renegades, they opened freedoms for countless people. As Mumford puts it, "Despite the power of the taboo and the strictness of its enforcement, the fact remained that for black men migrating to the North, the availability of white prostitutes in predominately black urban areas must have represented a significant change from life under Jim Crow. What was held up in the South as both most desirable and most taboo—white womanhood—was in the North readily available to the African American man able to spend five or six dollars."

Prostitutes set loose pleasures and freedoms that became part of legitimate American culture, but they were punished nonetheless.

SOCIAL PURITY

Beginning in the 1870s, prostitution was hit by waves of attacks. Some medical authorities and police officials wanted to force prostitutes to register with the state and be placed under close surveillance by doctors and police. The "regulationists" argued that prostitution could never be eliminated due to the "debauchery of the degenerate . . . already past hope of redemption." Far more successful was the movement to abolish prostitution entirely. Organizations formed all over the country that were devoted to the eradication of not just the oldest evil but also to newer ones such as pornography, which they defined broadly. What came to be called the "social purity" movement was the spiritual descendent of the Founding Fathers' virtuous republicanism, the abolitionists' attack on the debauchery of slavery, and the Freedmen's Bureau mission to civilize the ex-slaves. The movement was led largely by women who helped create modern feminism. Organizations such as the Women's Christian Temperance Union and the National Purity Association became training grounds for the suffrage movement and were enormously powerful lobbying groups between the 1870s and World War I. There were some men involved, and not every social purity activist supported women's suffrage or property rights, but, as Ruth Rosen puts it, "feminism and social purity were very much intertwined, with members of each movement supporting causes of the other."

In the 1910s, semilegal vice commissions were formed in virtually every major city with the goal of the "absolute annihilation of the Social Evil." They carried ominous names like the New England Watch and Ward Society, the New York Committee of Fourteen, and the Los Angeles Morals Efficiency Committee. Headed by august gentlemen but staffed mostly by female social workers, the vice commissions conducted investigations using undercover agents, publicized their findings in local newspapers, and lobbied aggressively for municipal and state authorities to take action against brothels, madams, prostitutes, and their clients. Between 1910 and 1915, some thirty-five vice commissions issued reports declaring that prostitution was "an intolerable fact of life." Special courts were established to handle the new wave of prosecutions, including the Domestic Relations Court in Philadelphia, the Morals Court in Chicago, and the Women's Court in New York. Several states built prostitute reformatories. Inmates were made to practice sewing, cleaning, and cooking. More often, judges sent convicted prostitutes to county workhouses. The federal government did its part in 1910 with the passage of the Mann Act, also called the White Slave Traffic Act, which made illegal the transportation of women across state lines for "immoral purposes."

Between 1909 and 1917, thirty-one states passed "red-light abatement" laws allowing courts to shut down buildings for "immoral purposes." Further, in the 1910s, most states specifically made illegal the keeping of a "disorderly house" or in any way managing prostitutes as a madam or a pimp. No city completely eliminated prostitution. "In most cases, however," reports Ruth Rosen, "the chief of police responded to civic pressure simply by ordering the closing of the [red-light] district." In cities from coast to coast, prostitutes were forced onto the streets. Arrests for street-walking "skyrocketed across the nation," and most of the arrested women were sent to reformatories and workhouses. Without the protection of a madam and the four walls of a brothel, facing hostile police and sometimes sadistic customers, prostitutes had nowhere to turn but to male criminals. "Given these conditions," writes Rosen, "it is not surprising that pimps began dominating the practice of prostitution." With its banishment, prostitution was moved from female power to male power. Though they were certainly exploited in brothels, "madams and prostitutes had wielded considerable power in their relations with customers. Now prostitutes became the easy targets of both pimps and organized crime. In both cases, the physical violence faced by prostitutes rapidly increased."

Responding to the argument made by moral reformers that sinful behavior was genetically determined, by 1913, twelve states had passed laws that allowed judges to order the sterilization of criminals, "perverts," "idiots," and the "feebleminded." Prostitutes were generally thought to belong to all four categories. As one investigator in Massachusetts put it:

> the general moral insensibility, the boldness, egotism and vanity, the love of notoriety, the lack of shame or remorse, the absence of even a pretense of affection or sympathy for their children or for their parents, the desire for immediate pleasure without regard for consequences, the lack of forethought or anxiety about the future—all cardinal symptoms of feeblemindedness—were strikingly evident in every one . . .

Maude Miner, a leading feminist and suffragist and director of the Waverly House for Women, a reformatory in New York City, claimed that one-quarter of prostitutes under her tutelage acquired their attitudes and behaviors from "some actively vicious element or clearly degenerate strain, drunkenness or prostitution." Between 1907 and 1950, some forty thousand American women were forcibly sterilized, most for selling sex.

Prostitutes joined the urban rabble and "bad niggers" as martyrs for our freedom.

Part Two

HOW WHITE PEOPLE LOST
THEIR RHYTHM

★ 5 ★

A RHYTHMLESS NATION

In its formal definitions, America has always been a rhythmless nation. And "good" Americans have never been able to dance. Indeed, one of the first accomplishments of the original settlers from Europe was to stop themselves from dancing.

The Puritan pilgrims left England in large part because it was full of people who used their bodies for pleasure. Next only to fornication, the most sinful use of one's body was to move in sensual and playful ways. In 1583 the Puritan writer Philip Stubbes had this to say about dancing:

> If you would have your son soft, womanish, unclean, smooth-mouth, affected to bawdry, scurrility, filthy rimes, and unseemly talking; briefly if you would have him, as it were, transnatured into a woman or worse, and inclined to all kinds of whoredom and abomination, set him to dancing school and to learn music, and then you shall not fail of your purpose. And if you would have your daughter riggish, bawdry and unclean, and a filthy speaker, and suchlike, bring her up in music and dancing and my life for yours, you have won the goal.

Another leading Puritan thinker, William Prynne, in 1632 denounced

> all mixt effeminate, lascivious, amorous dancing . . . [as] utterly unlawful unto Christians, to chaste and sober persons; as sundry Councels, Fathers, moderne Christian, with ancient Pagan Authors and Nations have resolved; though it be now so much in use, in fashion and request among us, that many spend more houres

(more dayes and nights) in dancing, then [*sic*] in praying, I might adde working too.

So once in America, where they had the opportunity to create a perfect world, the Puritans set out to lock bodily movements to the rules of God. In 1635 John Cotton, one of the principal ministers of the Massachusetts Bay Colony, declared that the new land should forbid "[l]ascivious dancing to wanton ditties, and amorous gestures and wanton dalliances . . . [which] I would bear witness against as a great *flabella Libidinis* [fanning of sexual desire]." In that same year Roger Williams, the founder of Rhode Island, saw in the dances of the Indians a near and dangerous temptation, "for after once being in their Houses, and beholding what their worship was, I durst never be an eye witnesse . . . [lest] I should have been partaker of Satans inventions and worships, contrary to Ephes. 5.14."

Early in their adventure, the Puritan pilgrims had to deal with what was perhaps the most renegade act in American history. In 1625 an Englishman named Thomas Morton organized a non-Puritan settlement, Merrymount, north of Plymouth at the present site of Quincy, Massachusetts. By many accounts, Merrymount was everything the Puritans feared. Whiskey and beer flowed freely, and whites and Indians cavorted, copulated, and danced wildly around a maypole, a Pagan invention that had become the symbol of fun and leisure in villages across England. Morton later recalled that the inhabitants of Merrymount:

> did devise amongst themselves . . . Revels and merriment after the old English custome; [they] prepared to sett up a Maypole upon the festivall day . . . and therefore brewed a barrell of excellent beare [beer] . . . to be spent, with other good cheare, for all commers of that day . . . And upon May day [a Pagan festival welcoming summer] they brought the Maypole to the place appointed, with drumes, gunnes, pistols and other fitting instruments, for the purpose; and there erected it with the help of Savages, that came thether to see the manner of our Revels.

Puritans in England and the New World called for banning the maypole and May Day festivals. But Merrymount's population grew at an alarming rate, and so in 1628 the Pilgrims in nearby Plymouth Colony dispatched

Captain Miles Standish and an armed force to destroy their libertine competitors. Morton was nearly killed in the assault, then hauled into a Plymouth court and deported back to England. The maypole was chopped down and burned.

Shortly thereafter, New England authorities made it illegal for men and women to touch each other while dancing, and many towns in the seventeenth century outlawed organized dances. "In fact," writes Bruce C. Daniels, a historian of early American leisure, "virtually no organized dances or mixed-sex dancing took place in the first generation of New England's settlement." But ministerial wrath and legal punishment did not eliminate dancing. People did it privately, inside their houses or away in the woods.

And then the French came. In the 1670s, migrants from the land of decadence arrived in New England, bringing with them expertise in decidedly lascivious movements. Worse yet, they opened schools in which they taught colonists dances that simulated carnal acts. When the authorities became aware of one of these schools of vice, they shut it down and prosecuted the proprietor. But the French dance schools continued to appear throughout the colonies. In 1684 Increase Mather set out to put an end to this with a precisely titled book, *An Arrow Against Profane and Promiscuous Dancing Drawn out of the Quiver of the Scriptures*. Not *all* dancing was bad, said Mather. It was perfectly appropriate "where men vault in their Armour, to shew their strength and activity," or when it was "sober and grave Dancing of Men with Men, or of Women with Women." (Mather did not anticipate later problems with same-sex dancing.) But "Mixt or Promiscuous Dancing" such as the kind he saw performed at a "frolick, reveling feast, and a ball, which discovers their corruption," or which he observed at "wanton Bacchanallian Christmasses," had "become customary amongst Christians" and "cannot be thought on without horror." Mather counseled governmental authorities to declare such dancing "to be utterly unlawful, and that it cannot be tollerated in such a place as New-England, without great Sin." Defining exactly what constituted "The unchast Touches and Gesticulations used by Dancers" that had "a palpable tendency to that which is evil" was a challenge. Certainly any dancing in which a man and a woman touched each other was evil. But what kind of bodily movement led one to hell? Mather called it "mincing," which biblical authorities had defined as a rapid and repeated swaying of the body. It was, according to Martin Luther, a "wag" or "waggle" resembling "the affected gait of coquettish females." It was feminine, irregular, disorderly, and sexual. It was authored by Satan and embodied in women. It was rhythm.

Many Americans continued to dance, but official America did not. William Penn, the founder of the province of Pennsylvania, attacked pleasure generally and dancing specifically in his treatises *The Frame of Government* (1682) and *No Crown, No Cross* (1697), which are widely considered to be the blueprints for the Constitution and, according to the eminent historian Bernard Bailyn, "could hardly have been more clearly fundamental, more manifestly constituent, in nature" to the American national system. In *The Frame of Government*, Penn insists that "stage plays, cards, dice, Maygames, masques, revels, bull-baitings . . . which incite people to rudeness, cruelty, looseness, and irreligion, shall be respectively discouraged, and severely punished." In *No Crown, No Cross,* Penn reprints lengthy, early Christian sermons arguing that "Dancing is the devil's procession, and he that entereth into a dance entereth into his procession, the devil is the guide, the middle, and the end of the dance; as many paces as man maketh in dancing, so many paces doth he make to go to hell." In 1700 Increase Mather's son Cotton, who more than anyone defined Puritan America, responded to the continued spread of formal dances and dance schools with his own published attack, *A Cloud of Witness Against Balls and Dances,* in which he called for an end to the dance craze "as it now prevails, and especially in balls, or in circumstances that lead the young people of both sexes unto great liberties with one another." A few decades later, George Whitefield, the leader of the "Great Awakening," which according to many historians laid the self-disciplining moral groundwork for the American Revolution, believed that dancing and music were "devilish diversions" and demanded that the people shun them. One night during a preaching tour of South Carolina in 1740, Whitefield attempted to convert an entire tavern full of dancers:

> I had not come to be their guest that night; for, it being New Year's Day, several of the neighbours were met together to divert themselves by dancing country dances. By the advice of my companions I went in amongst them whilst a woman was dancing a jig. At my first entrance I endeavoured to shew the folly of such entertain-

ments, and to convince her how well pleased the devil was at every step she took. For some time she endeavoured to outbrave me;
neither the fiddler nor she desisted; but at last she gave over, and
the musician laid aside his instrument. . . . Christ triumphed over
Satan. All were soon put to silence . . .

Those who heeded Whitefield's admonitions were more likely to adopt
the kind of discipline that the Founding Fathers would soon promote. But
not all the preacher's "converts" remained converted. Some were "so bent
on their pleasure, that notwithstanding all that had been said, after I had
gone to bed, I heard their music and dancing." Whitefield's sermons against
dancing achieved similarly mixed and comical results a few months later in
Philadelphia. A local newspaper reported,

Since Mr. Whitefield's preaching here, the Dancing School, Assembly and Concert room have been shut up, as inconsistent with
the doctrine of the gospel: And though the Gentlemen concern'd
caus'd the door to be broken open again, we are inform'd that no
company came last Assembly night.

Whitefield was more successful in Portsmouth, New Hampshire, where,
according to one observer after his visit in 1740, "music and dancing seems
to be wholly laid aside. Where you might formerly have heard jovial, and it
may be profane and obscene songs; you may now hear psalms and hymns
of praise sung to God, and to our Lord Jesus Christ." White people the far-
thest from civilization were the most likely to dance without shame, such
as the "inferior sort" of Scottish settlers in backcountry North Carolina
observed by an upper-class traveler in 1729:

Dancing they are all fond of, especially when they can get a fiddle, or bag-pipe; at this they will continue hours together, nay, so
attach'd are they to this darling amusement, that if they can't pro-
cure musick, they will sing for themselves. Musick, and musical
instruments being very scarce in Carolina.

When touring villages in remote parts of South Carolina, George Whitefield despaired to find

that in every little town, there is a settled dancing master, but scarcely anywhere a settled minister to be met with; such a proceeding must be of dreadful consequence to any, especially a new settled province. All Governors, if it were only from a policy of human policy, ought to put a stop to it. For such entertainments altogether enervate the minds of people, insensibly leading them into effeminacy, and unfitting them to endure those hardships, and fatigues, which must necessarily be undergone, to bring any province to perfection. True religion exalts a nation; such sinful entertainments are a reproach, and will, in time, be the ruin of any people.

The minister Joseph Bellamy of Connecticut, another leader of the Great Awakening and one of the Founding Fathers' principal clerical allies, preached against "the pernicious and insnaring practice of dancing." Before the Revolution, he warned of dancing as a "school of debauchery and corruption" that tends to "promote an idle and dissolute course of life" and "give[s] the mind a relish for nothing but carnal and sensual pleasures." Bellamy preached a lesson the Founders well understood: that dancing, like sensual pleasure generally, made the people "so very vain, and extravagant, and ungovernable."

When colonists fell "under the spell" of "primitive gyrations," their leaders were quick to discipline them. A member of James Oglethorpe's 1733 expedition recounted that an hour after they landed at what would become the city of Savannah, Georgia, the native residents welcomed the newcomers by "Dancing round a Large fire which They made upon the Ground." Some of the Englishmen were mildly disgusted by the Indians' "many antick Gestures, Singing and beating Time, with Their feet, and hands to admiration." Others were enthralled. And one went native.

One of the oldest of our people, Doctor Lyons, having slept away from our camp and gott a litle in drink, found his way up to the Indian town and joyned with the Indians in their dance indeavouring to mimick and ape them in their antick gestures, which I being informed of, sent for him, and desired that he would emediately repair home to our camp. Otherwise I assured him I would aquaint Mr. Oglethorp with his folly. He promised me that he would. But being so much in liquor he returned again to the Indians and danced with them as before, which being told to me I ordered severall white men who were there to carry him home by force.

Another member of Oglethorpe's party echoed what other settlers had said before, that the Indian dancers were similar to the "Morris" dancers in England. Morris dancing was a folk dance (possibly derived from dances performed by Moors from North Africa) involving rhythmic stepping with bent knees and elbows—moves not unlike the dances of Native Americans and American slaves. It was attacked by Puritans in England and banned in the New England colonies.

German settlers were similarly split over "primitive" and libidinal dancing. At a ball celebrating the signing of a treaty between European settlers and the tribes of the Six Nations at Lancaster, Pennsylvania, in 1744, the leader of the delegation of settlers was dismayed to see a number of German women who "danced [in] wilder time than any Indians. . . . The females (I dare not call them Ladies . . .) were, in general very disagreeable." In the 1750s, in the German town of Bethany on the Georgia frontier, the wife of the local school master was publicly censured and her husband dismissed from his position after she "conceived a lust to dance, and actually did dance" to the sounds of a dulcimer.

Nonetheless, many white colonists, especially in the South, continued to be inspired by the movements of Indians and slaves. In 1759 a clergyman of the Church of England was disturbed by the disorderly, black-inspired ways in which whites in Virginia amused themselves:

> They are immoderately fond of dancing, and indeed it is almost the only amusement they partake of: but even in this they discover great want of taste and elegance, and seldom appear with that gracefulness and ease, which these movements are so calculated to display. Towards the close of an evening, when the company are pretty well tired with country dances, it is usual to dance jigs; a practice originally borrowed, I am informed, from the Negroes. These dances are without any method or regularity: a Gentleman

and Lady stand up, and dance about the room, one of them retiring, the other pursuing, then perhaps meeting, in an irregular fantastical manner.

Another English traveler in Virginia, Nicholas Cresswell, noted the same phenomenon in 1775 and with the same disdain:

Last night I went to the Ball. . . . Here was about 37 Ladies dressed and powdered to the life, some of them very handsome and as much vanity as is necessary. All of them fond of dancing, but I do not think they perform it with the greatest elegance. Betwixt the country dances they have what I call everlasting jigs. A couple gets up and begins to dance a jig (to some Negro tune) others comes [*sic*] and cuts them out, and these dances last as long as the Fiddler can play. This is sociable, but I think it looks more like a Bacchanalian dance than one in polite assembly.

One Virginian who loved disreputable dancing was Thomas Jefferson's younger brother, Randolph, who, according to one of the family's slaves, "used to come out among black people, play the fiddle and dance half the night." This was in contrast to Thomas, who, according to one biographer, "seemed not the least bit curious about or interested in" the music of his or any other slaves. Several scholars believe that Randolph, rather than his brother, was the father of the child born to the family's slave, Sally Hemings.

There were even some bands of extreme renegade dancers among the white people of colonial America. In 1779 the *Independent Chronicle* of Boston reported on "a sect" in nearby Pepperell, "who, under the idea of religion, dance stark naked, &c. It proves indeed, that 'men will be guilty of great extravagances, when urged by a misguided conscience, and enthusiastic zeal.'" And then there were the Shakers of western Massachusetts, who, for a time during the American Revolution, reportedly "disclaimed the use of any kind of garment when engaged in their religious exercises; presenting themselves unpolluted by the vain and unchristian articles of dress, and performing all their dancing, turnings, jumpings, tumblings, twistings, and wrigglings, in that condition."

MIND THE MUSIC AND THE STEP

The founders of the United States learned from their intellectual forefather, John Locke, that children should be taught to dance only in a way that "gives graceful motions all the life, and above all things manliness." According to Locke, dance teachers should eliminate "apish affected postures" and "the jigging part" that leads children away from "perfect graceful carriage." More importantly, the Founding Fathers feared that sensual amusements would undermine the discipline necessary for a republic of self-governing individuals. Nothing was more subversive of order than animalistic lack of control, which certain types of dancing suggested. When he heard that his sister and her husband had changed their minds and would not send their children to dancing school, John Adams exulted. "[What] a sudden, and entire conversion is this! . . . it is from vanity to wisdom—from foppery to sobriety & solidity," he wrote. "I never knew a good Dancer good for any Thing else." Of the men who danced well, they gained neither "Sense or Learning, or Virtue for it." But rather than ban such amusements as "dancing, or Fencing, or Musick," Adams wrote that Americans "should be ignorant of em all than fond of any one of em." He was appalled by the gyrations of a white man named Zab Hayward he saw dancing in a tavern with a "rabble" and "Negroes with a fiddle":

> He has had the Reputation, for at least fifteen Years, of the best Dancer in the World in these Towns. Several attempted, but none could equal him, in nimbleness of heels. But he has no Conception of the Grace, the Air nor the Regularity of dancing. His Air is absurd and wild, desultory, and irregular, as his Countenance is low and ignoble. In short the Air of his Countenance, the Motions of his Body, Hands, and Head, are extreamly silly, and affected and mean.

Some of the Founding Fathers were torn between their private love of sensual pleasure and their public commitment against it. Adams's colleague Josiah Quincy II, who authored several of the most important pro-independence tracts, confided to his journal that he had attended several comedy-dance performances while visiting New York and was "upon the whole much gratified." Moreover, "if I had stayed in town a month I should go to the theatre every acting night." But, "as a citizen and a friend to the morals and happiness of society, I should strive hard against the admission and much more the establishment of a playhouse in any state of which I was a member." Benjamin Latrobe, the "Father of American Architecture" who designed the U.S. Capitol, saw whites performing the Virginia Jig and called it "the excess of detestability." A cousin of John Quincy Adams, Elizabeth Cranch, wrote of her love for dancing and her fear of the wrath of her cousin, who was "monstrously severe upon the follies of mankind." Given the Founders' feelings on the matter, it seems reasonable to conclude that the Continental Congress's 1774 declaration to discourage "every species of extravagance and dissipation," which was widely interpreted as including sensual dancing, formally established the American citizen as rhythmless. As the historian Bruce Daniels puts it, "Puritan asceticism found a new voice in the guise of republican simplicity."

One of the better-known Americans to have lost his groove during the Revolution was Yankee Doodle. Very few Americans know that this national icon was born a renegade. The term *yankee* was invented by British soldiers in the seventeenth century as an epithet against bawdy Dutch pirates in the West Indies. The first recorded use of the term in the American colonies was the listing of a South Carolina slave named Yankee in 1725. The British then used it in derisive reference to the "undisciplined" and "licentious" bumpkins of New England. During the first skirmishes of the War of Independence, British soldiers sang a song about a "macaroni"— slang for an ostentatious, hedonistic dandy—who "went to town" to find "the girls" with whom he was quite "handy." The character's surname, Doodle, was then a vernacular term meaning "simpleton," "fool," or "penis." To emphasize their point, the British often danced mock jigs to the song. Unfortunately, during the war, many Americans agreed with their enemies that this characterization was an insult rather than a compliment. And so they turned Yankee Doodle from a renegade into a soldier. Fife-and-drum units in colonial militias added a heavy, regimented "da-dum, da-dum" beat—free of irregular syncopation—and transformed the dance song into a march. New lyrics instructed soldiers to "mind the music and the step" and saluted "Cap'n Washington," who "sat the world along in rows, in hundreds and in millions."

Following in line, dance schools during the Revolution began to advertise themselves as teaching "only the genteelest dances." John Griffiths, the most influential dancing instructor of the early national period, taught classes throughout New York and New England and wrote a widely read manual that listed "Influences of Ill Manners, to be carefully avoided, by Youth, of both sexes." Among these were "Swinging the Arms, and all other awkward gestures," "Drumming with feet or hands in Company," "All actions that have the most remote tendency to Indelicacy," "All instances of that ill-judged Familiarity, which breeds contempt," and "every thing which may be called Sluttish or Slovenly." In the eighteenth century, the only folk dance deemed respectable was the contra dance, in which the movements were confined to walking stiffly in prearranged patterns, with no motion of the hips. The Marquis de Chastellux, a French general serving with the Americans, noticed considerable regimentation at formal balls in Philadelphia:

> Dancing is said to be the emblem both of gaiety and love; here it seems to be the emblem of legislation and of marriage; of legislation, inasmuch as places are marked out, the contredanses prescribed, and every proceeding provided for, calculated, and submitted to regulation; of marriage, since each Lady is supplied with a "partner," with whom she must dance the whole evening, without being allowed to take another . . . All the dances are previously arranged, and the dancers are called each in their turn.

Revolutionary-era balls were ruled by "managers." Chastellux was acquainted with one manager of whom it was said "that when a young Lady who was figuring in a square dance forgot her turn because she was conversing with a friend, he came up to her and loudly called out, 'Come, come, watch what you are doing; do you think you are here for pleasure?'"

This is not to suggest that the national effort to regulate bodily movement was entirely successful. One of Washington's soldiers reported in his journal that at the end of the epic winter of 1778, the Continental troops camped at Valley Forge celebrated with a renewal of an ancient renegade tradition:

> May 1st Last Evening May poles
> were Erected in everry Regt in

the Camp and at the Revelie
I was awoke by three cheers
in honor of King Tamany*
The day was spent in mirth
and Jollity the soldiers parading
marching with fife & Drum
and Huzzaing as they passd the
poles their hats adornd with
white blossoms
The following was the procession
of the 3d J Regt on the aforesaid
day
first one serjeant drest in an
Indian habit representing
King Tamany
Second Thirteen Sergeants
drest in white each with a bow
in his left hand and thirteen
arrows in his right . . .

*a seventeenth-century chief in
the Lenni-Lenape nation
of the Delaware Valley*

Having gone native, the soldiers were abruptly brought back to civilization by Washington himself:

The Non Commissiond
Officers and Soldiers being
drawn up in the afforsaid
manner on the Regimental
Parade gave 3 Cheers at their
own Pole and then Marchd
off to Head Quarters to do Honor
to his Excellency but just
as they were descending the
hill to the house an Aid
met them and informd
them that the Genl was
Indisposd and desird them
to retire which they did

with the greatest decency
and regularity—

Even commissioned officers in Washington's army were known to break
the new rules. A group of high-ranking officers who occupied a loyalist's
mansion in New Jersey was seen "dancing reels with some tawdry dressed
females." But when patriotic Americans danced in any way that exhibited
an earthy sensuality, they did so knowing that it was against the national
interest. This may account for why so many patriots danced so poorly.

By the nineteenth century, as we have seen, some slaves expressed pity
for white people's lack of rhythm. Others were amused. There are several
accounts of slaves mocking the movements of whites, such as a newspaper
report on a party held by slaves near Charleston in 1772. The entertainment
at the event was "men copying (or taking off) the manner of their masters,
and the women those of their mistresses, and relating some highly curious
anecdotes, to the inexpressible diversion of the company." One ex-slave
recalled, "Us slaves watched white folks' parties, where the guests danced a
minuet and then paraded in a grand march, with the ladies and gentlemen
going different ways and then meeting again, arm in arm, and marching
down the center together. Then we'd do it too, but we used to mock 'em
every step. Sometimes the white folks noticed it, but they seemed to like it;
I guess they thought we couldn't dance any better."

FROM WHITE CHIMPS TO YANKEE DOODLES: THE IRISH

In the nineteenth century, large numbers of white-looking people who were wickedly good dancers came to America.

First came the Irish, a notoriously funky people. Long before they arrived in America, the Irish were known as "a filthy people, wallowing in vice," as a twelfth-century English writer put it. They "live like beasts," "do not avoid incest," and "have not progressed at all from the habits of pastoral living." The poet Edmund Spenser wrote in 1596 that the Irish lived in "the most barbaric and loathy conditions of any people (I think) under heaven. . . . They do use all the beastly behaviour that may be, they oppress all men, they spoil as well the subject, as the enemy; they steal, they are cruel and bloody, full of revenge, and delighting in deadly execution, licentious, swearers and blasphemers, common ravishers of women, and murderers of children." British historian Thomas Carlyle visited Ireland in 1849 and found a "drunk country fallen down to sleep in the mud." The Irish, he wrote, were a "brawling unreasonable people," a "human swinery," and "a black howling Babel of superstitious savages." Clergyman Charles Kingsley was similarly shaken by his travels in Ireland. In 1860 he wrote to his wife, "I am haunted by the human chimpanzees I saw along that hundred miles of horrible country . . . to see white chimpanzees is dreadful; if they were black, one would not see it so much, but their skins, except where tanned by exposure, are as white as ours." Two years later, the British magazine *Punch* proclaimed the Irish as the "missing link" between man and simian:

A gulf certainly, does appear to yawn between the Gorilla and the Negro. The woods and wilds of Africa do not exhibit an example of any intermediate animal. But in this, as in many other cases, philosophers go vainly searching abroad for that which they could readily find if they sought for it at home. A creature manifestly between the Gorilla and the Negro is to be met with in some of the lowest districts of London and Liverpool by adventurous explorers. It comes from Ireland, whence it has contrived to migrate; it belongs in fact to a tribe of Irish savages: the lowest species of Irish Yahoo. When conversing with its kind it talks a sort of gibberish. It is, moreover, a climbing animal, and may sometimes be seen ascending a ladder laden with a hod of bricks.

Also in 1862, the ethnologist John Beddoe published his "Index of Negrescence," which measured the blackness of Europeans. Scoring lowest were the industrious, restrained, and "superior" Anglo-Saxons. Those with the highest scores were the Celts of Ireland, who Beddoe described in bodily, sensual, and animalistic terms. The Celtic "[l]eg and foot [is] usually well-developed, thigh long in proportion, instep high, ankle well-shapen and of moderate size; the step is very elastic, and rather springing." In the minds of some Americans, the Irish replaced African Americans at the bottom of the racial order. The famed diarist George Templeton Strong, for example, wrote that "the gorilla is superior to the Celtic in muscle and hardly their inferior in a moral sense." *Harper's* magazine in 1851 described the "Celtic physiognomy" as "simian-like, with protruding teeth and short upturned noses." Similarly, the 1871 book *New Physiognomy,* written by the American phrenologist Samuel Roberts Wells, described the Irish woman as being governed "by the lower or animal passions," "seeking her chief pleasure from things physical and animal," and unable to see "beauty in that which can not be eaten or used for the gratification of the bodily appetites or passions." She "is rude, rough, unpolished, ignorant, and brutish." Another proponent of the theory of natural Irish inferiority was James Anthony Froude, a professor of history at Oxford University. He described the Irish country folk as "more like squalid apes than human beings." The "wild Irish" were "unstable as water," while the English exemplified order and self-control.

The Irish were shiftless, too. Widely considered too stupid and lazy for skilled labor, most of the first large wave of Irish immigrants were hired to dig the canals that underlay the Industrial Revolution. Between 1827 and

1853, when Irish workers dominated the canal workforce, there were 57 strikes on U.S. and Canadian canals, as well as 93 incidents of labor rioting. Irish workers were known to sabotage equipment or even dynamite canals when they were dissatisfied with their wages or working conditions. In 1842, when Irish workers found none of the jobs that were promised them on the Welland Canal connecting Lake Erie and Lake Ontario, they took matters into their own hands. An estimated one thousand rioters looted stores, took flour from a local mill, and seized pork from a passing ship. Historians have noted that most of the strikes and rioting by early Irish American workers were spontaneous and, most importantly, outside the means of respectable, American, and "white" protest. "More than anything else," writes the historian Noel Ignatiev, "they resembled the strikes or rebellions of plantation slaves."

There was also widespread reporting by employers of Irish "malingering." One American philanthropist claimed that Irish immigrants "are content to live together in filth and disorder, and enjoy their balls and wakes and frolics without molestation." After visiting a work camp on the Illinois & Michigan Canal, the English traveler and author James Silk Buckingham concluded that the Irish "are not merely ignorant and poor—which might be their misfortune rather than their fault—but they are drunken, dirty, indolent, and riotous, so as to be the objects of dislike and fear to all in whose neighbourhood they congregate in large numbers." John MacTaggart, a manager of the Rideau Canal, declared the Irish incapable of becoming "useful labourers." They were too lazy to make themselves respectable. "You cannot get the *low Irish* to wash their faces, even were you to lay before them ewers of crystal water and scented soap; you cannot get them to dress decently, although you supply them with ready-made clothes." Instead "they will smoke, drink, eat murphies, brawl, box, and set the house on fire about their ears, even though you had a sentinel standing over with a fixed gun and bayonet to prevent them."

Most canal employers could not keep their Irish workers on the job if they did not supply them with a steady stream of alcohol. On average, Irish canal workers consumed three to four "gills" of alcohol during the workday—a total of twelve to twenty ounces. Even many Irish immigrants blamed the "poor drunken Irish" for their condition. Andrew Leary O'Brien, an Irishman trained for the priesthood who spent time working on the canals, found a great need for missionary work on the Pennsylvania

Canal: "There was plenty of liquor on the works . . . At night you could hear these wild Irish in their Bacchanalian revels fighting, singing, dancing, &c., all hours of the night." This, according to the historian Kerby Miller, was due to the fact that the early Irish immigrants were simply "unaccustomed to work practices in their adopted country."

Most of the Irish who weren't digging ditches were living in slums. Missionaries who went into the Five Points, the poorest neighborhood in New York City, believed the Irish there to be so degraded that they dragged down the African Americans around them. When in the presence of Irish, blacks wallowed in filth and idleness but "where the blacks were found by themselves, we generally encountered tidiness, and some sincere attempt at industry and honest self-support." One missionary claimed, "The Negroes of the Five Points are fifty per cent in advance of the Irish as to sobriety and decency." In 1857 a government investigating committee learned from landlords in the Five Points that "in some of the better class of houses built for the tenantry, Negroes have been preferred as occupants to Irish or German poor; the incentive of possessing comparatively decent quarters appearing to inspire the colored residents with more desire for personal cleanliness and regard for property than is impressed upon the whites of their own condition." Given the status of African Americans in the minds of most whites, this was saying something.

Largely in response to the great waves of hard-drinking Irish immigrants, the American temperance movement grew exponentially in the 1840s and 1850s. Temperance halls were established in every major city, and reformers marched through immigrant neighborhoods shouting at the newcomers to put down their cups. But the Irish were not ready to be good Americans. Temperance halls were set ablaze, sometimes by lone arsonists but often by volunteer Irish "fire companies." These fire companies were often simply fronts for Irish gangs who fought with each other over control of the slums. In Philadelphia, a government investigation of the Irish fire companies reported in 1853, "There is scarcely a single case of riot brought before the courts that has not its origin in the fire companies, their members, or adherents." A few years earlier, the *United States Gazette* had denounced the fire companies that "hinder the city of gains from the residence of capitalists who seek comfort and ease." But more than just wreaking criminal mayhem, the fire companies also defended Irish immigrants from attacks by anti-immigrant gangs and from intrusions by moral reformers. Antidrink marchers were assaulted in the streets by Irish gangs who were affiliated with or aided by the companies. Asked why the Irish rioted against the temperance movement, one man fresh from a grog shop said, "in this land of liberty, they expected to do as they liked."

Between the 1810s and 1850s, when more than one million Irish fled poverty and famine and came to the United States, they were frequently referred to as "niggers turned inside out" or simply as "white niggers." American observers found the cultural similarities between the two groups so strong that even blacks were sometimes called "smoked Irish." And in 1864, a Democratic Party campaign document warned, "There is the strongest reason for believing that the first movement toward amalgamation in this country will take place between Irish and Negroes." Indeed, the movement had already begun.

Cohabitation with blacks began immediately upon arrival, as the Irish were forced into the poorest neighborhoods in American cities. And there is abundant evidence that cohabitation frequently turned into something more intimate. In New York City in 1834, throngs of native-born whites responded to reports of rampant interracial sex by rampaging through the Sixth Ward, attacking blacks and Irish on the streets, demolishing the St. Philip's African Episcopal Church, and setting fire to black homes, Irish homes, and Irish taverns. A similar pattern of mixing and outrage in Philadelphia caused one missionary to complain of how common it was for an Irishwoman to be "living with some dirty Negro." In 1847 a census taker among the African American population in Philadelphia expressed his shock at this phenomenon: "My heart is sick, my soul is horror-stricken at what my eyes behold. . . . The greater part of these people live in with the Irish." A Philadelphia grand jury reported in 1853 on the great amount of mixing among Irish and African Americans in the city's poorest district, including in one tavern and lodging house where "men and women—blacks and whites by dozens—were huddled together promiscuously, squatting or lying upon the bare floors." In their study of black Bostonians before the Civil War, Lois Horton and James Horton found a substantial number of whites who lived in black neighborhoods or married across the color line, and that most were Irish: "The residential patterns of Boston facilitated personal contact between the poorest, most oppressed groups, increasing the likelihood of both friction and more amiable relationships among individuals." The *World,* one of New York City's major newspapers, reported in 1867 that "no spectacle in our city is more common than the sight of the lower classes of blacks and of whites living together in union, if not in miscegenation. . . . It is a somewhat remarkable fact that, although between an Irishman and a black man an antipathy is presumed to exist, yet between the Irish *woman* and the Negro there exists a decided affinity. In the majority of cases of miscegenation, the parties are black on one side and Irish on the other."

This commingling was most evident in the Five Points area of the Sixth Ward. According to journalist Herbert Asbury, the author of *Gangs of New York,* the district was occupied "for the most part, by freed Negro slaves and low-class Irish" who "crowded indiscriminately into the old rookeries of the Points." A missionary who visited a tenement in the Five Points reported coming across an "old Sambo over his brazier of coals." In the same room, from under:

> a long pile of rags . . . an Irish woman lift[ed] her tangled mop of a head . . . "Look here, gentlemen, look at this little codfish"; and with this she lift[ed] out from beneath the rags a diminutive mulatto child of a few weeks old, to the great delight of Sambo, who reveal[ed] all his ivory.

According to the missionary, the fate of the black-Irish child would be to have "rum its first medicine, theft its first lesson, a prison its first house, and the Potter's Field its final resting place." The largest tenement in the Five Points, a building known as the "Old Brewery," was a virtual temple of miscegenation. "During the period of its greatest renown," writes Asbury, "the building housed more than 1,000 men, women and children, almost equally divided between Irish and Negroes." Most of the rooms in the cellar "were occupied by Negroes, many of whom had white wives" but throughout the Old Brewery, "miscegenation was an accepted fact." The journalist George Foster, whose *New York by Gas-Light* provided a first-person account of the Five Points, noted not only the frequency of black-Irish romantic relations but also that the Irish women he observed regarded black men as "desirable companions and lovers." Once again, America's racial renegades came from the bottom of society.

There was some violence between blacks and Irish before the Civil War, but pleasurable activities in addition to sex appear to have been much more common. According to historian Graham Hodges, "strikingly little violence occurred between Irish and blacks" when the two groups dominated the Sixth Ward. "Even though interracial lovers, black churches, and abolitionists remained in the ward amidst an escalating Irish population, its residents did not participate in future riots against blacks . . . Dancing was the principal diversion during the early days of the Five Points, and scores of dance houses soon appeared on the streets surrounding Paradise Square." The most popular dance hall in the neighborhood was owned by Pete Williams, described as a "well-to-do, coal-black Negro, who has made an immense amount of money from the profits of his dance-house." An upper-class visitor to Williams's dance hall was shocked to see that "several very handsome mulatto women were in the crowd, and a few 'young men about town,' mixed up with the blacks; and altogether it was a picture of 'amalgamation,' such I had never before seen." A reporter from the *New York Clipper* agreed that "amalgamation" at the Orange Street establishment "reigned predominant, if we may judge from appearances." The dancing at places like this was, according to middle-class reporters and missionaries in the Five Points, nearly as bad as sex. Reverend Lewis Pease of the Five Points House of Industry orphanage saw this when a band played fast:

> The spirit of the dance is fully aroused. On flies the fiddle-bow, faster and faster; on jingles tambourine 'gainst head and heels, knee and elbow, and on smash the dancers. The excitement becomes general. Every foot, leg, arm, head, lip, body, all are in motion. Sweat, swear, fiddle, dance, shout, and stamp, underground in smoke, and dust, and putrid air!

At times, according to George Foster, the dancing was downright orgasmic:

> All observance of the figure [dance pattern] is forgotten and every one leaps, stamps, screams and hurras on his or her own hook. . . . The dancers, now wild with excitement . . . leap frantically about like howling dervishes, clasp their partners in their arms, and at length conclude the dance in hot confusion and disorder.

Many of the men who first imitated blacks on stage were Irish American, including such minstrel stars as Dan Emmett, Dan Bryant, Joel Walker Sweeney, and E. P. Christy; and Stephen Foster, the most prominent author of minstrel songs, was the grandson of immigrants from Derry. "There were thousands of Irish and Irish American performers" of blackface minstrelsy, writes historian Mick Moloney. "The list of Irish Americans on the minstrel stage goes on and on." To Noel Ignatiev, "it is surely no coincidence that so many of the pioneers of blackface minstrelsy were of Irish descent, for the Irish came disproportionately into contact with the people whose speech, music, and dance furnished the basis, however distorted, for the minstrel's art."

It is also perhaps no coincidence that, as historian Constance Rourke puts it, "the Negro seemed to pick up the Irish musical idiom with facility." One visitor to a black tavern in the Five Points heard a hybrid music: "In the Negro melodies you catch a strain of what has been metamorphosed from such Scotch or Irish tune, into somewhat of a chiming jiggish air." The scholar Eric Lott has noted, "The very instrumentation of minstrel bands followed this pattern: the banjo and jawbone were black, while the fiddle, bones, and tambourine (derived perhaps from an instrument called the bodhran) were Irish." Some of the most frequently performed minstrel songs overtly compared Irish and black experiences, such as "Tis Sad to Leabe Our Tater Land," an ode to Ireland in mock-black dialect, "Ireland and Virginia," and several Irish nationalist songs sung by Irishmen pretending to be slaves. Moreover, according to Lott, many minstrel skits "portrayed the Irish in terms identical to those in which they portrayed blacks." One of the more popular minstrel songs, "The Darkey's Lament," was written as a parody of "The Irish Emigrant's Lament."

Irish minstrels introduced the jig, the reel, and "the double" to the American public. One visitor to Ireland described the double as consisting "in striking the ground very rapidly with the heel and toe, or with the toes of each foot alternately. The perfection of this motion consists, besides its rapidity, in the fury in which it is performed." One of the greatest black dancers in the early United States was an Irishman. "Master" John Diamond was a featured performer in P. T. Barnum's traveling show. His performances of four dances, the "Negro Camptown Hornpipe, Ole Virginny Breakdown, Smokehouse Dance and Five Mile Out of Town Dance" were so good that Barnum invited local dancers to challenge him in a competitive "Negro breakdown." Diamond, according to one theater manager, "could twist his feet and legs, while dancing, into more fantastic forms than I ever witnessed before or since in any human being." Diamond and his black rival, "Master Juba," are widely credited by dance historians as having created the style that became tap dancing.

Tap dancing was not the only contribution by the renegade Irish. No matter who you are, you may very well owe much of your vocabulary to the filthy, primitive, and uncivilized Irish Americans of the nineteenth century. If you ever use or enjoy the terms "babe," "ballyhoo," "bee's knees," "bicker," "biddy," "big shot," "billy club," "blowhard," "boondoggle," "booze," "boss," "brag," "brat," "brisk," "bub," "buckaroo," "buddy," "cantankerous," "clout," "cockeyed," "cute," "feud," "fink," "fluke," "flunky," "freak," "gab," "galore," "gimmick," "giggle," "goof," "grifter," "hanker," "helter skelter," "humdinger," "malarkey," "mayhem," "moniker," "scoot," "scram," "scrounge," "shack," "shill," "shindig," "skedaddle," "skidoo," "slob," "slogan," "slop," "smithereens," "smudge," "snap," "snazzy," "sneak," "sneeze," "snide," "snoot," "so long," "spic-and-span," "spiel," "spree," "spunk," "squeal," "stocky," "stool pigeon," "stutter," "swoon," "tantrum," "taunt," "teeming," "throng," "twerp," "wallop," "whiz," "yack," or "yell," or if you have a "beef" with a young "buck" and have to "bounce" him because he talks a lot of "bunk" and doesn't mind his own "bee's wax," refer to the street you live on as your "block" or call a town a "burg" or a pirate a "buccaneer," call excrement "caca," are in "cahoots" with a "crony," get knocked on your "can" or have your "clock cleaned" while "chucking" a football or playing "chicken," call a police officer a "cop," make a wise "crack," dismiss a "crank" theory or just feel "cranky," play "craps," say that a dead person "croaked," "ditch" a job because you were "docked" pay for being late, "duke" it out with some "dude," "finagle" a deal that makes you "flush" with cash, are "framed" for a crime you did not commit, are a little old-fashioned and like to say "by golly" and "gee whiz," can't stand that "gawky" and "grouchy" old "geezer" who talks "gibberish" and "guzzles" beer, complain of "hack" politicians who take "graft," have a "hunch" that leads to a "jackpot," listen to "jazz," call someone a "jerk" for being a prostitute's "john," like to visit your favorite "joint," refer to a child or a pal as "kid," tell someone "kiss my ass," put money in a "kitty," are on the "lam" from the law, "lick" a man in a fight, see the ugly "mug" of a "mugger" who takes your money on a "muggy" night, pride yourself on being a "natty" dresser, give someone a "noogy," are either "nuts" or have the "nuts" to raise the bet but then get dealt the "nuts" hand in a game of "poker," have a "pet" animal or child or project or peeve, hate "phoneys" and young "punks" and "pussies," are proud or ashamed of being "queer" or just a little "quirky," complain about the neighbors' noisy "racket" or a corrupt business "racket," have a "rollicking" good time, think the promising "rookie" should be given playing time on the team you "root" for, call a gullible fool who falls for a "scam" a "sap," "shoo" away a fly or get the "skinny" on a "shoo-in," "skip" town, "slack" off, "slug" a shot of good Irish whiskey then "smack" the bar with the glass and "slug" a temperance reformer in the "smacker," know that many good things come out of the "slums," get a "square" deal, are just a working "stiff," create a "stink," laugh so hard you're in "stitches," are a "sucker" for "swanky" stuff, or say "uncle," you might have early Irish Americans to thank.

Lexicographers have found evidence that working-class Irish Americans either invented these terms, modified them from Gaelic origins, redefined them, or put them into common use.* Only their colleagues of the bottom, African Americans, have created as much of the language of the United States.

THE MAKING OF THE IRISH COP

Eric Lott and other scholars have argued that expressions of antiblack racism by Irish Americans—such as the lynchings of blacks during the New York City draft riots of 1863, or their invention of the word *coon,* or the deliberate attempts by some to belittle blacks in minstrel performances—were efforts to hide "their resemblance, in both class and ethnic terms, to 'blackness.'" As Noel Ignatiev puts it, "while the white skin made the Irish eligible for membership in the white race, it did not guarantee their admission; they had to earn it."

A minstrel song, written in 1844 after a series of Irish-led riots in Philadelphia, noted the beginning of a shift among white-skinned immigrants:

---

* A few critics have contested some of the broader claims made by Daniel Cassidy in *How the Irish Invented Slang: The Secret Language of the Crossroads* (Petrolia, CA: Counterpunch, 2007), from which this list was taken, but the sheer volume of the evidence strongly suggests that, at the very least, working-class Irish Americans greatly shaped American vernacular language.

Oh, den de big fish 'gin to fear,
Dey thought the burnin' was too near,
Dey call'd a meetin' to make peace,
An' make all white folks turn police.

One of those white folks was William "Bull" McMullen of Philadelphia, leader of the Irish American gang the Killers and its sister fire company the Moyamensing Hose. McMullen grew up among the smoked Irish and white niggers of the city's poorest neighborhoods. In the 1840s, he took part in several of the city's riots, including one in which he shot to death an anti-immigrant, and was charged with stabbing one policeman and injuring another. To avoid trial, McMullen and other Killers enlisted in the army. Soon after being shipped out to the Mexican War, the Killers physically overthrew the captain of their unit and replaced him with McMullen. By all accounts, McMullen and his crew became full-fledged Americans in Mexico, serving with discipline and loyalty and fighting so fiercely in the battle of Mexico City that they were cited for "the extremest of bravery." Like many other Irish Americans, McMullen moved immediately from service in the Mexican War to municipal politics. In 1850 he was elected president of the Democratic Party Keystone Club in Philadelphia, where he organized much of the Irish population to vote for a pro-Irish candidate for mayor. The candidate won and promptly named six members of the Moyamensing Hose Company to the police force. For his efforts, McMullen was appointed to the board of inspectors of Moyamensing Prison. The following year he was elected alderman, a position that allowed him to fill the Philadelphia police force with Irishmen.

The same pattern followed in New York, where in the nineteenth century the Irish transformed themselves from white niggers into white citizens. The Irish gangs in the city waged a relentless carrot-and-stick campaign to gain power and legitimacy. On the one hand, their riots, arson, and general criminal mayhem forced city officials to greatly expand the police and fire services. And on the other hand, the gangs' aggressive political organizing among immigrants—the Irish were known to vote "early and often" for candidates selected by gang leaders—forced mayors and police chiefs to fill the newly created jobs with Irishmen. In 1840, at the beginning of the great wave of Irish immigration, there was only a handful of Irish police officers on the force. But Mayor Fernando Wood, who was elected with most of the Irish vote in 1855, added 246 positions to the police force and filled half of them with Irishmen. By the end of the year, Irish made up more than one-quarter of the New York City police, and by the end of the century, more than half the city's police and more than 75 percent of its fire fighters were Irish Americans. In addition, Irish were disproportionately represented among prosecutors, judges, and prison guards. Soon, the Irish cop was a stock figure in American culture. Once known as apelike barbarians, the Irish were now able to show themselves as the most selfless and patriotic civil servants.

Through the nineteenth century and into the twentieth, Irish American community leaders waged a remarkably successful campaign of assimilation with the goal, as the Irish newspaper the *Boston Pilot* put it, to create "calm, rational, and respectable Irish Catholics of America." The movement was led at the grassroots by Irish Catholic priests such as Archbishop "Dagger John" Hughes of New York and Archbishops John Joseph Williams and William Henry O'Connell of Boston, who used the power of the church and Christian morality to make immigrants adopt the ways of their new country. Kerby Miller, the leading historian of Irish emigrants to North America, notes that Catholic discipline easily merged with American demands: "church teachings, as reflected in sermons and parochial school readers, commanded emigrants and their children to industry, thrift, sobriety, and self-control—habits which would not only prevent spiritual ruin but also shape good citizens and successful businessmen." Irish priests began the work of disciplining their flock during the canal-building period, when they were hired by employers to shame indolent and unruly workers. When laborers made trouble on the Welland Canal in the winter of 1843–44, a Father McDonagh "used the whip upon them with his priestly authority." And when Irish diggers put down their shovels in a spontaneous "turnout" on the Gallopes Canal, near Ontario, Father James Clarke pledged to the managers that "any assistance in my power to preserve order among the labourers is at your service." Clarke lectured the strikers on their duty to work and, according to one account, convinced them to return to their jobs and become "perfectly peaceable."

According to Miller, most Irish priests during this period "reflected both their church's concerns for order, authority, and spiritual conformity and their middle-class parents' compatible obsessions with social stability and their children's chastity." They therefore "condemned traditional wakes, fairy belief, sexually integrated education, crossroads dancing, and all other practices which threatened either clerical or bourgeois hegemony. . . . This 'iron morality' helped make the post-Famine Irish the world's most faithfully practicing and sexually controlled Catholics, but in the process it crushed many old customs which had given color and vitality to peasant life."

In America, the Church's worldview merged seamlessly with a ruthless determination by many Irish immigrants to make themselves one with their new nation. Archbishop Hughes, who did more than anyone to assimilate the New York Irish, insisted that "the Catholic Church is a church of discipline." To this end, he cajoled thousands of Irish New Yorkers to join temperance organizations and helped establish the Irish Emigrant Society, which placed immigrants in jobs and then monitored their diligence and commitment to the "work ethic." Workers who misbehaved were publicly shamed by the Emigrant Society and their parish priest. Hughes placed an army of nuns in major executive positions—managing hospitals, schools, orphanages, and church societies—where they inculcated, among other teachings, the "Marian doctrine." Girls were instructed to not only live chaste lives but also to ensure the purity of others. The Catholic schools established across the country by Hughes and other Irish priests punished children for using the "flash talk" that created so much of American slang and insisted on strict adherence to "proper" and respectable English.

By the end of the nineteenth century these efforts were apparently successful enough to allow Irish American newspapers to make bold new claims about Irish biology. Irish "racial" characteristics had become inherently American: Celts were declared to be naturally hard-working, orderly, loyal, and sexually restrained. The *Connecticut Catholic* newspaper claimed at the turn of the century that Irish Americans "are an exceedingly well behaved and orderly class of men." Rather than the stereotype of "idle, slovenly, and often vicious" beasts, the Irish actually "compare favorably . . . in all that goes to make up good citizenship . . . [and] the second generation are intensely American in their instincts."

All of this moralizing and re-racializing appears to have had some influence on the Irish, who by the end of the nineteenth century had left the ditches for good. Just one generation after the canals were dug, Irish were proportionally underrepresented in the lowest-paying occupations and overrepresented not only in police and fire departments but also in teaching, clerking, bookkeeping, and other white-collar jobs. Irishmen were elected mayor of New York in 1880, of Boston in 1884, and of Chicago in 1893. In the first two decades of the twentieth century, Rhode Island, Illinois, Massachusetts, and New York elected Irish governors. This was a great accomplishment, to be sure, but at what cost?

FROM JIGGING TO MARCHING

Like Irish Americans as a whole, Patrick Gilmore, Edward Harrigan, and Chauncey Olcott began their careers black and ended them white.

Soon after his arrival in Boston from Galway in 1849, Patrick Gilmore organized a blackface minstrel troupe called Ordway's Aeolians. Fourteen years later, while serving in the Union army, Gilmore took "Johnny I Hardly Knew Ye," an Irish antiwar song of a soldier returning from war blind and limbless, added elements of a Negro spiritual he had heard sung by a black street urchin, "dressed it up, gave it a name, and rhymed it into usefulness for a special purpose suited to the times." It became "When Johnny Comes Marching Home Again," one of the great patriotic—and often prowar—songs in American history. Gilmore penned several other wartime anthems including "God Save the Union," "Coming Home to Abraham," "Good News from Home," and "John Brown's Body." According to one historian, "In terms of creating a positive image in the eyes of Bostonians toward the Irish, no one did it better than Gilmore."

The son of Irish immigrants, Edward Harrigan grew up a stone's throw away from the heart of the Five Points during the heyday of the district's interracial carousing. As a teenager, he learned to play the banjo, the instrument invented by slaves that was the centerpiece of the minstrel stage. In the 1860s, Harrigan moved to San Francisco, where he established himself as a minstrel star, specializing in telling jokes in black dialect. During the 1870s, he moved back to New York and began writing and performing in comic plays depicting life among New York's lower classes, especially the Irish and African Americans. By the 1880s, Harrigan was the most successful playwright and theater producer of his era and had moved the Irish closer to respectability. At his shows, he offered "Pure Fun Only," declaring them an alternative to the overtly sexual entertainment in much of variety theater (see chapter 4). In effect, as one historian puts it, "Harrigan broke through the Anglo-Protestant representational hierarchy of ethnic and racial groups by injecting a positive Irish image onto the commercial stage." African American characters were featured in many of Harrigan's plays, usually as an uncivilized counterpoint to the Irish. The nineteenth-century literary critic William Dean Howells noted that while the Irish had moved out of their primitive state in Harrigan's characterizations, African Americans remained in theirs:

> All the Irish aspects of life are treated affectionately by this art-
> ist, as we might expect from one of his name; but the colored as-
> pects do not fare so well under his touch. Not all the Irish are good
> Irish, but all the colored people are bad colored people. They are
> of the gloomy, razor-bearing variety; full of short-sighted lies and
> prompt dishonesties, amusing always, but truculent and tricky;
> and the sunny sweetness which we all know in the Negro charac-
> ter is not there.

Harrigan drew laughs by poking fun at Irish drinking and brawling, but the overall trajectory of the Irish in his plots was upward into respectability. The main character in Harrigan's most popular series of plays, Dan Mulligan, immigrated from Ireland in 1848, fought in the Civil War, bought a grocery store, and served his community as a selfless politician.

Irish characters in Harrigan's plays had gained respectability but lost their rhythm. Songs written by Harrigan and his partner David Braham (also a former blackface minstrel) that depicted Irish American life were usually in the style of a jig but in a much slowed tempo and set to the regular cadence of a march. They were intended to evoke melancholy rather than movement. Rhythmic syncopation was reserved for the "cakewalk," or "celebration," songs sung by black characters and were among the classic tunes of the minstrel tradition, including "Walking for Dat Cake," "Dat Citron Wedding Cake," "Massa's Wedding Night," "The Old Barn Door," and "The Charleston Blues."

Like Harrigan, Chauncey Olcott started in show business with burnt cork on his face. The son of an immigrant mother who was raised in a "paddy camp" along the Erie Canal, Olcott ran away from home several times to join minstrel troupes and became one of the more celebrated blackface performers in the 1870s. But in the 1880s, as the effort got under way to make the Irish respectable by returning them to their imagined roots, Olcott was recruited to perform "authentic" Irish songs in an oper-atic, *bel canto* style. According to historian William H. A. Williams, after a visit to Ireland in the 1880s, his Irish accent was "good enough to last for hundreds of performances, as Olcott established himself as the reigning Irish tenor in American theater." Olcott specialized in sentimental ballads and melodramatic acting and pioneered "a new type of stage Irishman" who was utterly respectable and nonfunky. "Eschewing the excesses of the hard-drinking Paddy," Olcott "was a handsome, witty, attractive, yet sen-timental hero, who was not above shedding a manly tear for mother and motherland . . . He was a good-humored hero who, while capable of dar-ing-do, was more at home singing love songs and lullabies." Olcott wrote the lyrics to several sentimental ballads, including "My Wild Irish Rose" and "When Irish Eyes Are Smiling," which came to symbolize the sober, romantic, chaste, and nondancing Irish who were invented to replace the white simians of old. "Olcott and his associates gave Irish Americans a glorious, albeit fantastic, past upon which to build dignity and respect-ability."

INOFFENSIVE

In 1917 an investigator for the Juvenile Protective Association attended a "largely Irish" dance at the Thirtieth Ward Woodrow Wilson Club in Chi-cago. The investigator witnessed a considerable amount of drinking and some "kissing and hugging," "but nothing unseemly in the dance hall." The dancing, he reported, was "inoffensive." The "style was modern," a fox trot, but with a "clog effect." This movement away from offensive, sexu-ally suggestive dancing appears to have been widespread. Irish youth were noticeably underrepresented on the floors of the commercial dance pal-aces that became the rage in the 1910s and 1920s.* Many instead attended clubs in which only "traditional Irish music" was played. These clubs were

---

* There is no mention of Irish Americans participating in the dance crazes in David Na-saw, *Going Out: The Rise and Fall of Public Amusements;* Lewis Erenberg, *Steppin' Out: New York Nightlife and the Transformation of American Culture, 1890–1930;* or Ruth Alexander, *The Girl Problem: Female Sexual Delinquency in New York, 1900–1930* and the only mention of Irish Americans in Kathy Peiss, *Cheap Amusements: Working Women and Leisure in Turn-of-the-Century New York,* is in the reference to the popularity of dance halls in "a West Side tenement district inhabited by American, German, and Irish working people."

part of the movement led by the Gaelic League, which had branches in all major U.S. cities, to rid the American mind of Irish stereotypes and reinvent Irish culture as genteel, placid, and respectable. The league claimed with fury that true Irish dancing was never "vulgar," that it was "superior in grace, science, modesty, life and mental effects," and that any dance resembling "the fleshpots of Egypt" was "alien" to the Irish people. Branches of the league were instructed to ban "the Cat Walk, the Cake Walk and all foreign monstrosities" at their social functions. League members vowed to stop the Irish from practicing "pure music-hall dancing," an "un-Irish style [that] should not be tolerated." What the Irish were doing in commercial, unregulated dance clubs "is buck-jumping [a dance associated with Irish sailors and black slaves in America]. It is fiercely vigorous, but in its execution there is no attempt at gracefulness; no attention to positions, of which the old dancing-masters told us there were five; there was little attempt at step—it was simply 'jigging' or as sometimes called clog dancing." (In Irish clog dancing, the wooden footwear is used by striking the heel or toe against the floor to create percussive, syncopated, "off-beat" or "downbeat" rhythms. It was taken up by many African Americans in the nineteenth century and is the basis of both tap dancing and "stepping" in black fraternities.)

Sadly and ironically, the vigorous jigs and reels denounced by the Gaelic League were, according to Irish dance historian Helen Brennan, "the real local traditional dance" in the villages of the old country. In their place, writes John P. Cullinane, another chronicler of Irish dance history, the league instituted "A strict, almost regimental, approach to the performance" of group dances. "Prior to that, these dances were performed with more individual, nonprescribed spontaneous footwork" and were "robbed of enjoyment and spontaneity and becoming regimental in both footwork and hand movements." And so, when "traditional Irish" bands in the early twentieth century such as the Four Provinces Orchestra in Philadelphia or O'Leary's Irish Minstrels in Boston played jigs and reels, they played them with a lovely elegance rather than in the ragged and pounding rhythms of the early immigrant taverns.

Similar changes were taking place in depictions of the Irish in American popular culture. William H. A. Williams, in 'Twas Only an Irishman's Dream: The Image of Ireland and the Irish in American Popular Song Lyrics, 1800–1920, finds that "the clusters of words referring to the combination of drinking, fighting, dancing, and singing—all part of the stereotype of the stage Irishman—decline from an average of 26 percent of the songs for the last two decades of the nineteenth century to an average of 8 percent for the first decades of the new century." Williams concludes, "Whereas 'Irish' had once signified people who were considered wild, rowdy, and undisciplined, by the turn of the century the word was beginning to suggest attitudes that were conservative and old-fashioned. . . . The old negative elements that had once accompanied the image of the gregarious, fun-loving Irish were gone."

In 1916 a book written by a "naturalist" named Madison Grant redefined the racial status of immigrants in America and established the racial hierarchy that would guide public policy in the United States for much of the twentieth century. *The Passing of the Great Race: or, The Racial Basis of European History* placed Europeans into three distinct races: the "Mediterraneans" from southern Europe, the "Alpines" from central Europe, and the "Nordics" from northern Europe. The Nordics were the superior race; what Grant called "the white man *par excellence*." The Alpines had some potential for achievement but would never reach the greatness of the Nordics due to their biological deficiencies. The Mediterraneans were only slightly better than Asians and Africans and would never rise above a primitive agricultural state. The book argued for the exclusion of non-Nordic races from the United States. As for the Irish, they came to America as "ferocious gorilla-like living specimens of the Neanderthal man . . . easily recognized by the great upper lip, bridgeless nose, beetling brow and low growing hair, and wild and savage aspect." In the first Irish to land in America, one could see that "the proportions of the skull which give rise to this large upper lip, the low forehead, and the superorbital ridges are clearly Neanderthal characters. The other traits of this Irish type are common to many primitive races. This is the Irishman of caricature, and the type was very frequently in America when the first Irish immigrants came in 1846 and the following years."

But lo and behold, an amazing thing happened to the Irish gorilla. "It seems, however, to have almost disappeared in this country." In less than seventy years, Irish Americans had vaulted to the very top of the racial scale. Grant saw that in 1916, "the Irish are fully as Nordic as the English." They were made up of "precisely the same racial elements as those which enter into the composition of the English." Eight years later, when Congress passed the National Origins Act severely limiting immigration by all non-Nordic people, the Irish were allowed continued free entry.

The most famous Irish American during the ascendancy to Nordic status was George M. Cohan, the father of the Broadway musical. Though he was born July 3, 1878, Cohan's parents were so eager to prove their patriotism that they insisted he was "born on the Fourth of July." By the end of his life, Cohan was such a cultural icon that in 1942 Warner Brothers produced a film dedicated to his life story, *Yankee Doodle Dandy*. James Cagney, who succeeded Cohan as the most prominent Irish American, won the Academy Award for Best Actor for his performance in the lead role. Both the film and Cohan's life illustrate the fate of Irish American rhythm. When Cohan was still in diapers, he appeared on stage with his parents and sister as "the Four Cohans," a touring vaudeville act that presented black-Irish hybrid entertainment. Each show included one "authentic Irish" act, in which the members of the family dressed in leprechaun outfits and danced a jaunty jig. After a short intermission, they reappeared in the Irish alter ego, with painted faces, as black dancers.

As a young man, Cohan appeared frequently in blackface and became one of the country's most skilled performers of tap dance. Cagney, too, was an exceptional tap dancer, having learned to dance on the streets around the Five Points, a short walk from where he grew up. But Cohan and Cagney became great Americans by merging tap dancing with marching. In the 1900s, Cohan began writing some of America's most enduring patriotic songs, including "You're a Grand Old Flag," a march first performed as the finale of his 1906 Broadway hit *George Washington, Jr.* During the closing act, which is reenacted at the end of *Yankee Doodle Dandy*, the lead performer tap-danced solo, then fell in line with a grand, patriotic, military-style, one-two procession.

During World War I, Cohan penned "Over There," which became the most popular marching song among U.S. soldiers—and, in American popular culture, the theme song for the war. In 1936 President Franklin Roosevelt presented Cohan with the Congressional Gold Medal of Honor for his contributions to World War I morale. In the final scenes of *Yankee Doodle Dandy*, Cohan receives the medal from Roosevelt in the White House, then joins a military march as it proceeds down Pennsylvania Avenue.

This is not to suggest that the Irish American renegade disappeared entirely. During the dance crazes of the 1910s and 1920s, a few were spotted in the nightclubs. And some even used the occasion of Saint Patrick's Day to let loose some of the older, degraded customs. This caused the *Brooklyn Tablet,* the borough's leading Irish newspaper, to declare in 1915 that "the Saint would have been the first to repudiate levity and dancing on the eve of the Sabbath," and that "Saturday night dances for Catholics are an abomination." In Boston, Archbishop William Henry O'Connell forbade not only the new forms of dancing but also sexually suggestive literature, immodest dress, cosmetics, card playing, and "degenerate singing." Jazz, the archbishop rightly pointed out, was "a sensuous, luxurious sort of paganism."

The results of this aggressive assimilation are twofold. First, Irish Americans not only shed their status as a race apart from other whites, but are now rarely even considered as "ethnics." The second result is what is found in Irish American bars all over the country: Guinness on tap, sports on television, and more fistfights than dancing on the dance floor.

★ 7 ★

THE JEW WAS A NEGRO

In the 1890s, there was wide agreement among scholars that while the Irish were no longer black, the Jews were certainly of African origin. The University of Pennsylvania archaeologist and ethnologist Daniel G. Brinton argued in 1890 that the dark continent was "the cradle of the Semites." Nine years later, William Z. Ripley's widely influential *The Races of Europe* popularized Brinton's claim. After the turn of the century, according to historian Eric Goldstein, "Jews, ancient Israelites, and Semites were all linked to Africa with increasing frequency," and there was an "increasing tendency of government officials to classify Jews racially as 'Hebrews.'" Moreover, a congressional commission began compiling statistics on the "racial" characteristics of southern and eastern Europeans in order to justify restrictions on immigration, and the Census Bureau planned to add new categories for European immigrant "races," including Jews, on the 1910 census. In Philadelphia, public schools required students to fill out questionnaires on their racial makeup and did not allow Jewish students to identify themselves as American. A 1910 book by Arthur T. Abernethy established in print what many Americans believed. Here is the conclusion to *The Jew a Negro*:

> Thousands of years of effort to throw off their nigrescence have failed to eradicate those race characteristics, and the Jew of to-day is essentially Negro in habits, physical peculiarities and tendencies. . . . Their pitiable disregard—especially among the men—for the finer conventionalities of social life, as well as for the regularities restricting sexual indulgencies, has become a by-word. The

Jews, like the Negroes, whom this mania often drives to crimes against womanhood, are equally abnormally full-blooded. . . . In music the Jews excel—and in this exceptional case are equally similar to the Negroes who, also, are a musical people by nature and so far as opportunity will permit.

THE JEW IS NOT A NEGRO!

A number of American rabbis responded angrily to such claims. Rabbi Martin A. Meyer of San Francisco acknowledged that "the Jews who came out of the desert to settle Canaan were Semites," but insisted "today but little of that original Semitic blood will be found in the veins of any of us." Rabbi Samuel Sale of St. Louis looked to the "science" of phrenology— racial claims based on cranial dimensions—as proof that Jews were no longer African. "We can not get away from the bald fact, based on anatomical measurements, that only about five percent of all the Jews bear the characteristic mark of their Semitic origin on their body." Cyrus Adler of the American Jewish Committee declared in 1909 that it was time for Jewish scholars to issue "a very strongly worded declaration as to the practical identity of the white race" that made Jews unarguably white.

Anthropologist Maurice Fishberg answered the call. In a series of articles and a 1911 book, *The Jews: A Study of Race and Environment,* Fishberg declared that "the African origin of the ancient Hebrew, and even of the Semites generally, is not an established fact"; concluded from skull measurements that Jews in Europe and the United States held "no relation at all" with Africans; and moved the cradle of the Semites to "the mountainous regions of the Caucusus." And thus it was quite possible for Jews, unlike blacks, to become fully American. "It is clear that certain strata of the population cannot assimilate merely by adopting the language, religion, customs, and habits of the dominant race," he explained. "Negroes in the United States cannot be rendered white merely by speaking English [or] becoming Christians." Yet "the Jews, as whites, are by no means debarred from assimilating with their fellow men of other faiths." These findings "explai[n] our optimism as regards the ultimate obliteration of all distinctions between Jews and Christians in Europe and America."

After Booker T. Washington compared the lynching of blacks with pogroms against Jews in a 1906 speech, the Jewish newspaper the *Modern View* complained that he drew a "poor parallel" between African Americans, "who by carnal crimes bring their people into disrepute," and Jews, who are "thought to be too acquisitive and too able commercially, professionally, and otherwise." Though African Americans experienced less oppression than Jews in Russia, the paper claimed, blacks were marked by "ignorance and idleness that makes for criminality in the Negro," while Russian Jews managed to remain "peaceful, industrious, free from crime," and devout. The New Orleans *Jewish Ledger* rebuked Washington for his uppity claims: "To compare the Jew, who occupies the highest pinnacle of human superiority and intellectual attainment, with the Negro who forms the mud at its base, is something only a Negro with more than the usual vanity and impudence of his race could attempt." Similarly, Philip Cowen, the editor of the *American Hebrew,* claimed in 1900 that in American race riots sparked by claims of rapes committed by Jews or blacks, "there is not even one [Jew] who is guilty" but typically "one wicked Negro" responsible for bringing on the attack.

Of course, many Jewish leaders not only rejected such racist attacks but also committed much of their lives to the cause of black civil rights. Yet many such leaders were guided by a belief in Jewish cultural superiority and a paternalistic impulse to help the unevolved. Several prominent Jews used the claim of Jewish strength under adversity to argue for a moral duty to care for African Americans. Felix Adler, founder of the New York Society for Ethical Culture, declared in 1906 that Jewish aid to African Americans indicated "what manner of men we are, [and] how far we ourselves have progressed along the road of moral knowledge and moral development." Rabbi Max Heller, a leader of American Reform Judaism, wrote in 1911 that Jews, as "men who have been steeled in the furnace of persecution . . . ought to lend an uplifting hand to the weak fellow-man." Rather than dwell at the bottom with the "backward" race, Jews should "lift the younger brother as speedily as possible to our own level."

In popular culture, many Jews moved swiftly to distance themselves from blacks. *The Melting-Pot,* a 1909 play written by the Jewish immigrant Israel Zangwill, remains the most famous expression of immigrant assimilation into American culture. "More than any social or political theory," writes the cultural critic Werner Sollors, "the rhetoric of Zangwill's play shaped American discourse on immigration and ethnicity." Less well known is that *The Melting-Pot* told immigrants that to become American meant to become white. The play's protagonist is a young Jewish violinist who seeks to write a "symphony" that will define "the" culture of America. The music must not show the influence of "comic operas" or the "popular classics" favored by "freak-fashionables" who are "vulgarizing your high heritage" and "undoing the work of Washington and Lincoln." It will resist the popular demand for "the 'rag-time' and the sex-dances" of "the ex-African," as Zangwill put it in the afterword to the play. Rather, America's symphony will be derived from the high classics of Europe and written by "a Jew who knows that your Pilgrim Fathers came straight out of his Old Testament."

ABNORMALLY TWISTED

Despite the efforts of assimilationist Jews to convince themselves and the nation that they were one with white America, anti-Semitism actually escalated during the 1910s and 1920s. Universities established quotas limiting Jewish admissions. Similar barriers were erected in the job market. By the end of the 1920s, according to one study, Jews were barred from 90 percent of white-collar jobs in New York City. Jewish bankers were widely blamed for financing and profiting from the disastrous world war. After 1918, *The Protocols of the Elders of Zion*, a pamphlet allegedly produced by a Jewish cabal bent on establishing a world dictatorship, circulated among large portions of the American reading public—including several congressmen and officers in the Intelligence Division of the United States Army—and was assumed by many to be evidence of such a conspiracy. Lower-class Jews were considered (with some justification) to be little more than carriers of foreign, radical "Bolshevist doctrines."

Most damaging of all to the assimilationist cause was the continued association of Jews with primitive sexuality. In 1915, soon after a Jewish manager of a pencil factory in Atlanta named Leo Frank was convicted of raping and murdering a thirteen-year-old Gentile girl named Mary Phagan, the Southern politician Tom Watson wrote, "Every student of sociology knows that the black man's lust after the white woman is not much fiercer than the lust of the licentious Jew for the gentile." After a judge commuted Frank's death sentence to life imprisonment, a group calling itself "the Knights of Mary Phagan" kidnapped Frank from prison and hanged him from a tree. On October 16, 1915, exactly two months after the Frank lynching, members of the vigilante group helped to reestablish a new Ku Klux Klan, an organization dedicated to the proposition that "every influence that seeks to disrupt the home must itself be destroyed." Above all, the new Klan declared that "it is committed to the sacred duty of protecting womanhood; and announces that one of its purposes is to shield . . . the chastity of womanhood. The degradation of women is viola-tion of the sacredness of human personality, a sin against the race, a crime against society, a menace to our country, and a prostitution of all that is best, and noblest, and highest in life."

The Klan, which reached a membership of four or five million and a high degree of respectability by the middle of the 1920s, is most famous for lynching black people, usually for alleged sexual assaults against white women. But it spent much more of its time and resources policing the *vol-untary* sexuality of white women, in particular the female renegades of the age. The KKK focused most closely on dance halls and automobiles, both of which, the Imperial Wizard of the Klan warned, subjected weak-willed women to "seductive allurement." In hundreds of towns and cities where the Klan had organizations, it conducted campaigns against dance halls, which they called "vile places of amusement." They lobbied local govern-ments to regulate or shut down dance halls, and often, when that wasn't successful, they burned them down. The Klan always claimed to be pro-tecting white women from the aggressions of men from other races, but it seems that they were really protecting white women from their own de-sires. And they had good reason to be concerned. Most Klansmen in the 1920s were living in cities that were rapidly filling up with blacks, Jews, and Catholics, and with women—in particular white working-class women—who were eager to participate in the new, sexually liberated culture that was available there.

Arguments about "unassimilable" Jews were particularly compelling in Congress. In 1921 the chairman of the Committee on Immigration and Naturalization of the House of Representatives, Albert Johnson, quoted diplomats in eastern Europe who warned the country was in danger of be-ing overrun by "abnormally twisted" Jews, "filthy, un-American, and often dangerous in their habits." Congress then passed the Emergency Quota

Act, which severely restricted immigration from eastern and southern Europe.

Throughout the 1920s, newspapers, politicians, and ministers charged Jews with bringing radicalism and sex into the country. Auto magnate Henry Ford gained a wide following by publishing a series of articles in his *Dearborn Independent* newspaper on the menace of "The International Jew: The World's Problem." Ford's claims that Jews dominated the banking industry were overstated, and his allegations of an international Jewish conspiracy to destroy Anglo-Saxon culture appear to have been fantasy. But on the Jewish role in promoting sex, Ford was onto something. Musical theater had indeed become "a flash of color and movement—a combination of salacious farce and jazz music." There is no question that at the time Ford was writing, as he said, "the rage is for extravaganza and burlesque" featuring "fleshly spectacles set off with overpowering scenic effects, the principal component of which is an army of girls whose drapery does not exceed five ounces in weight." Who could deny that by the 1920s, "frivolity, sensuality, indecency" ran rampant in American popular culture? The new culture "gravitates naturally to the flesh and its exposure, its natural psychic habitat is among the more sensual emotions." It most certainly represented "a frontal attack on the last entrenched scruple of moral conservatism." The 1920s was the "age of the chorus girl, a voluptuous creature whose mental caliber has nothing to do with the concern of drama, and whose stage life cannot in the very nature of things be a career." And, yes, most of the theaters, dance halls, and movie palaces were "under Jewish control." No historian would deny Ford's claim that "in New York, where Jewish managers are thicker than they ever will be in Jerusalem, the limit of theatrical adventures into the realm of the forbidden is being pushed further and further." It is well documented that more than any other ethnic group, Jews owned and operated "the centers of nervous thrills and looseness." Yes, the "throngs who indulge in indecent dancing" did so in what Ford called "Jewish jazz factories." Largely because of such enterprises, American entertainment had become a "welter of sensuousness" and "voluptuous abandonment." Ford summed it all up by declaring, "the Jews have introduced Oriental [meaning Asian, Mediterranean, and African] sensuality to the American stage." All this was true.

JEWISH JAZZ FACTORIES

The eminent Jewish historian Howard Sachar estimates that in the first decades of the twentieth century, 75 percent of the prostitutes in New York were Jewish and 50 percent of the brothels were owned by Jews. In the 1920s roughly 20 percent of the prisoners in New York state jails were Jewish. Much of the liquor consumed in the United States during Prohibition was delivered by Jewish bootleggers. As we have seen, Jews were the pioneers in the underground contraceptives industry. They made another major contribution to sexual freedom in America by radically increasing the publication and distribution of pornography. Jews made up the major portion of those arrested for violating the Comstock Act and other obscenity laws between 1880 and 1940. As pornography expanded in the years between the world wars—a time described by one commentator as "sex o'clock in America"—Jews established themselves at the center of the industry. Historian Jay A. Gertzman argues that moral reformers during this period were "correct to claim that the traffic in 'pornography' was vigorous in the 1920s and 1930s, and that Jews were preponderant as distributors of gallantiana [erotic fiction], avant-garde sexually explicit novels, sex pulps, sexology, and the most flagitious materials."

Jews were a bodily people in many ways. Today few Americans know—or can believe—that Jews were once the most natural athletes in the U.S. The first professional basketball association, the American Basketball League (ABL), was dominated by Jewish players from its founding in 1925 into the 1950s. In the first two decades of its existence, the league's winningest teams were the Cleveland Rosenblums, led in the backcourt by the "Heavenly Twins" Marty Friedman and Barney Sedran; the all-Jewish Brooklyn Jewels; the Philadelphia SPHAS, an acronym for the South Philadelphia Hebrew Association; and the New York Celtics, who were led by the sport's first superstar, Nat Holman. Born and raised on the Lower East Side, Holman was described by one sportswriter as "an artist" on the court who "direct[ed] the short passing, weaving, meshing, game" and "revolutionized basketball." The SPHAS, who won seven ABL championships, featured many of the best players of the era, including Harry Litwack, Cy Kaselman, Moe Goldman, Shikey Gotthoffer, Irv Torgoff, Max Posnack, Jerry Fleishman, Inky Lautman, Red Klotz, Davey "Pretzel" Banks, the son of a Lower East Side pretzel maker, and the pride of Greenpoint, Brooklyn, Harry "Jammy" Moskowitz. The SPHAS dominated the American Basketball League, capturing seven league championships in twelve seasons. A writer for the 1926 *Reach Basketball Guide* called the SPHAS "one of the greatest, if not the greatest combinations in basketball history." Sports historian Peter Levine found that in the 1930s and 1940s, roughly half of the ABL's players were Jewish, and in a compilation of the ABL's top scorers for the 1940–41 season, "36 of the 61 names listed are clearly identifiable as Jewish." The top eight scorers that season were all Jewish, including the league's leading scorer, the SPHAS's Petey Rosenberg.

Jews dominated college basketball as well. In 1921 the *American Hebrew* declared that "the immigrant boys" on college basketball teams had achieved "supremacy of brawn, speed and skill." And in 1935 the *Jewish Chronicle* noted that in collegiate athletics, "basketball and Jewish stars are synonymous." Indeed, through the 1940s, colleges with predominantly Jewish student bodies wiped the hardwood with their Gentile rivals. Between 1919 and 1956, the nearly all-Jewish City College of New York team compiled a 423–190 record, and New York University, known by some as "NYJew," won 429 games and lost 235 from 1922 to 1958. Many pundits of the time tried to explain Jewish basketball prowess as biological: Jews were naturally more dexterous and had greater intrinsic athletic ability than non-Jews. Others, such as New York *Daily News* sports editor Paul Gallico, combined this belief with more traditional stereotypes. Writing in the 1930s, Gallico claimed that basketball "appeals to the Hebrew with his Oriental background [because] the game places a premium on an alert, scheming mind and flashy trickiness, artful dodging and general smart-alecness."

As "naturally" gifted as they once were in basketball, nowhere did Jews demonstrate their innate athletic gifts more convincingly than in the boxing ring. Between 1900 and 1940, more Jews won boxing world championships—twenty-six—than Irish, Italian, German, or African American fighters. During this period, most of the greatest stars in the sport were Jewish. Benny "the Ghetto Wizard" Leonard held the lightweight title for eight years and is still widely considered the greatest fighter in that weight class in the first half of the twentieth century. Maxie "Slapsie" Rosenbloom and Barney "Battling Levinsky" Lebrowitz each held the light-heavyweight championship for five years. And Barney Ross, born Dov-Ber Rasofsky and the son of a rabbi, was the first boxer to win three different weight divisions, capturing the lightweight, junior-welterweight, and welterweight crowns during his ten-year career. Jews were so prominent in the sport that nine times between 1920 and 1934, Jews fought each other in championship matches.

JEWISH NIGGERS

In the music industry, for many years Jews were blacker than Negroes. In the 1890s and early 1900s, the Jewish-owned company M. Witmark & Sons published and publicized many of the most important "syncopated" or "coon songs" of the era. Some of the Witmark brothers got their start in blackface minstrel troupes. The company also functioned, according to its historian, as "the amateur minstrel center of the country" largely through its "Minstrel Department." The house published not only minstrel songs but also a full line of joke books, "Negro acts," minstrel overtures, and finales. It supplied tambos, bones, slave costumes, and, of course, burnt cork. In 1899 the Witmark brothers published *The First Minstrel Encyclopaedia* and *The First Minstrel Catalogue,* which "covered every want of the amateur quite as well as the mastodonic Sears, Roebuck catalogue covers the needs of its vast patronage."

As the Irish faded out of blackface, Jewish immigrants stepped in with great enthusiasm. Historian Mark Slobin points to "the fact that virtually every Jewish American stage personality, from Weber and Fields through Al Jolson, Sophie Tucker, and Eddie Cantor, first reached out to American audiences from behind a mask of burnt cork." The Jewish influx into blackface minstrelsy was so pronounced that the *Morning Telegraph* was compelled to announce in 1899 that "Hebrews Have Been Chosen to Succeed Coons."

For a time, many Jews considered themselves to have even more musical facility than the descendants of American slaves. In 1910 the young Irving Berlin wrote "Yiddle on Your Fiddle, Play Some Ragtime," a tribute to Jewish rhythm. The song depicts a woman named Sadie at a wedding where "Ev'ryone was singing, dancing, springing." When she heard Yiddle playing ragtime, "she jumped up and looked him in the eyes," then shouted:

Get busy
I'm dizzy
I'm feeling two years young
Mine choc'late baby

Berlin's identification with blackness was even expressed in the way he taught himself to play music: he hit only the black keys, which he called "nigger keys," on what he called his "nigger pianos." Al Jolson was another chocolate Jew. According to his biographer Isaac Goldberg, Jolson was "the living symbol of the similarity" between blacks and Jews. As a young adult, Jolson was fascinated with black music and spent a great deal of time in Harlem, where in the 1910s he was the only white man allowed into Leroy's, a black musical cabaret. Jolson emerged as a star in the 1911 musical *La Belle Paree,* in which he appeared as Erastus Sparkle, "a colored aristocrat from San Juan Hill, cutting a wide swath in Paris." Among the featured songs was "Paris Is a Paradise for Coons," which was written by the Jewish composer Jerome Kern. Over the next two decades, Jolson rose to the top of show business, performing regularly in blackface.

In the same year that Jolson achieved blackface stardom, Irving Berlin penned his first hit, "Alexander's Ragtime Band," the first popular American song featuring syncopated rhythm. Its lyrics, which were meant to be sung in mock-Negro minstrel dialect, celebrated primitive musicality: "There's a fiddle with notes that screeches / Like a chicken / And the clarinet is a colored pet / Come and listen / To a classical band what's peaches . . . So natural that you want to hear some more." Berlin had learned syncopation by listening to ragtime pianists at a Chinatown nightclub where he worked as a waiter. Berlin went on to write many of the most famous "black songs," including "Harlem on My Mind" and "Supper Time."

In 1918, Al Jolson performed "Swanee," a minstrel song written by the young Jewish songwriter George Gershwin. The song told of an ex-slave's longing to be "among the folks in D-I-X-I-E," where "the banjos are strummin' soft and low" and "my mammy is waiting for me." Gershwin's subsequent career was built on black music, from *Rhapsody in Blue* to *Porgy and Bess.* He learned the sounds of spirituals, blues, jazz, and ragtime in Harlem nightclubs, which he began frequenting as a teenager. Jerome Kern, too, was both black and Jewish. In high school, he helped write a senior class minstrel show in which he played ragtime on piano. Kern's score for the 1927 *Show Boat,* a collection of spirituals, ragtime, blues, and jazz, including the classics "Ol' Man River" and "Can't Help Lovin' Dat Man," is usually considered his greatest artistic achievement. In that same year, Al Jolson achieved iconic status with the release of the first "talkie" motion picture, *The Jazz Singer,* in which Jolson's character repudiates his devout Jewish family for stardom in blackface theater.

While Berlin, Gershwin, Kern, and Jolson tried to straddle the line between African American music and mainstream sensibilities, Harold Arlen appears to have fully embraced his blackness. Arlen's father was a cantor with a reputed adeptness for improvisation. As a young musician, Arlen studied the "race" records of Louis Armstrong, King Oliver, Fletcher Henderson, and other foundational jazz musicians, and formed an association with the Cotton Club in Harlem. Arlen was put on the map in 1930 when his "Get Happy" was performed at the club. Over the next three decades, he wrote dozens of blues and jazz numbers, including songs for an "American Negro" suite in 1940 called *Reverend Johnson's Dream.* The blues singer Ethel Waters was so taken with Arlen's authenticity that she called him the "Negro-ist" white man she had ever known, and one of his songwriting colleagues claimed that more than just an imitator of African Americans, Arlen "was really one of them."

Many of the songs performed by Jewish entertainers were written by African American composers. Sophie Tucker, the "Coon Shouter" and "Last of the Red Hot Mamas," hired African American singers to give her lessons and African American composers to write her songs. Joe Sultzer of the Jewish vaudeville duo Smith and Dale credited black street performers on the Lower East Side in the 1890s as the inspiration for his act: "A colored fellow used to come and dance on our street. It was called buck dancing. He had sand and threw it on the sidewalk and danced. The sound of the sand and the shuffle of his feet fascinated me, and I would try to dance like him. It made me feel I wanted to go on the stage." Less famous Jews were similarly taken with black music. In the 1880s, the journalist and social reformer Jacob Riis noticed that the "young people in Jewtown [the Lower East Side] are inordinately fond of dancing." Jewish moral reformer Belle Moskowitz despaired that in Jewish neighborhoods, "the glare of lights and the blare of music strikes you on every side." In the 1910s and 1920s, Hadassah chapters and Jewish youth and recreation centers in cities across the country regularly staged shows featuring Jewish entertainers in black-face singing in mock black dialect and dancing the most intricate jazz steps of the day.

Jewish immigrants took over vaudeville theater in the early twentieth century and made it into a celebration of unseemly pleasures. Most disturbing to the disciplinarians of the time was the dancing of vaudeville performers—in particular the undulations of female dancers and the "tough dances" in which copulation was simulated.

Like the first Irish immigrants, eastern European Jews who settled in the United States seemed unaware or unconcerned with the American color line. According to historian Jeffrey Gurock, they "showed no easily recognizable unwillingness towards living with and among blacks." By the 1920s, thousands of Jews lived and operated businesses in the African American neighborhoods of Harlem and Chicago's South Side.

One of the more remarkable—and underreported—examples of Jewish identification with African Americans was the common use of *nigger* by Jews as a nickname. In Michael Gold's autobiographical novel *Jews Without Money,* the narrator's best friend is a "virile boy" named "Nigger." Jewish gangsters who ruled many big-city streets in the early part of the twentieth century often adopted the same *nom de guerre.* There was "Yoski Nigger" of the Yiddish Black Hand, "Nigger Benny" Snyder of the Greaser Gang, Harry "Nig" Rosen of Philadelphia's 69th Street Gang, and Isadore "Nigger" Goldberg of the Twentieth Ward Group in Chicago. There was even a Jewish brothel owner in New York known as "Nigger Ruth." And down on Pell Street in New York's Chinatown, there was a café owned and operated by a Russian Jew named "Nigger Mike" Salter, the man who hired Irving Berlin as a waiter.

Milton "Mezz" Mezzrow, the son of Russian-Jewish immigrants in Chicago and one of the great jazz clarinetists of his age, went so far as to declare his racial defection. After a teenaged excursion to Missouri, he remembered "the Southerners had called me a 'nigger lover' there."

> Solid. I not only loved those colored boys, but I was one of them—
> I felt closer to them than I felt to the whites, and I even got the
> same treatment they got. . . . By the time I reached home, I knew
> that I was going to spend all my time from then on sticking close

to Negroes. They were my kind of people. And I was going to learn
their music and play it for the rest of my days. I was going to be a
musician, a Negro musician, hipping the world about the blues the
way only Negroes can.

Mezzrow performed in otherwise all-black jazz bands, married a black
woman, and moved to Harlem. He not only declared himself a "voluntary
Negro" but also became a "bad nigger." In the 1930s, Mezzrow established
himself as the primary drug dealer in the jazz scene, and in 1940 he was
arrested and convicted of possession and intent to distribute marijuana.
When he arrived at Riker's Island, he told the guards he was black and was
sent to the segregated prison's Negro section.

In 1946 *Ebony* magazine honored Mezzrow in a feature story titled
"Case History of an Ex-White Man," for being "one of the few whites" to
have "passed through the Jim Crow portals of Negro life to live on equal
terms with its harried inhabitants." Of course, the article noted, "Physically
speaking," Mezzrow "couldn't pass for Negro by any stretch of the imagination; his skin is too white." Nonetheless, the article maintained, his "conversion to 'the race' has taken place largely within himself. In psychological
makeup, he is completely a black man and proudly admits it."

THE JEW IS A WHITE MAN

To many historians, Jewish attachment to jazz, basketball, dance halls, and
blackface was evidence of Jewish assimilation into American culture. Yet
those scholars do not appreciate that there have been many and conflicting
American cultures. The Jews who danced orgiastically and called themselves niggers became "bad" Americans.

To understand that even during the Jazz Age "good" Americans did not
have rhythm, we need only listen to the music that was played and the dances that were danced in institutions that trained immigrants to be American.
The historian Derek Vaillant has written that social workers among immigrants in the first decades of the twentieth century "moved swiftly to single
out specific musical forms, such as ragtime and jazz, and their audiences
for censure if they challenged conventional expectations of self-control,
women's place, sexual mores, and youth behavior, or if they appeared to

encourage social mixing." Fearing "the attendant evil of the modern styles of dancing," social workers and city officials banned the playing of "ragtime music or any other music with suggestive titles or words, or with any form of improper dancing" at dances catering to immigrants. Forbidden moves included "close dancing," "improper position," "a distorted position," and "freak, unnecessary or indecent movements" such as "suggestive wiggling, frequent low dipping, [or] extreme swaying." Dancers were allowed only to exhibit "self-control and self-government" in their movements.

Jewish American leaders were among the first to warn that improper dancing and other forms of un-American behavior were more likely to break out among immigrants who lived in close proximity to blacks. In 1911 a writer for the *Forward,* the leading Jewish American newspaper, decried the mixing of Jewish shopkeepers with blacks. "To make a living, the grocer must give up all of the comforts of the 'outside' civilization" and live among the "old, ramshackle ruins" of the "Negro neighborhood," where his children are "influenced by the half-wild and barbaric street life of the black." The grocer "learns the black's English, and finds himself at a very low station in life." In the Yiddish press of the 1920s and 1930s, according to historian Hasia Diner, "[t]here were probably more articles on black crime than on any other single black theme in the Yiddish press." The headlines for these articles "were either gruesome or explosive: 'Crazy Negro Kills 4 People in Chicago,' 'Mad Negro Bites Policeman, Who Dies,' 'Black Accused of Trying to Chloroform a White Girl and Rape Her,' and 'Negro Found Guilty of Murder of Girl: Two More Girls Attacked Brutally Yesterday,' typifies the Yiddish press style."

Most important, the Yiddish press highlighted the danger of mixing with blacks. "The *Forward* ran several long articles on Harlem nightlife, partly to discourage Jewish youth from slumming there." All the newspapers concluded that "it was dangerous for whites to patronize Harlem cabarets and saloons." In Diner's survey of Yiddish newspapers from 1915 to 1935, she found eight reports of Jewish women being attacked or raped by black men, several other articles on Jews being shot or stabbed by blacks for no apparent reason, and scores of reports of black violence against Jews during robberies, "not just of merchants but of Jews waiting on subway platforms, walking in the hallways of apartment buildings, passing on the streets, or in their homes."

At about this time, Jewish biology began to change. In the 1920s and 1930s, several Jewish American intellectuals argued that Jews were in fact a distinct "race" but one whose characteristics were perfectly consistent with American respectability. In his *Famous Musicians of a Wandering Race* (1928), Gdal Saleski argued that "the bloodstream of the Jew courses through the spiritual veins of every major art that modern civilization has risen to honor" and praised Jewish American composers whose work was "entirely free from the barbaric influence of jazz and from the lurid wail of the saxophone." Similarly, Mac Davis's *From Moses to Einstein: They Are All Jews* (1937) presented sixty biographical sketches of Jews who made "immense" contributions to civilization as "soldier, statesman, explorer, pugilist, poet, scientist, rabbi, actress, [and] business man" without mentioning any of the equally prominent Jews in blackface minstrelsy or jazz.

While some in the non-Jewish press noticed that Jewish athletes shared with African Americans a "natural" facility with their bodies, many prominent Jews steered attention to their upstanding demeanor. Harold Riegelman, a national leader of the Zeta Beta Tau fraternity, praised Jewish athletes for their "sportsmanship on the athletic field," "their reserve and decency of deportment," and "the inherent fitness of their character." The *American Hebrew* hailed University of Michigan football star Benny Friedman for his "character, intrinsic merit, and pleasing deportment" and basketball legend Nat Holman for his "dignified bearing" as "a man of culture," his "well-enunciated speech" and "poise," and his "clean, high-minded Americanism." The Jewish editor of *Ring Magazine,* Nat Fleischer, noted Benny Leonard's "hair-trigger brain." Even Leonard himself argued that "it was the Jewish fighters who put the science in the game." Jewish scholar Max Margolis helped counter comparisons to black physicality by declaring in a 1923 issue of the *B'nai B'rith News* that biologically, "the Jew is a white man." Some went so far as to claim that anyone who excelled with his body could not be a real Jew, as the *Daily Jewish Courier* said in 1923 about Jewish boxers:

> as for our highly honored members of the fighting fraternity, we may say that if the Jewish people has anything to contribute to the common civilization and culture of the race, such contributions are rather to be sought in the realm of their intellects than in their

fists. . . . As a matter of fact, none of these pugilists may be said to be Jews except in the accident of their birth.

Similarly, a 1939 booklet distributed by the Anti-Defamation League stated categorically that Jews had achieved whiteness. "Scientifically and correctly speaking, there are three great races in the world: the black, yellow, and white. Within the white race all the sub-races have long since been mixed, and we Jews are part of the general admixture."

Some who acknowledged Jewish participation in jazz credited Jews with civilizing the music. Critic Abraham Roback argued in 1927 that "The . . . people to bring into the wild gyrations of the original jazz a note of restraint, of anxiety and foreboding were the Jewish song writers who were versatile enough to catch the spirit of Negro music. . . . If you ask what America would have done without the host of Jewish . . . composers, and what the music of the street would have been like, the answer would be that jazz would still have had its day, but it would have been a more puerile and less varied kind of jazz. . . . The original Negro jazz is shapeless and chaotic. In most of the Jewish versions you can follow motifs."

Others simply wished that the Jews would leave black music alone. As Rabbi Steven Wise wrote in 1924, "Jazz is one of the inevitable expressions of what might be called the jazzy morale of mood of America . . . when America regains its soul, jazz will go, not before—that is to say, it will be relegated to the dark and scarlet haunts whence it came and whither un-wept it will return, after America's soul is reborn." Belle Moskowitz made it her life's work to rid her people of their rhythm. She told her brethren, "you cannot dance night after night, held in the closest of sensual embraces, with every effort made in the style of dancing to appeal to the worst in you and remain unshaken by it." Moskowitz and other reformers led a campaign to regulate the styles of dancing in dance halls, and by the 1920s, more than sixty city governments passed ordinances banning "lascivious," "de-bauched," and "sensual" movements on public dance floors. Jewish movie executives soon instituted a similar purification program in their indus-try. In 1934 they began to enforce the Motion Picture Production Code, which forbade, among many things, the presentation of "dances suggesting or representing sexual actions or indecent passions," "dances intended to excite the emotional reaction of an audience," "dances with movement of the breasts," and "excessive body movements while the feet are stationary."

RISE OF THE NERD

Yiddish-language newspapers during the 1920s and 1930s paid careful attention to black-Jewish relations and helped establish what might be called the liberal Jewish view on race. Influential, widely read papers such as the *Forward,* the *Morgen Journal,* and the *Tageblatt* "agreed upon very little," according to historian Hasia Diner, but "race and the lot of black Americans proved a striking exception." All the major Yiddish papers condemned legal segregation, supported civil rights, and praised black achievements. But they also made it clear that Jews and blacks should be culturally separate. Blacks had rhythm; good Jews did not. In the Yiddish press, according to Diner, "descriptions of Negro life in Harlem were replete with dancing, gyrating men and women, the sounds of bongo drums (which one *Tageblatt* writer called 'their national instrument') resounded, and exuberant vibrant music filled the streets." In one article, Maurice Schwartz, a star of Yiddish theater, "claimed in no uncertain terms that rhythm ran in the Negroes' blood." Similarly, the English-language *Jewish Tribune* wrote that one should "expect colored dancers to put about fifty times more pep into a performance than the average white girl cares to attempt." And the *American Hebrew* declared that "the rhythm of the Negro is vicious, it is of kinesthetic urge. One sways and bends with it." Overall, Jewish papers asserted that "musical and rhythmic expression were the most distinctive characteristics of black cultural life." But in the very same issues in which civil rights were championed and black musical genius celebrated, warnings were made to Jews who might cross the color line. Occasional references were made to the apparent affinity several Jewish entertainers had for black music, but any similarity between the two groups was attributed to suffering, not sensuality. As a *Forward* review of *The Jazz Singer* put it, the film's "Negro songs" contained "the minor key of jewish music, the wail of the Chazan, the cry of anguish of a people who had suffered. The son of a line of rabbis well knows how to sing the songs of the most cruelly wronged people in the world's history."

During World War II, with success demanding national unity, the federal government officially welcomed Jews into the white race. In 1943 the Immigration and Naturalization Service for the first time denoted all Europeans as "white" on its forms for immigrants seeking American citizenship. The military remained thoroughly segregated between black and white—

even blood supplies from black and white donors were kept separate—but extraordinary measures were taken to merge Americans of European origins. According to the historian Gary Gerstle, the military for the first time formed regiments of white men of every ethnicity and nationality.

> Sometimes together for as long as four years, these units became extraordinary vehicles for melding the many streams of Euro-Americans into one . . . And this assimilatory process was racialized from its inception because no blacks and few Asians were permitted to take part, in the sense that they were excluded from regiments defined as white.

The effect of this integration was profound. According to historian Eric L. Goldstein, "More than any other wartime development, the thorough integration of Jews and Catholics into the American military helped cement the public's view of these groups as unambiguously white." Suddenly, Jews and Italians were members of "ethnicities" rather than races. In the 1940s, best-selling books such as Ruth Benedict's *The Races of Mankind* and Ashley Montagu's *Man's Most Dangerous Myth: The Fallacy of Race* rejected the existence of races among Europeans and claimed that differences among whites were cultural rather than biological. Opinion polls conducted after the war showed that for the first time, a majority of Americans did not identify Jews as a race.

During and after World War II, Jews acted on the fears of racial mixing by moving en masse out of Harlem, the South Side of Chicago, and other neighborhoods that were taking in black migrants from the South. Soon fewer Jewish Americans were participating in renegade culture than observing it. As Goldstein notes, "countless memoirs record the fascination of Jewish youth of these years with African American jazz artists, whose performances in nightclubs and dance halls they would often attend." At the same time, the number of Jewish jazz musicians declined in the postwar period, and those who continued with the music—including such greats as Stan Getz, Lee Konitz, Herbie Mann, Red Rodney, Stan Levey, Lou Levy, Paul Desmond, Teddy Charles, and Shelly Manne—tended to follow the postwar trend away from swing and into nondanceable "cool jazz" and intricate, highly technical bebop.

Jews also abandoned sports, in particular sports considered to be less cerebral and more primitive than others. According to Jewish boxing historian Allen Bodner, "[b]y 1950, there were virtually no Jewish boxers, and their number has been minuscule ever since. A similar decline occurred among Jewish trainers, but Jewish managers, promoters, and matchmakers continue to maintain a presence." According to Peter Levine, by the late 1940s, "Jewish dominance of the American Basketball League was in clear decline." In the 1950 season, only ten of the top thirty-six scorers were Jewish, and in the following year, league rosters "indicate that only 9 percent, or 11 of the ABL's players, were Jewish." By the 1960s, "Jews were more likely to be found in NBA boardrooms than on the hardwood." The most telling symbol of the Jewish loss of physical dexterity was the fate of the great Philadelphia SPHAS. In the early 1950s, the SPHAS, then led by the talented point guard Red Klotz, defeated the all-black Harlem Globetrotters in two exhibition games. Klotz later bought the SPHAS and changed the name of the team to the Washington Generals. In 1953 Klotz entered into an agreement to make the Generals the regular "opponent" of the Globetrotters in exhibition games staged to show off the black team's spectacular skills. Between 1953 and 1995, the Generals won six games against the Globetrotters and lost more than thirteen thousand.

After World War II, a physically inhibited, highly talkative suburban family replaced the blackface dancers and basketball players as the most famous Jews in America. What began as a radio program in the 1930s about Jewish family living in a Bronx tenement, *The Goldbergs,* became a television program in the 1940s and 1950s about the same family relocated to the suburbs and obsessed with "fitting in" with their new Gentile neighbors. In 1950 *The Goldbergs* was the seventh-highest-rated series on television; the show's creator and star, Gertrude Berg, was awarded the Emmy Award for Best Actress; and Philip Loeb, who played the patriarch of the family, was named "Television Father of the Year" by the Boys Clubs of America. Whereas Jews in popular culture before the war whirled about the screen and performed high-tempo dance numbers, most of the action in the *The Goldbergs* takes place at the kitchen table or in the living room, where chess is played, classical music emanates from the phonograph, and the conversation focuses on how to become "more modern." The topic of one episode is the shame that Berg's character feels at not being able to participate in the new Latin dance craze. "You know I only waltz," she says.

Jews continued to be featured prominently in American entertainment, but further and further removed from the sounds and moves of blackness. In the 1960s and 1970s, the most famous Jewish entertainers were the great popularizers of classical music Aaron Copland and Leonard Bernstein; romantic balladeers like Eddie Fisher, Barbra Streisand, Eydie Gorme, Steve Lawrence, Burt Bacharach, Barry Manilow, and Neil Diamond; intellectual folk singers such as Bob Dylan, Paul Simon, Art Garfunkel, Carole King, Janis Ian, and Leonard Cohen; and a phenomenal number of film score composers including Alfred Newman, Elmer Bernstein, Bernard Hermann, Marvin Hamlisch, Danny Elfman, Jerry Goldsmith, Philip Glass, James Horner, Howard Shore, Alan Menken, and Randy Newman. The physically awkward but intellectually gifted *nebbish* was foregrounded in film and television by Woody Allen, Dustin Hoffman, and Richard Dreyfuss, and later by Jerry Seinfeld, Adam Sandler, Ben Stiller, and Larry David. By the late twentieth century, Jews had left the dance floor and arrived in America.

But Jewish Americans who wish to revive their renegade heritage can now find heroes in the unlikeliest places. Though most Americans now think of her as the kindly former judge on a popular talent contest—and are probably unaware of her ethnic background—Paula Abdul is as funky and as Jewish as any of the dancing Hebrews of the vaudeville era. Her father, Harry Abdul, is a Syrian Jew, and her mother, Lorraine Rykiss, was born into one of the few Jewish families in Saint Boniface, Manitoba. Abdul regularly attends Chabad of Bel Air, an orthodox synagogue in Los Angeles. Since 1988, she has placed five singles in the top forty of *Billboard*'s Hot R&B/Hip-Hop Songs Chart, formerly called the Black Singles Chart; and ten singles in the top forty of *Billboard*'s Hot Dance Club Play Chart, a weekly national survey of the most popular songs in dance clubs.

Jews have also made impressive inroads into hip-hop. The Beastie Boys, a group formed in the early 1980s by Michael Diamond, Adam Yauch, and Adam Horovitz, are one of the longest-lived and most successful hip-hop groups. Rick Rubin, who convinced the Beastie Boys to switch from punk rock to hip-hop early in their career, founded Def Jam Records and created much of the music in the 1980s that made hip-hop the dominant genre in the music industry. In the late 1980s, Michael Berrin of Far Rockaway, Queens, grabbed the mic and the stage name MC Serch, styled his kinky hair into a "high-top fade," busted MC Hammer–type dance moves, and became one of the leading rappers of his time. As front man for the group

3rd Bass and later as a solo act, Serch produced five top-twenty singles on the *Billboard* Rap Charts. The Beasties and Serch are often credited with creating the archetype of the "white nigga" or "wigga."

Today, two of the most sought-after producers of hip-hop beats are Scott Storch, an aficionado of "bling" jewelry and founder of Tuff Jew Productions, and Alan Daniel Maman, better known as the Alchemist, a master of combining disparate noises into hip-hop hits who took his name from the Sephardic Jews of the Middle Ages who mixed common metals into gold, silver, and potions for eternal life.

Mock them all you like as "inauthentic" wannabes, but Jewish wiggas might be truer to their heritage than any accountant, lawyer, or doctor will ever be.

★ 8 ★

ITALIAN AMERICANS: OUT OF AFRICA

In the 1830s, when there was only a trickle of Italian immigrants into the United States, a prominent gentleman in New York declared, "A dirty Irishman is bad enough, but he's nothing comparable to a nasty . . . Italian loafer." A few decades later, the eminent American historian and philosopher John Fiske concurred, estimating that "the lowest Irish are far above the level of these creatures [Italians]." The most common claim made against Italians was that they possessed "a natural inclination toward criminality," as the *New York Times* put it in 1876, but they were accused of other unsuitable behaviors as well, as the *Times* remarked in the same editorial: "The Italian is lazier, more gossiping, and fitter for intrigue than the American." The newspaper concluded that it was "hopeless to think of civilizing them, or of keeping them in order, except by the arm of the law." The philanthropist Charles Loring Brace wrote in 1872 of his failed attempts to reform new arrivals from Italy and concluded that Italian immigrants were "without exception, the dirtiest population I had met with." The dark skin of Italians and their home country's proximity to Africa made many suspect that the immigration service was allowing into the country a new population of Negroes—"black-eyed, swarthy, and wicked," according to an 1881 *New York Times* article. The *Times* was especially concerned that Italians wielded a primitive sexual power. There were "hundreds of romantic young women in this City whose imaginations have been fired" by the newcomers, since "the romantic nature craves something Southern, Latin, and intense."

Direct comparisons of Italians to the other "primitives" living in the United States were often made, especially in Louisiana and Mississippi, where Italians immigrated in large numbers to take jobs vacated by blacks who had fled to the North. A Sicilian immigrant who worked in the sugar-cane fields of Louisiana remembered that "the boss used to call us niggers" and "told us that we weren't white men." In 1890, after the chief of police of New Orleans was murdered, the New Orleans *Times-Democrat* accused Sicilian immigrants, "whose low, repulsive countenances, and slavery attire, proclaimed their brutal natures," of committing the crime. After nineteen Sicilian men were charged but acquitted, a mob broke into the jailhouse where they were being held, slashed limbs from the men and hanged them from trees. Over the next two decades, Italians were lynched in Denver, Tampa, Gunnison, Colorado, Tallulah, Louisiana, and Johnston City, Illinois.

Less murderous blackening of Italians was common as well. In the Mississippi Delta, attempts were made to segregate "white" and Italian schoolchildren and to disenfranchise the newcomers. A local newspaper in the Delta said in 1898, "when we speak of white man's government, they [Italians] are as black as the blackest Negro in existence." For these reasons, in the 1890s the term *guinea,* which had been used for slaves from the coast of West Africa, was applied to Italian Americans.

Comparisons of Italians with blacks became increasingly common in the North as well. *Leslie's Illustrated* reported in 1901 on the "instincts" of the Italian immigrant, which included many of the natural characteristics widely believed to be those of African Americans: "He plays cards, throws dice, gets up all kinds of gambling games, and stakes his all with the same shiftless indifference as though something other than his own purposes protected him." Of the Italian birth rate, "there is sixty per cent that is illegitimate. The papers are full of affairs between men and women . . . and girls little more than children have their children whose coming into the world was not sanctioned through law or sacrament." The following year, the president of Princeton University and future president of the United States, Woodrow Wilson, wrote that Italians who came to America constituted "the more sordid and hapless elements of their population, the men whose standards of life and of work were such as American workmen had never dreamed of hitherto." A 1904 commentary by *Popular Science Monthly* welcomed immigrants from northern Italy, who were "often of lighter complexion" and were very often "skilled in some trade or occupation" but warned against admitting "the southern Italian," who was "short of stature, very dark in complexion" and "invariably is an unskilled farm laborer." Like blacks and the first Irish and Jewish immigrants, Italians were perceived as a people completely of the body. The southern Italian's "intelligence is not higher than one could imagine in the descendant of peasantry illiterate for centuries," said *Popular Science Monthly*, but "nevertheless, they are wiry and muscular and capable of prolonged physical exertion" and "have a deftness of hand which adapts them to trades requiring manual skill." Accordingly, wages for Italian Americans were comparable to wages for African Americans in many labor markets.

In 1910 the *Chicago Tribune* sent anthropologist George A. Dorsey to Italy to study the source of the undesirable immigrants. Southern Italians in particular, concluded Dorsey, were clearly of "Negroid" ancestry and therefore "of questionable value from a mental, moral, or physical standpoint." And in its 1911 report, the United States Immigration Commission warned against admitting the southern Italian "race," which was "excitable, impulsive, highly imaginative, impracticable" and had "little adaptability to highly organized society." The commission's reports on the work habits of southern Italians echoed descriptions of the work habits of black slaves: "It seems generally agreed that the Sicilians are less steady and less inclined to stick to a job day in and day out than other races. They will take a day off now and then whether they lose their positions or not." Even more damning was the conclusion that "certain kinds of criminality are inherent in the Italian race." After receiving the commission's report, the U.S. House Committee on Immigration and Naturalization debated—with inconclusive results—whether one should regard "the south Italian as a full-blooded Caucasian."

In the 1910s, several scholars examined the racial lineage of Italians and were disturbed by what they found. Edward Ross, professor of sociology at the University of Wisconsin and president of the American Sociological Association, argued in a 1914 book that because there was "no small infusion of Greek, Saracen, and African blood in the Calabrians and Sicilians," they had reached only "a primitive stage of civilization." Ross reported that southern Italian immigrant children, "with the dusk of Saracenic or Berber ancestors showing in their cheeks, are twice as apt to drop behind other pupils of their age as are the children of the non–English-speaking immigrants from northern Europe." He also found that in the U.S. South, "a fear has sprung up lest the Italians, being without the southern white man's strong race feeling, should mix with the Negroes and create a hybrid." Ross described a number of characteristics in Italians that were commonly associated with blacks. Notably, they were "addicted to gambling," often resistant to work, and therefore prone to criminal behavior: "In an Italian quarter are men who never work, yet who have plenty of money. 'No,' they say, 'we do not work. Work does not agree with us. We have friends who work and give us money. Why not?' It is these parasites who commit most of the crime." The country from which they came "has from three to four times the violence of the North, while its obscene crimes, which constitute an index of sensuality, are thrice as numerous." To Ross, these racially determined behaviors meant that "half, perhaps two-thirds, of our Italian immigrants are *under* America, not *of* it."

Madison Grant's influential *The Passing of the Great Race* (1916), which moved the Irish to "Nordic" status, argued that, in contrast, southern Italians exemplified the lowest race in Europe. While Grant placed "Mediterraneans" within the "white" category, he made no bones about what many suspected: those people had a lot of black in them. "A study of the Mediterranean race shows that, so far from being purely European, it is equally African and Asiatic," he wrote. With similar pessimism for the prospect of Italian assimilation, the chairman of the Missionary Education Committee, a Protestant Evangelical organization, declared in 1917 that Italian immigrants "have very little or no knowledge of what Christian living means. Sunday to them is a fete day not a holy day; drinking is a matter of course; sexual morality is at a very low ebb among the men; and so far as their appreciation of the value of the truth is concerned, the less said the better."

Italians flunked a number of intelligence tests that were given to immigrants in the 1910s and 1920s. Dr. Arthur Sweeny administered one such test to several thousand immigrants among sixteen nationalities and concluded in 1922 that "we can . . . strenuously object to immigration from Italy," since 63.4 percent of the Italians who took the test scored in the "D class"—the bottom category of intelligence. The D class represented "a stage between imbecility and dull normality," and as a class of workers "was somewhat more useful" than the mentally retarded "but little more dependable." Only the Polish scored lower on the test. Owing to their lack of discipline, Italians "were in no sense soldier material," said Sweeny. Rather, they were best suited to dig ditches, clean latrines, and contribute "only in a muscular way to the work of the army." The shiftlessness of Italians was described in terms nearly identical to those used for the behavior of slaves: "Constant supervision of their work was necessary. Even simple tasks were beyond their powers if continuous labor was necessary. They wholly lacked initiative." And like blacks, while Italian immigrants were believed to lack rationality and discipline, they were also thought to be better able to perform and enjoy the pleasures of the body. "Men of the D class are physically well developed," Sweeny reported. "A large number of them are attractive," and, "by reason of their emotional instability, are regarded on first sight as unusually quick and responsive. They laugh easily and are with equal ease moved to tears." Some members of the D class were also marked by a "lack of inhibition" that made them value leisure over work, freedom over responsibility, and gratification over sacrifice: "What gives him pleasure is the height of his ambition."

In a 1919 study written by Harvard economics professor Robert F. Foerster, Italian immigrants were found to be sorely lacking the American work ethic. Foerster reported that employers often described the Italian worker as "lazy, shirking, tricky, a time server" and complained that Italians were known—just as slaves were once known—to "feign sickness in order not to have to work in bad weather." Their "bad qualities" included "low efficiency and inability to withstand cold weather," said one employer. Others interviewed by Foerster preferred black workers over Italians: "Our opinion is that generally the amount of work done per Italian laborer per day is not equal to the amount of work done per laborer per day by our other white laborers or by Negroes." Foerster reported that the results of a test conducted by a company to determine the efficiency of Italian workers showed that in a given time they completed only 35 percent to 50 percent of the same work done by nonimmigrant workers. In line with their poor work discipline was a lack of sexual control: "Plenty of testimony exists to show that loose living on the part of male Italians abroad is common. Our witnesses, who are generally also critics, affirm that there is often a ready frequenting of prostitutes" as well as a high rate of "wife desertion." Foerster attributed all these failings to the Italians' general lack of civilization. "In many things, the Italian has the mind of a child," he wrote. "Sometimes what is impressive is a sheer lowness of standards, a state of contentment with those modes of living which civilized people, as much by metaphor as by knowledge, surely, call primitive." For instance, the Italian's "universal vice was his dirtiness; he was dirtier than the Negro." For all these reasons "it is no compliment to the Italian to deny him whiteness, yet that actually happens with considerable frequency."

The biological claims about the blackness of Italians, in particular southern Italians, were not without merit. Since much of southern Italy is closer to Africa than to Rome and for millennia experienced flows of population to and from the "dark continent," it "should be no surprise," as historian Thomas Guglielmo puts it, "that many social scientists at the time considered *meridionali* [southern Italians] part African—in many cases they were (and are)."

During the great wave of immigration, most of the Italians who relocated to the United States moved even closer to Africans. They settled in neighborhoods in New York, Chicago, and New Orleans that were populated by African Americans, and many shared tenement buildings, workplaces, and recreational facilities with blacks. This, as Guglielmo says, "often meant the most intimate of contact." According to historian Robert Brandfon, since Italian immigrants in New Orleans and neighboring plantations did not hesitate to take "nigger work," "the Italians assumed the status of Negroes. One blended into the other, and Southern thinking made no effort to distinguish between them." Another scholar found that at the height of Jim Crow segregation in the southern states, "Italians, not schooled in the racial prejudice of the South, associated freely with the blacks, going against the accepted social order." Italian American newspapers in Chicago reported casually of marriages or sexual liaisons between Italians and African Americans. Social worker Jane Addams, who led the movement to assimilate immigrants through settlement houses and who may have observed more immigrants at the time than anyone, reported that Italians in Chicago "held no particular animosity toward Negroes, for those in the neighborhood were mostly from South Italy and accustomed to the dark-skinned races." Moreover, Addams concluded that the "Mediterranean" immigrants were "less conscious than the Anglo-Saxon of color distinctions, perhaps because of their traditional familiarity with Carthage and Egypt."

After the infamous "Red Summer" of 1919, when dozens of African Americans were killed by whites in rioting on the streets of Chicago, the city's leading Italian newspaper, *L'Italia,* sympathized with the black victims of the riots and condemned not only the white perpetrators but also the failure of Americans to live up to their official creed of universal equality and justice for all. According to Guglielmo, a few Italians participated in the mayhem, but "the vast majority of Italians do not appear to have taken part in the Color Riot of 1919." The Chicago Commission on Race Relations reported that in the area known as "Little Sicily," the rioting was "not serious" and that "immediately after the fracas, the Negroes and Italians were again on good terms." Three years later, the commission reported, "friendly relations exist between the Sicilians, who predominate [on the Near North Side] and their Negro neighbors. Some Negroes live harmoniously in the same tenements with Sicilians. Their children play together, and some of the Negro children have learned Sicilian phrases so that they are able to deal with the Sicilian shopkeepers."

Many African Americans in Chicago shared this view. In 1925 the National Urban League, the leading black civil rights organization in the city, noted that "Negro families often reported their Italian neighbors as being very friendly, visiting and even rendering assistance in some few cases of sickness and poverty." A University of Chicago social scientist who studied the city's ethnic groups in the 1920s found that African Americans "are usually found in close associations with Jewish or Italian communities. These two groups are, on the whole, the most recent immigrant groups in the city, and they do not seem to have acquired the marked prejudice against the Negroes which characterizes many of the older immigrant and American groups in the city." And in 1930 a director of the West Side Community Center remarked that the two largest unassimilated immigrant groups were the most willing to cross the American color line: "the Jew and the Italian seem to be the only people who will live in the same house with the Negroes. I think that is why the Italians are coming into this neighborhood—they follow right on the heels of the Negroes." Similarly, in New York, historian Salvatore J. LaGumina found numerous instances of recreational cooperation between Italian Americans and African Americans during this period and that "African American and Italian American relations were generally devoid of violence and antagonism before the 1930s."

Guglielmo's analysis of voting patterns in Chicago during the 1920s shows that "many Italians willingly voted alongside African Americans throughout these years." Furthermore, "some Italians never seemed overly concerned about belonging to the same party [Republican] as African Americans, even when the Democrats furiously fought to paint that party as 'Negro' through and through. Indeed, Italian-language newspapers openly advertised the point that Italians and African Americans held simi-lar party affiliations, and on one occasion, *L'Italia* held up African Ameri-cans as a model for Italian political organization and behavior." When the national political parties were demographically realigned in the 1930s, both Italian Americans and African Americans moved overwhelmingly to the Democratic Party and remained solid voting blocs for the Democrats for the next thirty years. Indeed, one of the greatest champions of black civil rights during the 1930s and 1940s was Vito Marcantonio, the left-wing New York congressman whose East Harlem district contained large num-bers of both Italians and African Americans. Marcantonio sponsored sev-eral civil rights bills, led the congressional fight against the discriminatory poll tax in southern states, and worked to make lynching a federal crime.

Though Italian Americans often resented comparisons to "primitive" blacks, for many years they did not respond to racial insults by aligning themselves with whites. Guglielmo notes that in the first five decades of mass immigration, when Italians in the United States identified them-selves publicly, "they did so in any number of ways—depending on the time and context, as Italians, South and North Italians, Sicilians, Luccese, Americans, Italian Americans, workers, women and men, Catholics, and so forth—but hardly ever as whites."

Even in their religious practices, Italian immigrants blurred American racial lines. Italian immigrant churches across the United States displayed paintings and statues that depicted the Virgin Madonna and several saints as black. Until the 1940s, Catholics in Italian Harlem annually staged a procession of the feast of St. Benedict the Moor: the son of black slaves brought from Ethiopia to Sicily whose life in the sixteenth century was so pure that he was known in the church—and in twentieth-century Italian Harlem—as "the Holy Negro." According to historian Robert Orsi, "it was not uncommon to see San Fratellan women [immigrants from the Sicilian village of San Fratello] barefoot, and in prayer, honoring the black saint."

ITALIAN CONTRIBUTIONS TO BAD AMERICAN FUN

Americans who like to drink owe a debt to the "primitivism" of Italian Americans, who did more than any other group to subvert Prohibition and did so precisely because they were unwilling to live up to the stan-dards of "good" Americans. A writer for the *Independent and Weekly Re-*

view reported in 1922 on the widespread resistance—both passive and aggressive—by Italians to Prohibition:

> To try to explain the theory of prohibition to a group of Italian workmen is very much like trying to explain to you, the reader, that in Siberia people walk on their ears. In other words, it sounds interesting, but it does not "get over" . . . People of this type, who are otherwise law-abiding and patriotic and well-intentioned, protect bootleggers and otherwise violate the Volstead Act with the same faith in the justice of their actions that a group of Middle Western Americans would have in evading a law that prohibited them from planting corn . . .

Of course, Italian American gangsters were the frontline troops in the war against Prohibition. Quite possibly a majority of the bottles consumed illegally in the United States at one point passed through the hands of a member of an Italian crime syndicate. Even Italian women fought on the home front in the good war. According to Guglielmo, "many women" in the Italian community of Chicago "were actively involved in the illicit home production of alcohol, upon which the city's entire bootlegging industry depended."

What many observers called the Italian immigrants' resistance to "discipline and control" was heard in their musical tastes as well. "Musical as few other peoples have been, the Italians have never developed much interest in choir singing," said Robert F. Foerster. Edward Ross described Italian American singing and dancing as "joyous, shameless gregariousness." University of Chicago researcher Gertrude Sager toured the Near West Side and found that southern Italians "would rather sit and sing all day than do any work and improve their surroundings." Almost as confirmation of their blackness, an extraordinary number of Italian immigrants were drawn to African American music. A sociologist working for Columbia University in 1904 studied a section of the Lower East Side of New York City inhabited by unassimilated immigrants and African Americans, and found that the defining element of its culture was disreputable dancing:

> Of all the different amusements possible to these tenement dwellers (Italians, Jews, and blacks for the most part), there is none that

appeals to both sense and emotion so strongly as dancing, especially dancing conducted to the wild music of blaring cornet and
loud-beating drum, with rattling sounds from a guitar and man-
dolin.

The ethnomusicologist Julia Volpelletto Nakamura argues that in the
early nineteen hundreds, Italian Americans began to duplicate the "black
rhythms of African work songs and ceremonial dances."

At the turn of the century, New Orleans was the Italian capital of the
United States. More people of Italian and Sicilian descent lived in the Big
Easy than in any other American city. Even before they landed on shore,
the immigrants were feared for their rhythm. A reporter for the New Orleans *Daily Picayune* sounded the alarm in his report of an "immigrant-
freighted vessel" from Palermo approaching the city:

> as it came gradually closer and closer to the shore and recogni-
> tion was possible from ship to landing, and from terra firma to the
> floating mass, there arose a chorus of excited yells, queries, excla-
> mations, calls, in high-pitched vernacular, that was positively deaf-
> ening. And the gyrations of arms, heads and bodily contortions
> which, strangely, seem to be indispensable with the exchanges of
> greetings among some of the Latin races, were enough to cause
> any sedate and practical onlooker to fear that a limb or two of the
> most vehement of the excited performers would suddenly be sev-
> ered and fly off.

Most of these "surly Sicilians" headed to the "Little Palermo" section of
the French Quarter. A visitor to the neighborhood called it "an area of gin,
cheap wine, and dope," with "half-naked children," "old, dark, fat men and
women sleeping on their stoops," and "the odor of garlic and rotten fruit
everywhere." This was where many of the funkiest men in American history were born.

Most of the early jazz clubs in New Orleans were owned and operated by Sicilian immigrants—many of them members of the Mafia—and
because of the immigrants' affinity with African Americans and the gangsters' disregard for social mores, they all featured both black and Italian

musicians in direct violation of segregation laws. Clubs such as Matranga's, Joe Segretta's, Tonti's Social Club, and Lala's Big 25 hosted the social laboratory that created America's classical music. The creators of that music were descendants of slaves like Joe "King" Oliver, Ferdinand "Jelly Roll" Morton, and Louis Armstrong, and men who had been the half-naked children of the old, dark, fat Sicilians of Little Palermo.

Dominic James "Nick" LaRocca, a self-described "poor dago boy from the wrong side of the track," claimed with some justification that he was "the creator of jazz," though he began his musical career by imitating the African American brass bands he heard as a child in New Orleans. Whether or not LaRocca invented the music, his Original Dixieland Jass Band spread its shockingly primitive sexuality to a national audience. In 1916 the band, featuring LaRocca on cornet and his fellow Sicilian American Tony Sbarbaro on drums, traveled to Chicago, where it gained national attention for making white people dance. Antivice activists in the city hoped to drive the "blatant scream of the imported New Orleans Jass Band" back down the Mississippi River but soon found that thousands of the band's fans were intent on "making the night hideous." As LaRocca remembered:

> The impact we had on the people of Chicago was terrific. Women stood up on the dance floor, doing wild dances. They had to pull them off . . . The more they would carry on, the better we could play . . . The crowd would start yelling, 'Give us some more jass.' I can still see these women who would try and put on a show . . . raise their dresses above their knees and carry on, men shrieking and everybody having a good time.

The following year in New York, the band made the first commercially issued jazz recordings, including LaRocca's composition "Tiger Rag," which became one of the most widely covered jazz standards of the twentieth century. The band's records and its performances in large New York venues gave rhythm to millions of white people. *Variety* magazine described a January 1917 performance by the (slightly renamed) Original Dixieland Jazz Band at Reisenweber's restaurant on Columbus Circle as both the moment when "jazz made its official bow in New York" and as a revolutionary learning experience for the audience:

The band disgorged its voltaic music—a far cry from the formal waltzes, one-steps, tangos, and fox-trots to which New York had been accustomed. The music, with its piercing sonorities, its complicated rhythmic patterns, seemed like so much tonal confusion, so much riot of sound. Bewildered by this strange music, the clients at Reisenweber's made no move toward the dance floor, but listened half perplexed, half magnetized. The band played one number after another and still no move was made toward dancing. At last the manager interposed with a polite explanation: "Ladies and gentlemen, this is jazz. It is meant for dancing!" There was some good-humored laughter, and the ice was broken. A few venturesome partners started dancing; others followed. . . . There is one thing that is certain, and that is that the melodies as played by the jazz organization at Reisenweber's are quite conducive to making the dancers on the floor loosen up and go to the limit in their stepping . . . anyone who could move his feet rhythmically across a dance floor was capable of performing creditably. . . . Jazz had come to New York. For better or for worse, it had come to stay.

One member of the audience that night was another funky Italian named Jimmy Durante. Durante had traveled downtown to the show from 125th Street in Harlem, where he was the piano player at a saloon in the basement of a burlesque club. The Brooklyn-born son of immigrants had been so inspired by the music of Scott Joplin that he dropped out of school in the eighth grade to become a full-time ragtime pianist. Soon known as "Ragtime Jimmy," Durante developed an especially "hot" musical style conducive to dancing and was naturally drawn to LaRocca's sound. After seeing the Reisenweber performance, Durante was inspired to assemble his own dance music group, called the Original New Orleans Jazz Band, which featured, in one of the first acts of racial integration in American popular music, a young African American clarinetist named Achille Baquet. During the 1920s, Durante also collaborated with a black songwriter named Chris Smith on several songs that were recorded by the great blues singer Mamie Smith. Ragtime Jimmy later moved into comedy and acting in vaudeville, radio, Broadway theater, movies, and television, and became one of the most famous personalities in American show business.

Wingy Manone and Joe Marsala were two other sons of Italy who helped pioneer hot dance music. Raised in Little Palermo near Nick LaRocca's home, Manone recorded several important swing songs including "Tar Paper Stomp," "Nickel in the Slot," "Downright Disgusted Blues," and "Tailgate Ramble," and was known for his facility with comedic "jive" talk. Marsala, a Chicago native, hosted what are considered to be the first regular interracial jam sessions for jazz musicians and in 1936 became one of the first white bandleaders to hire an African American musician when he employed the trumpeter Henry "Red" Allen. According to jazz historian Leonard Feather, "Joe Marsala was responsible in his quiet and unpublicized way for more attempts at breaking down segregation in jazz than Benny Goodman."

But none of these Italian Americans achieved musical fame as spectacularly as did Louis Prima. As a boy, Prima listened to the music pouring out of clubs near his home and early on established himself, according to his biographer, as "Louis Armstrong's biggest fan in Little Palermo." Prima began to imitate the cornet playing, singing, dancing, stage presence, and general style of his hero. "Honestagod," Prima recalled, "from the first time I heard Armstrong, I felt such a close understanding of his phrasing, his handling of a tune, that it was impossible for me to do some tunes without being like him." While still in high school, Prima formed two bands that specialized in "jive street jazz, a sort of raw Dixieland emphasizing Mediterranean and African melody lines." Soon, the man who called himself "America's Hottest Trumpeteer" headed to New York to make it on the national stage. But he was turned away because he was black.

By the middle of the 1930s, Fifty-second Street had supplanted Harlem as the jazz capital of the world. "Swing Street," a two-block stretch between Fifth and Seventh avenues, contained all the most important jazz clubs of the time. In the 1930s, a few of the clubs were willing to hire African American performers, but most—fearing that white patrons weren't ready for black entertainment—maintained strictly segregated stages. Billie Holiday remembered that "white musicians were 'swinging' from one end of Fifty-second Street to the other, but there wasn't a black face in sight on the street except [pianist] Teddy Wilson and me." Guy Lombardo, one of the white bandleaders who helped popularize jazz on Fifty-second Street, recalled that for many years "nightclub owners simply refused to break the color line, fearing financial consequences."

Lombardo had discovered Louis Prima in 1934 on a trip to New Orleans during Mardi Gras and arranged for the young trumpeter to meet with Eddie Davis, the owner of Leon and Eddie's, one of the most popular clubs on Swing Street. "I felt I could talk him into hiring Prima," Lombardo remembered. But when the club owner saw Prima, he took Lombardo aside and whispered, "I can't use him." According to Lombardo, "Eddie Davis, on first seeing olive-skinned and swarthy Louis Prima and knowing that he came from New Orleans, had simply assumed that he was a black man. The shame is not so much that he lost a gold mine but that he capitulated to the prejudice of the times." Prima's penchant for "hepcat talk" and loose movements certainly didn't help. "For six months," he recalled, "I couldn't get a job no matter what Guy or anyone else tried to do for me." Finally Prima was able to convince the new owner of the Famous Door that he was white and was given a regular spot with his new band, His New Orleans Gang. Soon tickets to the Famous Door were the hottest in town, and Prima was the new, swarthy face of New York jazz.

Though his credentials were newly Caucasian, Prima's music was decidedly not. *Billboard* magazine reported that Prima's band played "the music of a hot Negro orchestra made more compact, . . . that may explain why people like it—because it is savagely rhythmic, almost primitive in its quality." According to his biographer Garry Boulard, the savagely rhythmic man from New Orleans "forever changed the way 52nd Street was viewed by jazz musicians. Before Prima, the street was a nice place to drink and listen to dance band music. After Prima, it was the only spot in town where hot, swinging jazz of a kind never heard before in New York could only be found." According to the doorman at the Famous Door, Prima drove female patrons to "practically have an orgasm" with the "hoarse, horny voice of his." Moreover, "word got out that he was rather well-fortified, and there were lots of tables just bulging with females." Boulard attributes Prima's success to his exuberant blackness: "When he danced and coiled his way across the bandstand, he presented to his New York audiences a spectacle usually confined to the more suggestive black performances of Harlem. In fact, Prima's rather remarkable character traits were reminiscent of the more successful black entertainers of the day." Even his sartorial style violated the norms of respectable whiteness. "Long before male entertainers broke away from the conventional dark business suit required for stage appearances, Prima was wearing lavender coats or yellow suits or even red, white, and blue-striped pants . . . Loud patterns, flashy colors, and the unconventional were the predominant themes in Louie's clothing." His clothes, voice, mannerisms, dancing, musical style, "raw" sexual appeal, and ability to sing "scat" as well as any musician in history "prompted observers to compare Prima with various black performers." During his stand at the Famous Door, Prima made the first recordings of his songs, including "House Rent Party Day," in which Prima sings and speaks lyrics in the drum rhythms and which was therefore, according to *The Vibe History of Hip-Hop*, the first recorded forerunner of rap.

White jazz fans were not the only admirers of Prima's style. By the end of the 1930s, his band had played in black theaters in New York, Baltimore, and Boston, and was the only white band during the swing era that performed repeatedly at the Howard Theatre in Washington, DC, "the largest colored theatre in the world," and the Apollo Theatre in Harlem. Sammy Davis Jr. made his first appearance at the Apollo with Prima's orchestra, and remembered a certain racial confusion: "Half the people who came to the theatre thought Prima was black anyway. Mixed. So he was a big favorite." The host at the Apollo, Ralph Cooper, attributed Prima's success with black audiences to the fact that "his style merged with the Apollo. Being from New Orleans, and the Louie Armstrong–Joe Oliver background, I suppose that was one of the reasons his music appealed to us."

FROM *NERO* TO *BIANCO*

Despite his popularity, by the height of his career, Louis Prima was part of a dying breed.

In 1906 an Italian government official named Luigi Villari came to Louisiana to investigate alleged mistreatment of Sicilian agricultural workers. He found that most plantation owners considered the Italian immigrant to be "a white-skinned Negro" and treated him accordingly. Villari regretfully concluded that the "only way an Italian can emancipate himself from this inferior state is to abandon all sense of national pride and to identify completely with the Americans." Many Italian American leaders learned of Villari's dictum and were also aware that several influential American thinkers doubted the inherent ability of Italians to become "good" Americans. They knew that a growing number of powerful Americans agreed with the assessment of Edward Ross, the president of the American

Sociological Association, who wrote in 1914 of why Italians were among the least likely to assimilate:

> As grinding rusty iron reveals the bright metal, so American competition brings to light the race stuff in poverty-crushed immigrants. But not all this stuff is of value in a democracy like ours. Only a people endowed with a steady attention, a slow-fuse temper, and a persistent will can organize itself for success in the international rivalries to come.

Wise to the rules of America, Italian American leaders taught their people to be slow and steady.

This assimilationist campaign gained desperate urgency in the early 1920s, when Congress began curbing the immigration of "undesirable" groups. The 1921 Emergency Quota Act cut the flow of people from Italy and other southern European countries by roughly 75 percent. A year later, David Starr Jordan, the president of Stanford University, complained that the new law did not go far enough. Jordan called on Congress to completely bar immigration by southern Italians, who were "biologically incapable of rising either now or through their descendants above the mentality of a 12-year-old child." In 1923, in an article titled "Keep America 'White'!," the influential *Current Opinion* magazine demanded the tightening of quotas on immigration from southern and eastern Europe: "If the tall, big-boned, blue-eyed, old-fashioned 'white' American is not to be bred out entirely by little dark peoples, Uncle Sam must not simply continue the temporary quota law in operation, but must make its provisions much more stringent." The following year, in one of its many articles calling for an end to Italian immigration, the *Saturday Evening Post* argued that because southern Italians were part African, they were "incapable of self-government and totally devoid of initiative and creative ability." The *Post* claimed that "unrestricted immigration [into southern Italy] made a mongrel race of the south Italians" and that "unrestricted immigration [into the U.S.] will inevitably and absolutely do the same thing to Americans."

Amid the anti-Italian noise, the Order of the Sons of Italy in America sent a letter to Representative Albert Johnson, chairman of the House Committee on Immigration and a leading opponent of Italian immigration, arguing that Italians possessed a "physical vigor and strong mentality," were "sober, thrifty and industrious," and constituted "an unimpeachable racial factor in the formation of the American race of the future." Nonetheless, in 1924 Congress passed the National Origins Act, which further curbed immigration by southern and eastern Europeans and reduced the flow of Italians to four thousand annually, a reduction of 98 percent from its peak at the beginning of the century.

Italian American representatives continued to argue that they were inherently American, as when Chicago's *L'Italia* newspaper declared in 1928 that "the 200,000 Italians of Chicago represent an honest and laborious community." In the 1930s, when the Depression made competition over jobs and housing a life-and-death contest, many Italian Americans began to heed the calls to distance themselves from "bad" Americans. Newspapers reported a number of incidents of Italians angrily protesting or violently confronting the influx of African Americans into their neighborhoods. But the efforts to distance themselves from blacks did not cohere into a new Italian American racial identity and culture until the 1940s. As Thomas Guglielmo puts it, "Indeed, not until World War II did many Italians identify openly and mobilize politically as white." On the Near North Side, where large populations of Italians and African Americans lived in close proximity, "neighborhood hostility between Italians and African Americans was rare in the 1920s and 1930s." But in the 1940s, Italians waged several battles against black residents in their neighborhoods.

Father Luigi Giambastiani of St. Philip Benizi Church, the largest Sicilian church in Chicago, led a movement to keep Italians and blacks segregated in new public-housing projects. According to Guglielmo, "prior to the 1940s in his many public statements and essays in defense of Italians," Giambastiani "mentioned whites rarely," "defended Italians by highlighting their virtues as Italians, not as whites," and "even in his neighborhood battles against incoming African Americans in the mid-1930s, he shied away from explicit talk about whiteness." By the 1940s, however, "Giambastiani's language had changed dramatically, as Italians became 'whites' and race became color." In a 1942 letter written on behalf of his constituency to the Chicago Housing Authority, Giambastiani explained that "the cohabitation or quasi-cohabitation of Negro and White hurts the feelings and traditions of the White people of this community." Even more significantly, he declared a fundamental biological difference between his people and black people: "You know neither you, nor I, would cherish the idea of living next door to a neighbor from whom nature, tradition and culture have segregated us. By this cohabitation, the Negroes might be uplifted, but the Whites, by the very laws of environment feel that they will be lowered." After years of speaking only for "Italians" and "Sicilians," Giambastiani now represented "the white people of St. Philip" against "the newly come Negroes." At the same time, a director of the Cabrini public-housing project reported being told "repeatedly" by Italian prospective residents "that families would move in if the Negroes were segregated, but they would not if they are not segregated."

A University of Chicago researcher found during the 1940s that attempts by blacks to move into the Italian neighborhood on the Near West Side had "been blocked by the persistence and resistance of the Italian community," and that "the attempts of Negroes to use public facilities [there] . . . still meet with violence." In 1941 a group of young Italian men calling itself the Black Hand Gang began beating and shooting African Americans in the neighborhood, and two years later a riot involving several hundred blacks and Italians erupted after shots were fired into an African American's apartment. In 1943 local Italians organized a petition drive to persuade city officials and a property owners' association to buy all the available homes in the area to preempt blacks attempting to buy or rent them. During this time, arsonists set fire to several black homes, and Italian shop owners on the Near West Side began refusing to serve African American customers.

The rejection of blacks and the embrace of whiteness took on intellectual and political legitimacy during the war. Italian American newspapers and newspapers published by labor unions with large Italian memberships reproduced the basic points in Ruth Benedict's best-selling 1943 book *The Races of Mankind,* which included, as one newspaper put it, the point that "the three primary races of the world are: the Caucasoid, the Mongoloid, and the Negroid. The Aryans, the Jews, the Italians are not races." During the war, the Chicago city government regularly invited Italian Americans to participate in the annual "I Am an American Day" celebrations at Soldier Field, and the city's newspapers hailed "Chicago's Army of Italian Folk" who "have been assimilated and Americanized to a large degree" and were going all "out to win the war." In several major cities, the Order of the Sons of Italy in America launched drives to encourage Italian Americans to purchase war bonds, even though the funds for those bonds went partly toward defeating Italy. In the early 1940s, the U.S. naturalization application no longer required Italians to identify as a race separate from other whites. According to Guglielmo, in the first five decades of mass immigration, "Italians were often listed as southern or northern Italian for race and white for color. By the beginning of World War II, however, Italians, as well as many other groups like Armenians, Yugoslavians, Greeks, English, Syrians, and Mexicans, began offering the same answer for the race and color questions: white." Perhaps the most powerful evidence of the success of the campaign to assimilate Italians into American culture was the fact that, unlike Japanese Americans, no Italians Americans born in the United States were interned as threats to national security during World War II, even though most Italian American newspapers had supported the rise of Benito Mussolini's Fascist regime.

Relations between blacks and Italians did not improve after the war. In 1947 several hundred students at Chicago's Wells High School, led by three Italian youths, walked out of classes to protest the district's allowing "so many Negroes in our school." One month after the school strike, ten African Americans died in a Near West Side apartment building set ablaze by arsonists. And in 1951 in nearby Cicero, the National Guard was called in and martial law declared when arson and rioting greeted a black family who had moved into an all-white apartment building. Reports that most of the rioters were Italian Americans were affirmed by the *Baltimore Afro-American*, one of the leading national black newspapers, which identified them as "8,000 frenzied, blood-thirsty descendants of immigrants from the Mediterranean area of Europe." As Guglielmo concludes, "Whiteness was becoming, for the first time, a central part of Italians' public self-understanding."

Like their Irish predecessors, Italian Americans seized on the most militant forms of public service as a means to assimilate. Italian American newspapers encouraged their male readers to enlist in the armed forces and trumpeted the sacrifice and valor of the sons of Italy in the service of Uncle Sam. During the 1940s, Italian Americans also began to move in large numbers into municipal police forces—in many cases supplanting Irish Americans as the dominant ethnic group in law enforcement.

Frank Rizzo was one of many Italian Americans who used a law enforcement career to establish himself as both a good American and as an enemy of renegades. The son of immigrants, Rizzo joined the Philadelphia police force in 1943 and was assigned to the predominantly African American community of West Philadelphia. He rose through the ranks by raiding underground speakeasies and gambling parlors that were owned and patronized by blacks. In the 1960s, Rizzo, as deputy police commissioner and then chief of police, ordered what he called "my men, my army" to arrest nearly every civil rights and black power activist who demonstrated in the city, including Malcolm X, members of the Student Nonviolent Coordinating Committee, and a group of black teenagers who held a rally demanding more courses on African American history in the city's public schools. In 1970 Rizzo was applauded by many of Philadelphia's Italian Americans when his officers raided the local headquarters of the Black Panther Party, hauled six members into the street, and forced them to strip naked in front of a news photographer. "Imagine the big Black Panthers with their pants down," he said. Rizzo also cracked down on bad whites. He closed down beatnik coffeehouses and gay bars and banned hippies from the city.

In 1971, 86 percent of Philadelphia's Italian Americans voted for Rizzo in the mayoral election, helping to make him the first Italian American to hold the city's top office. As mayor, Rizzo opposed public housing in white neighborhoods, arguing that people there "did not want black people moving in with them." The political scientists Jack Citrin, Donald Philip Green, and David Sears have concluded that Rizzo transcended his Italian identity by becoming "an established symbol of hostility to blacks." He also, as historian Stefano Luconi puts it, helped Italian Americans replace "their ethnic sense of affiliation based on national ancestry" with a new "racial identity" as white.

NIGGAZ WITH SHORT MEMORIES

During the rise of Italian Americans into American respectability, Louis Prima and the hepcats of his generation were replaced by men who did not dance.

Like many Italians (and Irish before them), Frank Sinatra's parents moved from disrepute to citizenship through government work. In the 1910s and 1920s, Marty Sinatra worked as a prizefighter and bootlegger and operated a speakeasy with his wife, Dolly, who supplemented the family's income by performing illegal abortions. But Dolly worked her way up the ranks of the local Democratic Party, becoming leader of the Third Ward in

Hoboken, New Jersey, and through her political connections secured a job for Marty as one of Hoboken's first Italian American firefighters. Though they passed on to their son a racial liberalism that was becoming increasingly rare among Italian Americans, Frank Sinatra's racial identification was white from the beginning.

Whereas Louis Prima chose the black street musicians of New Orleans as his role models, Sinatra idolized the symbols of Caucasian performance of his day: the Protestant Anglo-Saxons Bing Crosby, a descendant of *Mayflower* pilgrims who grew up in Washington State, and Rudy Vallee, native of Maine and Yale graduate whose first band was called "the Connecticut Yankees." Crosby and Vallee popularized a new style of singing called "crooning," which employed the tones of black jazz singers but replaced the bodily sexuality of jazz with a romantic and spiritual eroticism. Both were known for wearing conservative suits, standing stock-still on stage, and for singing ballads instead of dance music. *Vanity Fair* magazine praised Vallee in 1929 for having "none of the dash or rhythm of the usual jazz player," while scholars have characterized Crosby's style as a "disembodied voice" and his personality as exuding "the traditional values associated with white Protestant hegemony: a good work ethic, morality, family, and small-town living." When a teenaged Frank Sinatra saw Crosby perform in New Jersey, he decided to "do that." The man who more than anyone reinvented the image of Italian Americans saw Bing Crosby as "the father of my career, the idol of my youth." The only problem this caused for Sinatra was when Hollywood executives asked him to perform a few dance numbers in movies. "I had never danced," remembered Sinatra. "I didn't know how to dance."

Along with Sinatra, an entire generation of tuxedo-clad, slow-moving Italian American crooners followed Crosby to stardom. Ruggiero Eugenio di Rodolpho Colombo (Russ Columbo), Pierino Como (Perry Como), Francesco Paolo LoVecchio (Frankie Laine), Dino Crocetti (Dean Martin), Anthony Dominick Benedetto (Tony Bennett), Vito Rocco Farinola (Vic Damone), Gennaro Luigi Vitaliano (Jerry Vale), and Francis Avallone (Frankie Avalon) all credited "der Bingle" of Spokane, Washington, as their primary influence.

This new generation of Italian American entertainers shared Sinatra's view of the new dance music that emerged in the 1950s. "Rock-and-roll is the most brutal, ugly, desperate, vicious form of expression it has been my misfortune to hear," Sinatra told Congress in 1958. "Rock-and-roll smells phony and false. It is sung, played, and written for the most part by cretin-ous goons, and by means of its almost imbecilic reiteration, and sly, lewd—in plain fact, dirty—lyrics . . . it manages to be the martial music of every sideburned delinquent on the face of the earth."

In response to the raw, driving sexuality of black-influenced rock, young Italian American men in New York and Philadelphia did to the new music what Sinatra and his generation had done to jazz. A style combining smooth vocal harmonies, romantic lyrics, and a stationary stage presence, doo-wop was invented in the 1940s by black youth on street corners, but it shot to the top of the pop charts in the late 1950s when Italian Americans adopted it as their own—just as most African American performers moved toward "soul music." From 1958, when Dion (DiMucci) and the Belmonts placed several songs on the pop charts, until the "British Invasion" of 1964, Italian American doo-wop groups dominated American popular music. All wearing conservative suits and exuding a benign romanticism, the Ca-pris, the Elegants, the Mystics, the Duprees, the Del-Satins, the Four Jays, the Essentials, Randy and the Rainbows, and Vito & the Salutations de-clared the arrival of Italians into American civilization.

During the rise of doo-wop and Frank Rizzo, Malcolm X mocked the newly white Italians. "No Italian will ever jump up in my face and start putting bad mouth on me," he said, "because I know his history. I tell him when you're talking about me you're talking about your pappy, your fa-ther. He knows his history. He knows how he got that color." Though fewer and fewer Italian Americans know the history of which Malcolm X spoke, some have reenacted it.

As Louis Prima faded as the symbol of Italian America, he nonetheless remained devoted to its primitive past. In 1947 he scored one of his last hits, "Civilization (Bongo, Bongo, Bongo)," a recording that might have served as the renegade immigrant's anthem. Singing "I don't wanna leave the Congo" and "I'm so happy in the jungle," Prima mocks the members of civilization who "hurry like savages to get aboard an iron train." When "they've got two weeks vacation, they hurry to vacation ground. They swim and they fish, ha, that's what I do all year round."

In the early 1950s, Prima joined with Sam Butera, another black Ital-ian from New Orleans, and Butera's band the Witnesses, and began playing a harder, wilder version of his music. Music critic Art Fein wrote thirty years later, "The music they were playing, and that Prima sensed was vital and even visionary, then had no name. It's taken historians thirty years to pinpoint it for what it always was—rock-and-roll." Prima further bucked the trend of Italian Americans toward civilization by proclaiming his admiration for the new jungle music. "There's nothing, but nothing, wrong with rock-and-roll," he said. "It's got that beat, and as long as the kids keep listening to it, they'll keep out of trouble—don't sell those kids short— they've got an instinct for the kind of music that's fun to listen to and dance to." Prima chided his generation for attacking rock-and-roll and thereby renouncing its primitive past. "I don't know what their parents are complaining about," he said. "They used to dance the black bottom—and that was downright vulgar."

In 1967, near the end of his career, Prima renewed his fame by performing a role in a film that was perfectly suited for him: as an orangutan. The character of King Louie in Disney's animated Oscar nominee *The Jungle Book* is the leader of the jungle apes and the host of a perpetual jazz party. In the film's most memorable scene, he sings, "I'm the king of the swingers, the jungle VIP," while dancing with what Prima's biographer calls "hip abandon." Prima admired his character: "This cat really rocks the jungle," he said. "In fact, the whole monkey tribe in the picture really swings. And they look a lot like me and Sam Butera and the Witnesses."

In the 1970s, Italian Americans appeared for a time to have regained their rhythm. Disco was incubated in underground parties in New York City that were attended largely by African Americans but which were run by Italian Americans. According to music historian Peter Shapiro, "Italian Americans mostly from Brooklyn largely created disco from scratch." Most of the DJs who developed the music in the early 1970s were of Italian extraction: Francis Grasso, David Mancuso, Nicky Siano, Michael Cappello, Steve D'Aquisto, Tom Savarese, Bobby "DJ" Guttadaro, Frankie Strivelli, and Richard Pampianelli. By the middle of the decade, disco dancing spread to nightclubs in Italian American neighborhoods, from where it moved into mainstream American culture. The 1977 film *Saturday Night Fever* tells the story of the young Italian Americans who ruled the dance floor at 2001 Odyssey in the Bay Ridge section of Brooklyn, the most famous early disco club in the city. In the first scene at the club, Tony Manero and his four buddies seem to be aware that they are living on a racial edge. One of them admires his own hair and new clothes and asks, "Looking sharp, huh?" to which another replies, "Any sharper, and you'd be a nigger."

Other, more recent Italian Americans have made careers out of crossing the racial and dancing divides. Scott Ialacci, better known as DJ Skribble, and James D'Agostino, who operates as DJ Green Lantern, are two of the most successful hip-hop producers in the early twenty-first century. And, of course, Madonna Louise Ciccone has made more money by singing and dancing to black-influenced music than any other American in history.

Despite the transgressions of these renegades, official Italian America remains willfully ignorant of its people's history. In 2002 Chuck Nice, an African American deejay at the hip-hop radio station WAXQ-FM in New York City, commented on air that "Italians are niggaz with short memories." The Order of the Sons of Italy in America, which eighty years earlier had insisted to Congress that Italians were inherently white, promptly announced that they were "puzzled by the statement" and demanded an apology from the station.

Of course, given the renegade history of Italian Americans, Chuck Nice's statement is hardly puzzling. But more importantly, let us use that history, as well as the histories of all the "primitive" and "black" European immigrants who contributed so much to our freedoms and pleasures, to turn what the Sons of Italy viewed as an insult into a compliment.

Part Three

FIGHTING
FOR BAD FREEDOM

★ 9 ★

SHOPPING:
THE REAL AMERICAN REVOLUTION

If you were a typical American living in the early part of the nineteenth century, you had to plant, tend, harvest, slaughter, and process your own food. You had to make your own clothing, and all of it had to be strictly utilitarian: no decorations, unnecessary colors, or "style." You worked from before dawn until late at night. Your only source of entertainment was books, and most that were available were moral parables. You spent your entire life within a fifty-mile radius of your home. You believed that leisure was bad. There was no weekend.

By the end of the nineteenth century, you as a typical American bought most of your clothing from stores. You owned clothes whose sole function was to make you attractive. You ate food that had come from all over the country. You drank cold beer and ate ice cream. If you lived in a city, you went shopping at Montgomery Ward, Sears, Roebuck, Macy's, Abraham & Straus, Jordan Marsh, Filene's, or Wanamaker's. If you lived in the country, you shopped from the same stores by mail order. You read dime novels whose sole purpose was to provide you with fun. If you lived in a city, you went to amusement parks, movie theaters, and vaudeville shows. You went dancing. You rode on trains. You worked fewer hours than your parents and many fewer hours than your grandparents. You believed that leisure was good.

Who was responsible for this revolution in everyday American life? Scholars have attributed it to the vast natural resources of the North American land mass; the lack of trade barriers among the states; the building of mass, integrated industries such as railroads, steel, oil, wheat, lumber, and meat; the early development of the modern corporation in the United

States; technological advances in production such as rubber vulcanization, the sewing machine, refrigeration, the Bessemer and open-hearth steel processes, the assembly line, and electric light and power; as well as the assistance of the federal government to economic development in the form of protective incorporation laws, land grants, the authorization of stocks and the backing of bonds, protective tariffs to shield American companies from foreign competition, and armed intervention against labor strikes.

And yet not a single consumer good would have been produced if people did not want them or did not allow themselves to seek them. Without desire there would have been no demand. Without demand there would have been no production. What was necessary for the consumer revolution to take place was a radical change in the way Americans thought about desire, pleasure, leisure, and spending. Without renegades, we'd all still be farmers.

THE "AMUSEMENT PROBLEM"

Looking back from the twenty-first century, it may be hard to imagine that most Americans in the nineteenth century believed that materialism was evil, thrift was virtuous, and the pursuit of pleasure was dangerous at best. But American politicians, clergy, intellectuals, business leaders, and labor leaders were virtually unanimous in condemning "indulgence." Francis Wayland, a prominent theologian, antislavery activist, and longtime president of Brown University in the decades before the Civil War, spoke for many of the cloth when he warned that "thoughtless caprice," "sensual self-indulgence," and "reckless expense" were not only sinful but also socially ruinous. "We consume values in the lower gratifications of sense when we expend money for shows, for mere delicacies of the table, and for any thing which the only result is, the gratification of a physical appetite." The first markets for consumer goods were merely "new avenues to temptation" that undermined the virtue on which the republic depended. To Wayland, "objects which yield no other utility than the mere gratification of the senses, or, which are rendered necessary by command of fashion, or the love of ostentation" were worthless. Henry Ward Beecher, another major religious thinker and social reformer, argued in his widely read *Lectures to Young Men* (1848) that "satisfaction is not the product of excess, or of indolence, or of riches; but of industry, temperance, and usefulness." Secular thinkers were no less hostile to the buying of things for pleasure. The great writer Henry David Thoreau represented an entire generation of American intellectuals who denounced "games and amusements" and embraced "Spartan simplicity" as the only condition for happiness. These and other spokesmen for the American way of life agreed that the people should resist food that exceeded what one needed to function, clothing that was fashionable not functional, homes that provided more than just adequate shelter, and goods that were mere playthings.

The first study of the spending habits of ordinary Americans, authored in 1875 by Carroll D. Wright for the Massachusetts Bureau of Statistics of Labor, found an increasing and alarming amount of purely pleasurable items in American homes. Most troubling was the quantity of alcohol being consumed, its effects on general spending habits, and the resulting aggressiveness of workers for higher wages. Wright argued that temperance "induces frugal habits, and frugal habits prevent strikes." What was needed was the creation of the "sober, industrious, and thrifty" worker who rejected "riotous living," "the display of enervating luxury," and "the insane attempt to keep up appearances which are not legitimate."

Even the wealthy attacked spending. Andrew Carnegie amassed one of the largest fortunes in history but renounced the pleasures it could bring. Carnegie's family emigrated from Scotland and settled in Pittsburgh in 1848, when he was thirteen. To help support the family, young Andrew worked as a steam engine tender, a messenger, and a telegraph operator. A Pennsylvania Railroad official noticed his talent and drive and offered him a job with the railroad. Carnegie quickly worked his way up the company hierarchy, earning enough money to invest in his own businesses. After the Civil War, he decided that steel was the future of America, and in 1873 he invested all of his assets into developing the first steel mills in the United States. Over the next twenty years, as the chief of the global steel industry, Carnegie made himself into one of the wealthiest men in the world. And yet he worked nearly every day of the year, normally beginning before first light and finishing near midnight, and rarely indulged in luxury. By the end of his life, he had given away almost all of his fortune to charities.

In 1889 Carnegie wrote an article that supported the system of industrial capitalism but attacked the pleasures it produced. "The Gospel of

Wealth" preached a fundamental tenet of what some have called "bourgeois" culture: that one must accumulate wealth but not enjoy it. The only "proper use" of one's money was "for public ends" that "would work good to the community." Rather than spend money for his own pleasure, the rich man should "attend to the administration of wealth during his life, which is the end that society should always have in view, as being that by far most fruitful for the people." To ensure that "the selfish millionaire's unworthy life" would be redeemed, Carnegie proposed massive estate taxes on the wealthy so that they would be forced to "have enormous sums paid over to the state from their fortunes." Rich men should be self-sacrificing patriarchs:

> This, then, is held to be the duty of the man of wealth: first, to set an example of modest, unostentatious living, shunning display or extravagance; to provide moderately for the legitimate wants of those dependent upon him; and after doing so to consider all surplus revenues which come to him simply as trust funds which he is called upon to administer, and strictly bound as a matter of duty to administer in the manner which, in his judgment, is best calculated to produce the most beneficial results for the community—the man of wealth thus becoming the mere agent and trustee for his poorer brethren, bringing to their service his superior wisdom, experience, and ability to administer, doing for them better than they would or could do for themselves . . .

The only man wealthier than Carnegie was John D. Rockefeller, the "titan" who during his career from 1870 to 1897 as head of Standard Oil Company owned most of the world's petroleum supply. Rockefeller never smoked, drank, or traveled for pleasure. He neither attended nor gave parties. He taught his four children to abstain from candy, forced them to share a single bicycle, and dressed them in hand-me-downs. His son, John Jr., was the youngest and the only boy, and so until the age of eight he wore only dresses. Rockefeller's biographer Ron Chernow calls him "a prisoner to the Protestant work ethic" who "attacked recreational interests with the same intensity that he had brought to business," "engaged in strenuous rituals of austerity," and "grimly sought to simplify his life and reduce his wants." Curious that men with such great wealth refused to enjoy it, the German social scientist Max Weber concluded that they became capitalists not so that they could enrich themselves, but because they felt a responsibility to manage society—to be superpatriarchs. To them, this was a religious "calling" that, if fulfilled, would grant them redemption and grace.

Ordinary Americans who preferred leisure over work had no spokesmen. All the major American labor organizations in the nineteenth and early twentieth centuries were as deeply committed to the work ethic as were the first Puritan settlers. In 1866 William H. Sylvis founded the National Labor Union, the first federation of trade unions in the United States, not only to protect the economic interests of its members but also to "elevate the moral, social, and intellectual condition" of all workers. This meant, above all, instructing them that to labor was to "carry out God's wise purposes." The Knights of Labor replaced the National Labor Union as the major national labor organization in the 1870s and 1880s but carried forward the commitment to work over leisure. In 1879, when Terrence Powderly, a Pennsylvania machinist, took over the Knights, he opened its ranks to women, blacks, immigrants, and unskilled workers. This was a radical step in a period when most craft unions would admit none of them. But Powderly's intention was to spread a conservative message to the uninitiated. All new members of the organization were required to recite a "Ritual of Initiation" that declared, "In the beginning, God ordained that man should labor, not as a curse, but as a blessing." The purpose of the organization was "to glorify God in [labor's] exercise." Powderly and the Knights advocated reducing the number of labor hours but only because they believed excessive work undermined the work ethic—men became machines unable to appreciate the glory of labor.

The American Federation of Labor, which dominated the labor movement from its founding in 1886 to the 1930s, was no less committed to the work ethic. The AFL's longtime president, Samuel Gompers, derided "unmanly, dishonorable, puerile" avoidance of work. Like the Knights, the AFL campaigned for shorter hours not to increase the leisure and freedom of workers but to keep them from hating work. Even radicals loved work and hated leisure. Eugene Debs, the principal leader of the Socialist Party at the turn of the century, declared it his mission to "plant benevolence in the heart of stone, instill the love of sobriety into the putrid mind of debauchery, and create industry out of idleness."

This ascetic ideal was one of the criteria of respectability in nineteenth-century America. Indulgence in luxury was seen by both the wealthy and large portions of the working class as un-American.

The generation of "progressive" intellectuals—the founders of what is now called liberalism—differed with business, religious, and labor leaders on many issues but shared the belief in the evils of leisure and consumption. Writing at the turn of the twentieth century, during the first great thrust of industrial production, these thinkers hoped to find a way to keep a society newly awash in pleasure from sinking into chaos. They faced what the historian Daniel Horowitz calls "the dilemma materialism posed to the values of hard work, saving, and self-discipline." Simon Patten, one of the most influential economists of the early twentieth century, argued for an increase in the material wealth of ordinary Americans, but only so that they would not seek solace from their poverty by succumbing to "debasing appeals to pent-up passions." With stomachs full and heads adequately instructed, workers would be able to resist the temptations of the nickelodeon, the burlesque show, and the amusement park. "Raised above grinding necessity," as Horowitz describes Patten's argument, "immigrants and the poor would become willing puritans." Thorstein Veblen produced the most influential progressive critique of consumption in a series of books and articles, most notably the scholarly classic *The Theory of the Leisure Class* (1899). Like Patten, Veblen feared that the impoverishment of workers was leading them to lives of undisciplined pleasure-seeking. He found "a substantial ground of truth in the indictment" of working-class Americans as "improvident and apparently incompetent to take care of the pecuniary details of their own life." The miserable conditions of workers produced a "growing lack of deference of and affection for" the "conventional features of social structure." Untrained in the art of restraint, when workers did gain more than subsistence wages, they spent it on useless fun. What others had "euphemistically spoken of as a rising standard of living," Veblen saw as simply the "cumulative growth of wasteful expenditures."

A host of progressive studies of working-class spending habits aimed to determine the exact degree of material wealth—and not one dollar more—that would provide "the power to ensure one's primary faculties, supply one's essential needs, and develop one's personality." The conclusion of most of these studies was that to avoid socially harmful "excesses," the "minimum amount of goods and opportunities" should also be the maximum amount. Typical was Robert Chapin's *The Standard of Living Among Workingmen's Families in New York City* (1909), which labeled "visits to cafes, ale houses," tobacco, gambling and lotteries, "ornaments (personal)," "theater and public festivities," and even candy, soda water, and ice cream for children as "luxuries" and "extravagances." Progressive investigators such as Mary Kingsbury Simkhovitch called for a reduction in working hours so that workers would have *less* fun, not more. "The hotter the pace at which work is set, the more recreation will sink to the sensual and the exciting," she concluded.

> The longer and the intenser the hours of labour, the more debasing the forms of recreation become . . . the saloon will exist as long as there is overwork. . . . Dancing is another of the pleasures of the senses, innocent and delightful in itself but often debased to the most vicious uses, and, when accompanied by drinking, as is often the case with the public dance halls, is frequently provocative of sensuality. Dancing often is loved as drink is loved. It is the element of abandon, of relief from the absolute deadness that comes from overwork that can find pleasure only in the most highly stimulating forms of amusement.

According to the progressive economist Frank Streightoff, low wages, irregular employment, and "the physical and nervous strain of his work" debauched the working man and caused him to spend his money wildly:

> In his intellectual and moral life the workman is by no means all that could be desired. He thinks and talks impurely, his home life is largely a matter of convenience, there is often little or no spiritual comradeship between husband and wife. The saloon exacts a terrible tribute, both directly in money, and indirectly in physical and mental suffering. Amusement tends strongly to the sensual, dancing leads frequently to gross immorality . . .

The solution to what Streightoff called "the amusement problem" was "social and literary functions similar to those so much enjoyed in the settlements, and by instruction public lectures upon subjects of real educational value." Similarly, in her study of working women in Boston, Louise Marion

Bosworth found spending on "innumerable forms of amusement and in-dulgence" and blamed it on overwork. "Long hours and low wages do not supply the surplus vitality demanded for the proper enjoyment of these evening privileges" such as lectures, classical music concerts, and classes at settlement houses, where immigrants were taught to be American. "If the wages were sufficient to provide nourishing food and generally comfort-able living conditions, and if the working day were short enough to allow more time for recuperation, the working girl might make good use of these chances for intellectual, physical, and social development." As Horowitz puts it, "In numerous unexamined ways, the budget studies" undertaken by progressives "attacked immigrant and working-class culture, hoping to replace it with the bourgeois emphasis on self-help and personal disci-pline."

Opposition to shopping grew especially severe during World War I, when bourgeois disgust over the new working-class culture took the form of well-organized campaigns against drinking, prostitution, and venereal disease, and in the moral condemnation of working-class spending hab-its. Shortly after the United States entered the war in 1917, Senator Porter McCumber issued a warning about the "moral dangers resulting from our orgy of opulence." He said that "this revelry in extravagant habits, this un-quenchable demand for amusements, for continuous mental intoxicants" threatened to bring the nation to its knees. A number of government of-ficials and intellectuals saw the war as an opportunity for America to re-deem itself by renouncing its desire for more stuff. When the Bureau of Labor Statistics and the National War Labor Board reported in 1918 that on average, "wage earners and the low or medium salaried families" had more than doubled the percentage of their spending on items other than food, shelter, and clothing since 1875, government policymakers and intel-lectuals set out to establish a "minimum comfort" budget for working-class families that would be frugal and thus patriotic. Leading progressive econ-omist Stuart Chase, who in 1917 joined the Federal Trade Commission and publicized an ascetic "War Budget for the Household," wrote that it was "not only a personal necessity but a patriotic duty to eliminate waste and extravagance" by cutting back on luxuries and that to be a good American was to eliminate spending on "baubles, surfeits, and poisons that serve no rational human need, and only succeed in polluting and perverting our national life and character." Chase hoped that Americans would embrace a new frugality "in peace no less than in war."

THE HIGHEST OF HEELS

Had the ascetic ideals of nineteenth-century America remained dominant, there would be no movie theaters, no shopping, and no weekend. But those ideals were eroded by a generation of young Americans who simply chose to live differently. This is the story of a revolution, but a revolution without leaders or manifestoes or militias. It was driven by hundreds of thousands of obscure working-class women—women such as the Jewish garment workers on the Lower East Side who went uptown to shop for flowered hats and to Coney Island to shop for boys; packinghouse workers from the Polish section of Milwaukee Avenue in Chicago who went to the movies several times per week; and Italian sausage makers in South Philadelphia who shopped at Wanamaker's "every chance we got."

Agnes M. was one such revolutionary. Born in 1883 in Treves, a German city on the border with France, Agnes was raised by nuns at a Catholic reform school, where she lived for most of her childhood, and by a mother who was "very stern" and "was almost a stranger to me." In a memoir she wrote for a magazine in 1903, Agnes told of how at the age of fifteen she began work as an unpaid apprentice for a milliner, laboring from eight o'clock in the morning until six o'clock and sometimes as late as nine o'clock in the evening. Despite a life filled with restraints, Agnes was "used to plenty of play." She flirted with boys, danced, "had a good voice for singing," and had "plenty to say for myself." Though the boys and girls at her school were kept separate, she "found means of conversing" and fell in love with "a tall, slim, thoughtful, dark-haired boy named Fritz." The couple carried out their illicit relationship through the bars of the fence that divided the playground. When they were caught laughing at one of the nuns, Agnes was whipped on the hands with a rod.

While working for the milliner, she began to think of leaving her life: "I grew more and more tired of all work and no play, and more and more anxious to go to America." Her mother, who "could not understand that I wanted amusement," finally surrendered to her wish for freedom and sent her to live with her sister in New York City. For the first time, Agnes made her own money and could spend it as she pleased. "I wanted more plea-sure," she remembered. She took a job as a baby nurse for a wealthy family, in part because it gave her more free time. Agnes seized her days off. She traveled with friends to the beaches of Long Island and Brooklyn. "If we go on a boat, we dance all the way there and all the way back, and we dance nearly all the time we are there." But the place that moral reformers called "Sodom by the Sea" was her favorite destination. "I like Coney Island best of all," she said. "It is a wonderful and beautiful place."

What Agnes most liked to do was dance. Most remarkably, like the slaves who pitied the awkward moves of their masters, Agnes looked down upon the elite and the moral reformers who believed that Coney Island and dance halls were beneath them. "The trouble is that these high people don't know how to dance," she said. "I have to laugh when I see them at their balls and parties. If only I could get out on the floor and show them how—they would be astonished."

Like many in this generation of renegade young women, Agnes threw off the cultural expectation that she should marry immediately. "I don't want to get married yet, because when a girl marries, she can't have so much fun—or rather, she can't go about with more than one young man." In New York she found a "tall, dark" man and was impressed that he was an assistant in a large grocery store "and soon will go into business himself." But she thought that she might marry him for a more important reason. "I like him, because I think he's the best dancer I ever saw."

Agnes M. was part of a massive movement of women into the streets. In the early nineteen hundreds, nearly 60 percent of all women in New York City aged sixteen to twenty worked outside the home, most were sin-gle, and a substantial number lived alone. These were dangerous, renegade "women adrift." According to historian Kathy Peiss, they "pushed at the boundaries of constrained lives" by refusing to limit themselves to the ob-ligations of daughters, wives, and mothers. They were the first generation of American women who lived to a great degree for their own pleasures and freedom. Taking jobs freed them from their fathers' homes and re-duced their economic dependency on men. Though they often hated their work, they loved the liberties it brought them. By bringing them out of the confines of the home and away from the regulation of parents and po-lice and priests and rabbis, the world of work gave a generation of women the kind of freedoms that previously had been enjoyed only by very "bad" ladies. For the first time in American history, great numbers of women made their own wages, spent their own money, lived much of the day on their own, walked the streets unescorted, and established their own liaisons with men. Ironically, many saw work as an avenue to pleasure. "Far from inculcating good business habits, discipline, and a desire for quiet evenings at home," says Peiss, "the workplace reinforced the wage earner's interest in having a good time."

Moral reformers and vice investigators noticed greater numbers of women in previously male domains. By the 1910s, according to Peiss, "women increasingly frequented saloons." A Committee of Fourteen investigator took note of this tendency in 1917 when he observed that not all the women in a West Side saloon were prostitutes: "2 of the women that were here seemed to be respectable, they had been out marketing and had their market bags with them." Working-class women also opened the door to gambling. Historians have found evidence that women in large cities during this period were avid players of daily lottery games known as "policy" or "numbers." One newspaper reported that "many of the players are women who live in the tenement districts and spend almost every cent they earn in playing 'gigs,' 'horses,' and 'saddles.'"

These women typically worked ten to twelve hours a day at taxing, menial labor but shocked many with the energy they still had for fun. The manager of a dressmaking factory noted with amazement that her employees "all took Sunday for a gala day and not as a day of rest. They worked so hard having a good time all day, and late into the evening, that they were 'worn to a frazzle' when Monday morning came." This ferocious love of pleasure was perhaps best articulated by a New York saleswoman who helped many of these women prepare for nights out: "You see some of those who have complained about standing spend most of the evening in dancing." This was of no small concern to employers, such as the training supervisor at Macy's. "We see that all the time in New York," he said, "many of the employees having recreation at night that unfits them for work the next day."

Another Committee of Fourteen investigator in 1914 observed the loose behavior of women workers in a restaurant: "They were putting on their aprons, combing their hair, powdering their noses, . . . all the while tossing back and forth to each other, apparently in a spirit of good-natured comradeship, the most vile epithets that I had ever heard emerge from the lips of a human being." Even at Macy's, where managers worked to enforce the highest standards of respectability among the female employees, one investigator found "salacious cards, poems, etc., copied with avidity and passed from one to another, not only between girls and girls, but from girls to men." Though not all the workers behaved with such wanton disregard for proper behavior, there was "more smutty talk in one particular department than in a dance hall." Many working-class women formed social clubs in which, according to Peiss, "young women's desire for social freedom and its identification with leisure activities spilled over into behavior unsanctioned by parents and neighbors, as well as middle-class reformers." Female mail-order clerks at Siegel-Cooper Dry Goods Store formed the Bachelor Girls Social Club as a place where "we enjoy our independence and freedom." In many clubs, independence and freedom meant shattering conventional notions of womanhood. One club member reported to a moral reform group that "in all [clubs] 'they have kissing all through pleasure time, and use slang language,' while in some they 'don't behave nice between young ladies.'"

Like nineteenth-century slaves who dressed above their station, working-class women of the early twentieth century crashed through the limits placed on their bodies. Middle-class author Bertha Richardson remarked in 1904,

> Did you ever go down to one of our city settlements full of the desire to help and lift up the poor shop girl? Do you remember the chill that came over you[?] . . . There must be some mistake, you thought. These could not be poor girls, earning five or six dollars a week. They looked better dressed than you did! Plumes on their hats, a rustle of silk petticoats, everything about them in the latest style.

Even female factory workers dressed far above where they were expected to be. During a 1909 strike of shirtwaist makers in New York City, a reporter for *Collier's Weekly* magazine was stunned to see the high fashion on display:

> Lingerie waists were elaborate, puffs towered; there were picture turbans and di'mont pendants. . . . This was a scene of gaiety and flirtation. My preconceived idea of a strike was a somber meeting

where somber resolutions were made, . . . "But they don't look as if they had any grievance," I objected. It is always painful to renounce a preconceived picture.

Newspaper reports of the strike similarly noted that the picketing women, none of whom earned above a poverty wage, were "in their best gowns, were picturesque enough, and looked far from starving or downtrodden" and "all looked prosperous." Mary Augusta LaSelle, author of *The Joy in Work* and other moral lessons for young women, reported in 1914 that:

> comparatively few girl wage-earners dress in a proper manner when at their work. The hat is usually freakish, either in size, shape, or color . . . the wide collar is of cheap and gaudy lace; the suit is of inappropriate material and color; the much embroidered and oftentimes unclean lingerie waist is too low in the neck and too short in the sleeves, and many times insecurely fastened in the back . . . the feet even in January are enclosed in gauze stockings and pumps with the highest of heels . . . the girl who wears the fresh tailored waist with its clean white collar and tidy little jabot or tie presents a far more attractive appearance than does the flashily-dressed girl in her attempts at finery; and in any store or office the girls who are most quietly and tidily dressed are, as a rule, the ones who are of greatest service to their employer . . .

Just as nineteenth-century whites attacked slaves for "foolishly" imitating aristocrats in their dress, LaSelle called the high aspirations of working-class women stupid:

> The unsuitable dressing of the working girl is also due to the fact that she lacks sufficient judgment to discriminate concerning a style of dress suitable to a woman of wealth who rides down the avenue in her limousine, who walks in her thin silk stockings and tiny slippers only upon thickly-carpeted floors, and whose gorgeous hat may not be out of place when it adorns the head of a wearer in a private equipage. The working girl's hat, shoes, dress, and general attire are in too many cases a fantastic imitation of the costly costumes of women of large incomes. It seems difficult for

our girls to discriminate between a style of dressing suitable to a wealthy woman of leisure and that suited to a girl in an office on a salary of possibly $12 per week; or to distinguish between really valuable clothing and pinchbeck imitations.

Women such as these were also the vanguard of a new sexual revolution.

When researchers surveyed one thousand public school children in New York in 1910, nearly 90 percent of the girls but only one-third of the boys reported they knew how to dance. According to Peiss, in the large public dance halls "promiscuous interaction of strangers was normative behavior." A vice investigator in 1917 described the scene in one of the city's more reputable dance halls:

I saw one of the women smoking cigarettes, most of the younger couples were hugging and kissing, there was a general mingling of men and women at the different tables, almost every one seemed to know one another and spoke to each other across the room, also saw both men and women leave their tables and join couples at different tables, they were all singing and carrying on, they kept running around the room and acted like a mob of lunatics let lo[o]se.

Moral reformer Julia Schoenfeld reported that in New York dance halls "vulgar dancing exists everywhere, and the 'spiel,' a form of dancing requiring much twirling and twisting, . . . is popular in all." The kind of social dance called "spieling," in which a couple spun around seemingly out of control, "particularly cause[d] sexual excitement" because of "the easy familiarity in the dance practiced by nearly all the men in the way they handle the girls." One investigator who observed this new culture reported that "most of the girls are working girls, not prostitutes, they smoke cigarettes, drink liquors, and dance [dis]orderly dances, stay out late and stay with any man, that pick them up first."

Dancing, which became massively popular in the 1920s, was central to the sexual revolution. In 1924, in New York City alone, six million women and men attended dance halls. Over 10 percent of the women and men between the ages of seventeen and forty in New York went dancing at least once a week, and the numbers were almost certainly comparable in other large cities. This was a trend among whites and blacks, immigrants and native born, and virtually every ethnicity. For the first time in American history, women and men socializing, dancing, and displaying their sexuality in public was both commonly accepted and practiced by the majority. More than sixty city governments attempted to regulate the styles of dancing in the dance halls to make it less sexual and "safer" for young women, but the dance craze grew only stronger through the 1920s and into the 1930s and 1940s.

WOMEN AGAINST GIRLS

When feminists spoke of "freedom" for women, they did not mean the freedom of desire. Bertha Richardson spoke for her fellow feminist reformers when she reported that after seeing well-dressed working girls, "you went home thoughtful about those girls who wasted their hard-earned money on cheap imitation, who dressed beyond their station, and you failed to see what enjoyment they got out of it." The mission of women's leaders was clear: "to those who have little and try to look as if they had more, we teach morals and standards." The feminist social worker Lillian Wald, who founded the Henry Street Settlement on the Lower East Side of New York City, recalled her failure to change one young woman's love of material pleasure. "A girl leading an immoral life was once sent to me for possible help," Wald remembered in her memoir. Raised in poverty, the girl had worked demonstrating products in a department store,

> where the display of expensive finery on the counters and its easy purchase by luxurious women had evidently played a part in her moral deterioration. Her most conscious desire was for silk underwear; at least it was the only one she seemed able to formulate! And this trivial desire, infinitely pathetic in its disclosure, told her story.

This reaching beyond one's social status was what Bertha Richardson called the "vulgar vanity" of the girls who were forced to work but lived to play. Leaders of the labor union that organized the shirtwaist strike were so disturbed by the finery of the strikers that they attempted to impose a limit on the amount of money that each member of the union could spend on clothes.

Feminists were almost universally opposed to the new culture of young, working-class women. One feminist group, the New York Association of Working Girl's Societies, counseled women to avoid lowbrow popular entertainment so "that the tone of womanhood be raised." The group's journal warned that young girls not "be anxious to acquire personal popularity in the work room, if the price of it be the sacrifice of purity of thought." Some members of the NYAWG nonetheless complained of the group's rejection of fun. One working woman noted in the journal that the group's membership had declined and asked, "Is it not because, as our name implies, we are *working girls* and though desirous of mental, physical, and spiritual culture, we *most* need *pleasant recreation*?"

At the center of the culture of leisure and pleasure were movies, amusement parks, and dance halls, three phenomena widely considered to be causes and exemplars of social disorder. The Reverend John J. Phelan of Toledo, Ohio, was one of many moral reformers who set out to study the dangers of the new fun. In 1919 Phelan conducted a survey of amusements in his city and was shocked to learn that in the downtown area alone there were "fifty-four rooms used for dancing purposes" and that they were all located "in the neighborhood of the picture houses." The close proximity of the two types of venues was no coincidence, Phelan concluded: "From personal observation, it was noted that a hasty and promiscuous acquaintance is often made at the picture shows which later develops in patronage of these dances." This slippery slope from movies to dance halls to sex was frequently noted by progressive and religious authorities concerned with the great numbers of young people who moved into the cities—either from rural areas or overseas—during the Industrial Revolution and especially during the military buildup of World War I. These people had left "the restraining and refining influences of the established home" and were "outside the fold." Phelan found that because the cities lacked sufficient moral regulations, "'cheap' popular shows—in all that the name implies—and the many unsupervised and commercialized forms of amusement are greatly patronized." The sheer numbers of potential renegades were overwhelming. In Toledo, a medium-sized city of just over 243,000 at the time, Phelan estimated "that at least 20,000 young persons live in the 300 rooming houses which are located within walking distance of the picture houses." Most disturbing to Phelan was the report of "an authority in the business" that despite their relative poverty, "the larger part of these persons attend two or three times a week, and a considerable number, nearly every night in the week and Sundays." Historians have found similar rates of moviegoing in Chicago and New York at the time.

Reverend Phelan outlined an awesome number of "general dangers" at the movies, including "promiscuous mingling with undesirables," "physical contact with the unclean," "laxity of home-control," "promiscuous mingling with feebleminded," "incapacity of sustained mental application," "creation of adult standards for immature youth," "exaggerated viewpoints of life," "awakening of morbid curiosity," "lack of discrimination of what constitutes travesty and serious," "false conceptions of sin," "development of an abnormal imagination," "creation of sickly sentimentalism," "vivid portrayal of loose ethics as affecting home-ties, relation to state and society," and "false delineation of what constitutes true Americanism." The dangers for girls were especially acute: "It is estimated that two-thirds of the girls who appear before the Court charged with immorality owe their misfortune to influences derived directly from the movies, either from the pictures themselves or in the 'picking up' of male acquaintances at the theatre!"

A REVOLUTION OF DESIRE

In 1919, the year after the war in Europe ended, four million American workers—a staggering 22 percent of the country's workforce—went on strike, the most ever in a single year in the United States. The immediate cause of the strikes was the government's repeal of wartime price controls, which caused skyrocketing inflation. The strikes were so large that they shut down telephone service in New England, the police force in Boston, the fire department in Cleveland, and nearly the entire city government in Chicago. They halted almost all the railroads in the country, almost all the coal mines, the entire steel industry, and the whole city of Seattle. Many in the government believed that the strikes were led by radicals acting in concert with the Bolsheviks—the communist revolutionaries who had taken control of Russia. This belief provided the basis for what came to be called the Red Scare. Attorney General A. Mitchell Palmer initiated a series of mass arrests of immigrants who were suspected of being subversives. Several thousand people were detained during the Palmer raids, and some six hundred were deported back to their countries of origin. While most historians now condemn the Red Scare as an unwarranted attack on civil liberties, there is nonetheless wide agreement that most of the strikes of 1919 were, in fact, led by radicals. Some scholars even argue that the great strike wave was a moment of revolutionary, anticapitalist potential in the United States. Yet there is far more evidence that the strikes of 1919 were part of the emerging mass consumer culture than they were a move against capitalism.

Though many labor *leaders* were radical anticapitalists, only a tiny fraction of the rank and file was associated with a left-wing organization. Virtually all the strikes of 1919, even the few that were led by radical labor leaders, were carried out to demand higher wages, shorter hours, better working conditions, or union recognition—and nothing else. Not one significant strike was carried out by workers with the goal of taking control of their industry. In fact, one would be hard pressed to identify a strike in 1919—or any strike in the United States in the twentieth century—that was not for the so-called bread-and-butter objectives of more money and less work. In other words, the so-called Red strikes were more likely an effort by millions of ordinary people to improve their material lives—to make more money so they could spend more money, and to work less so they could enjoy, among other things, the new pleasures available with that money.

Indeed, several magazines and newspapers specifically blamed working-class consumption for the labor upheavals that were taking place. A writer for *Harper's* argued that because of the scarcity of labor during the war, workers had become "so pampered, so flattered, so kow-towed to," and that after the war they were "demanding money, not for the necessities of life, but for the luxuries . . . [They want] motor-cars and the delicacies of the table, the jewels and the joy rides." Albert Atwood, a writer for the *Saturday Evening Post*, announced that workers "are today gratifying wants long felt and never before possible of realization." He criticized working-class people, but especially women and African Americans, for their attempts to live above their station. Atwood mocked factory girls and black workers who bought fancy clothes without asking about the price. Ordinary laborers refused to invest in worthwhile things, he said, and instead put their money "into mere show, into clothes, diamonds, and the like." Many commentators after the war, including Attorney General Palmer, argued that instilling frugality into the minds of working people would stop the strikes and social unrest that threatened the nation's security.

THE CUSTOMER IS QUEEN

Most historians of the "consumer revolution" argue that it came from above, directed from the offices of advertising agencies. The standard story is that advertisers created desires and invented false needs in the minds of consumers. They seized consumers' minds, established "cultural hegemony," and were nothing less than the "captains of consciousness," according to the title of one of the leading histories of the advertising industry.

However, in the eighteenth century, the first mass marketers of consumer goods understood that to be successful meant to treat the "consumer as king"—or, more precisely, as queen. Josiah Wedgwood and Thomas Bentley, the first manufacturers of pottery and among the first capitalists to seek broader markets for consumer products, acknowledged to each other that they could not allow their own tastes to determine what they produced. When Wedgwood found that a particular vase which he thought unattractive was widely popular, he did not hesitate to mass produce it. "I do not see any beauty in it but will make something of it," he told Bentley. To guide their production, Wedgwood and Bentley spent as much time as possible in their London shop, observing what customers purchased and asking them their opinions. According to business historian Regina Lee Blaszczyk, the partners "acknowledged consumer sovereignty and crafted a strategy aimed at meeting demand, rather than shaping it." They "perfected techniques that registered the nuances of consumer taste and channeled this information into the factory's design shops." At first responding only to the preferences of the London elite, Wedgwood and Bentley found that the principle of consumer sovereignty applied to the lower classes as well. Rather than seeking to dictate taste to "the Middling Class of People," the pair acknowledged that "Their character is established" and would only "buy quantitys" of products that they already knew they liked. By the end of the eighteenth century, this strategy made Wedgwood the best-selling pottery line on both sides of the Atlantic. Similarly, Frederick Hurten Rhead, one of the leading Anglo-American potters of the early twentieth century, learned that only consumers, and not style experts, could "tell the manufacturer what to make."

In the 1920s, what *Nation's Business* called the "economic necessity" of "fact finding" compelled the creation of the audience survey. Procter & Gamble pioneered the method by sending questioners door-to-door in neighborhoods across the country, keeping track of the number of items returned, and interviewing shoppers about their likes and dislikes. The company would not launch a product that had not gone through rigorous vetting with consumers. Paul T. Cherington, research director of the J. Walter Thompson advertising firm, said in 1931, "the consuming public imposes its will on the business enterprise." The company promised to get "the facts from the real consumer." The central problem for any business, according to Cherington, was to understand the "fussy and troublesome ideas" that consumers had about particular products. The most successful enterprise would attempt not to manipulate but "to please and satisfy the public." To Cherington, the consumer held "the balance of power" in the marketplace, and "the measure of the manufacturer's or merchant's skill" was the extent to which it knew and satisfied the consumer's desires.

By the end of the nineteenth century, every major business that catered to consumers was conducting market research surveys to find out what they wanted, then producing it as soon as they could. Ordinary Americans with new, extraordinary desires were voting with their feet and their hard-earned money every day, electing new lives for themselves and a new way of life for everyone.

Anyone who believes that advertisers control consumers need only be told a few names: Tucker, Henry J., Ford, Edsel, Mercury Park Lane, Studebaker, Wagonaire, Lincoln Blackwood, AMC Marlin, Buick Reatta, and Eagle Premier. These were among many automobiles that were marketed strenuously by their manufacturers but quickly discontinued due to weak sales. Moreover, of the 30,000 new products introduced in grocery stores after 1960, more than 80 percent were pulled from the shelves by 1980. In the 1980s, consumers rejected even more products. Of the 84,933 grocery store products introduced after 1980, fully 86 percent did not survive to 1990. And ask any Hollywood executive how easy it is to please the customer. There have been thousands of big-budget, highly advertised films that lost millions for studios. Indeed, it has been estimated that at least 80 percent of Hollywood productions have lost money, while many have lost fortunes.

No less an authority than Carl Laemmle, founder of Universal Film Manufacturing Company, spoke to the inability of Hollywood to control its audience. Testifying before a congressional committee in 1916 on the moral content of his films, Laemmle reported that he had sent a survey to twenty-two thousand theater owners titled "What Do You Want?" The studio chief said that he expected 95 percent of the respondents to ask for clean and wholesome films, but "instead of finding 95 percent favoring clean pictures, I discovered that at least one-half, or possibly 60 percent, want pictures to be risqué, the French for smutty. . . . They found their patrons were more willing to pay money to see an off-color than a decent one." Because "one after another [theater owner] said that it would be wise to listen to the public demand for vampire pictures," Laemmle argued that film producers could not be the "guardian of public morals."

From early in the history of American marketing, producers understood that, in the words of the advertising trade journal *Printers' Ink* in 1929, "The proper study of mankind is *man*, but the proper study of markets is *woman*." This was especially true in the burgeoning markets for fun. Several historians have shown that the early motion picture industry was driven largely by female consumption. According to historian Nan Enstad, "during the same years that working women went on strike in unprecedented numbers, they were creating a motion picture 'craze'" when "neighborhood theaters, called nickelodeons, boomed after 1905." Though women possessed far less money and had far fewer opportunities for leisure than men, they comprised nearly half of movie audiences in the early years of the motion picture industry. Consequently, producers increasingly geared their films to female audiences, including "a long line of motion picture serials featuring female heroines" such as the long-running and enormously popular series *What Happened to Mary* and *Hazards of Helen*.

Working-class women flocked to amusement parks as well and helped make them the living symbols of the end of the Victorian age. "Coney Island in effect declared a moral holiday for all who entered its gates," the historian John Kasson has written. "Against the values of thrift, sobriety, industry, and ambition, it encouraged extravagance, gaiety, abandon, revelry." At first catering to a "sporting" male subculture in the 1870s—with venues for horse racing, prizefighting, and prostitution—by the end of the nineteenth century, newly liberated working-class women made Coney Island their own. To cater to what was becoming the resort's most ardent patrons, proprietors built dancing pavilions up and down the boardwalk. These open-air dance halls became the scene of "thousands of girls who are seized with such madness for dancing that they spend every night in the dance halls and the picnic parks," as one observer put it.

The mostly female crowds that flocked to the dancing pavilions drove the rapid growth of Coney Island at the turn of the century, spurring the construction of amusement parks to lure in the throngs. Three parks—Dreamland Park, Luna Park, and Steeplechase Park—catered to the new sexual culture of New York's working girls. Rides at the amusement parks "encouraged closeness and romance" by deliberately jostling patrons so as to cause patrons to bump into one another. The Barrel of Love, a revolving drum at Steeplechase Park, went even further by tumbling riders on top of one another. Other rides, such as the Canals of Venice and the Tunnel of Love, simply sent patrons into dark passageways. Without a population of women wishing for such encounters and willing to experience them in public, Coney Island and American amusement parks as we know them would not have existed. As Kathy Peiss puts it, "the desires of such working women as Agnes M., who loved to dance, see the men, and have a good time, shaped the emergent mass culture."

The generation of working-class women who drove the American revolution of leisure and pleasure overcame the opposition of protective parents who didn't want them to work outside the home or have their own money. They broke through the common belief that women seeking pleasure in public spaces were immoral and degenerate. And they simply ignored the Puritan and Victorian proscriptions against "indolence," "extravagance," and "dissipating luxury." They created the weekend, and for this alone, they should be considered national heroes. But they accomplished something even more phenomenal. Against all odds, they created American fun.

★ 10 ★

HOW GANGSTERS MADE AMERICA
A BETTER PLACE

Imagine an America without jazz. Imagine an America in which alcohol is still illegal. Imagine an America without Broadway, Las Vegas, or Hollywood. Imagine an America in which all gays and lesbians are in the closet. All you have to do is imagine American history without organized crime.

WORST PLACES, BEST MUSIC

As we have seen, the first members of the Sicilian mafia to emigrate to the United States arrived in New Orleans in the 1860s. By the 1880s, some three hundred mafiosi controlled substantial portions of the city's economy, most significantly the many brothels, saloons, and nightclubs that defined New Orleans as the pleasure capital of the South. Several historians have argued that it was precisely the gangsters' disregard for social norms that made them the most likely to enter illicit economies. Indeed, by the turn of the century, when respectable Americans shunned jazz as black and criminal jungle music but many at the lowest orders of society—mostly black and Italian dockworkers along the Mississippi waterfront—nonetheless demonstrated a willingness to pay to hear and dance to it, New Orleans gangsters happily made it their business. We have seen that Italian Americans were among the first to play the music, and also that the first buildings in which jazz was played professionally—brothels in the Storyville district near the French Quarter—were owned by Sicilian mobsters. In 1917 a teenaged Louis Armstrong received his first wages for playing the trumpet at a tavern owned by Henry Matranga, leader of the Matranga family and arguably the most powerful criminal in the early-twentieth-century United

States. According to Armstrong, Matranga disregarded the color line as blithely as he ignored other social mores. "He treated everybody fair, and black patrons loved him very much." Armstrong and the other black inventors of jazz such as Buddy Bolden, Freddie Keppard, and King Oliver also received their early pay from George Delsa, manager of Anderson's Rampart Street cabaret, one of the first clubs to feature jazz, who used his Mafia connections to protect the club and the prostitutes who worked there from the police.

In Chicago and New York, Italian and Jewish gangsters operated many of the most important early jazz clubs. Al Capone, who controlled several of the clubs in Chicago that introduced jazz to mainstream audiences, was an aficionado of the music and was the first to pay performers a better than subsistence wage. The pianist Earl Hines remembered that "Scarface got along well with musicians. He liked to come into a club with his henchmen and have the band play his requests. He was very free with $100 tips." Most importantly, Capone supplied steady and professional incomes to jazz musicians who had previously lived in poverty. The singer Ethel Waters fondly recalled that Capone treated her "with respect, applause, deference, and paid in full."

Mob-owned clubs on State Street in Chicago, where, according to the writer Langston Hughes, "gangsters were coming into their own," employed the musicians who made jazz a national phenomenon, including bands fronted by Louis Armstrong, King Oliver, Fletcher Henderson, and Benny Goodman. According to one performer, "the worst places on State Street always had the best music." The same was true in New York City, where, as another jazz musician remembered, the clubs where the music was being invented were "run by big-time mobs, not tramps . . . who had a way of running them better than anyone else." According to the scholar Jerome Charyn, "There would have been no 'Jazz Age,' and very little jazz, without the white gangsters who took black and white jazz musicians under their wing."

Similarly, very few people were more important in the development of Broadway as an entertainment center than Arnold "the Brain" Rothstein, a man credited with turning organized crime into big business. Rothstein gained massive wealth first by investing in speakeasies, underground casinos, and horse tracks, then by gambling on poker games, horse races, and sporting events (including the 1919 World Series) that he "fixed." In the 1920s, Rothstein moved into bootlegging and narcotics trafficking and by

1927 was considered to be in control of virtually the entire U.S. drug trade. Along the way, Rothstein, whose unofficial office was Lindy's restaurant at Forty-ninth Street and Broadway, invested heavily in the burgeoning musical theater industry in midtown Manhattan. He financed the opening of several venues, including the famous Selwyn Theater on Forty-second Street, as well as various productions that brought tens of thousands of patrons to Broadway and helped establish it as the first entertainment capital of America.

PUBLIC ENEMIES, PUBLIC HEROES

Today there is nearly universal consensus that Prohibition—the period from 1919 to 1933, during which the sale, manufacture, and transportation of alcohol for consumption were banned nationally as mandated in the Eighteenth Amendment to the United States Constitution—was a puritanical disaster. And yet it is seldom acknowledged that organized criminals were primarily responsible for making Prohibition the most spectacularly unsuccessful moral reform movement in American history.

Beginning on January 16, 1920, the date the Eighteenth Amendment went into effect, rumrunners employed by Italian and Jewish crime syndicates delivered liquor all along the coasts of the Pacific, Atlantic, and the Gulf of Mexico. In the North, giant sleds carrying cases of liquor were pulled across the border from Canada. Thanks to these efforts and the overwhelming desire of Americans to drink, consumption of sacramental wine increased by eight hundred thousand gallons during the first two years of Prohibition. Speakeasies, many of which were owned by criminals, could be found in every neighborhood in every city in the country. In Manhattan alone, there were five thousand speakeasies at one point in the 1920s. Women, who had been barred from most saloons before Prohibition, were welcome in speakeasies and became regular customers. When a rumrunner boat escaped a Coast Guard ship off Coney Island one summer day, thousands of people on the beach stood and cheered. All of this helps explain why gangsters became the heroes of the Prohibition era, both in the movies and in real life.

In 1931, in a poll conducted by *Variety* magazine, a broad cross section of the American public was asked to identify a list of names of public figures. *Variety* reported that the names most familiar to Americans in

1931 were those of film stars. But the next most familiar names belonged to gangsters. Third on the list were athletes. And fourth were politicians. The celebrity status of gangsters can be explained, first, by the publicity they received during Prohibition. But their greatest promotion came from the gangster genre film, which was by far the most popular variety of motion picture during the last years of Prohibition. Three of the largest grossing films of this period were *Little Caesar*, released in 1930, *The Public Enemy* (1931), and *Scarface* (1932). *Little Caesar* and *Scarface* were based on the life of Al Capone, and *The Public Enemy* told a fictionalized account of the life of Hymie Weiss, the leader of a major Jewish gang of the 1920s. These three films established the prototype of the American gangster film of the early 1930s. In these films, the story is told from the point of view of the gangster, whereas previously criminals had been portrayed as objects of moral disapproval. In other words, these were the first films to treat the gangster with empathy and with sympathy. W. R. Burnett, the author of *Little Caesar*, who essentially invented the genre, said this about why his film was revolutionary:

> [The reason it] was a smack in the face . . . was the fact that it was the world seen completely through the eyes of a gangster. . . . It had never been done before then. You had crime stories but always seen through the eyes of society. The criminal was just some son of a bitch who'd killed somebody and then they got 'em. I treated them as human beings.

In *Little Caesar*, the protagonist, played by Edward G. Robinson, rises from a small-town crook to become the leader of a major crime syndicate in Chicago. The film shows his success as the product of courage, intelligence, and determination, and his death as tragedy rather than as justice. Like Robinson in *Little Caesar*, James Cagney's character in *The Public Enemy* starts out as a petty criminal and works his way up to the top of a criminal empire. He is smart, ruthless, and entirely out for himself. Not one policeman makes an appearance in the movie. The death of the Cagney character comes from a rival gang, and, again, it is portrayed as tragedy. *Scarface*, which censors rightly claimed glorified gangsters, was perhaps the most blatant example of the genre. Paul Muni plays Tony Camonte, a thinly disguised Al Capone, whose motto is: "Do it first, do it yourself, and keep on doing it." Camonte is released from prison by a crooked lawyer who finds a loophole in the law, and when he walks out of the prison, he strikes a match on a policeman's badge, lights his cigarette, and waves a mock salute. In these three films, as with gangster movies of the period generally, the filmmakers clearly intended the audience to identify with and admire the renegade protagonists.

The gangster of early Depression films had a female counterpart, via another highly popular genre during the period: what film historians have called the "fallen woman genre." Hollywood produced a number of successful films that portrayed women who used their sexuality to gain wealth and power. They manipulated men, they were highly intelligent and independent, they loved luxury, and they rejected the traditional roles of wife and mother. Nearly every female star in Hollywood appeared in at least one "fallen woman" film, including Greta Garbo, Marlene Dietrich, Joan Crawford, Claudette Colbert, Jean Harlow, and Tallulah Bankhead. *Red-Headed Woman*, starring Jean Harlow, generated enormous publicity, much of it attacks by moral reformers, because it depicted a working-class woman who seduces her wealthy, seemingly happily married boss. Her use of sex as a means to gain material rewards and power over men is bluntly shown, and in one scene she barges into an exclusive country club and forces her rich, respectable boyfriend to kiss her in a phone booth. The film ends with the heroine shooting her rich husband and laughing over his body with her boyfriend. In *Blonde Venus*, Marlene Dietrich separates from her husband and supports herself by performing in a cabaret in a sleazy part of town. Though seldom regarded as a feminist, the Dietrich character refuses to be a loyal and monogamous wife. In one of her performances in the film, Dietrich sings these lyrics:

Things look bad—stocks are low
So today, my best beau
Went back again to live with his wife
Why should I care a lot?
So he's gone—well, so what?
It doesn't mean a thing in my life.

BOSSES AND QUEENS

Though famous for their ultramasculinity, gangsters were nonetheless instrumental in fostering and protecting the gay subculture during the hostile years of World War II and the 1950s. Vito Genovese and Carlo Gambino, leaders of the largest and most powerful crime families in New York, began investing in gay bars in the early 1930s. Some have speculated that Genovese learned of the bars from his wife, Anna Petillo Vernotico, who was a regular at the bars and for many years was openly involved in a lesbian relationship. Genovese not only approved of her sexuality but also had her first husband murdered so that she could be unbound by what she considered a loveless marriage and freely involve herself with women.

By the 1950s, most of the gay bars in New York were owned by the mob. Because of the Mafia's connections with the police department and willingness to bribe officers, patrons of mob-owned bars were often protected from the police raids that dominated gay life in the 1950s. The

Vito Genovese, leader of one of the most powerful crime syndicates in American history and owner of many of New York City's first gay bars.

Stonewall Inn on Christopher Street in Greenwich Village had been a straight restaurant and a straight nightclub for many years when it was purchased in 1966 by three associates of the Genovese family, led by "Fat Tony" Lauria, a mob don known for weighing 420 pounds and for preferring men as sexual partners. Partly to facilitate his own yearnings and partly in recognition of the great demand among gay men and lesbians for bars protected from the police, Lauria converted the Stonewall into a gay bar and began paying officers in the Sixth Precinct headquarters $2,000 per week to shield it from raids. Despite the bribes, Stonewall provided a huge profit for its mob owners. Many of the mafiosi who managed the Stonewall and other gay clubs were themselves gay, and several had penchants for drag queens. An enormous bouncer known as "Big Bobby," who worked the door at Tony Pastor's, a popular Mafia-run gay club at Sixth Avenue and MacDougal Street, carried on an open relationship with a Chinese drag queen named Tony Lee, who performed ballet at the club.

The Stonewall Inn seems to have had more than the usual number of gay mobsters. According to the historian Martin Duberman, a gangster-bouncer named "Petey," who worked various gay clubs, including the Stonewall, "had a thick Italian street accent, acted 'dumb,' and favored black shirts and ties." He was "the very picture of a Mafia mobster—except for his habit of falling for patrons and coworkers." Petey was especially fond of an Italian drag queen named Desiree who frequented the Stonewall. The Stonewall's manager was a man named Ed "the Skull" Murphy, a lifelong hood and ex-convict who chose to work as a bouncer at many of New York's first gay clubs because he found it an easy way to meet and have sex with men. Murphy was also known for his fondness for black and Latino men, which contributed to the Stonewall's reputation as the most racially diverse bar—gay or straight—in New York City.

The famous 1969 raid on the Stonewall was actually part of a federal sting operation directed at the mob. The Sixth Precinct was not notified of the operation until the last minute, when it was forced by federal officers—who were not on the mob payroll—to conduct the raid. Over the next decade, Murphy and the Genovese family funded the gay pride parades in New York that became annual, international demonstrations of sexual freedom, and Murphy rode the route every year in an open-top car wearing a crown and a sash that declared him "the Mayor of Christopher Street."

MAKING VEGAS

Today the most visited tourist destination in the United States, the Strip in Las Vegas, would be just a street in the desert were it not for gangsters. As with other illicit but popular amusements such as early jazz and sexy movies, alcohol during Prohibition, and gay bars before Stonewall, gambling was first made profitable by those who most thoroughly disregarded social norms. In the 1930s, Meyer Lansky, leader of a Jewish crime organization known as the Syndicate, controlled more gambling operations in the western hemisphere than anyone, with major casinos in Miami, Saratoga Springs, New York, and Havana, Cuba. In 1934 Lansky sent two of his lieutenants, Moe Sedway and Benjamin "Bugsy" Siegel, to explore the possibilities of developing casinos and hotels in Nevada, where gambling had been made legal three years earlier. Soon Sedway was working with William Wilkerson, a hotel developer who wanted to take advantage of the state's new law but needed the mobsters' knowledge of running gambling operations.

By 1945, Wilkerson, Sedway, and another of Lansky's lieutenants, Gus Greenbaum, had broken ground in the desert for what would become the Flamingo hotel and casino. Though the war had ended, wartime regulations and restrictions on construction remained, making building materials scarce and expensive. A year later, the project appeared on the verge of collapse, with Wilkerson running out of funds and unable to obtain sufficient construction materials. So in stepped Bugsy Siegel, a rising star in Lansky's syndicate and a prominent playboy who headed the mob's operations in Los Angeles. With his various shady connections and through a series of illegal payoffs, Siegel obtained black-market building materials at low enough prices for construction to resume on the Flamingo. Soon Siegel forced Wilkerson out of the project, established the Nevada Project Corporation of California as owner of the Flamingo, and named himself as president. By the summer of 1946, the Flamingo, which became the foundation on which Las Vegas as we know it was built, was wholly owned and operated by the mob.

Though the Flamingo ultimately thrived, Siegel did not. The ambitious gangster's desire to run the casino entirely on his own terms along with unaccounted losses soon after its opening led Lansky to believe that Siegel was skimming money from the enterprise. On the night of June 20, 1947, Siegel was shot repeatedly, including twice in the head, while reading the newspaper at the home of an associate in Beverly Hills, California.

After Siegel's murder, Greenbaum, Davey Berman, and Morris Rosen, three of the Syndicate's chief authorities, took over the hotel and renamed it the Fabulous Flamingo. These gangsters essentially invented what is known as the "complete experience" resort. Instead of limiting its offerings to just a casino and simple accommodations, as had been the norm until then, the Flamingo staged spectacular theater productions and featured lavish rooms and massive swimming pools. Guests had no reason to ever leave the grounds. From then on, the hotel proved a smashing success, encouraging the Syndicate to devote much of its resources to building more resorts along the Strip. By the mid-1950s, the Strip was lined with hotel-casinos, most of which were owned and operated by professional criminals, and Las Vegas was made.

BAD JEWS, THOMAS EDISON, AND THE INVENTION OF HOLLYWOOD

Soon after he invented the motion picture camera and projector, Thomas Edison formed his own movie production and distribution company. In 1908 Edison joined with nine other film companies—owned mostly by upper-class WASPs—to create the Motion Picture Patents Company, a monopoly that attempted to control the making, distribution, and showing of all movies in the United States. Edison and "the Trust" pledged to make only movies that promoted wholesome, Christian, and "American" values. But on the Lower East Side, a group of entrepreneurial Jewish immigrants used Edison's inventions to produce and screen their own films, which were shown in hundreds of nickelodeons—five-cent movie theaters—in working-class neighborhoods all over the country. These "outlaw" filmmakers started out as vaudeville and burlesque promoters, and many of their movies were sexier, more violent, and far more entertaining than the bland fare put out by the Trust.

The great inventor was furious that "Jewish profiteers" were stealing his patent, getting rich from it, and using it to spread "smut" across America. So too were newspapers and law enforcement officials. In 1907 the *Chicago Tribune* denounced nickelodeons as being "without a redeeming feature to warrant their existence" and "ministering to the lowest passions of child-hood." It was "proper to suppress them at once," since their "influence is wholly vicious." The new, cheap theaters "can not be defended," the paper concluded, and "are hopelessly bad." A judge in Chicago concurred, writing that "these theatres cause, indirectly or directly, more juvenile crime com-ing into my court than all other causes combined." Progressive reformer Jane Addams called for tight regulation of the moral content of the mo-tion pictures shown in nickelodeons, allowing only stories that encouraged thrift, sobriety, communal sacrifice, and the work ethic. Shortly thereafter, the Chicago City Council passed an ordinance granting power to the chief of police to censor motion pictures played in the city. In New York in 1907, soon after the police commissioner recommended that nickel shows be wiped out entirely, Mayor George McClellan Jr. was so moved by the evi-dence of immoral motion pictures polluting the minds of his citizens that on Christmas Day he ordered that all of the illicit motion picture houses be shut down. Not until the producers of nickelodeon movies agreed to censor their own material did the mayor rescind his order.

Moral condemnations and court injunctions didn't stop the prolifera-tion of nickelodeons that showed unseemly fare and violated Edison's pat-ent, so the inventor and his colleagues hired squads of thugs to shut them down. They seized film, beat up directors and actors, forced audiences out of theaters, smashed the nickelodeon arcades, and set fire to entire city blocks where they were concentrated. But fortunately, the Jewish renegades lived and operated in neighborhoods where hundreds of soldiers stood ready and able to protect them—men like "Big" Jack Zelig, "Lefty Louie" Rosen-berg, Harry "Gyp the Blood" Horowitz, Joe "the Greaser" Rosenzweig, and the leaders of the notorious Yiddish Black Hand, Jacob "Johnny" Levinsky and "Charley the Cripple" Vitoffsky. There were even women ready for the fight—fierce, well-armed gun molls like Bessie London, Tillie Finkelstein, Birdie Pomerantz, and Jennie "the Factory" Morris.

Cameras, projectors, film, and sound equipment disappeared from the storerooms of Edison companies and showed up on makeshift movie lots on the Lower East Side. Bullets rained down on the Trust's enforcers from the rooftops of nickelodeons. And fires destroyed the Edison distributors' warehouses in the Bronx, Philadelphia, and Chicago. In 1915 a federal court ruled the Trust an illegal monopoly, but by then the outlaw film-makers had moved west, where they could make bigger and better movies.

Who were the men who, with the help of their nicknamed friends, fought Thomas Edison and the law and won? They were Marcus Loew of Loews Theatres and Metro-Goldwyn-Mayer, Carl Laemmle of Universal Pictures, Adolph Zukor of Paramount Pictures, William Fox of Twentieth Century-Fox, and the brothers Harry, Albert, Sam, and Jack Warner.

★ 11 ★

"BEHOLD A DICTATOR": FASCISM AND THE NEW DEAL

It is absurd to claim, as a few have done, that the New Deal, the basis of what we now know as "liberalism," was identical to either German Nazism or Italian Fascism. But it is equally absurd to ignore, as all our textbooks do, the fact that the New Deal and European fascism grew from the same ideological roots, produced strikingly similar policies, and fostered national cultures that, if not identical, bore the resemblance of siblings. Though we think of Hitler's and Mussolini's regimes as pathological, even psychotic, and entirely alien to our political tradition, in fact, they were organically connected to the most influential American political movement of the twentieth century.

The policies initiated during Franklin D. Roosevelt's presidency redefined the relationship between the federal government and American society. The ideas behind those policies overthrew the laissez-faire ideology that had dominated the nation's political culture since its founding. Most fundamentally, the New Deal brought about an age of communal morality and made social regimentation a primary value in American popular culture. The margin of freedom between the individual and society was at its narrowest in the age of Roosevelt.

Though many see the New Deal era as a rebellious moment, when American culture embraced the interests of the lowest classes, in fact— like the War of Independence, abolitionism, and Reconstruction—it was one of the great antirenegade moments in the history of the United States.

THIS GREAT ARMY

In the spring of 1934, one year into his first term as president, Roosevelt was assailed by the left, the right, and even members of his own party. Leading Republicans took turns denouncing the "new dictatorship" in Washington. Typical was the claim made by GOP Congressman James M. Beck of Pennsylvania that Roosevelt's New Deal had transformed the government into a "socialistic state of virtually unrestricted power." Voices on the left were no less caustic. The Communist Party officially labeled the president a "Fascist." Also critical of Roosevelt's "heavy-handed" approach and "radical" policies were several Democrats, including former presidential candidate Al Smith and former Democratic National Committee chairman John J. Raskob, who helped form the anti-Roosevelt American Liberty League.

Of course, Roosevelt also had many loyal supporters. One of his admirers sent word to the White House encouraging the president to stand his ground and be proud of his "heroic efforts in the interests of the American people." The president's "successful battle against economic distress," wrote the German chancellor, Adolf Hitler, "is being followed by the entire German people with interest and admiration."

The New Deal had many critics, but it would not have captured American political life were it not enormously popular. Roosevelt won four elections, all by landslides, and the Democratic Party, whose platform was rebuilt on New Deal ideas, controlled the federal government for most of the mid-twentieth century. Industrial workers and African Americans moved *en masse* into the Democratic Party as a result of New Deal policies. A generation of intellectuals celebrated the "Roosevelt Revolution," academic discourse is still dominated by its partisans, and Roosevelt continues to be widely considered one of the greatest presidents in American history. But when the New Deal was created, few of its supporters in the United States were as effusive in their praise as were German and Italian fascists.

In July 1933, just four months after Roosevelt had taken office, the newly elected Hitler praised "Mr. Roosevelt," who "marches straight to his objectives over Congress, lobbies, and the bureaucracy." Hitler's compliments were not merely attempts to curry favor with the leader of the world's most powerful nation. Nazis continued to honor the New Deal as a project akin to their own. In January 1934, the Nazi Party's newspaper, the *Völkischer Beobachter*, applauded Roosevelt's "dictatorial" measures. "We, too, as German National Socialists are looking toward America. . . . Roosevelt is carrying out experiments and they are bold. We, too, fear only the possibility that they might fail." Many of the most favorable reviews of Roosevelt's books, *Looking Forward* (1933) and *On Our Way* (1934), were written by German critics who saw the New Deal and National Socialism as parallel enterprises. In 1934 a biography by the German author Helmut Magers, *Roosevelt: A Revolutionary with Common Sense,* lauded the New Deal as "an authoritarian revolution" with "surprising similarities" to the Nazi seizure of power.

Through the first two years of the Roosevelt presidency, the *Völkischer Beobachter* continued to find many similarities between Hitler and the "absolute lord and master" of the United States. "If not always in the same words," the Nazi newspaper wrote, "[Roosevelt], too, demands that collective good be put before individual self-interest. Many passages in his book *Looking Forward* could have been written by a National Socialist. In any case, one can assume that he feels considerable affinity with the National Socialist philosophy." Roosevelt put forward "the fictional appearance of democracy," but in the United States "the development toward an authoritarian state is under way." The newspaper praised "Roosevelt's adoption of National Socialist strains of thought in his economic and social policies."

Hitler himself saw a kindred soul in the American president. He told the U.S. ambassador to Germany, William Dodd, that he was "in accord with the president in the view that the virtue of duty, readiness for sacrifice, and discipline should dominate the entire people. These moral demands which the president places before every individual citizen of the United States are also the quintessence of the German state philosophy; which finds its expression in the slogan 'The Public Weal Transcends the Interest of the Individual.'" Dodd's successor, Hugh R. Wilson, reported to Roosevelt in 1938 that he had told Hitler that "you were very much interested in certain phases of the sociological effort, notably for the youth and workmen, which is being made in Germany, and that one of my first tasks would be to report to you on how these were being carried out." Even as late as 1940, when it was apparent that Roosevelt was eager to intervene militarily against Germany, Joseph Goebbels's weekly newspaper *Das Reich* continued to insist on a kinship between Nazi and New Deal policies. An article entitled "Hitler and Roosevelt: A German Success—An American Attempt" lamented that the American "parliamentary-democratic system" kept the New Deal from becoming fully realized. According to the historian John A. Garraty, "It is clear, however, that early New Deal depression policies seemed to Nazis essentially like their own and the role of Roosevelt not very different from the Führer's."

Fascists in Italy were similarly impressed with the New Deal. In Roosevelt, Benito Mussolini found a comrade. "The appeal to the decisiveness and masculine sobriety of the nation's youth, with which Roosevelt here calls his readers to battle," Mussolini wrote in his review of *Looking Forward*, "is reminiscent of the ways and means by which Fascism awakened the Italian people." When he heard that the National Industrial Recovery Act (NIRA) of 1933 gave the president unchecked power over much of the national economy, Mussolini exclaimed, "Behold a dictator!"

Self-proclaimed fascists were not the only ones drawing such comparisons. Many of America's leading liberals and Democratic Party stalwarts were drawing them as well. George Soule, the editor of the *New Republic*, wrote, "We are trying out the economics of Fascism without having suffered all its social and political ravages." Oswald Garrison Villard, the publisher of the *Nation*, came to regret his early endorsement of Roosevelt. "No one can deny that the entire Roosevelt legislation has enormously enhanced the authority of the president," Villard wrote in 1934, "given him some dictatorial powers, and established precedents that would make it easy for any successor to Mr. Roosevelt, or for that gentleman himself, to carry us far along the road to Fascism or state socialism." Two of the founders of *Consumer Reports*, J. B. Matthews and Ruth Shallcross, wrote in *Harper's* magazine in 1934 that "if developed to its logical conclusion," the principle behind early New Deal policies "arrives at the Fascist stage of economic control."

The New Deal's resemblance to European fascism was most striking in the first two years of the Roosevelt administration. Both Roosevelt and Hitler came to power in the depths of the Depression, and both argued that their extraordinary accumulation of authority and the establishment of a martial society were necessary in a time that was as perilous, they claimed, as war. "Turbulent instincts must be replaced by a national discipline as the guiding principle of our national life," Hitler declared to the German people in 1933. "If you preserve the same discipline, the same obedience, the same comradeship, and the same unbounded loyalty in the future—then nothing will ever extinguish this movement in Germany." He called on all Germans to make themselves into a military force. "Today millions are pouring into our ranks," he said. "But the greater part of them must learn now what this brown army has practiced for years; they must all learn to face what tens of thousands of our comrades have faced, and have paid for with their blood, their lives." In that same year, in his inaugural address, Roosevelt said this:

> If we are to go forward, we must move as a trained and loyal army willing to sacrifice for the good of a common discipline, because without such discipline no progress is made, no leadership becomes effective. We are, I know, ready and willing to submit our lives and property to such discipline, because it makes possible a leadership which aims at a larger good. This I propose to offer, pledging that the larger purposes will bind upon us all as a sacred obligation with a unity of duty hitherto evoked only in time of armed strife. With this pledge taken, I assume unhesitatingly the leadership of this great army of our people dedicated to a disciplined attack upon our common problems.

Roosevelt was probably not the only president to wish for such power, but he was the only one willing to demand it. Should the country fail to make itself into one great fighting force, "I shall not evade the clear course of duty that will then confront me," he said from the east portico of the Capitol. "I shall ask the Congress for the one remaining instrument to meet the crisis—broad executive power to wage a war against the emergency, as great as the power that would be given to me if we were in fact invaded by a foreign foe." Roosevelt was the only president to achieve this power.

Two days after taking office, Roosevelt, invoking a "national emergency," took an unprecedented step toward autocratic power. For the first time in United States history, a president closed the nation's banks. Then, on March 9, Congress transferred much of its power to the president and gave him sole authority over a large swath of the nation's economy. The Trading with the Enemy Act of 1917 was amended to declare that during time of war "or during any other period of national emergency declared by the President, the President may, through any agency that he may designate, or otherwise, investigate, regulate, or prohibit, under such rules and regulations as he may prescribe, by means of licenses or otherwise, any transactions in foreign exchange, transfers of credit between or payments by banking institutions as defined by the President, and exporting, hoarding, melting, or earmarking of gold or silver coin or bullion or currency." Congress effectively gave the president unchecked control over banks and financial transactions in general, and everything concerning gold in particular. More ominously, the new law allowed the president to alone decide when to acquire and exercise that power.

The Roosevelt administration's next major step, the National Industrial Recovery Act (NIRA), passed in June 1933, became the defining legislation of the so-called "First New Deal." It created an economic system that was virtually identical to the national economies established in Italy and Germany, and further consolidated power in the hands of the president. In a stunning reversal of laissez-faire and a repudiation of the American devotion to free and competitive markets, the NIRA and the National Recovery Administration (NRA), which put the law into practice, suspended all federal antitrust laws and created cartels of businesses in every major industry that—instead of market forces—decided how much products would cost, how much workers would make, and how much companies would produce. These cartels were called "code authorities." In Italy they were called "corporatives." In Germany they were known as "industrial cartels." But in all three nations they held the same powers, and in all three nations they could be overruled only by the head of state: Mussolini in Italy, Hitler in Germany, and Roosevelt in the United States.

How could such a radical policy come about in the United States? Many of the men who conceived of the NIRA were opposed to free markets, disdainful of democracy, and committed to a centrally controlled economy. The architects of the early New Deal had their roots in progressivism and shared that movement's obsessions with social order, discipline, rationality, and the merging of the individual's identity with the nation. These obsessions were a transatlantic phenomenon in the first half of the twentieth century, but they were particularly powerful in the United States, Italy, and Germany.

According to historian John P. Diggins, whose 1972 book *Mussolini and Fascism: The View from America,* was the first academic acknowledgment of fascist sympathies among American elites, "Mussolini's Fascist dictatorship drew more admiration from democratic America than from any other Western nation." Many leading American intellectuals and political figures from the progressive generation were drawn to fascism in the 1920s. The famous progressive muckrakers Lincoln Steffens and Ida Tarbell visited Italy and wrote glowing accounts of the Blackshirt regime. One of the most enthusiastic supporters of both the early New Deal and Italian fascism was Charles Beard, a Columbia University professor and the leading member of the school of "progressive historians." In an article in the *New Republic* magazine, Beard argued that Americans should look past Mussolini's use of violence and suppression of civil liberties and recognize that fascism was the most effective modernizing force in the world:

> [It is] an amazing experiment . . . an experiment in reconciling individualism and socialism, politics and technology. It would be a mistake to allow feelings aroused by contemplating the harsh deeds and extravagant assertions that have accompanied the Fascist process to obscure the potentialities and the lessons of the adventure—no, not adventure, but destiny riding without any saddle and bridle across the historic peninsula that bridges the world of antiquity and our modern world.

Another group that was overwhelmingly supportive of Italian fascism was American big business, which praised Mussolini for bringing order and stability to the Italian economy. The president of the U.S. Chamber of Commerce, Julius Barnes, repeatedly declared in speeches and magazine articles that "Mussolini is without question a great man." James Emery of the National Association of Manufacturers praised Il Duce at a NAM convention for "leading through the streets of a reunited country a great body of citizens" who rescued Italy from "the blighting hand of radical socialism." Referring to the American economy, the *Wall Street Journal* titled an editorial "Needed A Mussolini." Thomas W. Lamont, head of the J. P.

Morgan banking network, called himself a "missionary" for fascism and devoted himself to "quiet preaching" on its behalf. According to Diggins, "With few exceptions, the dominant voices of business responded to fascism with hearty enthusiasm." Many later directed their firms to donate money to the Nazi Party.

One of those businessmen was Gerard Swope, the chairman of General Electric, who also wrote the first draft of the NIRA. In 1931 Swope published what he called the "Swope Plan," which argued that antitrust laws had to be suspended so that companies in a given industry could free themselves from market forces and collectively determine prices, wages, and production levels. Running through Swope's argument, as in the arguments of many New Dealers, was a hostility toward democracy. "Shall we wait for society to act through its legislatures," he asked, "or shall industry recognize its obligation to its employees and to the public and undertake the task?" His answer was to replace the U.S. Congress with corporate cartels: "Organized industry should take the lead, recognizing its responsibility to its employees, to the public, and to its stockholders—rather than that democratic society should act through its government." Herbert Hoover, the president at the time, called the Swope Plan a "prescription for Fascism." That prescription was filled in the first month of Roosevelt's presidency, when, according to Leon Keyserling, one of the principal authors of the NIRA, "The original draft of the act grew out of the so-called Gerard Swope plan for recovery."

The men who made the New Deal were driven by dreams of a machinelike society, in which all members, from the leaders of government to the lowliest workers, would be parts designed, built, and employed entirely for their function within the whole apparatus. But to their dismay, these men found that most Americans rejected such dreams, except during times of crisis. The First World War was the first such crisis, and they embraced that opportunity to discipline America. But then came the peace and prosperity of the 1920s, a long time of waiting for another national emergency that could make their fantasies of social order come true.

SOCIAL MACHINERY

In the 1920s, the offices in the buildings along the eastern edge of the Columbia University campus looked from the hills of Morningside Heights out over Harlem. Rexford Tugwell, a professor in the economics department, occupied one of those offices. From behind his desk in Hamilton Hall, Tugwell could not hear the music but he could see the nightclubs, dance halls, and speakeasies that defined the Jazz Age. And so he waited.

Tugwell had been shut off from the pleasures of the body as a child, when asthma and persistent illnesses kept him confined to bed in his rural and isolated hometown in far-western New York State. He grew into an extraordinarily handsome man, with the dark looks and wavy hair of a silent-screen star. But his illnesses continued, and by the time he reached maturity, he had retreated into a world of books. He was a fan of utopian science fiction, such as H. G. Wells's *In the Days of the Comet,* in which mankind, fearing destruction from an onrushing comet, remakes world society into a cooperative commune. Tugwell spent much of his youth conjuring perfect worlds inhabited by perfect people. As an undergraduate at the University of Pennsylvania in the 1910s, he fell under the spell of the young economics professor Scott Nearing, who had recently published a book calling for the creation of just such a world. "The kind of social philosophy I was developing under the tutelage of Nearing, reinforced by other instruction," Tugwell later recalled in his autobiography, "is perhaps best defined in a little book called *The Super Race: An American Problem,* which Nearing published in 1912." Nearing argued that the United States should develop, through selective breeding, a race of supermen who would create the world's first utopia. These ideas, which were bastardized versions of Friedrich Nietzsche's philosophy, were then in vogue among German intellectuals who would become the intellectual founders of Nazism.

Tugwell's other mentor in college was the prominent progressive economist Simon Patten, who had been trained in German universities. "He taught me the importance of looking for uniformities, laws, explanations of the inner forces moving behind the façade of events," Tugwell remembered. "One of these was the conclusion that our pluralistic system— laissez-faire in industry, checks and balances in government, and so on—must be shaped into a unity if its inherent conflicts, beginning to be so serious, were not to destroy us." From where did Patten get this benign-sounding idea? "He thought that the Germans had the key to that unity in philosophy, in economics, and perhaps in politics. He saw the conflict, now so ominously coming up over the horizon, as one between the living wholeness of the German conception and the dying divisiveness of English pluralism." Even more ominous was the belief that Patten shared with his German colleagues—who would supply the intellectual basis for Nazism—that industrial capitalism and technological advances had softened and emasculated the people. "Every improvement which simplifies or lessens manual labor," explained Patten, "increases the amount of the deficiencies which the laboring classes may possess without their being thereby overcome in the struggle for subsistence that the survival of the ignorant brings upon society." Patten's solution to this problem was swift, simple, and breathtakingly ruthless. "Social progress is a higher law than equality, and a nation must choose it at any cost," and the only way to progress is the "eradication of the vicious and inefficient." But the prescriptions of Nearing and Patten were just academic wishes. Tugwell wished to make them real.

The world war was a godsend. When America entered the European conflict in 1917, Tugwell, like many progressives, saw it as a chance to create "an industrial engineer's Utopia." The government agencies that seized control of major industries and directed the national economy from Washington, the campaigns against vice to maintain the country's discipline and racial vigor, and the creation of five million regimented, physically fit men through the draft, filled Tugwell with hope. "We were on the verge of having an international industrial machine," he later remembered. But peace dashed his dreams. "Only the Armistice prevented a great experiment in control of production, control of price, and control of consumption." Through the 1920s, Tugwell looked wistfully out the window of his Columbia office and wrote a series of articles calling for a return to a wartime society, when "social control" and the "scientific management of human life" would be the order of the day.

The stock market crash of 1929 provided his next opportunity. In the early years of the Great Depression, Tugwell wrote a book that he thought America, now in its most desperate hour, could finally take seriously. *The Industrial Discipline and the Governmental Arts* argued for making all of society into a great factory. The book called for removing "the dead hand of competitive enterprise" and replacing it with central planning. "When industry is government and government is industry, the dual conflict deep in our modern institutions will have abated," he said. Naturally, he admired the Italian government for doing just this. Mussolini, he said, had done "many of the things which seem to me necessary. And at any rate, [Italy] is being rebuilt physically in a systematic way."

On a frigid winter day in 1932, while walking down the street near his office, huddled in his tweed jacket and overcoat, Tugwell encountered a colleague from the political science department named Raymond Moley. Moley asked if he would like to meet Franklin Roosevelt, then the governor of New York and a candidate for the presidency, to discuss joining Roosevelt's team of advisors. Tugwell, thrilled, accepted the offer, and within a few weeks he was a member of the famous "Brains Trust," a small group of academics who built the New Deal. Tugwell would conceive and craft several major initiatives of the New Deal, including the NIRA, the public works programs, and many of Roosevelt's agricultural projects. But soon after he started his new job in Washington, Tugwell began to envy his hero in Rome. "Mussolini certainly has the same people opposed to him as F. D. R. has," Tugwell later said. "But he has the press controlled so they cannot scream lies at him daily. And he has a compact and disciplined nation, although it lacks resources. On the surface, at least, he seems to have made enormous progress." Democracy was the problem, and fascism was "the cleanest, neatest, most efficiently operating piece of social machinery I've ever seen. It makes me envious."

While Tugwell came to his love for regimentation through the life of the rationalistic mind, General Hugh Johnson came to his through another major source of New Deal culture: the military. With a round Irish face reddened by alcoholism, Johnson looked and drank like W. C. Fields, but he did not share the comedian's individualism and irreverence toward authority. As a teenager in the Wild West town of Alva, Oklahoma, Johnson voluntarily participated in twice-weekly drills with the local militia company. He was so enamored with thoughts of war that when he was fifteen he attempted to enlist with Teddy Roosevelt's Rough Riders to fight in the war against Spain. Foiled from becoming a child soldier by his father, Johnson nonetheless enrolled at West Point when he was just seventeen. Later, as an officer in the army, he relished directing drills, roll calls, parades, reviews, and marches, and was known to scream at soldiers for the smallest violations of protocol. While serving in the army, Johnson began a side career as a writer of short stories for magazines in which boys in the military learn discipline, loyalty, and self-sacrifice, and make themselves into men.

Like Tugwell and many future New Dealers, Johnson saw the Great War not as the worthless horror that most Americans considered it to be but as a long-awaited opportunity to militarize all of society. Because only 73,000 men volunteered for service in response to President Wilson's call to create an army of millions, the federal government was forced to institute the first draft since the Civil War. Several military leaders recognized that few people were better suited to the job of creating a vast army of conscripts than Johnson, and he was brought to Washington to implement the new Selective Service System. The registration of 10 million men for compulsory military service, which resulted in 4 million actually being shipped to training camps, 117,000 killed in action, and more than 200,000 wounded, "was one of the most spectacular developments of the war," Johnson recalled. He also devised a plan to make useful the undrafted men, "who stood in saloons and pool rooms watching their contemporaries marching away to war." All deferred men who were either unemployed or engaged in "nonessential work" were warned that they would be inducted into the military if they did not find work that was essential for the war effort. Johnson boasted that the "work or fight" order forced 137,255 "bartenders, private chauffeurs, men hairdressers, and the like that are pansies" to take jobs that the government considered essential.

During the 1920s, Johnson retreated into the private sector, waiting for the world to turn in favor of the martial life. In 1932, at the bottom of the Depression, Johnson saw his chance. He wrote a plan of action and circulated it privately among friends in the Democratic Party. With the heading, "By MUSCLEINNY, Dictator pro tem," Johnson's "Proclamation" called for him to "assum[e] the dictatorship of the Republic." The time was right to do away with democracy. "In this crisis, and especially in this political year, divided powers were wholly inadequate," he wrote. "*The sole cure was singleness of control and immediate action.*" He demanded that the president, vice president, "and all members of Congress" be removed from the country and that elections be suspended. One month after writing his proclamation, Johnson was invited into the inner circle of the Roosevelt campaign. He later recalled that "from the principle of taking active charge of events through several of the principal acts that were found to be necessary more than eight months later, *Muscleinny pretty accurately diagnosed the situation and at least dimly anticipated much of the Recovery Program.*"

When it came time to draft the National Industrial Recovery Act, Johnson successfully argued for the president alone—rather than Congress—to have supervisory power over the code authorities. When the act was passed, Roosevelt—perhaps out of gratitude—made Johnson the first administrator of the NRA. By then, Johnson had discovered the writings of the Italian fascists. He distributed books written by Mussolini's education minister to other members of the Roosevelt cabinet, and in a speech called the Italian dictator the "shining example of the twentieth century."

Johnson brought in Donald Richberg, a progressive labor lawyer who helped craft the NIRA, to be the general counsel of the NRA. Richberg recalled that the drafting of the law grew out of a desire to end parliamentary democracy and establish autocratic rule in America. "America did not want to reform its bad habits," he said, and someone had to do it for the people. "America is not going to choose to do anything which a large number of Americans do not wish to do—so long as democratic government can endure and politicians can evade a perilous issue," Richberg wrote. What he called "the inefficiencies and corruptions of popular government" were replaced by a single leader. "We called for a Man of Action, and we got one . . . The American people might well go down upon their knees and thank God that . . . there came into power the man who alone could save them—the Man of Action." As the legal historian James Q. Whitman puts it, "The two leaders of the NIRA were marked antiparliamentarians; the true creatures of the crisis atmosphere of 1932–33."

Two other creatures of that crisis, Roosevelt and Hitler, shared a devotion to the soil and a belief that their nations could be redeemed by merging with it. First, they both established control over agriculture. In the United States, through the Agricultural Adjustment Act of 1933, and in Germany, through the Estate for Agriculture, the national government decided how much farmers would produce and how much they would charge for it. Roosevelt and Hitler both saw the family farm as the root of national virtue. For the president, the country was the only place "to establish a real home in the traditional American sense." For the führer, peasants were "the foundation and life source" of Germany and "the source of national fertility." As governor of New York, Roosevelt established a program to pay for city families to move to farms so that "they may secure through the good earth the permanent jobs they have lost in overcrowded cities and towns." As president, he launched a program designed by Tugwell called Subsistence Homesteads, which provided families with "a modern but inexpensive house and outbuildings, located on a plot of land upon which a family may produce a considerable portion of the food required for home consumption." Likewise, the Nazis subsidized the construction of homes in rural areas in order to encourage self-sufficiency and to alleviate overcrowding in the cities. In Italy, one of Mussolini's most ambitious projects was the draining of a three-hundred-square-mile marshland near Rome and the establishment of independent family farms on the reclaimed land. As the German cultural historian Wolfgang Schivelbusch has written, "Fascism, National Socialism, and the New Deal all made the garden-settlement into a cornerstone of their plans for a new form of civilization, feeding popular enthusiasm with appealing words, images, and projects."

Roosevelt's favorite New Deal initiative was the Civilian Conservation Corps, also created in 1933, which placed young men in military-style camps and put them to work in the nation's hinterland. The Nazis, too, improved much of the German countryside through the labor of youth housed in work camps. "There was, furthermore, little difference in appearance or intent," according to John Garraty, "between the Nazi work camps and those set up in America under the Civilian Conservation Corps." Roosevelt praised the CCC for getting young men "off the city street corners." Hitler said the Nazi work camps saved German youth from "rotting helplessly in the streets." Both the New Dealers and Nazis designed the programs to shape young men into citizen-soldiers. The U.S. Army was put in control of the hundreds of thousands of volunteers who enlisted in the CCC. "Corpsmen" were required to stand at attention, to address their superiors as "Sir," and to attend morning and evening flag-raising ceremonies. One corpsman remarked in a letter home, "The engineers and technicians teach us to be soil soldiers, a name they call us here, because we are the army who are training to repel the enemies of the land."

Toward the end of the 1930s, as America moved closer to war, this militarization of youth became the undisguised purpose of the CCC. In 1940 Congress mandated noncombat military training for all CCC enrollees. The director of the program, James J. McEntee, explained that the military emphasis was necessary for "converting unemployed young men without work experience into strong, vigorous young men who could drive trucks, tractors, which are the first cousins to tanks, build roads, bridges, telephone lines . . . which would aid in the advancement of industrial defense and in the strengthening of the military forces."

The New Dealers, Mussolini, and Hitler were united in the belief that the conditions of the working class had to be greatly improved. The Fascist and Nazi regimes outlawed trade unions, but they worked hard to make factories safer, cleaner, and more pleasant workplaces, and also provided subsidized housing, low-cost vacations, and sports programs to millions of workers. In the U.S., more money was spent on public works projects than on any other part of the New Deal. The Works Progress Administration (WPA), established in 1935, was the largest such program. It made up half the federal budget and employed an average of 2.1 million workers per year between 1935 and 1941. WPA workers built highways, roads, sidewalks, libraries, schools, stadiums, parks, airports, sewage treatment plants, bridges, and swimming pools. Of the three regimes, the Third Reich was the most effective in delivering a new life to the workers. The Nazis instituted a full employment program that within three years of Hitler's rise to power had virtually eliminated unemployment in Germany. A massive public works project, the *Reichsarbeitsdienst* (RAD), rivaled the WPA in size and scope. Functioning as a militarylike unit, the RAD built the Autobahn, countless surface roads, and bridges. It reclaimed marshland for cultivation, constructed dykes, improved drainage systems, and completed vast tree removal operations. During the war, the RAD built bunkers, underground facilities, and entrenchments all over Europe.

In both the U.S. and Germany, government-sponsored employment programs were in large part directed toward military purposes. The Nazis put hundreds of thousands of Germans to work building weapons, planes, and tanks. In the U.S., workers employed by the Public Works Administration built two aircraft carriers, four cruisers, several smaller warships, more than one hundred fighter planes and bombers, close to fifty military airports, and the air force headquarters. The German and American public works programs served another important function too: they regimented large portions of the American and German workforces and inculcated national cultures of discipline, order, sacrifice, and loyalty to the state. It is striking to see how similar were the ways in which the New Dealers and Nazis promoted their programs. In the thousands of posters produced by both governments, loyalty to the state frames the messages, work is extolled as a means to dignity, masculinity and manual labor are glorified, and homoerotic overtones abound.

Left: Poster promoting Works Progress Administration.

Right: "You are the front."

Left: WPA poster.

Right: "Workers of the mind and hand: Vote for the front soldier Hitler!"

There was a widespread belief in both nations that the dissolution of the family in the sexually liberated 1920s was both a cause and result of social disorder. Consequently, New Dealers and Nazis undertook propaganda campaigns to promote motherhood and merge it with the national interest. According to the manifesto of the Nazi women's organization, "To be a woman means to be a mother, means affirming with the whole conscious force of one's soul the value of being a mother and making it a law of life." The German Law to Reduce Unemployment of 1933 replaced women workers by funding work projects and occupational training programs that excluded women. Likewise, under the New Deal, federal and state governments were given the power to enforce motherhood. The Social Security Act of 1935, a major piece of legislation in the so-called Second New Deal and one of the few to survive into the twenty-first century, included an old-age pension system and an unemployment insurance program. Because the unemployment and pension programs excluded domestic workers, most women who worked were excluded from work-related government aid. The Social Security Act was designed to give aid to only a certain kind of woman: a woman who contributed to the nation as the producer of workers, soldiers, and citizens. The law established Aid to Dependent Children (ADC), a welfare program intended to keep mothers in the home. According to the committee that drafted the ADC provision in the law, it was "designed to release from the wage-earning role the person whose natural function is to give her children the physical and affectionate guardianship necessary not alone to keep them from falling into social misfortune, but more affirmatively to rear them into citizens capable of contributing to society."

THE DISCIPLINE OF A DEMOCRACY

In both the U.S. and Germany, censorship of the press increased dramatically during the era of the New Deal and Nazism, but more often the press censored itself to support the state, avoid punishment, or simply to abide by the norms of cultures that were increasingly hostile to free expression. In Germany, hundreds of journalists enthusiastically joined the Ministry of Propaganda. For others, according to Schivelbusch, "Mere knowledge of the consequences of noncompliance with the often unwritten rules sufficed to encourage most of them to toe the line, and enforce the most effective and invisible form of control—self-censorship." In the U.S., there was some heavy-handed censorship but far more willing submission by the press itself.

Roosevelt appointed loyalists to the Federal Communications Commission who made it clear that licenses would be revoked for broadcasters who aired programs critical of the government. In 1934 the Yankee Radio Network of New England promised to give the president "a lot of support" after it received warnings from an FCC commissioner. An executive for another network said that the fear of government intervention would "blue pencil a dozen programs for every one that an official censor might object to." In the first weeks of the Roosevelt administration, NBC instituted a policy barring the president's critics from its broadcasts. Henry Bellows of CBS told Roosevelt's press secretary immediately after the inauguration that "the close contact between you and the broadcasters has tremendous possibilities of value to the administration, and as a lifelong Democrat, I want to pledge my best efforts in making this cooperation successful." In 1935 CBS celebrated the second anniversary of the New Deal with *Of the People, by the People, for the People,* a program in which professional actors re-created great moments in the administration's first two years. The U.S. Office of Education mandated that civics classes in public schools play the two-hour program for students. Boake Carter of CBS was a popular political commentator until 1938, when he was fired for his increasingly critical remarks about the president. Both CBS and NBC continued to ban critics of the New Deal through the 1930s and into the war.

Hollywood, the chief transmitter of national social norms, underwent a profound transformation during the New Deal. As we have seen, in the 1920s and especially in the early 1930s, rogues were the heroes of the silver screen, as Hollywood movies reflected and promoted the sexual liberation and disregard for authority that were evident in American culture at the time.

The Catholic Church and other moral reformers pressured Hollywood to clean up its movies. In 1930 the Motion Picture Producers and Distributors of America, better known as the Hays Office after its chairman, Will Hays, issued a code of self-censorship for the industry. But it was not enforced for several years. According to Hays, Hollywood and America were not yet ready to limit their freedom of expression. "Trying to preach morality in a cataclysm of that sort was like a voice sounding off in the desert," he said. The so-called Hays Code was not implemented until March 6, 1933, two days after Roosevelt took office. This indicated, according to film historian Giuliana Muscio (author of the only scholarly study of the New Deal and Hollywood), "that the industry was afraid that an administration that championed federal intervention like the New Deal would interfere with film affairs." That is, the studio chiefs understood that if they didn't censor themselves, Washington would do it for them.

The Hays Code was as thoroughgoing a restriction of expression as any system of censorship imposed in Germany and Italy. It also far outlived the Nazi and Fascist regimes. For more than thirty-two years, until it was replaced in 1967 by the film rating system, virtually all motion pictures produced in the United States adhered to the code. To begin, the code stated broadly, "No picture shall be produced that will lower the moral standards of those who see it." Only "Correct standards of life, subject only to the requirements of drama and entertainment, shall be presented." The third section of the code, which mandated that "Law, natural or human, shall not be ridiculed," was undoubtedly well received by a federal government that was then producing a massive and unprecedented system of regulatory laws.

The depiction of sexuality was severely restricted. "The sanctity of the institution of marriage and the home shall be upheld," the code stated. "Pictures shall not infer that low forms of sex relationship are the accepted or common thing." More to the point, "Scenes of passion . . . should not be introduced when not essential to the plot." What were the forbidden "low forms" of sexuality? "Excessive and lustful kissing, lustful embraces, suggestive postures and gestures, are not to be shown . . . In general, passion should so be treated that these scenes do not stimulate the lower and baser element." Of course, "Sex perversion," referring to homosexuality, "or any inference to it is forbidden," but so was "white slavery," "miscegenation" (sex relationships between the white and black races), mention of "sex hygiene and venereal diseases," and even "indecent movements" in dancing. To keep audiences from drawing illicit connections, "The treatment of bedrooms must be governed by good taste and delicacy" and "scenes of actual child birth, in fact or in silhouette, are never to be presented."

In language virtually identical to the Third Reich's laws against "degenerate art," the code proclaimed that it was intended to produce "correct entertainment" and prevent the creation of "wrong entertainment" that "lowers the whole living conditions and moral ideals of a race." While the Nazis were purging German museums of thousands of works of "immoral" art, the most popular art form in the United States was being produced according to a set of rules organized around the belief that "Art can be morally evil in its effects. This is the case clearly enough with unclean art, indecent books, suggestive drama."

It is well known that the state and the media were merged in Italy and

Germany. In the United States, the merger of the New Deal and Hollywood was less formal but no less complete. It began even before Roosevelt
was elected. In September 1932, Jack Warner of Warner Bros. staged the
Motion Picture Electrical Parade and Sports Pageant at Los Angeles Olympic Stadium, which according to Muscio was "a spectacle in the style of
a gigantic Busby Berkeley film" and "an unequivocal political promotion
of Roosevelt as a presidential candidate." It featured giant electrical floats
and "human geometrics of bodies reminiscent of the mass choreography
typical of Nazism." Warner Bros. continued to be an unofficial propagan-
dist for the New Deal after the election. In 1933 the studio released *The
Road Is Open Again,* which served precisely the function performed by
the Nazi propaganda offices. In this film, the spirits of presidents Washington, Lincoln, and Wilson praise the current president:

WASHINGTON: Well, Abe, it looks as though we can stop worrying
about our country. Roosevelt has it headed right again.

LINCOLN: All it needed was a plan of action . . . and a man with
the courage to carry it through.

WILSON: There isn't a person in America who won't benefit by the
NRA, if every man, woman and child does his part.

WASHINGTON: You can always depend on Americans.

Another Warner Bros. film released in 1933, a box-office smash called
Footlight Parade, features a grand finale, choreographed by Busby Berkeley,
in which marching soldiers form themselves into images of an American
flag, a portrait of FDR, and the NRA eagle.

Other studios did their share for the New Deal as well. Fox's biggest
star in the early 1930s was Will Rogers, who was also the leading supporter of the New Deal in American popular culture. Rogers had been a
vaudeville and silent movie star in the 1910s and 1920s, but he gained his
greatest fame during the first three years of the Roosevelt administration.
He starred in twelve films between 1933 and 1935, and during that time
established what came to be known as the "Will Rogers formula." Typically, Rogers played a plain, pure-of-heart character from a rural town
who is victimized by big-city businessmen. The plot normally involved

the collective work of ordinary Americans like himself to overcome their oppression. In nearly all of his films, work—in particular direct, physical labor carried out cooperatively and for the community rather than for individual gain—is portrayed as noble, while the desire for material comforts and luxuries is shown as the source of corruption. Rogers campaigned vigorously for Roosevelt in the 1932 election, then used his radio show to promote New Deal policies. He called himself "the Number One New Dealer." Rogers was also a great admirer of another world leader. "Mussolini, he's the biggest thing in the world today," he said on a speaking tour in 1927, one year after he met Il Duce in Italy. "Anyone who can put those dagoes to work is some guy." Later, in a speech to a crowd of his fans, the Number One New Dealer praised Mussolini's militarism:

> He knows the Nations that are great are the ones that have something in the way of side arms. He knows that without an Army and Navy they will never be able to find room for his growing population. That fellow has kept Italy on the up-grade for all these years, and all the time everybody says, "Oh, he can't last." I have said ever since I met him in '26, that he was by far the greatest Guy I had ever met, and there has never been a day since then that I have changed. He has done more for his Country than any man ever did for one in a like time. You don't see 'em shooting at him any more do you. He is a Whiz, that baby is. I have never yet seen him propose a fool thing.

After he died in a plane crash, Rogers was replaced at the top of the box office charts by Shirley Temple, whose breakthrough film was *Stand Up and Cheer,* released by Fox in 1934. In the film, the president of the United States, who looks very much like Franklin Roosevelt, appoints a secretary of amusement to cheer up the country. The secretary recruits vaudeville acts, in opposition to a gloomy group of businessmen called the "bluenoses" who have a financial interest in prolonging the Depression. His star performer is a four-year-old girl played by Temple, who wins over the nation with her singing. At the end of the film, a crowd shouts into the camera, "The Depression is over! Men are going back to work!"

The Roosevelt administration appreciated the efforts of the Hays Office, which was busily purifying Hollywood films according to the Motion Picture Production Code. In 1938 Eleanor Roosevelt wrote in *Photoplay* magazine that she was happy to see that movie producers had taken on the responsibility of "creating good taste" in the American public. And without the slightest embarrassment, she declared that censorship and the narrowing of artistic expression served the national interest:

> The highly cultured people of the world are those who have good taste . . . some things in literature and the arts have always presaged decadence. Those things must be kept from the drama if we are to promote good taste. Here is the great challenge to the movie producer of the future—will movies be an instrument in the development of good taste and are we growing up to be a nation with artistic knowledge and appreciation?

In 1941 Will Hays received a letter of encouragement from Franklin Roosevelt, in which the president praised him as the engineer of "the greatest propaganda machine in the country." Urging the Hollywood censor to continue his work, Roosevelt wrote, "You are the kind of Czar that nobody could call 'a Dictator' because you are fair-minded and do not use a whip but still get things done for the general good." Indeed, the leaders of the American movie industry enjoyed extraordinarily close relationships with both Roosevelt and Mussolini.

In 1935, Charles Pettijohn, general counsel for the Motion Pictures Producers and Distributors of America, met with Mussolini and suggested making a documentary about the Fascist state. He guaranteed that it would be shown in "about 14,500 American theatres" so that "about 70 million Americans would have understood better Italy's position." In 1936 Hays himself traveled to Italy when some Fascist officials suggested blocking the importation of American movies. Hays convinced Mussolini that the code's "reformation" of American movies had aligned them with the moral values of the Italian state. After that meeting, Mussolini allowed more than 250 American films to be shown in Italy per year. Hays then appointed Pettijohn to serve as an unofficial liaison between the U.S. and Italian governments. In 1937 Pettijohn met with Vittorio Mussolini, Il Duce's son, who was on his way to Hollywood to establish a production company with studio chief Hal Roach, who had made stars out of Laurel and Hardy, the "Our Gang" kids, and Will Rogers. The company was called RAM Films, for "Roach and Mussolini," and it made documentary newsreels promoting Italy. Pettijohn wrote to the Roosevelts' son-in-law, John Boettiger, that the young Mussolini was "a fine, quiet, modest, young man," who "expressed a very sincere desire to meet the president before he goes back to Italy." Pettijohn's letter revealed friendly relations between the Roosevelt and Mussolini families. "The president's son [John Roosevelt] met his father [Benito Mussolini] in Rome, and I just suspect that the president would permit this boy [Vittorio] to return the call." Shortly thereafter, Vittorio Mussolini had tea with FDR in the White House.

Regimentation, the hallmark of Nazi and Fascist culture, was a prominent theme in Hollywood musicals and federal propaganda during the New Deal. Busby Berkeley and Warner Bros. put out several enormously popular films in the early years of the New Deal that were openly partisan for the Roosevelt administration. *Gold Diggers of 1933, 42nd Street, Footlight Parade,* and *Dames* all featured tightly synchronized movements by large numbers of dancers and implicit collectivist messages. Berkeley acknowledged that designing parade drills as an army lieutenant during World War I was the "best apprenticeship" for his career as a choreographer.

Martial imagery was a staple of New Deal culture, and it was common for public officials to speak of bringing order and discipline to daily life. In 1932 Roosevelt pledged during his election campaign to mobilize "the infantry of our economic army." A few months into his presidency, the National Recovery Administration distributed badges to be worn by participants in what Roosevelt called the "great offensive against unemployment."

> In war, in the gloom of night attack, soldiers wear a bright badge on their shoulders to be sure that comrades do not fire on comrades. On that principle, those who cooperate in this program must know each other at a glance. That is why we have provided a badge of honor for this purpose, a simple design with a legend, "We do our part," and I ask that all those who join with me shall display that badge prominently. It is essential to our purpose.

In 1937 Roosevelt used similar language to ask Congress for new public works programs. "You and I cannot afford to equip ourselves with two rounds of ammunition where three rounds are necessary," he said. "If we stop at relief and credit, we may find ourselves without ammunition before the enemy is routed. If we are fully equipped with the third round of ammunition, we stand to win the battle against adversity." Roosevelt's cabinet members often spoke of him as though he were the leader of a conquering army. Harold Ickes, the secretary of the interior, said in 1934 that FDR "grasped this acute situation with a firm hand and proceeded to restore order."

> In my judgment here is the leader you have been looking for for more years than you would like to remember. And, miracle of miracles, this leader in a great forward movement for a new and better social order is actually occupying the seat of the mightiest ruler in the world today. Strong in the faith of the people, entrenched in their confident affections, he will not fail us unless we fail him. He is the master of a stout ship, sailing in the right direction. Granted any sort of a favoring breeze, he will bring us safely into the harbor of a fairer land.

Washington, DC, and many German cities were remade during the period of the New Deal and Nazism. Hitler's architects designed several buildings that became characteristic of a distinctive "Nazi architecture," including the Olympic Stadium, the new Reich Chancellery, the Tempelhof Airport, the Ministry of Aviation, the Japanese embassy in Berlin, and the House of German Art. Hitler also worked with his favorite architect, Albert Speer, on a complete redesign of Berlin that included an immense domed "Great Hall" connected by a three-mile-long avenue to the chancellery. While planning these buildings, Nazi architects implemented the theory of "ruin value," which was enthusiastically supported by Hitler. According to this theory, all new buildings were designed to leave imposing ruins thousands of years in the future that would stand as testaments to the greatness of the Third Reich. The theory was realized in monumental stone constructions that imitated ancient Greek and Roman styles.

The monumentalist, neoclassical style was also favored by architects hired by the Roosevelt administration to design the buildings that came to define modern Washington, including the Federal Triangle, the National Gallery of Art, the National Archives, the Supreme Court Building, the Pentagon, the Department of Justice Building, and the Jefferson Memorial. The architectural historian Thomas S. Hines has noticed that this was a transatlantic phenomenon: Roosevelt's "architectural tastes were grandly conservative, not far removed from those of his contemporaries, the dictators of Italy and Germany." Particularly striking were the similarities between the designs of Albert Speer and Roosevelt's favorite architect, James Russell Pope. Hines suggests that historians begin to make "overt comparisons, formally and culturally, of the architecture of Pope and the frequently similar work of the German architect Albert Speer." Another architectural historian, John W. Reps, has noted the "supreme irony" that an architectural style "originally conceived to magnify the glories of despotic kings and emperors came to be applied as a national symbol of a country whose philosophical basis was so firmly rooted in democratic equality."

Certainly, there was one obvious difference between the New Deal and Nazism, which is that in the United States there was never a mass murder of Jews—or of gypsies, the disabled, communists, or homosexuals—in the name of "racial purity." There was, however, a different form of racial purification attempted in the U.S., one that was carried out by Jews against themselves.

Before the New Deal, Jewish heroes filled the eyes of moviegoers. Jewish and Gentile filmmakers told stories set in eastern European *shtetls* and the Lower East Side. American audiences saw rabbis, cantors, street peddlers, and Yiddish-speaking heroes. Unambiguously Jewish movie stars, such as Vera Gordon, Molly Picon, Eddie Cantor, Fanny Brice, Al Jolson, and the Marx Brothers played unambiguously Jewish characters named Cohen, Goldberg, Rubens, Feinbaum, and Rabinowitz. Even the famous WASP (and racist) director D. W. Griffith made a sentimental film about a young seamstress in the Lower East Side who struggles with the death of her mother. Remarkably, the heyday of Jews in films took place during the 1920s, which was also the heyday of American anti-Semitism, when more than four million people joined the Ku Klux Klan, books and newspapers warning of "the international Jew" sold by the millions, and immigration was cut off from eastern Europe. One group of Jewish filmmakers in Philadelphia responded by deliberately producing even more films on "the every-day life of the Jew." More remarkably, in the midst of a viciously anti-Semitic culture, when Jews were widely blamed for the Depression, some of the most successful Hollywood films celebrated Jewish–Gentile intermarriage. Following the premise of the enormously successful *Abie's Irish Rose* (1928), *The Cohens and Kellys* series—a string of seven comedies made by Universal Pictures during the early Depression—told the story of a marriage between a Jewish woman and an Irish-Catholic man.

By the time of the New Deal, Jews had taken over much of the American film industry. Seven of the eight major Hollywood studios during the 1930s were owned wholly by immigrant Jews. A 1936 study found that 62 percent of studio employees engaged in production were Jewish. But these Jews had a different mission than their predecessors. They played golf and polo. They married Gentile women. Louis Mayer, the head of MGM, claimed that he had lost his birth records while immigrating from Russia and took July 4 as his birthday. Harry Cohn of Columbia Pictures delighted in telling "Jew jokes," and when asked to contribute to a Jewish relief fund, yelled, "Relief *for* the Jews! How about relief *from* the Jews?" All the Hollywood moguls threw lavish Christmas parties, rarely if ever attended synagogue, and made a point of working on Rosh Hashanah, Yom Kippur, and Passover. They mocked Kosher dietary rules.

Film historian Neal Gabler, author of *An Empire of Their Own: How the Jews Invented Hollywood,* has described the anti-Semitism of Hollywood Jews in the 1930s in terms of a cultural holocaust: "Above all things, they wanted to be regarded as Americans, not Jews; they wanted to reinvent themselves here as new men." Assimilation among immigrants was nothing new, "but something drove the young Hollywood Jews to a ferocious, even pathological, embrace of America. Something drove them to deny whatever they had been before settling here." The men who controlled Hollywood "embarked on an assimilation so ruthless and complete that they cut their lives to the pattern of American respectability as they interpreted it." They "launched a war against their own pasts."

Hollywood films of the New Deal era were an exercise in what historian Gary Gerstle calls "ethnic erasure." Jews were removed from American culture. "The dominant tendency of the thirties is the repression of ethnic and cultural differences and the representation of the average American—the final result of the great 'melting pot,'" writes film historian Patricia Erens, author of *The Jew in American Cinema*. "By 'average' Hollywood meant White Anglo-Saxon Protestant. Thus for most of the thirties, the Jew as a recognizable character practically disappears from the screen." The Hays Office disallowed the use of the words *Jew* or *Jewish* and any reference to religious practices. In films set in Europe, Jews were designated as "non-Aryan," a Nazi term. Studio executives insisted that Jewish actors "Americanize" their names, so Emanuel Goldenberg became Edward G. Robinson, Betty Perske became Lauren Bacall, David Kaminsky became Danny Kaye, Bernard Schwartz became Tony Curtis, and Issur Danielovitch Demsky became the square-jawed, all-American Kirk Douglas. Stories taken from the Yiddish theater were translated into films with Gentile characters and settings far from the ghetto. Even movies about famous episodes of anti-Semitism, like *They Won't Forget* (1937), about the Leo Frank case, and *The Life of Emile Zola* (1937), about the Dreyfus affair, made the victims into Gentiles.

Racial purity was a prominent theme in New Deal culture. "Eugenics," a doctrine organized around the belief that the human race can and should be perfected by encouraging breeding among superior people and preventing breeding among the inferior, is commonly associated with the Nazi regime. However, Nazis learned much of what they knew about eugenics from Americans. And while the Roosevelt administration never officially promoted eugenics as the Nazis did, its forerunners introduced the doctrine, and the New Deal was born during the heyday of American eugenics. By the mid-1930s, forty-one states prohibited marriage among the "feebleminded" and insane, and thirty allowed eugenic sterilization. In Alabama, those considered by the state to be "feebleminded" were involuntarily sterilized. In California, the law also allowed for "habitual criminals," "idiots," and "mental defectives" to be forced to have the surgery. Connecticut committed "those with inherited tendency to crime" to be sterilized. Laws in fourteen states applied to epileptics. "Moral degenerates" and "sexual perverts" were sterilized in North Dakota, Oregon, and Washington; "morally degenerate persons" in Idaho and Iowa. In Wisconsin, the law applied to "criminal persons."

According to the historian Steven Selden, author of *Inheriting Shame:*

The Story of Eugenics and Racism in America, "Eugenic ideology was deeply embedded in American popular culture during the 1920s and 1930s." Films such as *The Black Stork* promoted the sterilization of "unfit" women. Many ministers taught their congregations that genetically superior people should be careful to avoid marrying someone from an inferior gene pool. State fairs across the country featured "Fitter Families" exhibits that offered free eugenic evaluations. Those who received low scores were warned that they might be among those Americans who were "born to be a burden on the rest." High scorers were given medals proclaiming, "Yea, I Have a Goodly Heritage." In the 1930s, most high school science textbooks included lessons on eugenics, including the concept of "fit" and "unfit" races and the need to sterilize the unfit to preserve American culture. Harvard, Columbia, Cornell, and Brown were among hundreds of colleges and universities that offered courses on eugenics.

American eugenics and the New Deal were both progeny of the progressives. A large number of progressives who established many of the principles and policies that were later developed by the Roosevelt administration—including Margaret Sanger, David Starr Jordan, Robert Latham Owen, William Allen Wilson, Harry Emerson Fosdick, Robert Latou Dickinson, Katherine Bement Davis, Virginia Gildersleeve, and Rexford Tugwell's mentors, Simon Patten and Scott Nearing—were deeply involved with the eugenics movement. They saw in it a means to extend their mission of social planning into the bedroom and the maternity ward, to regulate the population at its genesis. Paul Popenoe, the most influential American eugenicist, was a leader in the progressive movement for "social hygiene." During World War I, Popenoe served as a captain in the U.S. Army Sanitary Corps, in charge of controlling liquor and vice in army camps—a major progressive cause. After the war, Popenoe's research and advocacy helped make California the leader in eugenic sterilizations. His book *Sterilization for Human Betterment* was one of the first American books translated into German by the Nazi government, and it was widely cited by Hitler's "racial hygiene" theorists to justify the Nazis' own sterilization programs. In 1934 Popenoe praised Hitler for establishing "his hopes of biological regeneration solidly on the application of biological principles of human society." Other American eugenicists expressed envy for their more successful German colleagues, as did Dr. Joseph S. DeJarnette, director of Western State Hospital in Virginia, in 1938:

> Germany in six years has sterilized about 80,000 of her unfit while the United States with approximately twice the population has only sterilized about 27,869 to January 1, 1938 in the past 20 years. . . . The fact that there are 12,000,000 defectives in the US should arouse our best endeavors to push this procedure to the maximum.

However, DeJarnette could take some solace in the fact that more sterilizations took place during the New Deal than at any other time in American history. The leading historian of the American eugenics movement, Daniel Kevles, found that "through the nineteen-twenties, the national sterilization rate had annually run between two and four per hundred thousand" in the American population. "In the mid-thirties the rate shot up to fifteen and climbed to twenty by the end of the decade. . . . Moreover, from 1932 to 1941, sterilization was actually practiced—as distinct from merely legislated—in a greater number of states than before."

In 1940 the Pioneer Fund, a leading eugenicist organization, embarked on an experiment with the help of Roosevelt's secretary of war, Harry H. Woodring, to find a way to improve the human race. The group offered $4,000, the equivalent of a middle-class salary, for the education of additional children born to U.S. Air Corps officers who already had at least three offspring—a group they considered to be genetically superior. The air corps (the precursor to the air force) promoted the program among its officers and provided the Pioneer Fund with extensive personnel records, including information on parentage, race, and religion. Twelve children received scholarships from the fund before the war ended the experiment.

The Second World War appeared to many contemporary observers, and still appears to many historians, as proof of a fundamental antagonism between fascism and the American way of life. Many have seen the war as evidence that, in particular, the New Deal–liberal way of life was hostile to fascism. After all, while many Republicans and other enemies of the New

Deal were opposed to fighting fascism abroad, Roosevelt led the nation to war against Germany, Italy, and Japan. More than four hundred thousand Americans died in the fight, and the Roosevelt administration made sure to not just defeat the fascist regimes but to obliterate them. But the evidence of their similarities suggests that the New Deal and fascism went to war not over ideas or values or a way of life. Rather, it seems, the war was a struggle between brothers for control of the world family.

★ 12 ★

JUST HOW POPULAR WAS WORLD WAR II?

It might have been "the Greatest Generation," as the television journalist and author Tom Brokaw calls the cohort of Americans who lived through the era of World War II, but it was far less willing to go along with the war effort than we are led to believe. Moreover, the resistance to the national mobilization in the midst of what many believe to be the most patriotic era in American history helped give flower to stunningly renegade cultures.

Unlike in many other wars, when majorities of able-bodied men readily volunteered to fight for a cause, and despite loud and sustained calls by government officials for American men to enlist in the military, most Americans during World War II were less than eager to make the ultimate sacrifice of citizenship when called upon to do so. Some two-thirds of the American soldiers who fought in the war did not volunteer; they were drafted, which alone indicates that the desire of Americans to fight was limited.

Even before the attack on Pearl Harbor, the Roosevelt administration, hopefully anticipating U.S. entry into either the war in Europe or a new war to stop the advance of Japan across the Pacific—yet pessimistic about the will of Americans to fight—urged Congress in 1940 to pass the nation's first peacetime draft legislation. The Selective Training and Service Act, signed into law by Roosevelt in September 1940, required that men between the ages of twenty-one and thirty-five register with local draft boards. The military draft was hailed by the president as having been since the Revolution the "keystone in the arch of our national defense." Yet in the months following the bombing of Pearl Harbor on December 7, 1941, it became clear that not enough men were volunteering to win the war and that many of those who enlisted voluntarily were unfit to fight. So on December 5, 1942, Roosevelt issued an executive order ending voluntary enlistments. From then through the war, the War Manpower Commission oversaw the involuntary induction of an average of two hundred thousand men per month. Some ten million American men were forced to fight in "the Good War." According to the historian Forrest C. Pogue, "it was the Selective Service Act of 1940 . . . that made possible the huge United States Army and Air Force that fought World War II."

The government also made it clear that those who refused to fight would be punished. Some six thousand people who either refused to serve in the military after being drafted or who did not register for the draft were punished with prison time or forced labor. And in 1940, Congress passed the Smith Act, which made it illegal to say or write anything that would encourage refusal of duty in the armed forces, even in peacetime.

Several books have celebrated the African American contributions to the armed services during World War II, but they ignore the fact that African Americans comprised 35 percent of the nation's delinquent draft registrants and more than 18 percent of those imprisoned for draft evasion. This was despite the strenuous efforts of the National Association for the Advancement of Colored People, the Urban League, and black newspapers to promote what they called the "Double-Victory" or "Double-V" campaign, meaning that the fight against the Axis was just as important as the fight against racism in America.

There is ample evidence to show that African Americans did not feel that it was their war—the overwhelming majority of the seven hundred thousand African Americans who served in the military during the war were drafted. There is also substantial anecdotal evidence that during the war, large numbers of black men feigned illness or insanity to evade the draft. In the cities, where drugs were widely available, many black men obtained 4-F status ("physically unfit") by ingesting amphetamines that "made your heart sound defective" before taking their medical inspections at induction centers. A young Malcolm X convinced his local draft board that he was psychologically and politically unfit for service:

In those days only three things in the world scared me: jail, a job, and the Army. I had about ten days before I was to show up at the induction center. I went right to work. The Army Intelligence soldiers, those black spies in civilian clothes, hung around in Harlem with their ears open for the white man downtown. I knew exactly where to start dropping the word. I started noising around that I was frantic to join . . . the Japanese Army. When I sensed that I had the ears of the spies, I would talk and act high and crazy. . . . The day I went down there, I costumed like an actor. With my wild zoot suit I wore the yellow knob-toe shoes, and I frizzled my hair up into a reddish bush of conk. I went in, skipping and tipping, and I thrust my tattered Greetings at that reception desk's white soldier—"Crazy-o, daddy-o, get me moving. I can't wait to get in that brown"—very likely that soldier hasn't recovered from me yet. . . . The room had fallen vacuum-quiet, with me running my mouth a mile a minute, talking nothing but slang. . . . Pretty soon, stripped to my shorts, I was making my eager-to-join comments in the medical examination rooms—and everybody in the white coats that I saw had 4-F in his eyes. . . . One of the white coats accompanied me around a turning hallway: I knew we were on the way to a head-shrinker—the Army psychiatrist. . . . I must say this for that psychiatrist. He tried to be objective and professional in his manner. He sat there and doodled with his blue pencil on a tablet, listening to me spiel to him for three or four minutes before he got a word in. . . . Suddenly, I sprang up and peeped under both doors, the one I'd entered and another that probably was a closet. And then I bent and whispered fast in his ear. 'Daddy-o, now you and me, we're from up North here, so don't you tell nobody. . . . I want to get sent down South. Organize them nigger soldiers, you dig? Steal us some guns, and kill us crackers!' That psychiatrist's blue pencil dropped, and his professional manner fell off in all directions. He stared at me as if I were a snake's egg hatching, fumbling for his red pencil. I knew I had him. I was going back out past Miss First when he said, "That will be all." A 4-F card came to me in the mail, and I never heard from the Army anymore, and never bothered to ask why I was rejected.

In a similar vein, John "Dizzy" Gillespie, a pioneer of bebop jazz, gained 4-F status by sharing these thoughts with his recruitment officer:

Well, look, at this time, at this stage in my life here in the United States whose foot has been in my ass? The white man's foot has been in my ass hole buried up to his knee in my ass hole! . . . Now you're speaking of the enemy. You're telling me the German is the enemy. At this point, I can never even remember having met a German. So if you put me out there with a gun in my hand and tell me to shoot at the enemy, I'm liable to create a case of "mistaken identity," of who I might shoot.

Virtually announcing their indifference toward citizenship, tens of thousands of black and Mexican American youths adopted the zoot suit style, which many whites considered to be outrageous and lacking proper respectability. The zoot-suiters were called unpatriotic slackers who were more interested in having a good time than in helping the war effort. This was largely true. Since the U.S. War Production Board had declared illegal the use of excess fabric for clothing, the zoot suit's baggy trouser legs, exaggerated shoulders, and accompanying wide-brim hat were patently unpatriotic. Many of the zoot-suiters were involved in street gangs, all of them were deeply immersed in the swing dance craze, and they were well known as draft dodgers. One zoot-suiter wrote a letter to the police and the draft board that included the following poem:

Yea, so it be
I leave this thought with thee
Do not attempt to fuck with me.

In early June 1943, local newspapers in Los Angeles played up a story that Mexicans had beaten up a group of Anglo sailors. In response, thousands of marines, sailors, soldiers, and civilians imposed a reign of terror on Mexican American neighborhoods in LA, assaulting zoot-suiters, stripping off their clothes, and cutting their long hair. No one was killed, but more than one hundred people were injured in the violence.

During the war, much of the racist hatred normally directed at African Americans was diverted toward the Japanese. It became commonplace to talk about the Japanese as a distinctively devious, sadistic, and cold-blooded "race" of people. This anti-Japanese racism, combined with the fact that there were only 127,000 Japanese in the United States at the time, made it relatively easy for the federal government to take action against what it thought was an internal threat to national security. Many in the State Department believed that Japanese living in Hawaii had helped plan the attack on Pearl Harbor and that Japanese in California were conspiring to help an invasion of the West Coast. In February 1942, Roosevelt signed an executive order, called the Civilian Exclusion Order, authorizing the army to place all people of Japanese descent living in the United States—even those *born* in the United States—in what were called "relocation centers." Roosevelt then issued another executive order creating the War Relocation Authority to oversee the project. Nearly all Japanese Americans were imprisoned in relocation centers, which were spread out in remote locations across the West.

Indeed, many Japanese Americans were *not* loyal to the United States. Just before the war began, more than 10,000 Japanese Americans joined the Japanese Military Servicemen's League, which paid dues to the Japanese army, and close to 5,000 were members of the Imperial Comradeship Society, which pledged to carry out sabotage against the U.S. The league's prospectus proclaimed, "whenever the Japanese government begins a military campaign, we Japanese must be united and everyone must do his part." Meetings of the two groups commenced with the singing of the Japanese national anthem and concluded with declarations of loyalty "for our emperor, our country, our race, our posterity." At one league meeting in Gardena Valley, near Los Angeles, members were told "to encourage the proudest Japanese national spirit which has ever existed, to fulfill the fundamental principle behind the wholesome mobilization of the Japanese people, to strengthen the powers of resistance against the many hindrances which are to be faced in the future," and to "assist in financing the war with the utmost effort on the part of both the first and second generation Japanese and whoever is a descendant of the Japanese race. Now is the time to awaken the Japanese national spirit in each and everyone who has the blood of the Japanese race in him. We now appeal to the Japanese in Gardena Valley to rise up at this time." The combined membership of the two groups comprised more than 12 percent of the total Japanese American population.

Other Japanese American organizations promoted similar loyalty to the home country. The Society for Defending the Country by Swords was made up of former soldiers in the Japanese military, and the Togo Kai raised money for the Japanese navy. Moreover, the historian John Stephan found that people of Japanese descent living in Hawaii purchased 3 million yen ($900,000, or $12 million in current dollars) worth of Imperial war bonds and gave 1.2 million yen ($350,000, or $4 million in current dollars) to the Japanese National Defense and Soldiers' Relief Fund between 1937 and 1939. Reportedly, Japanese living in Hawaii contributed more per capita to the National Defense Fund than did people living in Japan at the time. Japanese-language newspapers in California were staunchly pro-Japanese before wartime censors shut them down. A few months before the Pearl Harbor attack, the *New World Sun,* based in San Francisco, declared that Japanese in California were "ready to respond to the call of the mother country with one mind" and that "our fellow Japanese countrymen must be of one spirit and should endeavor to unite our Japanese societies in this country." Japanese-language newspapers in Hawaii referred to the Imperial Army as "our army" and to Japanese fighter pilots as "our angry eagles." Stephan also found that the tone and content of the English sections of Japanese American newspapers were far different than the sections in Japanese: "Treatment of Japan in the English sections was comparatively detached. However, the sections written in Japanese reverberated with [pro-Japan] patriotic rhetoric." Similarly, inscribed above the altar in Buddhist temples across Hawaii and California was the command "Now let us worship the Emperor every morning."

Virtually all Japanese American children attended Japanese-language schools, where they were taught not only the Japanese language, the making of sushi and origami, and the sport of sumo wrestling, but were also commanded to devote themselves to the Emperor. U.S. Senator Daniel Inouye, who attended one of the schools in Hawaii, recalled the intensely nationalistic teachings of the instructors:

> Day after day, the [Buddhist] priest who taught us ethics and Japanese history hammered away at the divine prerogatives of the Emperor. . . . He would tilt his menacing crew-cut skull at us and solemnly proclaim, "You must remember that only a trick of fate has brought you so far from your homeland, but there must be no

question of your loyalty. When Japan calls, you must know that it
is Japanese blood that flows in your veins."

Another observer reported that the school day began with the instructor
ordering students to "line up in ranks at stiff attention like miniature soldiers. The teacher would then hold up a picture of the emperor or a famous
Japanese general or admiral and the students would raise their hands in
a salute and shout '*Banzai*.'" Japan's Department of Education supplied
many of the textbooks used in the American Japanese-language schools.
One junior high school textbook declared, "We must never forget—not
even for a moment—that we are Japanese." The historian Page Smith calls
these schools "in practical fact agencies of Japanese nationalism." At the
time of the attack on Pearl Harbor, thirty-nine thousand *nisei* (American-
born children of Japanese immigrants) in Hawaii and eighteen thousand
in California were enrolled in Japanese-language schools. During the war,
several thousand American citizens of Japanese ancestry answered the call,
fled the United States, and joined the Imperial Army or Navy.*

This is *not* a defense of the internment of Japanese Americans. Nor is
it an attempt, made by many conservatives who have publicized this evidence, to support racial profiling and anti-immigration measures. It is,
however, part of an argument that America was far less united than we are
led to believe.**

Perhaps the most important battle on the home front was the battle for
production, or more precisely, the battle to make workers *produce*. Tom
Brokaw has told us all about Rosie the Riveter, victory gardens, and bond
drives, but we hear nothing about the workers in defense plants who went
on strike—and were called selfish, unpatriotic, and even traitorous.

The Office of Price Administration, which had been created during

---

* Estimates of the number of Nisei who joined the Japanese military during the war range
from the Japanese government's official figure of 1,648 to 7,000. These estimates do not include
the number of Japanese in the United States who assisted the Imperial Army and Navy as spies
and saboteurs.

** Several scholars have challenged Michelle Malkin's use of intercepted Japanese diplo-
matic communications—known as the "MAGIC cables"—to support her claim of an espionage
network inside the United States (*In Defense of Internment: The Case for Racial Profiling in World
War II and the War on Terror*), arguing that the messages do not contain clear evidence of such
a network. These scholars do not challenge the evidence of Japanese-American loyalty to Japan
that is presented here.

the war to control inflation, and the War Production Board, set strict limits on wages in most industries. Many workers made less per hour than they would have without the controls, since the labor market was so tight. Because of this, but also because of the strict discipline that had been instituted in the war industries, including mandatory overtime, there were more than fourteen thousand strikes involving more than six million workers during the war. Most of these strikes were in defense industries despite the no-strike pledge taken by the leaders of both labor union federations, and because of this, most were "wildcat" strikes in which the unions in the industries denounced the strikes and attempted to punish the strikers. In most cases, the unauthorized walkouts were responses to speedups, mandatory overtime, and disciplinary measures by plant managers. But the strikes were another indication that the willingness to sacrifice for the war effort was not as deep as the government would have liked. Workers who struck in the war industries were denounced for being unpatriotic, for putting their own interests above the interests of the wartime state. Those criticisms were largely true.

There were also two quite unintended and highly ironic consequences of the war that helped create the greatest *renegade* generation. First of all, the war was a watershed for gays and lesbians. Millions of gay people in isolated towns moved to cities or bases where they were able to find one another. Gay men who joined the military called it the turning point in their lives, and joining Women's Auxiliary Corps became well known among lesbians as the thing to do. Many gay men of the "Greatest Generation" have told of having their first sexual experiences in the military. Bob Thompson's happened on a troop train from San Diego to Madison, Wisconsin. "At the end of some cars," he remembered, "there were little compartments that would sleep maybe four. I think four of us had the same idea when we got on the train. We just rushed for one of those compartments, and all of us were gay. So it was something at night when we closed that door."

A captain in the Navy Surgeon General's Office reported in August 1942 that "the problem of the homosexual in the Naval Service and what to do with him is ever before us. . . . It seems likely," the captain predicted, "that under these circumstances homosexuality may become more widespread in the service as the war progresses." William Menninger, a psychiatrist who served as chief consultant to the surgeon general of the army, became convinced that the culture of the wartime army rapidly increased homosexual activity. In his study of the role of psychiatry in wartime, published in 1948, Menninger shocked many by characterizing the U.S. military during World War II, in a "technical, psychiatric sense," as "fundamentally a homosexual society." The success of any military endeavor, Menninger argued, "depended on the ability of men to get along with, live with, and work with other men, and to accept the almost total exclusion of women from their lives." To meet these demands, "certain adjustments were required of the 'normal'" trainee—most importantly the establishment of intimate bonds with other men. "Many men discovered satisfaction in a physical interest in other men, which often surprised them." And while the culture of the military appeared to be producing homosexual feelings in "normal" men, it was also being flooded with unambiguously homosexual men. Menninger surmised that "for every homosexual who was referred or came to the Medical Department (to be diagnosed and discharged), there were five or ten who never were detected."

"I found that it was quite easy to have sex in the army," recalled Robert Fleischer. "It was very furtive at first, because even the gay ones were afraid to expose themselves because they didn't know if you were going to turn them in or not turn them in. And after a while, you knew who was [gay], who wasn't, who [was] to be trusted, who not. There seemed to be available and interested men all through my basic training."

Soon after its establishment in May 1942, the Women's Army Corps gained a reputation as a hotbed of lesbianism. Increased screening found that many women chose the WAC from motives including "loves a uniform and what it stands for," "always wanted to be a boy and join the army," seeks "companionship of girls with similar patriotic desire," wants the "opportunity to mix with other girls," and so on. When Pat Bond went to enlist in the WAC, she recalled that the women "looked sort of like all my gym teachers in drag. Stockings, little earrings, her hair slicked back and very daintily done so you couldn't tell she was a dyke, but I knew!" Bond explained that many "butch" lesbians she knew applied for the WAC "wearing men's clothes" and despite these women's masculine appearances, the psychiatrists admitted them. "By God, when I got into basic, I thought I had transferred to hog heaven! . . . Everybody was going with someone," Bond remembered, "or had a crush on somebody or was getting ready to go with somebody."

Betty Somers, who went through basic training at women marines boot camp at Cherry Point, North Carolina, recalled that she never saw "any particular reaction" to "women being affectionate with each other." In particular, she remembered, women who volunteered for the motor pool, which provided the transportation of personnel and supplies in trucks and other military vehicles, were likely to be gay. At Somers's base, the women marines who drove the trucks were "really a sort of up-front, out-and-out lesbian group" with an especially strong softball team.

So great were authorities' perceptions of homosexuality in the services that they attempted to channel "abnormal" impulses into behavior conducive to military discipline. Trainees who exhibited "potential homosexual tendencies" could be "deterred from active participation" in gay sex by instructing them to redirect their sexual desires into a "'heteroworship' type of reaction." Similarly, WAC officers attempted to channel lesbian tendencies into nonsexual obedience to superiors. A good officer, "by the strength of her influence," could "bring out in the woman who had previously exhibited homosexual tendencies a definite type of leadership which can then be guided into normal fields of expression, making her a valued member of the corps."

One of the more striking but little acknowledged features of military life during World War II was the ubiquitous GI drag show. "From Broadway to Guadalcanal, on the backs of trucks, makeshift platforms, and elegant theater stages," writes historian Allan Bérubé, "American GIs did put on all-male shows for each other that almost always featured female impersonation routines." The Army Special Services Headquarters, which provided instructions for soldiers to stage their own entertainment, virtually codified the drag scene that is central to gay culture. The Special Services handbook for the show *Hi, Yank!* contained more than eight pages of patterns and illustrations for dresses to be worn by male soldiers, including instructions for making a "G.I. showgirl" gown out of an army blanket and a tutu out of a military-issue "T-shirt dyed pink." Many of the shows put on by soldiers were written by playwrights who were themselves gay and had developed the "camp" style of gay theater. Several army bases saw productions of *Private Maxie Reporting*, which featured an overtly gay character named "Pfc. Bloomingslip" who "wears a green carnation" and reports to Officer Candidate School because, as he says, "to be an officer would just be too, too queer!" The all-female satiric play *The*

Women, which had become a gay camp classic before the war and would be a staple of gay theater through the 1950s and 1960s, was one of the most popular shows put on by GIs. *Life* magazine singled out the cross-dressing performers for praise in its review of a production of the play at Lowry Field in Colorado: "Despite their hairy chests, size-16 shoes and bulging biceps, these 'actresses' did a good job with the play, present[ing] it as straight comedy. . . . After the first hour, the audience forgot that 'the women' were men, remembered only when they talked about having babies in their bass voices."

But the most popular Special Services theatrical production was *This Is the Army,* which according to Bérubé "became the prototypical World War II soldier show and established the three basic wartime styles of GI drag." These were the comic "pony ballets" of masculine men dancing and singing in dresses, highly skilled drag performances of songs, and what would become the centerpiece of postwar gay entertainment: impersonations of female celebrities. Reviewing one performance of *This Is the Army,* the New York *Herald Tribune* concluded that it "has everything except girls, and the terrible truth is that you don't miss them." In 1943 the War Department and Warner Bros. coproduced a film version of the play that featured several major Hollywood stars, including George Murphy, Joan Leslie, Alan Hale, and Ronald Reagan. Bérubé notes that the great influx of women into the military services beginning in 1942 and many attempts to stage male-and-female productions did not reduce the demand among GIs for all-male drag shows.

Perhaps the most important and lasting consequence of the war for gay culture was the emergence of gay and lesbian bars and clubs in cities near military bases. Were San Francisco not adjacent to Treasure Island Naval Base, Hunters Point Naval Shipyard, and Naval Air Station Alameda, it would not have been the site of so many well-known gay bars, such as Finnochio's, the Top of the Mark, the Black Cat, the Silver Dollar, the Silver Rail, the Old Crow, Li-Po's, and the Rickshaw, and would not have become the gay capital of the western United States.

The other unintended and ironic consequence of the war had to do with production for the military. In early 1942, Japan cut off supplies to the U.S. of coarse fibers from Asia, which were vital in the making of several war materials. In response to this, the federal government encouraged American farmers to grow hemp, also known as marijuana, which could be used as a coarse fiber in defense production. Marijuana had been effectively outlawed in 1937, but during the war all American farmers were required to attend showings of the USDA film *Hemp for Victory*, sign that they had seen the film, and read a hemp cultivation booklet. Hemp harvesting machinery was made available at low or no cost. Farmers who agreed to grow hemp were waived from serving in the military, along with their sons. During the war, 350,000 acres of marijuana were cultivated for the war effort, and the seeds for the pot culture of postwar America were literally planted.

If World War II was a war for freedom, these are the reasons why.

Part Four

WHICH SIDE ARE YOU ON?

★ 13 ★

HOW JUVENILE DELINQUENTS
WON THE COLD WAR

After World War II, Soviet soldiers brought the virus home from the western front. It soon infected large portions of the Soviet population, then spread to other Eastern Bloc countries. Within a few years, the Communist Party leadership feared it would destroy the socialist fatherland from within. But it was not a biological disease that threatened Communism. Soviet Premier Joseph Stalin and his commissars called it an "amoral infection" in the minds of Soviet youth. It was "American primitivism," "capitalist cultural imperialism," and "bourgeois cosmopolitanism." But it was really American renegade culture.

In 1946, soon after Stalin's chief aide Andrei Zhdanov warned that jazz would "poison the consciousness of the masses," the Central Committee of the Communist Party ordered all state orchestras to stop playing the music. Also banned were saxophones, wah-wah trumpet mutes, the plucking of bass strings, the deliberate lowering of tones to create "blue notes," and the playing of drums with too much rhythm. Brigades of music patrols monitored theaters and dance halls to ensure that nothing jazzy was being played. Couples caught dancing anything other than the waltz, the polka, or Russian folk dances were subject to arrest. Members of jazz bands were rounded up and sent to Siberian prisons or exiled to remote cities, where they were supposed to undergo "rehabilitation."

Soviet authorities were right to fear jazz, but they could not stop it. Bootleg recordings were sold by the millions on the black market. *Stiliagi*, or "style hunters," appeared on the streets of all the major cities in the Soviet bloc, wearing zoot suits and ducktails if they were male or tight dresses—"stretched tightly over their figures to the point of indecency," according to one state-run Soviet newspaper—and bouffant hairdos if they were female. They refused to work and loved to drink, "hang out," read American comic books, and listen to African American music. With little access to American-made products, the *stiliagi* were forced to re-create them on their own. To make flashy, multicolored ties, they literally painted over their drab, state-issued ties, or affixed to them American cigarette packages. Because there were no hairstylists behind the Iron Curtain who could or would give them the look of their American idols, the style hunters used heated metal rods on one another's hair. So, many sported not only fashionable ducktails but also burns on their necks. Instead of American chewing gum, many chewed paraffin wax. They smuggled as many of the real sounds of renegade America as they could but were forced to copy them in an ingenious way. A jazz-loving Soviet medical student discovered that he could inscribe sound grooves on the surface of X-ray plates, and invented a machine that allowed him to produce low-quality but sufficient copies of music recordings. From there, the *stiliagi* used the technique to take over the black market in American music. Swing and boogie-woogie were early favorites, then bebop and rhythm and blues.

Every nation of the Eastern Bloc had its own *stiliagi*. In Poland, they were the *bikiniarze*. In Hungary, they were the *jampec*. And in Czechoslovakia, *pásek* overran the streets. When the police in these countries didn't arrest the renegades, they gave them impromptu street haircuts or slashed their clothes.

In East Germany, which had been granted to the USSR by the U.S. and Great Britain as part of the Soviets' sphere of influence at the close of the war, so-called Hot Clubs for jazz sprang up in several cities in 1945 and 1946. According to the historian Uta Poiger, these clubs were "notorious for jam sessions where musicians improvised and played long solos, while the audience danced and clapped." The popularity of jazz—especially the styles conducive to dancing—were seen by East German authorities as nothing less than the leading edge of American imperialism. The East German newspaper *Neues Deutschland* charged the United States with dumping "a mudslide of boogie-woogie" on Communist youth. And in 1950 one East German culture official, Kurt Hager, saw the ultimate symbol of American conquest in the bouffant, "rockabilly" hairstyle of East German youth who emulated Hollywood movie stars: "The hair is styled in such a manner that it rises from the base of the neck like the mushroom cloud of an atomic bomb." That same year, another East German official declared that by resisting jazz, his countrymen were defending their "national cultural tradition" against both "American imperialist ideologies" and "barbarization by the boogie-woogie 'culture.'" Also in 1950 East German authorities disbanded informal jazz bands, barred jazz from East German radio, and confiscated jazz records at border crossings. As an alternative, East German youth agencies offered lessons for dancing "in a civilized fashion," which meant no "excessive movements" of the hips, arms, or legs.

In the 1950s, *Halbstarke*—young, aggressive males influenced by American popular culture—were accused of subverting the discipline of the Communist state. During the trial of Werner Gladow and his gang, which had conducted a spree of armed robberies across East Germany, Communist authorities blamed American cultural influences for creating the criminals. One East German newspaper argued that Gladow was shaped by "the sluttish kitchen of American gangster movies, of crime stories, of murder and [other] sensational trials, to whose influence he succumbed."

Communist authorities accused *Tangojünglinge* (Tango-boys) and other young males wearing American-style clothing of waging "provocations" that led to a massive popular uprising against the Communist regime in June 1953. For two days, thousands of people—mostly young—demonstrated across the German Democratic Republic. Demands of the protesters included shorter work hours, free elections, and in some cases the removal of the Communist government. Demonstrators in East Berlin tore down the Soviet flag from the Brandenburg Gate, while in other cities prison inmates were freed and members of the secret police were beaten on the streets. The uprising was crushed on June 17 when Soviet tanks rolled into the center of East Berlin and East German troops opened fire on stone-throwing demonstrators. The major East German newspapers immediately laid the blame for the demonstrations primarily on American cultural influences. "Saviors of the culture of the Christian West" in striped socks and half-long pants (part of the early rockabilly style), as the *Junge Welt* put it, had filled the East Berlin streets. The *Neues Deutschland* featured a photograph of one of the rioters wearing a T-shirt with a cowboy printed on it, "a Texas tie with a picture of nude women," a bouffant hairstyle, and "a criminal's face," and identified him as one of "the typical representatives of the American way of life." The East German prime minister, Otto Grotewohl, concurred with this assessment, alleging that "the Western provocateurs with the colorful plaid striped socks, with cowboy pants [jeans], and Texas shirts wanted to cause a large-scale political provocation." Grotewohl's speech, according to Uta Poiger, "was part of an outright campaign in the East German press that put West German or West German-influenced youths who sported Americanized fashions at the center of the June events." Nonetheless, in response to the riots, East German authorities adopted economic polices that steered more resources toward consumer goods and entertainment.

By 1954, when it was apparent that more East German youths than ever were sporting American styles, listening to jazz, and dancing the "boogie woogie," leaders of the GDR were forced to soften their positions against American popular culture. The major Communist Party youth newspaper began to publish photos of jazz bands, though usually those associated with the "cool" rather than "hot" styles of the music.

Unfortunately for the Communist leadership, the emergence of jazz fans behind the Iron Curtain was only the beginning of a process that ended in 1991. The historian Julia Hessler has written that, "in a real sense, the *stiliagi* heralded the advent of an individualistic, self-expressive approach to consumption characteristic of the consumer societies of the postwar West." Not only did this "vulgar" and "decadent" culture continue to spread, but as the 1950s ended, it mutated into something even worse: rock-and-roll.

ROCK THE BLOC

In East Germany, when authorities eased restrictions on jazz, demands for even more renegade "*Ami-Kultur*" increased. In 1954, when rock music first made its way across the Iron Curtain, *Halbstarke* appeared on streets in virtually every East German town and city, and demonstrations calling for greater cultural freedom and access to consumer goods often resulted in riots. West Berlin theaters showing Hollywood movies and playing jazz and rock lined the border with East Berlin. Alarmed by what appeared to be a great number of East Germans crossing the border daily (this was before the building of the Berlin Wall), officers of the GDR conducted a study in 1956 and 1957 and found that each day, on average, some twenty-six thousand East Berlin youths attended movies and dances at the West Berlin "border theaters." In some theaters, East Berlin teenagers made up 90 percent to 100 percent of the customers. At government-sponsored public forums designed to address the demands of East German citizens, many youth asked why Hollywood movies—especially music films with "hits"—were not allowed, why East German fashions were below Western standards, and why jeans and other tight pants were not available in the GDR. In 1956 riots broke out in front of several East German movie theaters that showed only patriotic or educational films.

In 1957 East German authorities responded to the youth rebellion with justified despair for the future of Communism. Alfred Kurella, head of the new Commission for Culture in the Central Committee of the Socialist Unity Party (the ruling, Soviet-controlled party in the GDR), warned of the "danger of growing decadent influences" that were spurring the "animalistic element" in East German youth. Kurella announced that it was time for good Communists to "save the cultural and social life of the . . . nation from this destruction" and to preserve "the true national culture." The party's Culture Conference in October 1957 declared that in recent years "damaging influences of the Western capitalist nonculture" had "penetrated" the GDR. By the following year, rock-and-roll had replaced jazz as the most dangerous of Western cultural products. In a 1958 announcement on rock, General Secretary Walter Ulbricht condemned "its noise" as an "expression of impetuosity" that characterized the "anarchism of capitalist society." Defense Minister Willi Stoph distributed a warning, published in East German newspapers, that "rock 'n' roll was a means of seduction to make the youth ripe for atomic war." Stoph singled out Bill Haley and the Comets, who had toured West Germany in 1958. "It was Haley's mission," Stoph said, "to engender fanatical, hysterical enthusiasm among German youth and lead them into a mass grave with rock & roll." State-run newspapers broadcast these warnings. *Neues Deutschland* called Elvis Presley a "Cold War Weapon," and *Junge Welt* counseled its young readers, "Those persons plotting an atomic war are making a fuss about Presley because they know youths dumb enough to become Presley fans are dumb enough to fight in the war."

Hoping to steer rock fans toward "better" music, officers of the Socialist Unity Party heavily promoted Alo Koll, a Leipzig bandleader who played thoroughly safe music, and commissioned three dance teachers to invent a refined, respectable, civilized, "socialist" dance step, which became known as the "Lipsi."

East German youth weren't interested. In 1959 groups of adolescents staged pro-rock, anti-Socialist Unity Party demonstrations in Leipzig and Dresden. They marched through the streets shouting, "We want no Lipsi and want no Alo Koll, instead we want Elvis Presley and rock 'n' roll." In Leipzig, one member of the "Elvis Presley Hound Dogs" shouted "Long live Walter Ulbricht and the Eastern Zone [East Germany]," to which the rest of the marchers answered "Pfui, Pfui, Pfui" [the German equivalent of booing] and chanted "Long live Elvis Presley!" That year internal reports on juvenile delinquency listed groups of "Presley admirers" in at least thirteen East German municipalities. Arrests of the pro-rock demonstrators and leaders of the Presley gangs, as well as the formation of a special police force to monitor state-run youth functions so that no improper dancing took place and to "extinguish the remainders of the capitalist way of life among adolescents" did not stop the rebellion. A 1959 report to the Secretariat of the Central Committee of the Socialist Unity Party showed that rock-and-roll protests, illegal trips to West Germany, acts of "outrageous instigation" against the GDR leadership, and youth crime had all increased rapidly. The report concluded that most of the youth in these incidents were "rock 'n' roll admirers." The following year, the Department for Youth Affairs of the Central Committee reported that despite an overall drop in crime, juvenile delinquency was 61.4 percent higher in 1959 than in 1950. The reason for this, the department asserted, was that Americans and West Germans "had increased their efforts to bring the youth of the GDR under their influence." Among their "means of seduction" were music, comic books, and fashion.

And so when East German authorities built the Berlin Wall in 1961, they did so not only to keep East Germans in but also to keep American cultural products out. They called it the "antifascist protection dam."

Despite the corrosive effects of American popular culture on Communist regimes, U.S. authorities refused for many years to promote it in the Eastern Bloc. From 1946 to 1955, American cultural centers (*Amerikahäuser*) set up in West German cities to spread U.S. influence provided libraries with open stacks, lectures, classical music concerts, and showings of educational films but did not show Hollywood movies or sponsor concerts of jazz or rock-and-roll. In fact, as Uta Poiger has pointed out, Eastern Bloc authorities learned to attack jazz, rock-and-roll, and Hollywood from others. Of course, the Nazis had condemned jazz as "decadent" and "degenerate," but they too learned those terms from others. "The vocabulary of 'decadence' and 'degeneration' was not the invention of Soviet or East German authorities," Poiger writes. "Rather . . . European and American writers from across the political spectrum had leveled such attacks against various forms of art as well as mass culture since the nineteenth century."

THE ENEMY WITHIN

As we have seen, until well into the twentieth century, jazz was attacked in the United States more often than it was praised. But no music has been the object of more apocalyptic fears than rock-and-roll in 1950s America. Liberal and conservative political leaders frequently found common cause in attacking the music. Committees in both houses of Congress conducted hearings through the second half of the 1950s on the power of disk jockeys to impose rock on the masses. As one witness before Representative Emmanuel Celler's House Judiciary Anti-Trust Subcommittee put it in 1956, deejays and record companies were "responsible for rock-and-roll and the other musical monstrosities which are muddying up the airwaves. . . . It's the current climate on radio and television which makes Elvis Presley and his animal posturings possible . . . it's a set of untalented twitchers and twisters whose appeal is largely to the zoot-suiter and the juvenile delinquent."

In an effort to stop "the airwaves of this country" from being "flooded with inferior music," in 1957 and 1958 senators John F. Kennedy and Barry Goldwater vigorously supported a bill that would have radically curtailed the ability of radio stations to "artificially stimulate" demand for rock—or as one witness in hearings for the bill put it, the "forced feeding of rock 'n' roll music to the public." One witness in hearings on the bill, a professor of music at Brown University, told the sympathetic senators that "we owe it to our children and our families to limit the consumption of cheap and questionable music on the air and at least provide light music of the best grade at our disposal." Several members of a House subcommittee investigating rock-and-roll in 1959 declared their intentions to save the public from the "horrible things" being played on the radio. The chairman of the subcommittee, Oren Harris of Arkansas, asserted that "when this type of music, if you call it music, that is anything but wholesome is forced onto them at that age, I think it is the worst possible service that the medium could be used for."

Several cities banned rock performances, including Washington, DC, Boston, Baltimore, Hartford, Atlanta, Houston, Jersey City, Newark, Cleveland, Santa Cruz, San Antonio, Burbank, New Haven, and New Britain. In Tennessee, a judge ordered a local radio station to replace its new rock format with its older playlist of classical music. Police in San Diego and Florida forced Elvis Presley to sing without moving while on stage. In 1958 a scheduled State Department–sponsored tour of American disk jockeys through Europe was canceled when U.S. Senator Norris Cotton complained that it would damage the international reputation of the United States. The president of the National Council of Disk Jockeys for Public Service, Murray Kaufman, guaranteed that no rock would be played by his organization's members in Europe and that all "hops" would be on U.S. Army bases under the supervision of the United Service Organizations. As the historians Linda Martin and Kerry Segrave have noted, the U.S. government rarely made an issue of Soviet and East German censorship of rock music "because the U.S. government did not like it either."

THE SOUNDTRACK OF GLASNOST

Like rock-and-roll, Hollywood movies and comic books received just as much scorn from American political leaders as they did from Eastern Bloc authorities. Concerns over the rising rates of juvenile crime and the general sexualization of American teenagers spurred several members of Congress to look for their causes in popular culture. In 1955 Senator Estes Kefauver conducted a series of hearings on juvenile delinquency and its connections to sex and violence in popular culture. Dr. Leopold Wexberg, chief of the Mental Health Division of the Bureau of Disease Control in the Department of Public Health, testified that movies, television programs, and comic books did indeed contribute to juvenile delinquency. Kefauver concluded that the federal government was "not fully exercising the powers presently vested in it to protect the public interest, and especially to protect the Nation's [sic] children from the magnitude of programs dealing with crime and violence." FBI Director J. Edgar Hoover vowed to suppress "trash mills which spew out celluloid poison destroying the impressionable mind of youth."

Meanwhile, in the Eastern Bloc, the introduction of reel-to-reel tape recorders in the 1960s helped create a vast underground culture of fans of rock, rhythm and blues, and later disco and hip-hop. In the 1960s the newspaper *Sovetskaia Rossia* warned: "The epidemic of bawdy and vulgar songs copied from tape recorders is spreading faster than a flu virus." By far, the biggest dance during the Khrushchev era was the twist, which had been introduced in the United States by the black rocker Chubby Checker. In Czechoslovakia alone, there were an estimated two hundred "twist ensembles" that performed the dance in underground theaters. Increasingly, however, Soviet Bloc youth listened to native musicians who made the music their own.

Though they avoided the explicit racism of their capitalist rivals, Communist authorities clearly understood the source of the corruption. A Bulgarian newspaper called young rockers "arrogant monkeys, dropped into our midst as if from a foreign zoo." Soviet cultural magazines referred to jazz and rock as "mud music" produced by an "ape culture." East German Communists more frankly dismissed it as "*Negermusik.*" But the youth in those countries apparently took the association with African Americans as a compliment. The first rock band in Poland, formed in 1958, was originally named Rhythm and Blues and subsequently changed its name to the Reds and Blacks.

By the 1970s, desire for music frequently turned to hatred for the Communist regime. Riots broke out at several rock concerts, where the targets were usually authorities who attempted to stop the performances. Then disco swept the Soviet Bloc, soon after it was created in New York City nightclubs. It was particularly popular in the Baltic republics, where dance clubs were the sites of several uprisings against the police. A Latvian newspaper called the country's three hundred discos the "incubators of violence."

The Kremlin was forced to acknowledge that popular music could no longer be contained. Instead, as the historian Timothy W. Ryback has put it, it became "the soundtrack of *glasnost.*" In the 1980s, performance spaces were opened with official approval from Moscow, the censorship of recordings was eased, giant rock concerts were staged all over Eastern Europe, and by the end of the decade, major American and British pop acts were allowed to perform behind the Iron Curtain. Polls of Soviet youth showed that they had far greater knowledge of rock stars than of Marx, Lenin, or Stalin. When the Berlin Wall came down in 1989, East Germans flooded West Berlin record shops.

Why, then, did the culture of American renegades get so little praise from the would-be evangelists of democracy? If jazz, rock, comic books, and "vulgar" movies helped bring down Communism, why were they not promoted by American political leaders as beacons of freedom? The answer might be that, by necessity, leaders of all political varieties—from the American presidents to Communist commissars—share a devotion to social order and are therefore natural enemies of renegades.

"A PROCESS OF SELF-PURIFICATION": THE CIVIL RIGHTS MOVEMENT'S ATTACK ON AFRICAN AMERICANS

In the summer of 1957, a Baptist preacher in the segregated South issued a series of fiery sermons denouncing the laziness, promiscuity, criminality, drunkenness, slovenliness, and ignorance of Negroes. He shouted from pulpits about the difference between doing a "real job" and doing "a Negro job." Instead of practicing the intelligent saving habits of white men, "Negroes too often buy what they want and beg for what they need." He suggested that blacks were "thinking about sex" every time they walked down the street. They were too violent. They didn't bathe properly. And their music, which was invading homes all over America, "plunges men's minds into degrading and immoral depths."

The preacher's name was Martin Luther King Jr. And the immoral black people he denounced did more to destroy segregation than did the civil rights movement.

BLACK CITIZENS AND "BAD NIGGERS"

Since emancipation, many African Americans have struggled against the barriers to citizenship and the behaviors that set them apart from it. Members of the black middle class as well as what has sometimes been called the "respectable black working class" have understood what historians of the modern civil rights movement often have not, that the project of making black citizens required a radical reformation of African American culture.

For Martin Luther King Jr. and many of the leaders of the civil rights movement, the requirements of citizenship merged with Christian asceticism. In his sermons and writings, King called for African Americans to work hard, to shun immoral forms of sexuality, and to curb their materialism. They would no longer abdicate familial and social responsibilities and would undergo "a process of self-purification" to produce a "calm and loving dignity befitting good citizens."

In advocating nonviolence, King asked African Americans to "present our very bodies" as living sacrifices to attain citizenship and respectability, and offered himself as a model of self-abnegation. After his house was bombed during the Montgomery Bus Boycott in 1956, King issued a statement to the press in which he sounded not only like the Apostle Paul but also like a citizen-soldier willing to die for his country. "The consequences for my personal life are not particularly important," King said. "It is the triumph of a cause that I am concerned about." In 1957 King cemented his position as national spokesman for civil rights with three interlocking projects: the founding of the Southern Christian Leadership Conference, the launching of a voting rights effort called the Campaign for Citizenship, and an evangelical crusade to rid black people of un-Christian and un-American habits. The first two projects have been noted by historians as marking King's ascendancy to leadership of the civil rights movement. What is remarkable, however, is the almost complete silence among chroniclers of King's career on his moral reform crusade among African Americans.

In the summer of 1957, King delivered a series of sermons under the title "Problems of Personality Integration." The sermons were intended to prepare African Americans for entry into mainstream American culture. King encouraged "those who are giving their lives to a tragic life of pleasure and throwing away everything they have in riotous living" to "lose [their] ego in some great cause, some great purpose, some great ideal, some great loyalty." By doing so, King said, they would create in themselves what he called "the integrated personality."

In subsequent speeches, as well as in an advice column he began writing for *Ebony* in 1957 and in a book he published the following year, King endorsed Christian self-abnegation as a means to attain "first-class citizenship." To become citizens, African Americans must "seek to gain the respect of others by improving on our shortcomings." King called for blacks to stop drinking and gambling and to curtail their desires for luxuries. On the causes of black crime, he blamed not only poverty and structural racism but also the lack of discipline and morality in the ghetto. "The church must extend its evangelistic program into all of the poverty-stricken and slum areas of the big cities, thereby touching the individuals who are more susceptible to criminal traits. By bringing them into the church and keeping them in touch with the great moral insights of religion, they will develop more inner stability and become more responsible citizens," King wrote.

King even attributed poverty in large measure to what he considered the profligacy and laziness of African Americans. On these issues he approvingly paraphrased Booker T. Washington: "There is a great deal that the Negro can do to lift himself by his own bootstraps. Well has it been said by one that Negroes too often buy what they want and beg for what they need. Negroes must learn to practice systematic saving." King was particularly concerned that African Americans had rejected the white work ethic:

> Don't set out to do a good Negro job. . . . If it falls your lot to be a street sweeper, sweep streets like Raphael painted pictures; sweep streets like Michelangelo carved marble; sweep streets like Beethoven composed music; sweep streets like Shakespeare wrote poetry; sweep streets so well that all the host of heaven and earth will have to pause and say: "Here lived a great street sweeper, who swept his job well."

King recognized that black sexuality posed a special threat to his assimilationist project. "We must walk the street every day, and let people know that as we walk the street, we aren't thinking about sex every time we turn around," he told one audience. In *Ebony* he impugned readers to avoid rock-and-roll, which "plunges men's minds into degrading and immoral depths."

When white southerners spoke of African Americans in these terms, they commonly referred to "bad niggers."

TOO BLACK

One of the great untold stories of the civil rights movement is the flourishing and subsequent destruction of black ministers in the postwar period who were anathema to aspiring black citizens. It would not be an exaggeration to say that two of these ministers in particular, James Francis Jones, who was known as Prophet Jones, and Charles Manuel Grace, who operated under the moniker Sweet Daddy Grace, were the most popular religious figures among the black working class in the 1940s and 1950s, even more popular than the rising group of ministers who would lead the civil rights movement.

Prophet Jones headed the two largest Pentecostal congregations in Detroit during this period. He also broadcast a live weekly sermon over Canadian station CKLW, whose fifty-thousand-watt signal reached several Midwestern cities with sizable African American populations, and in 1955 began hosting a Sunday-night program on WXYZ-TV, making him the first African American preacher in Detroit to host a weekly television program. The radio and television shows, were, according to several sources, the most popular programs among the city's African American population. With the help of sustained national mainstream media attention, including feature articles in *Life, Time, Newsweek,* and the *Saturday Evening Post,* by the mid-1950s, Jones's admirers made up a substantial portion of the African American population as a whole. And he was almost certainly the most popular minister among Detroit's black working class. A researcher at Wayne State University who studied one of Jones's congregations wrote, "The devotees of the cult appear to constitute largely that class of persons who are near the bottom of the social and economic ladder." In 1955 the Detroit-area circulation for the *Saturday Evening Post* jumped 30 percent when the magazine ran an extensive and flattering profile of Jones.

Jones reveled in materialist self-aggrandizement. He spoke not from a pulpit but from a $5,000 throne. In public he often wore a full-length white mink coat draped over European suits, and at home he liked to relax in satin slippers and a flowing robe decorated with sequins and an Elizabethan collar. He was doused with cologne and festooned with enormous jeweled rings, and drove a massive white Cadillac. But most impressive of all was his fifty-four room mansion, called Dominion Residence, which included a perfume parlor, barber shop, ballroom, and shrine to his longtime companion, James Walton, who died in 1951. Jones had the mansion painted a different color each season of the year. Perhaps most astonishing, nearly all of his wealth came from gifts he received from his followers, whose devotion to Jones was never cooled by the press's constant exposure of his homosexuality.

Like Prophet Jones, Sweet Daddy Grace was a fount of self-love and an idol of the black working class. Beginning in Charlotte, North Carolina, in the 1920s, then expanding into Washington, DC, New York City, and finally New England, Grace built a Pentecostal empire up and down the East Coast that by the 1950s included at least five hundred thousand members in three hundred congregations in nearly seventy cities. Declared by *Ebony* to be "America's Richest Negro Minister," Grace made every effort to demonstrate the validity of the title. His shoulder-length hair splayed across the collar of his gold and purple cutaway coats, which often framed chartreuse vests and floral-print ties. More striking still were his five-inch-long fingernails, usually painted red, white, and blue. Grace, who immigrated from Cape Verde and worked as a dishwasher and migrant farm laborer before becoming a preacher, said the nails represented his rejection of work. It may be no coincidence that in the late twentieth century, this style of extraordinarily long and elaborately decorated fingernails became common among black, working-class women—many of whom worked at keyboards and cash registers but who refused to subordinate themselves to their jobs.

Grace rode in a custom-built Cadillac limousine, and he bought some of the most prestigious real estate in Manhattan, including the El Dorado on Central Park West, which was then the tallest apartment building in the world. By the mid-1950s, his total net worth was estimated at $25 million. And again, like Prophet Jones's fortune, most of it came from donations by Grace's working-class devotees. In many of his churches, the members constructed enormous, arklike containers covered with dollar bills, behind which sat Grace's throne. Grace's services were also sexually charged. They began with him slowly walking down the red-carpeted aisle as his followers pinned ten-, twenty-, fifty-, and sometimes hundred-dollar bills onto his robe. While a rhythm and blues band played, the congregants danced ecstatically. Asked why he promoted such libidinous revelry, he replied, "Why should the devil have all the good times?" Grace gave himself the title "Boyfriend of the World," and his theme song featured the chorus "Daddy, you feel so good."

The civil rights movement ended the careers of Prophet Jones and Sweet Daddy Grace. In January 1955, after years of neutral coverage of Jones, the *Michigan Chronicle,* Detroit's leading black newspaper, published a broadside attack against the preacher, calling him a "circus-type headline seeker operating under the guise of religion." Three months later, after NBC scheduled an appearance by Jones on the *Today* program, the Detroit Urban League and the Detroit Council of Churches organized a successful protest to keep the prophet off the air. The most strident attacks came from C. L. Franklin, father of Aretha Franklin, pastor of New Bethel Baptist Church, and the emerging leader of the Detroit civil rights movement. Franklin had been friendly toward Jones for many years, but now he called the prophet "degrading not only to local religious circles but, more significantly, a setback of hundreds of years to the integration of all races who are this time seeking democratic as well as Spiritual brotherhood."

Soon after the attacks on Jones, he was arrested for allegedly attempting to perform fellatio on an undercover police officer who had been assigned to investigate rumors that Jones ran a numbers-running operation. The local black press cheered the arrest. The *Michigan Chronicle* called it a victory for "an increasingly vociferous element in the community" who demanded that people like Jones, "who exist by the skillful intermixing of religion, fear, faith in God, and outright fakery solely for personal aggrandizement be driven from their lofty perches." The *Detroit Tribune,* which in previous years had praised Jones, now denounced him for giving the impression to whites that the black race was "under the guidance of a sex-deviate." On the national level, *Ebony* devoted four punishing pages to Jones's trial, calling it a "day of reckoning." Yet despite his ostracism by the black leadership, Jones's followers remained as loyal as ever. They packed the courtroom every day of his trial, and when the jury declared him not guilty, hundreds of them raucously celebrated and shouted, "All is well!" Jones was subsequently shunned by the press and lost his visibility as a representative of the black working class, but his enduring popularity was confirmed by the crowd of more than two thousand people who attended his funeral in 1970, where his bronze casket was draped with his famous white mink coat.

Daddy Grace faced a similar fate. In 1957, Louvenia Royster, a retired Georgia schoolteacher, filed a lawsuit against Grace, claiming that he had been married to her in the 1920s but deserted her shortly after the birth of their child. Though the court quickly rejected the claim, the black press delivered a guilty verdict. *Jet*'s headline read, "The Past That Haunts Daddy Grace—Dismissed Alimony Trial Reveals Secret of 1st Wife." The magazine called the preacher "America's richest cultist" and speculated hopefully that the trial would "shake [the] kingdom of Daddy Grace." Joining the attack, Martin Luther King pointed a damning finger at the profligacy and irresponsibility of preachers like Grace. He told his congregation in Montgomery:

> Leaders are needed all over this South, in every community, all over this nation: intelligent, courageous, dedicated leadership. Not leaders in love with money, but in love with justice; not leaders in love with publicity, but in love with humanity.

The greatest threat posed by Grace and his followers was to the cause of integration. They were, according to King, too black:

> [If] we're going to get ready for integration, we can't spend all of our time trying to learn how to whoop and holler. . . . And we've got to have ministers who can stand up and preach the gospel of Jesus Christ. Not a Negro gospel; not a gospel merely to get people to shout and kick over benches, but a gospel that will make people think and live right and face the challenges of the Christian religion.

The subjects of Grace's kingdom were unfazed. His supporters filled the courtroom to overflowing, and, eight months after the trial, tens of thousands attended his annual parade through downtown Charlotte. Yet by the time Grace died in 1960, the kingdoms of Sweet Daddy Grace and Prophet Jones had been conquered by a new generation of leaders.

The civil rights leaders faced other competitors for the loyalty of African Americans, most famously black nationalists. But while the nationalists rejected integrationism and nonviolence, they shared with the civil rights leaders a contempt for the decadence of Jones and Grace as well as the ethic of sacrifice. Malcolm X and the Nation of Islam insisted on strict discipline, hard work, and the renunciation of drugs, tobacco, liquor, gluttony, laziness, emotional display, and promiscuity. They promised a new black nation "where we can reform ourselves, lift up our moral standards, and try to be godly." Whereas "the black man" in his current condition was "not fit for self," the "new black man" would relinquish his desires for "the good life" in service of the nation. According to Malcolm X, Islam taught black people "to reform ourselves of the vices and evils of this society, drunkenness, dope addiction, how to work and provide a living for our family, take care of our children and our wives." With a similar mission, the Black Panther Party, founded in 1966, organized itself into a semimilitary organization in which duty to the "community" took precedence over what they called "decadent and bourgeois" desires for wealth and pleasure. Black cultural nationalists such as Amiri Baraka, Ron Karenga, and Nikki Giovanni routinely denounced attachment to "materialistic fetishes" as "the white boys' snake medicine" and as the product of a "slave mentality." The Last Poets, an avant-garde musical group that grew out of the Black Arts Movement, condemned "niggers" whose alligator shoes, Cadillacs, and preoccupation with sex made them "scared of revolution."

SLEEPING ON THE FLOOR

Significantly, among the most ardent ascetics in the "black freedom movements" were whites. Applications for the Mississippi Freedom Summer Project in 1964 reveal that many of the white college students were attracted to the poverty and suffering of black Southerners. In explaining his motivations for participating in Freedom Summer, one volunteer wrote, "This is not a struggle to be engaged in by the mere liberal, for the liberal can't be counted on to make the sacrifices required. . . . I have rejected my 'birthrights' and voluntarily identified with the suppressed classes." Another declared, "I am against much of what my family stands for. I realize that four families could live comfortably on what my father makes—[that is,] comfortably Mississippi Negro style." In one application, a graduate student wrote that he would end his career as an academic to join the movement. "I can simply no longer justify the pursuit of a PhD. When the folks in [Mississippi] have to struggle to comprehend the most elementary of materials on history and society and man's larger life, I feel ashamed to be greedily going after 'higher learning.' And when I reflect on the terrors and deprivations in daily lives here, I cannot return to the relative comforts and security of student life." Some of the volunteers could not contain their rage at those who chose to live in material comfort. In response to advice from white leaders of the National Council of Churches that the volunteers should project a respectable, middle-class image, one wrote:

> We crap on the clean, antiseptic, decent middle-class image. It is that decency we want to change, to overcome. So crap on your middle class, on your decency, mister Church man. Get out of your god-damned new rented car. Get out of your pressed, proper clothes. Come join us who are sleeping on the floor. . . . Come with us and walk, not ride, the dusty streets of Gulfport.

The white volunteers devoted considerable energy to teaching black Mississippians the value of the ascetic life, thus suggesting that the people they actually encountered on the streets of Gulfport and elsewhere in the state did not share their calling. Many of the white volunteers helped establish "freedom schools" for poor black children and served as teachers. Staughton Lynd, a white radical who was then a professor at Spelman College, oversaw the freedom schools and developed their curriculum. A central purpose of the schools, as stated in the basic curriculum written by Lynd, was to inculcate values in black children that were antithetical to white middle-class life. One lesson was intended "To find out what the whites' so-called 'better life' is really like, and what it costs them." Another was "To help the students see clearly the conditions of the Negro in the North, and see that migration to the North is not a basic solution."

An entire unit of the Freedom School curriculum was devoted to explaining the differences between what were called "Material Things," which were associated with whites, and "Soul Things," which were associated with blacks. The purpose of this lesson was "To develop insights about the inadequacies of pure materialism." Among the "ideas to be developed" with the students were that "The possessions of men do not make them free" and that "Negroes will not be freed by: (a) taking what the whites have; (b) a movement directed at materialistic ends only." A list of questions designed to lead to these ideas included the following:

Suppose you had a million dollars. You could buy a boat, a big car, a house, clothes, food, and many good things. But could you buy a friend? Could you buy a spring morning? Could you buy health? And how could we be happy without friends, health, and spring?

This is a freedom movement: Suppose this movement could get a good house and job for all Negroes. Suppose Negroes had everything that the middle class of America has . . . everything the rest of the country has . . . would it be enough? Why are there heart attacks and diseases and so much awful unhappiness in the middle class . . . which seems to be so free? Why the Bomb?

An exchange between a white Freedom Summer organizer and his black constituents indicates that they did not share the same aspirations. When black teenagers in Greenwood, Mississippi, demanded that violent tactics be used to gain access to a whites-only movie theater, Bob Zellner, the son of a white Methodist minister and a lead organizer of Freedom Summer, was brought in to change their minds. At a community forum, Zellner argued that rather than focus on the movie theater, the teenagers should focus on "more important" matters. "We feel that our concentration has to be on voter registration now," he told them. "Integrating all the movies in the South won't achieve anything basic." A sixteen-year-old girl then responded. "You say that we have to wait until we get the vote," she said. "But you know, by the time that happens, the younger people are going to be too old to enjoy the bowling alley and the swimming pool." When the white volunteers arrived in Mississippi, they and the people they sought to emulate were often headed in opposite directions.

TOO BAD FOR INTEGRATION

While it is undeniably true that the civil rights and black nationalist organizations inspired great numbers of African Americans with visions of black uplift, movement leaders did not succeed in creating a mass commitment to the responsibilities and sacrifices necessary for revolution or for citizenship. The aversion to communal obligation was far greater among the black working class than among whites. As W. E. B. DuBois, Langston Hughes, James Baldwin, and more recent scholars such as Robin

D. G. Kelley, David Roediger, Saidiya Hartman, and Roderick Ferguson have suggested, the relatively liberated character of black American culture might very well have been the result of the fact that for most if not all of their history, African Americans have been to some degree excluded from citizenship and therefore far less likely to internalize its repression. It is certainly arguable that having created a culture of freedom out of slavery, segregation, and compulsory labor, when citizenship appeared attainable in the post–World War II period, the black working class demonstrated an unwillingness to relinquish the pleasures of that culture in exchange for their rights. As scholars have moved away from studies of black leaders and toward an examination of African American working-class culture, evidence of this resistance has mounted.

Draft evasion as well as insubordination against commanding officers in the military remained far greater among African Americans than among whites from the two world wars through the Korean and Vietnam wars. During World War I, the only black combat division in the American Expeditionary Force frequently ran away during battles, resulting in the removal of the entire division from the front. There is also substantial anecdotal evidence that during both world wars, large numbers of black men feigned illness or insanity to evade the draft. We have seen that during World War II, black men were more likely than whites to evade the draft. Similarly, historian Gerald Gill has found that draft law delinquency during the Korean War was extraordinarily high in black urban neighborhoods. In the early months of the war, it was estimated that 30 percent of eligible men in Harlem were delinquent in registering. At the national level, approximately 20 percent of those arrested for violating the Selective Service Act from 1951 through 1953 were African American. Black resistance to patriotic obligation peaked during the Vietnam War, when African Americans made up fully one-half of the eligible men who failed to register for the draft.

It is unlikely that this resistance to military service was motivated chiefly by pacifism. Indeed, evidence produced by several scholars has corroborated Timothy Tyson's claim that nonviolent integrationism, rather than combative and autonomous opposition to racism, "is the anomaly" in African American history, even during the civil rights era. This research has revealed mass uprisings against racist violence in Decatur, Mississippi,

Monroe, North Carolina, and Columbia, Tennessee, as well as countless examples of individual acts of violent self-defense throughout the South. In northern cities, violent responses to poverty and police brutality were, of course, commonplace, and in the major uprisings in Watts (1965), Detroit (1967), and Newark (1967), they were coupled with militant demonstrations of material desires in the form of looting.

Robin D. G. Kelley, Tera Hunter, and other historians have found a long tradition of resistance to labor discipline among black working men and women. According to Kelley, this most often involved "evasive, day-to-day strategies: from footdragging to sabotage, theft at the workplace to absenteeism, cursing and graffiti." Kelley criticizes scholars who, in attempting to counter racist stereotypes, "are often too quick to invert them, remaking the black proletariat into the hardest-working, thriftiest, most efficient labor force around." Rather, he says, "if we regard most work as alienating, especially work performed in a context of racist and sexist oppression, then we should expect black working people to minimize labor with as little economic loss as possible."

African Americans escaped the obligations demanded of "good" citizens in other, often clandestine ways.

Though many commentators have argued that the tax revolt of the 1970s was largely driven by resentful whites, African Americans were waging something of a tax revolt of their own, less visible and perhaps less consciously "political" than the white rebellion, but far broader. Studies of Internal Revenue Service records have shown that noncompliance to tax laws was significantly greater among African Americans in the 1960s and 1970s than among whites. Furthermore, these studies do not take into account the vast, untaxed underground economy, which economists have estimated produced between 8 percent and 14 percent of the total national income in the 1970s, and whose participants were disproportionately black. A study conducted by the Department of Labor in 1971 estimated that one of every five adult inhabitants of Harlem lived entirely on income derived from illegal enterprises.

Perhaps most tellingly, the black popular culture that arose in the 1950s and 1960s—a phenomenon ignored by nearly all historians of the civil rights movement—showed a distinct lack of interest in King's project.

Despite civil rights leaders' admonitions to African Americans to forego personal gratification for a higher purpose, the most popular black urban folk tales during the period continued the oral tradition of venerating "bad niggers" who rejected the "jive-ass jobs" assigned to them, defeated white opponents in athletic, sexual, and mental contests, and accumulated luxuries surpassing those of "Vanderbilt, Goldberg, and Henry Ford." Some of the most popular "party records" of the 1960s and 1970s were recordings of Rudy Ray Moore's stand-up comedy acts, in which he often recited X-rated versions of classic "bad nigger" tales such as "Dolemite," "Shine," "Pimpin' Sam," and "The Signifying Monkey." Similarly, Redd Foxx and Richard Pryor gained mass audiences with routines that unabashedly endorsed the sensuality of black culture. These performers established a dominant genre in African American comedy that proudly asserted black culture's embrace of pleasure and freedom over the repressive morality of whiteness. Moreover, these expressions of the superiority of African American "badness" were not exclusively masculine. No black comedian of the postwar period was more popular than Moms Mabley, whose orations on sex and soul food brought hundreds of thousands of black patrons to theaters across the country.

In film portrayals of African Americans, by the early 1970s, the sexless and self-sacrificing characters played by Sidney Poitier during the civil rights era had been replaced by hypersexual superheroes who had achieved spectacular wealth by means other than "working for the Man." The so-called blaxploitation genre was created not by Hollywood but by the independent black producers, writers, and directors of two films, *Sweet Sweetback's Baadasssss Song*, which was released in 1971, and *Superfly*, released in 1972. The hero of *Sweet Sweetback* is brought up in a brothel and becomes a pimp to pursue a life of fine clothes, fancy cars, and unlimited sex. After witnessing two white policemen savagely beating a young black man, Sweetback kills the cops and escapes across the Mexican border. *Ebony* called the film "trivial" and "tasteless," but the black working class voted with its feet. When the film opened at the Grand Circus Theater in Detroit, it broke the record for opening-night box office receipts. *Sweet Sweetback*, which was made for $150,000, went on to gross more than $15 million. It was then the most successful independent film ever released. *Superfly* was even more popular among black audiences, grossing more than $18 million, and it too was attacked by the civil rights leadership. The film portrayed a Harlem cocaine dealer who escapes the drug business and the ghetto by ripping off a white syndicate boss and overpowering corrupt cops. The hero rejects both his position of power and the work ethic, preferring a life of pleasure and freedom.

In popular music, the lyrics of African American songs in the era of civil rights and black power represented nearly all the desires the movements' leaders struggled to repress. Materialist aspirations were heralded by such enormously popular songs as "Money Honey," "The Payback," and Barrett Strong's "Money (That's What I Want)." Another staple of rhythm and blues lyrics was the rejection of compulsory labor. Fats Domino, Sam Cooke, and Smokey Robinson sang of hating "Blue Monday" and having "Got a Job," but also of loving the liberation brought by the weekend. And, as if in response to King's plea for hard work and frugality, in "Rip It Up" Little Richard wailed, "Well, it's Saturday night and I just got paid / Fool about my money, don't try to save / My heart says Go! Go! Have a time / 'Cause it's Saturday night and I feel fine." Of course, R & B was also well stocked with paeans to sexual revelry, from the Clovers' "Good Lovin'" in the 1950s to James Brown's "Sex Machine" in the 1960s and Marvin Gaye's "Let's Get It On" in the 1970s.

These sentiments were triumphant in the rise of disco, the most popular music of the 1970s. Having originated in black and Italian, gay working-class nightclubs, by the middle of the decade, disco dominated the airwaves, the Billboard music charts, and the dance floors. More generally, it was also at the center of the most sexually open era in American history. Disco culture celebrated the body, rejected work, and represented the antithesis of family values. Perhaps most striking, as many observers of the phenomenon noted, disco clubs were the most racially integrated public spaces in the United States. In one of the great ironies in the history of American race relations, a queer and entirely renegade creation produced more integration through desire than the civil rights movement ever achieved through moralism and legislation.

Not surprisingly, some of disco's harshest critics came from the heirs of Martin Luther King. Virtually quoting King's condemnation of rock-and-roll in the 1950s, Jesse Jackson attacked disco as "sex-rock" and as "garbage and pollution which is corrupting the minds and morals of our youth." Jackson threatened a boycott against stores that sold disco records, and his Operation PUSH held a series of conferences on the evils of the music. Disco did fade from the scene, but it gave birth to a cultural form that proved even more vexing to the remnants of the civil rights leadership. Since its arrival in the late 1970s, hip-hop has moved ever farther from King's vision. Today, the two dominant genres in the music and its visual accompaniments are the violently anti-integrationist "gangsta style," and "bling," a carnival of conspicuous consumption and sensual gratification.

Significantly, the achievements and failures of the civil rights movement correspond with the desires and antipathies expressed in contemporary African American culture. Despite the insistence by Ella Baker and other movement leaders that the objectives of the sit-in movement were, as Baker said, "bigger than a hamburger" and "not limited to a drive for personal freedom," testimonies by sit-in participants indicate that many African Americans in the South welcomed the desegregation of public space as their entry into the consumer culture. After the lunch counter at the largest department store in Atlanta was desegregated, sit-in organizers were dismayed that the first black people to eat there honored the occasion by dressing in their finest clothes, including fur coats.

THE WHITE FREEDOM MOVEMENT

Despite the efforts by the civil rights movement to reform it, the black working class brought at least a degree of liberation to whites who rejected the obligations of citizenship and were attracted not to the suffering and deprivation of African Americans but to the joys of their culture. A common theme in the writings of the most famous imitators of African Americans in the postwar period, the Beats, is the attempt to overcome their alienation as white middle-class youth through participation in black culture. In "Howl," Allen Ginsberg's "best minds" crashed through bourgeois barriers and into the Negro ghetto to revel in sex, drugs, and emotional catharsis. Jack Kerouac made this desire to be black and free explicit in *On the Road*. When the novel's hero arrives in Denver, he heads to the black neighborhood. "I walked . . . in the Denver colored section, wishing I were a Negro, feeling that the best the white world had offered was not enough ecstasy for me, not enough life, joy, kicks, darkness, music, not enough night." Like many white "race traitors," the Beats often reduced black culture to its most sensual aspects, but in doing so, they found a vehicle through which to escape the confines of whiteness and citizenship.

The Beats were only a very small part of what became a mass movement of white youth toward African American culture. In the 1950s, the revenue produced by black music grew from less than 5 percent of the total market to nearly 75 percent, and by the early 1960s, untold numbers of white Americans owned, listened to, and danced to rhythm and blues records. As was understood by white anti-integrationists who declared that "jungle rhythms" turned "white boys and girls" to "the level of the animal," the appeal of the sensual and emotional liberation represented by R & B threatened to subvert the social basis of their culture. This threat was manifested most powerfully by the masses of young white women who flocked to R & B concerts, where they were allowed to shed their sexual inhibitions and break racial taboos on the dance floor. Chuck Berry was candid about the meaning of black music for many white women. In songs such as "Brown-Eyed Handsome Man" and "Sweet Little Sixteen," Berry proclaimed that white sexual taboos were being violated, not by the black predations of the racist imagination, but by the desires of white women. Berry's boasts were essentially verified by the campaign conducted against him by law enforcement agencies in the late 1950s. He was arrested twice for violation of the Mann Act, which prohibited the transportation of minors across state lines for immoral purposes. One of the cases was dropped after the alleged victim, a white woman, declared not only that her relationship with Berry was entirely consensual but that she had initiated it. In the second case, Berry was found guilty and sentenced to three years in a federal penitentiary. And in 1959, the singer was arrested after a show in Meridian, Mississippi, when a white teenaged fan grabbed him by the neck and kissed him.

White men as well found black music enormously liberating, and were often militant in defending their access to it. In the late 1950s and early 1960s, a black deejay named Shelley Stewart cultivated a large white following in the Birmingham area with his R & B shows on the local black radio station and by spinning records at a weekly whites-only sock hop. During one of the sock hops, eighty members of the local Ku Klux Klan surrounded the building and threatened to do bodily harm to Stewart for his alleged attempts to "dance with white girls." At that point, a large group of the young male dancers, estimated to be several hundred strong, attacked the Klan, allowing Stewart to escape.

By the late 1950s, the popularity of R & B among white youth had become so great that it paved the way for the integration of several Southern universities. At Tennessee's Vanderbilt in 1958, editors of the student newspaper extended their love for R & B into a sustained critique of segregation in higher education. In a series of editorials, they compared white opposition to black music with violent repression of civil rights demonstrators, and called for the immediate integration of their campus. At the University of Alabama in 1962, while the administration was refusing to admit the first black applicants in the school's history, the Cotillion Club conducted a poll among the all-white student body to determine which entertainers should be invited to perform on campus. Though no African Americans were listed among the performers on the poll, Ray Charles won by what the campus newspaper called "an overwhelming majority with a write-in vote." The soul singer was duly invited by the president of the Cotillion Club, but the university administration refused to allow him to perform on campus. Charles won the poll again in 1964, and was again barred by the administration. The following year, the chairman of the Southern Student Organizing Committee, a white civil rights group, reported a surprising degree of pro-integration sentiment at the university. And in 1966, facing a student revolt, the administration welcomed none other than James Brown to campus.

The musicians who made rock-and-roll the chief rival of country music on the popular music charts during the 1960s and early 1970s were deeply influenced by black working-class culture. As has been well documented, many white rock performers found their calling in black juke joints and nightclubs or by listening to R & B on the radio, and the music they created challenged all the tenets of American citizenship. These refugees from citizenship and whiteness sought what Dan Emmett and other early blackface minstrels so desperately wanted. Rather than accept their place in American civilization, what W. E. B. DuBois called "so pale and hard and thin a thing," these whites envied what DuBois called the slaves' "sensuous receptivity to the beauty of the world."

THE FRUITS OF VIOLENCE

Martin Luther King is rightly thought of as the American apostle of non-violence, but he participated in one of the great attempted murders of the twentieth century. The victim of the attempted murder was the Bad Nigger.

During World War II, the Bad Nigger gained the attention of whites as the zoot-suiter, who infected much of American youth with a renegade spirit. The riots in LA and Harlem, the zoot suit culture, and rebellious youth in general were widely seen as threats to national security. The Bad Nigger bore the primary responsibility for this. And so a plot to kill him was hatched.

After the riots, Earl Warren, the governor of California, ordered a study of the social conditions that created the zoot-suiters. In Harlem, a young black psychologist named Kenneth Clarke interviewed black zoots who had participated in the riot and published an article in the *Journal of Abnormal Psychology* which attempted to explain the antisocial behavior that had caused the riots. During this time, a Swedish social scientist named Gunnar Myrdal was traveling through the ghettoes of American cities conducting field research for a study that would solve the American race problem once and for all. The study, which was titled *An American Dilemma: The Negro Problem and Modern Democracy,* was published in 1944, the year after the riots. It was a national bestseller, and it remains one of the most revered works of American social science. Its pages contained the first plan since Reconstruction to destroy the Bad Nigger.

An American Dilemma argued that black "pathologies" were the product of slavery and segregation. To Myrdal, the most debilitating of these pathologies were an antiwork ethic, hostility toward whites, sexual deviancy, and what he called the "instability of the Negro family." *An American Dilemma* directed African Americans to seek inclusion within the nation and "become assimilated into American culture," but warned that they would not be accepted until they embraced the norms from which they had diverged and acquired "the traits held in esteem by the dominant white Americans."

Though Myrdal counseled African Americans to assimilate, his sternest admonitions were directed at whites, in particular those in government and business who were undermining the nation's strength by

allowing segregation to continue. Sounding very much like the abolitionists who argued that slavery created sloth, Myrdal maintained that
integration and assimilation were required for the efficient working of
America:

> Not only occasional acts of violence, but most laziness, careless-
> ness, unreliability, petty stealing and lying are undoubtedly to be
> explained as concealed aggression. . . . The truth is that Negroes
> generally do not feel they have unqualified moral obligations to
> white people. . . . The voluntary withdrawal which has intensified
> the isolation between the two castes is also an expression of Negro
> protest under cover.

Anxiety about the inefficiency of segregation plagued the leading racial liberals of the postwar era. The Truman administration's push to integrate the
armed forces followed the report issued in 1947 by the President's Committee on Civil Rights, which argued that so long as blacks were segregated,
they would be poor soldiers and workers.

> Perhaps the most expensive results [of segregation] are the least
> tangible ones. No nation can afford to have its component groups
> hostile toward one another without feeling the stress. People who
> live in a state of tension and suspicion cannot use their energy
> constructively. The frustrations of their restricted existence are
> translated into aggression against the dominant group. . . . It is
> not at all surprising that a people relegated to second-class citizen-
> ship should behave as second-class citizens. This is true, in vary-
> ing degrees, of all of our minorities. What we have lost in money,
> production, invention, citizenship, and leadership as the price for
> damaged, thwarted personalities—these are beyond estimate. The
> United States can no longer afford this heavy drain upon its hu-
> man wealth, its national competence.

No one was more important in popularizing the language of racial liberalism than Eleanor Roosevelt. She had been the most aggressive proponent
of civil rights in her husband's administration, and was the most prominent member of the boards of the NAACP and the Congress on Racial

Equality after the war. In hundreds of articles and speeches, she insisted that the United States would not live up to its democratic promise until it gave full citizenship to African Americans. But she, like other racial liberals, understood that citizenship was not just a package of benefits. In 1943 Roosevelt contributed to a series of columns written by whites in the *Negro Digest* called "If I Were a Negro." She acknowledged that African Americans had reason to be angry, but reminded them that citizenship required work and sacrifice.

> If I were a Negro today, . . . I would know that I had to work hard and to go on accomplishing the best that was possible under present conditions. Even though I was held back by generations of economic inequality, I would be proud of those of my race who are gradually fighting to the top in whatever occupation they are engaged in.
>
> I would not do too much demanding. I would take every chance that came my way to prove my quality and my ability and if recognition was slow, I would continue to prove myself, knowing that in the end good performance has to be acknowledged . . .
>
> I would try to sustain my own faith in myself by counting over my friends and among them there would undoubtedly be some white people.

Traditionally, the Supreme Court's 1954 decision in *Brown v. Board of Education* has been interpreted as a gift to African Americans, but in fact, the court's principal justification for its decision was that educational integration would benefit employers and the state. The court made explicit that non-normative black behavior was at odds with the integration of African Americans into the body politic. In ruling segregation in education unconstitutional, the court explained that by depriving blacks of full citizenship, the United States was also depriving itself of the opportunity to create a new class of disciplined and productive workers and soldiers. The unanimous decision by the justices argued that the schools should be integrated in order to take advantage of this opportunity:

> Today, education is perhaps the most important function of state and local governments. Compulsory school attendance laws and

the great expenditures for education both demonstrate our recognition of the importance of education to our democratic society. It is required in the performance of our most basic public responsibilities, even service in the armed forces. It is the very foundation of good citizenship. Today it is a principal instrument in awakening the child to cultural values, in preparing him for later professional training, and in helping him to adjust normally to his environment.

The *Brown* decision contained one footnote: a reference to Gunnar Myrdal's *An American Dilemma*. The argument in *Brown* that segregation made blacks pathological was authored by Kenneth Clarke. And the man who wrote the decision was Chief Justice Earl Warren. The Bad Nigger haunts every word of the decision to integrate America's schools.

For the first time in American history, black leaders were offered real integration by the federal government. They seized this opportunity to replace the Bad Nigger with the Black Citizen.

In Montgomery, Alabama, local civil rights leaders spent much of the year after the *Brown* decision looking for a person to serve as a catalyst and symbol for a bus boycott they had decided to launch. The leaders agreed that the symbol would be female, because they believed a black woman would receive more sympathy than a black man. Early in 1955, a candidate did emerge, but she did not meet the requirements of respectability. In March, a fifteen-year-old girl named Claudette Colvin was forcibly ejected from a bus after disobeying the city's segregation ordinance, and the leaders considered launching a boycott to protest her act of defiance, until it was revealed that Colvin was pregnant and unmarried. Unlike Colvin, Rosa Parks was able and willing to project an image of feminine domesticity and respectability. Because she was married, restrained, and an active member of a church, Parks was well suited for her role as the founding mother of the civil rights movement. During the bus boycott, local civil rights leaders described her to the press as "mild-mannered and soft-spoken," a "lady . . . [who] was too sweet to even say damn in anger," and "a typical American housewife." One white supporter of the boycott said that she "looks like the symbol of Mother's Day."

Of course, the Bad Nigger lived on, in cities all over America. And what our textbooks don't tell us is that in the 1960s the Bad Nigger accomplished something quite remarkable. Without assimilating or integrating, he opened the doors of the segregated South.

Historians agree that the events of 1963 in Birmingham were pivotal in the history of American race relations. The Civil Rights Act was signed into law the following year, making segregation of public accommodations illegal. Historians also largely agree that the nonviolent demonstrations in May 1963, which allegedly provoked the use of fire hoses and dogs by Bull Connor and his notoriously brutal police department, shamed the local white power structure into forcing desegregation of the Birmingham commercial district.

As the story goes, nationally televised images of well-dressed children marching into jail, and of protesters being blasted with hoses and attacked by German shepherds, at a time when the United States was engaged in a competition with Communism for the hearts and minds of dark-skinned people in the Third World, made segregation a contradiction that had to be eliminated. And indeed, shortly after the airing of the police attacks, representatives of the Birmingham city government and chamber of commerce signed an agreement to open all parts of the downtown shopping area, including previously segregated jobs, to blacks. It was also during this time that Martin Luther King, who called for the "children's crusade," penned his famous *Letter from Birmingham Jail,* which quickly entered the canon of American letters and established nonviolent protest in American culture as not only morally correct but also the most effective means of social change.

But nonviolence was not just a strategy. In his letter, King pointed to its deeper political implication. The nonviolent civil rights movement sought not just desegregation, not just access to space and to the privileges of whites, but *integration,* which for King and the leaders of the civil rights movement meant the complete merger of the races. It was this goal that made nonviolence a necessary strategy, for as King understood, violent resistance to whites made it impossible for blacks to be welcomed by them. It also damaged what he called the "inescapable network of mutuality" that tied all people "in a single garment of destiny."

But what is missing from the narratives of the desegregation of Birmingham is the majority of black people in the city, namely those who did not participate in the movement. Their story is not one of nonviolence and integration but of violence and the defense of autonomy.

The records of the Birmingham Police Department contain hundreds of reports filed by police officers in the four years prior to the civil rights campaign that provide detailed descriptions of white encounters with African Americans. These reports indicate with stunning vividness that the all-white, notoriously racist, and brutal Birmingham police force and the city's equally famous segregationist civilian population did not go unchallenged, and that the violence in the streets went in both directions. The reports tell of hundreds of ordinary black people punching, kicking, biting, and even stabbing and shooting whites who encroached, even in the slightest ways, on their freedom.

Another striking aspect of the police reports is how many women participated in these street wars, and how fiercely they did so. On the night of April 29, 1962, two police officers arrived at the house of John Carter to deliver a citation for a parking violation. The report that documented the subsequent events tells of one ordinary black woman's sense of entitlement and willingness to defend it with means that fell well outside the norms of bourgeois respectability:

> While the officers were writing the citation, John Carter's wife came out of the house and told John not to sign the citation. The officers told her to go back in the house. She refused to do this and began hollering and causing a scene, which drew a crowd of other colored people. She told the officers that this was a public street and that there was no one that could tell her to leave. The officers placed her under arrest and she began to fight and scratch at the officers. She attempted to bite officer Jack Parker's hand. While Officer Parker was scuffling with this black female her husband made an attempt to jump on Officer Parker.

The department studied the number of women arrested during 1959 and found that seventeen black women had been arrested for carrying a concealed weapon, while only one white woman faced a similar charge during that year.

Several reports tell of spontaneous acts of solidarity against police encroachments on black spaces, such as an incident at the Three Sisters Café, a club in the black Southside district, on May 7, 1960. When two officers entered the café and arrested a man and a woman for drunk and disorderly conduct, "this caused several other Negroes to become belligerent and to begin cursing the police," and "several other patrol cars had to be dispatched to the scene" to handle the ensuing melee. Similarly, following a sporting event at the Municipal Auditorium in the summer of 1956, violence broke out between two large groups of whites and blacks when a black married couple, Harold and Vinia Lay, with an infant in tow, confronted and cursed out a white man they accused of hitting them with his car. The couple was placed under arrest, but fought against the police and had to be dragged through the street to police headquarters. During the trial, the judge told the couple that their actions nearly caused a "race riot."

Some of the reports of resisting arrest must be approached by the historian with caution, since they may have been efforts to justify instances of police brutality. However, they date from the late 1950s and early 1960s, before police brutality against African Americans had entered the national discourse and before *any* Birmingham police officer had been convicted or punished for unwarranted violence against an African American. Also, most of the reported incidents involved only slight injuries to the suspects or none at all. There are also many reports of incidents in which an officer involved was injured and the suspect was not. Indeed, during one eighteen-month period that was studied by the department, on average, one officer per month was seriously injured in a case of resisting arrest.

Similar kinds of resistance were directed at white civilians as well. Police and newspaper reports contain numerous accounts of blacks brazenly challenging the power of whites to maintain segregated spaces.

In the summer of 1955, white farmers at a downtown market told a group of black youths to leave their stall. When the youths refused, a farmer kicked one of them. The three teenagers then left and returned shortly with two older youths carrying pistols. With the armed guard, one of the boys began taunting the farmers. "The older boys in the background dared us to make the boy move from in front of our wagon," one farmer reported to the *Birmingham News*. "When we started after him, the older boys opened fire." Two of the farmers were wounded and three others narrowly missed being hit by bullets.

In 1960 white residents of the Kingston neighborhood, which was divided by race along railroad tracks, complained to the police about groups of black youths using their streets as a shortcut to a housing project, and threatened to arm themselves after their houses were stoned by the trespassers. Over the next several years, whites in this borderland area continued to complain that blacks attacked their homes and then escaped arrest by running back to the black side of the tracks.

On the other hand, white incursions into black neighborhoods were often met with violent reprisals. In September 1962, a group of white teenagers drove back and forth along a main thoroughfare in a black neighborhood, and, according to testimony one of them later gave to the police, were "yelling and hollering at Negroes, especially Negro girls." When they parked the car, two black men "grabbed them and beat them up and then went on." A police report filed one month later told of a similar incident, in which a patrol car responded to a call regarding a stabbing. When the officers arrived at the scene, they found three white teenagers, one of whom, Gary Hopkins, had been stabbed in the back. Hopkins said that as he was entering a drug store he "accidentally bumped into a black male standing in front of the store."

> He [Hopkins] stated that the black male had his hand on his hip with the elbow sticking out and this is the part of the Negro's body that he bumped. After he bumped the Negro they both started threatening and curs[ing] each other. This black male told Hopkins that he had better never see his face up there again, and then stabbed Hopkins in the back.

On a Saturday night in October 1960, a black man entered a café that was frequented by whites, approached the counter, ordered food, and handed the waitress money. At that point, according to the police report, two white customers told the man that he couldn't purchase food there. The waitress told him to wait outside for her to bring it to him. As he walked out of the café, several white men followed him but stopped at the front door. A group of twelve or so black men then came to the front door and, according to the waitress, "began cussing and calling names and inviting them outside." At that point, several of the white men rushed outside but were met by gunshots. One of the whites was wounded, and the black men escaped.

Perhaps the most dramatic act of violent resistance in Birmingham was authored by a twenty-year-old black woman named Matilda Cunningham.

She told the police that on the afternoon of August 8, 1960, three white men came to the rear door of her apartment and demanded entrance.

> When she refused them entrance to her residence, they forced the screen door open and entered. They searched the house inside, and then asked Matilda where her husband was. She told them that he was at work. They then told her that they were looking for him to beat him up. They stated that he was a "Smart Nigger" and that he had been seen coming out of a white woman's house in West End. They left at this time, and told her they would be back.

According to Cunningham, three days later the three men returned to her apartment.

> She stated that when she saw them coming, she went to the rear door to see what they wanted. They told her they were coming inside. She asked them to wait a moment, and went back inside the house. She stated that she got a shotgun and went to the rear door and they started walking off hurriedly. She then fired twice at the men as they were going away, however, no one was hit, and one of the men hollered back that they would return.

By 1956, white anxieties about black violence were so great that in the adjacent industrial city of Bessemer, whites became convinced that blacks had organized what they called "Push Day," when crowds of blacks would invade the downtown area and push white people off the streets. All off-duty police in Bessemer were called in to patrol downtown, but Push Day never happened.

At first glance, several incidents of blacks attacking whites appear to have been nothing more than acts of criminal malice. In August 1958, a young white couple walking in a deserted area late at night was set upon by four black men who smashed bottles over their heads and cut them with the jagged edges. In a similar incident, in March 1961, a group of six black people, four men and two women in their twenties, encountered a lone white man walking down a street, pounced on him, pummeled him, and cut him in the shoulder and hand. There is no evidence to suggest that the black attackers in incidents such as these were motivated by any explicit political mission, but their actions proved to be crucial in the desegregation of Birmingham.

Perhaps the most famous image of the civil rights movement was created in May 1963, when Bull Connor loosed fire hoses and police dogs on black people during the nonviolent protests led by King. What is not well known about that image is that the victims in it were *not* the nonviolent protesters. Rather, they were what historians of the Birmingham movement have described as "bystanders," "onlookers," "spectators," and people "along the fringes." These descriptions serve two functions. First, they efface the history of autonomous resistance by ordinary African Americans in the city, who, it now seems, were far more representative of black Birmingham than were the sons and daughters of civil rights activists who marched themselves into jail. Second, these descriptions assign to African Americans a victimhood that was precisely the identity that King sought to construct in the service of integration and assimilation. Yet, the people who were attacked by Connor's cops were hardly victims, and their actions, before and during the demonstrations, evinced no desire to be integrated or assimilated.

In fact, during the May demonstrations, there were far more people throwing rocks and bottles at the police than there were nonviolent protesters. And it was their violence that forced Connor to employ his brutal tactics. The Birmingham Police papers show that four officers were injured by rocks, bottles, and bricks in the first week of May, *before* the use of the hoses and dogs. It was not until May 7, when the rioting had grown

The confrontational attitude of these bystanders was far more common at the Birmingham anti-segregation demonstrations in May 1963 than the 'respectable' behavior of the civil rights activists who marched peacefully to jail.

so severe that six more police officers were injured, that Connor took the course of action that brought him eternal notoriety. Over the next several days, the rioting continued to grow in intensity, as thousands of the black residents of the Southside poured out of their homes and into the streets, where they met the police not just with fists and rocks and bottles but also with knives and guns. More than ten officers were injured during this street war, including one who received stab wounds and another who was wounded during what he described as a "gun battle."

But what did all of this accomplish? The answer can be found in the pivotal moment in King's *Letter from Birmingham Jail,* when he presents the city's white elite with a choice. He wrote that he stood between two forces in the black community: the complacent and conservative middle class that had accepted segregation and what he called a force of "bitterness and hatred." "I have tried to stand between these two forces," King wrote, "saying that we need emulate neither the 'do-nothingism' of the complacent nor the hatred and despair of the black nationalist."

> If the philosophy of nonviolence had not emerged, by now many streets of the South would, I am convinced, be flowing with blood. And I am further convinced that if our white brothers dismiss as "rabble-rousers" and "outside agitators" those of us who employ nonviolent direct action, and if they refuse to support our nonviolent efforts, millions of Negroes will, out of frustration and despair, seek solace and security in black-nationalist ideologies, a development that would inevitably lead to a frightening racial nightmare.

With our knowledge of the history of black resistance in Birmingham that was not respectable, loving, or seeking reconciliation and inclusion, we can understand why King's threat carried so much weight. If Birmingham's whites did not negotiate with him to open public spaces to blacks, they would have to continue to deal with the forces of hatred and bitterness—those bad people in the streets. Indeed, after several days of rioting, white business and government leaders sat down with the civil rights leader and signed an agreement that allowed blacks full access to commercial and public spaces in the city and desegregated jobs in downtown stores. This was not *integration,* in that it did not compel African Americans to live with or like whites, but it did allow them to come and go where they liked and as they pleased. And it was won not by appealing to the conscience of whites, nor by seeking admission to the American family, but by making the price of segregation too high to pay.

Sidney Smyer, the president of the Birmingham Chamber of Commerce who brokered the deal with King and the SCLC, said at the time that he was motivated not by a love for the Negro but by the need to regain control of the city. He called himself a "segregationist from top to bottom," but said, "what I'm doing is of more interest to our stockholders than anything else I could do for them." He told the *Wall Street Journal,* "Every dime of our assets is in Birmingham, but 30 percent of our property is vacant and unproductive. We've got to have growth if we want to develop it, and you can't have it in a city of hate and violence." Smyer later remembered, "I wanted some peace, too, and that's the honest truth."

The Bad Nigger desegregated the South and, in one of the great ironies in American history, he did so by speaking through the man whose mission was to wipe him from the face of the earth: the apostle of nonviolence, Martin Luther King.

★ 15 ★

GAY LIBERATION, AMERICAN LIBERATION

Gay people weren't always renegades. But once they rejected the goal of becoming "good" Americans, they broke open myriad freedoms and pleasures for all Americans.

The first gay political movement in the U.S., the "homophile" movement of the 1950s and 1960s, sought "civil rights," "full citizenship," and "recognition that we are just like heterosexuals." When America most vigorously defined itself as heterosexual, homosexual activists sought inclusion rather than freedom.

The crusade against sexual deviancy began in earnest in February 1950, when a State Department official testified to Congress that the department was riddled with homosexuals. This inaugurated a five-year period in which the Senate investigated "perverts" in government, the FBI conducted surveillance of thousands of Americans' sexual practices, the armed forces doubled the number of discharges of alleged deviates, President Dwight Eisenhower banned homosexuals from federal jobs, prospective employees were required to undergo screenings of their sexual histories, municipal police departments conducted thousands of raids on gay bars and cruising areas, and newspapers reported the names and addresses of men and women arrested for illicit sexual practices.

In response to the antihomosexual culture of the 1950s, members of the Mattachine Society, the Daughters of Bilitis, and the Janus Society, the three major homophile organizations, adopted the "politics of respectability" of the civil rights movement. Members of the organizations wore business suits and conservative dresses. They were expected to adhere to "Ivy League fashion"; no "swishing" and no "bottled-in-blond men, limp wrists and lisping" were permitted. At social gatherings, they showed only "scientific documentaries about homosexuality" that had "been approved by the Supreme Court." No "muscle movies" were allowed. The groups explicitly banned drag queens and "bull dykes" from their meetings. And their political activities were limited to seeking sympathetic scientists to conduct research that would demonstrate that homosexuality was "normal." The Mattachine Society adopted a resolution disavowing "any direct, aggressive action" in pursuit of its goals. Virtually repeating the words of Martin Luther King Jr. and other assimilationist leaders of the civil rights movement, the Janus Society urged "all homosexuals to adopt a behavior code which would be beyond criticism and which would eliminate many of the barriers to integration with the heterosexual world."

Early in the history of the Mattachine Society, one of its founding members argued for a different way. Chuck Rowland, who had grown up in a small town in South Dakota, where homosexuality was never discussed, and who had served in the army during World War II, knew the straight world as well as anyone. Yet at a 1953 convention of the Mattachine Society, Rowland attacked the politics of assimilation. "We must disenthrall ourselves of the idea," he said, "that we differ only in our sexual directions and that all we want or need in life is to be free to seek the expression of our sexual desires." The dominant, heterosexual culture had excluded them, and "as a result of this exclusion, [we] have developed differently than have other cultural groups." Rowland called for Mattachine members to affirm rather than hide their desires, pleasures, behaviors, and identities, and to focus on creating "an ethical homosexual culture." This was the last call for gay affirmation and autonomy for a generation. Rowland was defeated at the convention by leaders of the organization who committed it to the position that "the sex variant [homosexual] is no different from anyone else except in the object of his sexual expression" and that homosexuals should adjust themselves to a "pattern of behavior that is acceptable to society in general and compatible with [the] recognized institutions . . . of home, church, and state."

At the 1963 conference of the East Coast Homophile Organizations, according to one magazine report, "deadly respectability was the keynote" and "everyone was conservatively dressed." On the floor of the conference, "no swishing was allowed in public" and "a couple of local queens who sashayed up to one session were told politely but firmly to go home and come back only if they were properly dressed and behaved." The report concluded that "because they are so earnestly seeking respectability, the organizations discourage the obvious effeminates." The keynote speaker for the conference, a "big but pretty woman" named Joan Fleischmann, later said that "masculine men and feminine women were good public relations" for the homophile movement and that she was selected as convention chair in part because she did not look like "the stereotypical bulldyke."

When homophile organizations staged protests, they consisted of marching in silence for a few minutes, then departing quickly and without a word. The groups demanded that in public their members demonstrate not the slightest hint of sexuality, "not even touching or hand holding." Leaders of the organizations insisted again and again in their public statements that "the majority of homosexuals are, in everything but their sexual inclinations, no different than anyone else." They enforced a code of silence about sex and attacked the "swishy type of homosexual who brought contempt and derision on the majority of homosexuals." They sought to erase the renegade history of the gay subculture and to make themselves into respectable Americans. One could certainly argue that the strategy of respectability was necessary in the conservative era of the 1950s and early 1960s, but it was also an abject failure. The respectable movement failed to end police harassment (it actually increased in the 1950s and 1960s), won no civil rights, and, by eliminating the most powerful form of sexual dissent in American culture, actually contributed to the sexual conservatism of the time.

Something else entirely happened in the early morning hours of June 28, 1969, at the Stonewall Inn in New York's Greenwich Village. When police from the city's Public Morals Squad arrived to arrest gay patrons and the mafiosi running the bar, many of the two hundred patrons resisted arrest. Some ran away, some refused to produce their identification, and others marched out of the bar flaunting their sexuality. Several of the customers who made it out the front door staged mock performances for the crowd by posing and saluting the police in an exaggerated fashion. As one newspaper report put it, "Wrists were limp, hair was primped, and reactions to the applause were classic." Black, white, and Puerto Rican drag queens in high heels and butch lesbians wearing crew cuts and leather jackets threw bricks and bottles at the officers, set fire to the building, and, most stunningly, chanted, "We're faggots and we're not going home!"

Sylvia "Ray" Rivera, who was in full drag and had been in the Stonewall during the raid, remembered: "You've been treating us like shit all these years? Uh-uh. Now it's our turn! . . . It was one of the greatest moments in my life."

When the Tactical Police Force arrived to quell the riot, several members of the mob began an impromptu chorus-girl kick line, singing, "We are the Stonewall girls / We wear our hair in curls / We don't wear underwear / We show our pubic hairs." One observer recalled a scene that was the virtual opposite of what the homophile organizations had counseled—and one of the great renegade moments in American history:

> I saw a bunch of guys on one side and the cops over there, and the cops with their feet spread apart and holding their billy clubs straight out. And these queens all of a sudden rolled up their pants legs into knickers, and they stood right in front of the cops. There must have been about ten cops one way and about twenty queens on the other side. They all put their arms around one another and started forming a kick line, and the cops just charged with the [nightsticks] and started smacking them in the heads, hitting people, pulling them into cars. I just can't ever get that one sight out of my mind. The cops with the [nightsticks] and the kick line on the other side. It was the most amazing thing. What was more amazing was when the cops charged. That's when I think anger started. And the cops were used to us calling [them] Lily law, so the cops were used to some camp coming from us. And all of a sudden that kick line, which I guess was a spoof on their machismo, making fun of their authority. I think that's when I felt rage. Because . . . people were getting smashed with bats. And for what? A kick line.

Randy Wicker, who had marched for gay "citizenship" in a business suit in front of the White House in 1965, said the "screaming queens forming chorus lines and kicking went against everything that I wanted people to think about homosexuals . . . that we were a bunch of drag queens in the Village acting disorderly and tacky and cheap."

The next night, an even larger crowd showed up at the bar. Another riot broke out, and protests were held every night for the next five days. Poet Allen Ginsberg, who as a teenager in 1943 had discovered in himself "mountains of homosexuality," noticed a new countenance on the Stone-wall rioters: "You know, the guys there were so beautiful, they've lost that wounded look that fags all had ten years ago."

Whereas homophile movements had avoided using the word *gay* in any of their publications, a group calling itself the Gay Liberation Front (GLF) formed soon after Stonewall. Within six months, New York activists launched newspapers called *Gay, Gay Power,* and *Come Out!* Their com-bined readership climbed to between twenty thousand and twenty-five thousand within a year. The so-called gay liberation movement that fol-lowed ended police harassment, broke open notions of what it meant to be a man or a woman, and broadened the sexuality of a whole generation of Americans—queer and straight.

Before Stonewall, it was commonly assumed that homosexuality was a sickness or an evil, and gay meeting places were officially illegal in ev-ery city. But in 1970, one year after Stonewall, tens of thousands of men and women gathered in New York's Central Park and in Griffith Park in Los Angeles for enormous, organized coming-out parties, and the first gay pride parades were held across the country to commemorate the rebellion. Through the 1970s, several gay liberation organizations were founded in the United States as well as in countries around the world. Gay and lesbian studies programs were established in universities. Homosexuality became a common theme in Broadway plays and Hollywood movies. Most dra-matically in the lives of gays and lesbians, city governments ended police harassment of gay bars and bathhouses. In the years after Stonewall, gay bars even in small towns no longer camouflaged themselves, and by 1977, there were at least 129 openly gay bathhouses in the United States.

For heterosexuals, gay liberation transformed life in countless ways. Sex was brought not just out of the closet but also out of the home. The rampant and unabashed public gay sex of the 1970s, pioneered on the Christopher Street docks, in the backs of trucks parked in the meatpacking district, at St. Mark's Baths, in the sand dunes of Fire Island, in gay clubs, and in West Village doorways, induced America to take off its clothes. Nonmarital, nonprocreative, purely recreational sex—the only kind ho-mosexuals could practice—was legitimated for the first time in American culture. Soon after Stonewall, *The Joy of Sex,* which only a few years earlier would have been banned as pornography for its hundreds of pictures of copulating couples, spent seventy weeks on the *New York Times* best-seller list and introduced millions of heterosexuals to sexual positions previously thought to be degraded and perverted. As we have seen, before Stonewall, oral sex was considered to be the practice of prostitutes and homosexuals. The medical sexologist Edwin Hirsch wrote in 1934 that oral sex is "generally regarded as loathsome and indicative of a sad degree of sexual perversion." Through the 1960s, medical experts commonly referred to oral sex among heterosexuals as a "disorder" and "deviation of aim." The first medical "experts" on homosexual practices, such as David Reuben, whose best-selling *Everything You Always Wanted to Know About Sex but Were Afraid to Ask* appeared in 1969 just before the Stonewall riots, averred that oral sex played "a big role" in homosexual activity but that for most heterosexuals the "big question" was "Should you do it?'" After Stonewall, almost everyone was doing it.

Before Stonewall, Fire Island—the playground of thousands of New York gay men—was the only beach in America where nudity was tolerated by authorities. After Stonewall, illegal nudity at beaches along both coasts increased markedly. By 1973, substantial sections of various beaches, including Cape Cod National Seashore, Moonstone Beach in Rhode Island, Venice Beach in Los Angeles, and Black's Beach in San Diego, had been colonized by nudists. That year, Eugene Callen and other heterosexual nudist activists founded Beachfront USA as a protest and lobbying group to establish legal nudity on American beaches. By the following year, it was estimated that more than one thousand nudists appeared daily on Venice Beach. "Naturism" spread on the East Coast shortly thereafter. Portions of beaches from Florida to Maine (where the hardiest of naturists ventured) were taken over by nudes in noticeably greater numbers by the mid-1970s. In 1978 Lee Baxandall, who found his passion among the clothes-free crowds at Cape Cod, began publishing *Free Beaches* magazine and created the Free Beaches Documentation Center, collecting data from all over the world on nude beaches. Later he published *Lee Baxandall's World Guide to Nude Recreation,* a color guidebook locating places to go nude all over the world, which became the bible of international naturists. Baxandall and Callen later launched, without government approval, "National Nude Weekend" and "National Nude Week."

Until Stonewall, psychologists not only considered homosexuality to be a mental illness but also thought of masculinity and femininity as inversely proportional within an individual. The more feminine a person was, the less masculine he or she was, and vice versa. After Stonewall, the psychological profession, as well as the culture at large, changed its mind on both notions.

Emboldened by Stonewall and the burgeoning gay freedom movement, in May 1970 activists with the Los Angeles chapter of the Gay Liberation Front (GLF) infiltrated a conference on behavior modification by the American Psychiatric Association (APA). During a film demonstrating the use of electroshock therapy to decrease same-sex attraction, GLF members shouted "torture!" and "barbarism!" then seized the microphone to declare that doctors who prescribed such therapy for their homosexual patients were complicit in torturing them and that homosexuals were not mentally ill. Two years later, apparently sensing a national mood change, the APA invited gay activists to speak at the organization's national conference. And in 1973, the APA Board of Trustees voted to remove the category of homosexuality from the *Diagnostic and Statistical Manual of Mental Disorders*. That same year, the psychological profession adopted the Bem Sex-Role Inventory, a scale that measured masculinity and femininity as separate and coexistent within an individual. Thus, Americans began to speak not just of feminine and masculine personalities but also of "androgynous" types—people who were both masculine *and* feminine, or neither.

Today's movement for gay marriage—a renewal of the homophile movement—ended gay liberation, is helping to end straight liberation, and seeks to return all of us to the 1950s. Like the homophile movement, the gay marriage movement demands that, in order to gain acceptance as full citizens, its constituents adopt the cultural norms of the American citizen: productivity, selflessness, responsibility, sexual restraint, and the restraint of homosexual expression in particular. Proponents of same-sex marriage have justified their demand by presenting homosexual partners as devoted, self-sacrificing, and industrious adults.

Unlike the post-Stonewall gay pride movement, whose annual marches featured masses of naked and semi-naked people in celebrations of sexual openness, the gay marriage movement presents its constituents as sexless and their relations as platonic. Calls have been made by leaders of the movement to ban drag queens from Pride marches and to institute a dress code for marchers. The suppression of sex and the language of respectability are evident on the websites operated by gay, lesbian, bisexual, and transgender civil rights organizations. In the early 2000s, the website of

Lambda Legal featured profiles of gay and lesbian couples, all of whom were identified as long-term couples with respectable jobs, and many of whom were described as committed parents and grandparents. Among the featured couples was Colonel Margarethe Cammermeyer and Diane Divelbess, respectively the recipient of a Bronze Star "for distinguished service in Vietnam" and "an accomplished former professor." In the site's section on gays in the military, scores of homosexual members of the armed services offered lengthy accounts of their military accomplishments and nothing on their sexuality. This exchange of desire for responsibility was well illustrated by Carolyn Conrad, whose "civil union" with Kathleen ("K.P.") Peterson was the first of its kind in the United States following the enactment in 2000 of a Vermont law allowing same-sex couples to become legal spouses. "When I first met K.P., I loved her because she rode a motorcycle," Conrad said. "And now I love her because she makes the payments on her motorcycle." Advocates for gay marriage insist that such a reform is necessary to acquire many long-denied rights, yet virtually all those civil rights have been won in Europe through "domestic partner" laws and in the majority of major companies in the United States, which give full benefits to nonmarried domestic partners.

The implications for gay, lesbian, and transgender people are clear. But for straights, they are no less world defining. The homophile and gay marriage movements tell us that the nuclear family is the destiny for all of us who wish to be healthy. Above all, they tell us not just that homosexual acts should be hidden and contained, but as the Puritan strain in American culture has told us from the beginning, *all* sex should be hidden and contained. For those who reject that notion, the queers of the Stonewall era should be national heroes.

★ 16 ★

ALMOST FREE: THE PROMISE AND TRAGEDY
OF REDNECKS AND HIPPIES

White people might have lost their rhythm during the twentieth century, but they didn't lose all of their renegade nature. During the 1960s and 1970s, millions of ordinary white Americans refused to be good citizens for at least a time. But more often than not, they returned to the values of the Puritans and the Founding Fathers.

There were plenty of white people during the 1960s who acted like renegades. Most famous among these were the hippies and antiwar protesters. But there were also many ordinary-looking white folks who acted like "shiftless" slaves. It is a little-known fact that during the 1960s, an extraordinary number of white workers more often demonstrated a desire to leave the workplace than to take responsibility for it. This was especially true in the automobile industry. Daily absenteeism in auto plants doubled during the decade, and the incidence of strikes unauthorized by a union in all industries also doubled, reaching more than two thousand in 1969. In addition, there was a marked increase of workplace sabotage, insubordination toward managers and union stewards, and other forms of industrial disobedience.

Yet while many whites resisted the American work ethic during this period, a great number celebrated their "Americanism." To gauge the depth of white working-class cultural identification with the nation-state, one need not look any further than popular reactions to American military ventures since Pearl Harbor. Even during the Vietnam War, hostility toward the antiwar movement was most intense in white working-class quarters. The largest prowar demonstrations were led by predominantly white trade unions, and in the spring of 1970, white construction workers in New York, St. Louis, and Tempe, Arizona, violently attacked antiwar protesters.

The rise of country music as a leading working-class cultural form amply demonstrated this commitment to the flag. During World War II, country music emerged as both a popular and patriotic genre. By the end of the war, at least sixty-five recording companies were putting out country records, and the popularity of country music continued to grow after the war, spreading well beyond its traditional roots in the South. In 1947 *Billboard* magazine noted that country stars were enormous box-office draws across the country, and that Pennsylvania, Ohio, and Michigan were among the largest markets for the music. Many country songs during World War II contained patriotic themes, including Roy Acuff's "Cowards over Pearl Harbor," Bob Willis's "Stars and Stripes on Iwo Jima" and "White Cross on Okinawa," and Carson Robison's bluntly titled "We're Gonna Have to Slap the Dirty Little Jap (and Uncle Sam's the Guy Who Can Do It)." One of the most popular songs of any genre during the war was "There's a Star Spangled Banner Waving Somewhere," recorded by the "hillbilly singer" Elton Britt, which tells the story of a crippled "mountain boy" who pleads with Uncle Sam to let him fight. "God gave me the right to be a free American," Britt sang, "and for that precious right I'd gladly die." In 1942 *Billboard* noted the pronounced patriotism in country music:

> [The] popularity of fighting country tunes in the music boxes calls attention to the fact that [country music], far more than the pop field, has come through with war tunes of the type asked for by government officials.... The output has continued ... doing a fine morale job.

Country musicians' commitment to the nation continued into the cold war, with such stridently anticommunist songs as Harry Choate's "Korea, Here We Come," Jimmie Osborne's "Thank God for Victory in Korea," Jimmie Dickens's "They Locked God Outside the Iron Curtain," and Elton Britt's "The Red We Want Is the Red We've Got (In That Old Red, White, and Blue)." Hank Williams said "No, No, Joe" to Stalin, and in "Advice to Joe," Roy Acuff warned the Soviet dictator of the day to come "when Moscow lies in ashes."

In the 1960s, despite the rise of the "counterculture," country music continued to be the music of much of the white working class. The number of radio stations with an all-country format grew from 81 in 1961 to 328 in 1966, and by then the popularity of the music was clearly no longer just a "country" phenomenon. According to a market research study, by the mid-1960s, the typical country listener was a skilled or semiskilled worker living in or near a metropolitan area.

The content of country music became even more militantly patriotic during the Vietnam War, when country musicians led the attack against the antiwar movement. Scores of songs not only denounced the "hippies" and "doubters" who would "rather go to prison than heed their country's call" but often threatened violence against them. Merle Haggard warned that antiwar protesters were walking on "The Fighting Side of Me." In Pat Boone's "Wish You Were Here, Buddy," the soldier-narrator promises his draft-dodging friend that at the end of the war, "I'll put away my rifle and uniform, and I'll come a-lookin' for you." And Victor Lundberg vowed in his "Open Letter to My Teenage Son" to disown his offspring if he were to burn his draft card.

Country music and the masses of white Americans who consumed it demonstrated other commitments to cultural citizenship as well. The nuclear, heterosexual family—the bedrock of the American nation—was honored and defended in country songs, especially songs sung and written by women. Tammy Wynette's "Stand by Your Man," the best-selling country record ever recorded by a woman, and "Don't Liberate Me, Love Me" became anthems of the pro-family backlash against the women's movement. The other major women country stars of the period, Loretta Lynn and Dolly Parton, expressed more assertiveness in their songs than did Wynette but consistently upheld the virtues of the devoted, self-sacrificing housewife against those who "march for women's lib." Songs performed by women country singers of the 1960s and 1970s that promoted motherhood, chastity, monogamy, and child rearing outsold country songs about women expressing their sexuality, cheating on their mates, dancing at honky-tonks, or drinking. Several scholars have noted that in country lyrics—even in the "outlaw" country movement that projected images of wayward, hard-drinking, womanizing "cowboys"—"satisfactory male-female relations are equated with good marriage."

On the great American work ethic, postwar country music expressed a deep and painful ambivalence. Songs such as Merle Travis's "Sixteen Tons," Johnny Paycheck's "Take This Job and Shove it," and Johnny Cash's "Oney" and "One Piece at a Time" told of small-scale rebellions against the dictates of the boss—similar to many of the wildcat strikes and other forms of individual workplace resistance discussed above—but did not challenge the moral obligation to work. Rather, country music lyrics simultaneously expressed a hatred of work and a pride in doing it. Merle Haggard, one of the biggest country stars of the late 1960s and early 1970s, best represented this contradiction. In the hit song "Workin' Man Blues," Haggard sings of the hardship of working with his "nose to the grindstone" to support "nine kids and a wife," which leads him to the tavern every night and a longing to "catch a train to another town." But family and the respectability of work keep him from leaving:

> *I go back working,*
> *Gotta buy my kids a brand new pair of shoes . . .*
> *I ain't never been on welfare*
> *And that's one place I won't be*
> *I'll be workin'*
> *Long as my two hands are fit to use.*

This attachment to the work ethic was demonstrated in several songs scorning welfare. Loretta Lynn's argument that "They Don't Make 'Em Like My Daddy Anymore" is supported by her claims that her father was "one heck of a man that worked for what he got" and that he "never took a handout." Guy Drake was more explicit when he mocked the owner of a "Welfare Cadillac" who "never worked much" but who was able to purchase his luxury automobile with payments "from this here federal government." That these enormously popular songs represented the attitudes of broad sections of white America seems undeniable. But they may also point us to an explanation for the lack of a widespread or sustained shorter-hours movement in the twentieth-century United States, as well as for the fact that by the end of the century, American employees worked on average from one hundred to three hundred hours more per year than did workers in western Europe.

It was certainly no coincidence that country music became the soundtrack to the rise of the "new right." The Alabama segregationist George Wallace, who promised the "average citizen who works each day for a living" that he would bring tax relief, an end to welfare and foreign aid, a strengthened military, and a crackdown on antiwar protesters, made country music bands a central feature of his presidential campaign tours in 1964, 1968, and 1972, and received endorsements from several country performers. One of the most notable aspects of the Wallace campaigns was the enthusiastic support he received in the industrialized North, in particular among automobile workers. The movement for Wallace within the United Automobile Workers in 1968 was so great that the liberal UAW leadership mobilized six hundred full-time staff members and devoted a half million dollars to stop it. Nonetheless, four years later, Wallace won the Democratic primary in Michigan, by most estimates taking the largest share of the union vote. Many of Wallace's working-class supporters were moved by his implicit attacks on African Americans in his references to welfare cheaters, crime, and busing, just as many country fans no doubt attached black faces to the loafers and urban predators mentioned in their favorite songs. But Wallace's *explicit* attacks were always directed at the white elite, "bureaucrats" and "theoreticians," who, like the New Deal liberals who had dominated American political culture since the 1930s, imposed their grand schemes of social management on the hard-workers and taxpayers of the country.

Richard Nixon, who virtually repeated Wallace's pledges in his successful campaigns in 1968 and 1972, was endorsed by country stars Tex Ritter and Roy Acuff and invited Merle Haggard and Johnny Cash to perform at the White House. Likewise, Ronald Reagan found the winning formula in 1980 when he declared that "work and family are at the center of our lives; the foundation of our dignity as a free people," and vowed to protect that foundation with tax cuts and an aggressive military. The year of Reagan's victory over incumbent Jimmy Carter, more than two hundred radio stations switched to all-country formats, and between 1977 and 1983, the number of country stations doubled from 1,140 to 2,266. Reagan, who as governor of California had pardoned Merle Haggard for his previous conviction on felony burglary charges, invited the "Okie from Muskogee" to the White House on several occasions.

The "new right" and its cultural expressions combined a renegade rejection of elite social control with a fierce defense of obligations—to nation, family, and work—that comprised the responsibilities of American citizenship in the postwar period. As in earlier periods, citizenship and whiteness were constructed in tandem, with African Americans serving as the model of the noncitizen. Moreover, this dual investment in Americanness and whiteness was always presented as a self-regulating paternalism. The (normally male) individual would work hard to support his family without assistance from the state, and would sacrifice himself to protect the family from its enemies, be they loose women, criminals, or communists.

BACK TO THE (AMERICAN) LAND

While a majority of white Americans followed the route of Merle Haggard into a half-renegade, half-citizen contradiction, others—like white zoot-suiters, rock-and-rollers, and the Beats—hoped to break entirely from their heritage.

The best-known offshoot of the rock-and-roll movement, the hippies of the 1960s and 1970s, are well known for their libertine attitudes but, ironically, they found themselves in the same contradictory place as their redneck archenemies. We typically think of hippies as free-loving, work-avoiding, pot-smoking, acid-dropping, nature-loving vagabonds. And indeed, many hippies—especially those who remained in cities and did not fully realize the hippie commitment to "natural living"—did maintain an essentially renegade lifestyle of avoiding labor, monogamy, and service to country. But those who carried out the logic of their creed ended up living lives that in many ways were more constrained, more onerous, and less free than the lives of the "square" Americans they shunned.

In the late 1960s, hundreds of hippies left the cities and suburbs to establish self-sustaining communes. These "intentional communities" were typically established in remote locations so as to re-create agrarian, preindustrial society. Such remoteness also made necessary agrarian levels of work. Though they disparaged the "rat race," hippies on most rural communes—at least those that were not funded by the inheritances of independently wealthy members—were forced to work *more* than the average American worker. Water was hauled from natural sources, wells were dug with shovels, food was grown without farming machinery, daily quotas of bread were baked in homemade ovens, clothes were made without sewing machines, and dwellings were built, log by log and brick by brick, by hand. Labor-saving technology was generally eschewed for more "authentic" means of production. In many hippie communes, according to sociologist Gilbert Zicklin, "the naturalists stood opposed to the use of advanced technology, preferring at times to substitute the muscle power of people and beasts." In one intentional community, some members grew tired of deliberately avoiding labor-saving devices and called for the use of a gasoline-powered tractor to pull the plow, but they were denounced by those who believed that the use of anything but the hoe and rake would violate the founding principle of the commune. At Haney, a commune in the mountains of northern Oregon, members traveled by donkey several miles to the nearest town for supplies. Other communes sought to go back to even *before* the agrarian era. Lelain Lorenzen remembered her experience of "gathering wild foods. Sometimes we would go gather a lot of walnuts, and we would gather sorrel, you know sheep sorrel, kind of sour. We'd make a soup out of that."

At many communes, the sexual division of labor was violated only enough to increase the amount of work done by everyone. At the Total Loss Farm in Vermont, one of the more famous communes of the 1960s, most of the cooking and cleaning was done by women and most of the hauling, carpentry, and wood splitting was done by men. But because the modern sexual division of labor did not yield sufficient production for agrarian survival, *additional* work was required for both sexes. On top of their traditional labor, women helped slaughter the pigs, milk the cows, and dig the well, while many of the men worked in the kitchen after a day of outside labor. One woman remembered the amount of work required just for preserving food:

> It seemed like that's all we did during September and October. If you figured up the hours and multiplied our labor by a dollar-sixty an hour, I suppose that economically we didn't come out that far ahead of buying our food. But we're not living this way just to do things cheaply.

Indeed, it seems that they were living that way also to do things *arduously*.

Though professing to be radicals, many hippie women proudly recalled their lives as similar to the experiences of the paragon of American conservative virtue: the pioneer woman. Ayala Talpai, who lived off the land with her husband and five children, remembered that when it was "time for supper, I'd pick up a basket and go out to the garden, that's how it started. . . . I just milked twice a day. So I was making cheese and butter and cottage cheese and yogurt and buttermilk and whipped cream and ice cream and everything. . . . But that was a major dent in my time, you know. I was cooking on a wood stove. So I was doing everything on this wood stove, and I was knitting my husband's socks out of yarn that I'd spun and dyed myself, and he'd go off to work with his sandwiches of homemade bread and mayonnaise and homegrown lettuce and homemade cheese and a hand-knitted hat on his head and homemade shirts, and oh my God." Nonie Gienger also lived "naturally" with her husband and children and gathered "seaweed and nettles, plantain and dandelion, berries and wild apples, too. . . . But we were even grinding our own flour to make bread. I was a pioneer housewife, and we were living off very little money. But it felt good because I knew where everything came from." One of her sons contracted dysentery from contaminated water: "One day I found him outside crying, and his intestine was hanging out. I didn't know what happened. I was horrified." Gienger then treated him with herbal remedies.

Marylyn Motherbear Scott described her life as a back-to-the-earth hippie in language reminiscent of countless pioneer novels: "When we went up there, there was nothing on the land except a cattle trough. So we were building homes, building water tanks, building roads, just building, building, building. And having babies still . . . I had my babies at home. I nursed my babies. I slept in the same bed. I schooled them at home. We'd get up and do the gardening, build houses, and cooked from scratch. Everything. I made my own bread. I made my own cheese. I made my own tofu. I gardened and had vegetables. I was even the first person I knew who grew blue corn and a lot of new food stuffs like that. I raised every kind of seed, every kind of bean, and every kind of vegetable."

Some members of naturalist communes aligned themselves with the image of ascetic Native Americans against the consumerist ways of other peoples of color. "Lakshmi," a woman who lived in an adobe hut on a commune near Taos, New Mexico, acknowledged the local Indians who "showed us how to build our houses, and how to plant the crops. We couldn't have made it without them. The Indians and the Chicanos, they're really on different trips. I mean, the Chicanos want all kinds of things, they really want to make it. But the Indians just want to live close to the land. They don't want very much, and they understand our trip."

Charles Reich, one of the first scholars to write about the hippie counterculture, noted that his subjects shared the dominant culture's commitment to work. "Unsympathetic observers of the new generation frequently say that one of its prime characteristics is an aversion to work. The observers are prevented by their disapproving, puritanical outlook, from understanding the real significance of what they see. . . . The new generation is not 'lazy,' and it is glad enough to put great effort into any work that is worthwhile, whether it is hours of practice on a musical instrument, or working on a communal farm, or helping to create People's Park in Berkeley." Judson Jerome, who with his wife, Marty Jerome, founded Downhill Farm in rural Pennsylvania and later became one of the leading scholars of 1960s hippie communes, noted that in communes "a strong work ethic has been established, but the bias against profit . . . is as rigorous a discipline as the old culture's bias in its favor." Jerome cautioned that the work ethic of "the new culture" was "not to be confused with the 'Protestant work ethic.'" Yet he nonetheless defined it as did the Calvinist settlers of New England: "The work ethic of the new culture is one in which work is valued for itself, indeed becomes a form of leisure."

Though some communes expelled members for seeking "exclusive possession" of love partners, most were made up of essentially monogamous heterosexual couples. According to Gilbert Zicklin, "Sexuality in communes, at least in naturalist communes, was often confined to couples who were attempting to make it together into the very indefinite future, rather than practiced promiscuously or *en groupe*." Virginia Stem Owens, a member of the Moriah commune in New Mexico, remembered that "what we desired was innocence, not debauchery."

Among the small number of ordinary white Americans who avoided the self-imposed obligations of rednecks, hippies, and American citizens and embraced the gift of renegades were the workers at the General Motors plant in Lordstown, Ohio, who in 1972 staged a walkout in rebellion against their employer and their union, the UAW. The national media noted that the strikers did not resemble the typical white workers of the time. Rather, they wore long hair and shaggy beards, indulged unreservedly in drugs and alcohol, opposed the war in Vietnam, and listened to rock every minute they could. Most stunning of all, they unashamedly rejected the work ethic. Many spoke publicly about committing acts of sabotage on the assembly line, spontaneous slowdowns and shutdowns, showing up late to work or not at all, general "goofing off," and "fucking up any time I can." While the immediate issue in the strike was a speedup imposed by General Motors, the workers quickly turned it into a rebellion against the UAW—"our union, Miss Goody Two Shoes"—which they accused of being more concerned with maintaining high production standards than with defending the freedom of the members. The rebels at Lordstown rejected not only the notion promulgated by New Deal liberals that they should take responsibility for their workplace, they also refused to abide by the cultural obligations of Americans.

If we allow ourselves to step out of the desire to be "good" and to appreciate the desires that have been called "bad," we have much to learn from the strikers at Lordstown. Like so many of the renegades in this book, they said very little but did a great deal that many of us envy. For at least a moment, they let themselves be free of the society in which they lived. There may have been other times in their lives when they wished to sacrifice themselves for their community or their nation. But if that is all they had ever done, how much would have been lost? How much would *we* have lost? Indeed, if Americans throughout history had *only* sacrificed themselves and made themselves "good," what kind of society would we live in now? To answer that question, you might count the things in this book that you value in your own life or wish to enjoy, then imagine them as impossibilities. Renegades made illicit joys not only possible but real. They didn't intend their actions as gifts to us. But now is our chance to accept them as gifts, take the side of the renegades when the guardians of social order try to keep them down, and take more.

Acknowledgments

Many people helped make a wild idea into this book.

Casper Grathwohl, Bill Clegg, and Tim Bartlett gave early encouragement and advice. Victoria Hattam, Mark Carnes, Kevin Kenny, Joshua Brown, and my mother, Leslye Russell Larson, all read and commented on portions of the manuscript.

Joshua Sperber and Mir Yarfitz read the entire manuscript and offered enormously helpful comments. Sasha Gronim provided wonderful research assistance.

Kate Van Winkle Keller and Kerby Miller generously helped me track down sources.

Dominick Anfuso, Bruce Nichols, Leah Miller, Maura O'Brien, and Jonathan Evans at Free Press did an amazing job with a demanding manuscript and author.

One of the best decisions I've ever made was to hire David Kuhn, the wizard of lower Fifth Avenue, as my literary agent. David changed my life. Billy Kingsland at Kuhn Projects not only gave me critical advice on the book but also inspired me to reach higher with it.

The ideas presented here were developed from years of conversation with Jonathan Cutler, the most original and brilliant thinker I have ever known. They were first made public in the classrooms of Columbia University, Barnard College, Eugene Lang College, and the New School for Social Research. I simply would never have attempted this book were it not for my students.

Sources

★ CHAPTER 1 ★

Agresto, John T. "Liberty, Virtue, and Republicanism, 1776–1787." *Review of Politics* 39 (1977): 473–504.

Burg, B. R. *Sodomy and the Pirate Tradition: English Sea Rovers in the Seventeenth-Century Caribbean*. New York: New York University Press, 1995.

Cott, Nancy F. *Public Vows: A History of Marriage and the Nation*. Cambridge: Harvard University Press, 2000.

Franklin, Benjamin. *The Autobiography of Benjamin Franklin*. New York: The MacMillan Company, 1927.

Gilfoyle, Timothy J. *City of Eros: New York City, Prostitution, and the Commercialization of Sex, 1790–1920*. New York: W. W. Norton, 1992.

Gilje, Paul A. *Liberty on the Waterfront: American Maritime Culture in the Age of Revolution*. Philadelphia: University of Pennsylania Press, 2004.

Godbeer, Richard. *Sexual Revolution in Early America*. Baltimore: Johns Hopkins University Press, 2002.

Horsmanden, Daniel. *The New York Conspiracy Trials of 1741: Daniel Horsmanden's Journal of the Proceedings with Related Documents*. New York: Bedford/St. Martin's, 2004.

Kann, Mark E. *Punishment, Prisons and Patriarchy: Liberty and Power in the Early American Republic*. New York: NYU Press, 2005.

Kross, Jessica. "The Sociology of Drinking in the Middle Colonies." *Pennsylvania History* 64: 1 (January 1997): 28–55.

Lender, Mark Edward and James Kirby Martin. *Drinking In America: A History*. New York: Free Press, 1982.

Linebaugh, Peter and Marcus Rediker. *The Many-Headed Hydra: Sailors, Slaves, Commoners, and the Hidden History of the Revolutionary Atlantic*. Boston: Beacon Press, 2000.

Lint, Gregg L. and James C. Taylor. *Papers of John Adams*. Cambridge, Mass.: Harvard University Press, 2008.

Locke, John. *Some Thoughts Concerning Education*. 1693.

Lyons, Clare A. *Sex Among the Rabble: An Intimate History of Gender and Power in the Age of Revolution, Philadelphia 1730–1830*. Chapel Hill: University of North Carolina Press, 2006.

———. "Mapping an Atlantic Sexual Culture: Homoeroticism in Eighteenth-Century Philadelphia." *William and Mary Quarterly* 60 (2003): 119–54.

Morgan, Edmund S. *The Birth of the Republic, 1763–1789*. Chicago: University of Chicago Press, 1977.

——. "The Puritan Ethic and the American Revolution." *William and Mary Quarterly* 24 (1967): 3–43.

Rorabaugh, W. J. *The Alcoholic Republic: An American Tradition*. New York: Oxford University Press, 1979.

Salinger, Sharon V. *Taverns and Drinking in Early America*. Baltimore: Johns Hopkins University Press, 2002.

Thompson, Peter. *Rum Punch and Revolution: Taverngoing and Public Life in Eighteenth-Century Philadelphia*. Philadelphia: University of Pennsylvania Press, 1999.

Warren–Adams Letters. Whitefish, MT: Kessinger Publishing, 2008.

Wulf, Karin. *Not All Wives: Women of Colonial Philadelphia*. Ithaca: Cornell University Press, 2000.

★ CHAPTER 2 ★

Block, Sharon. *Rape and Sexual Power in Early America*. Chapel Hill: The University of North Carolina Press, 2006.

Camp, Stephanie M. H. *Closer to Freedom: Enslaved Women and Everyday Resistance in the Plantation South*. Chapel Hill: The University of North Carolina Press, 2004.

Clinton, Catherine. *The Plantation Mistress: Woman's World in the Old South*. New York: Pantheon Books, 1982.

Cockrell, Dale. *Demons of Disorder: Early Blackface Minstrels and Their World*. New York: Cambridge University Press, 1997.

D'Emilio, John and Estelle B. Freedman. *Intimate Matters: A History of Sexuality in America*. New York: Harper & Row, 1988.

David, Paul A., et al, eds. *Reckoning with Slavery: A Critical Study in the Quantitative History of American Negro Slavery*. New York: Oxford University Press, 1976.

Escott, Paul D. *Slavery Remembered: A Record of Twentieth-Century Slave Narratives*. Chapel Hill: The University of North Carolina Press, 1979.

Fogel, Robert William and Stanley L. Engerman. *Time on the Cross: The Economics of American Negro Slavery*. Boston: Little, Brown, 1974.

Genovese, Eugene D. *Roll, Jordan, Roll: The World the Slaves Made*. New York: Pantheon Books, 1974.

Glenn, Myra C. *Campaigns Against Corporal Punishment: Prisoners, Sailors, Women, and Children in Antebellum America*. Albany: State University of New York Press, 1984.

Gutman, Herbert. *Slavery and the Numbers Game: A Critique of Time on the Cross*. Urbana: University of Illinois Press, 1975.

Kaye, Anthony E. "The Personality of Power: The Ideology of Slaves in the Natchez District and the Delta of Mississippi, 1830–1865." PhD diss., Columbia University, 1999.

Lane, Horace. *The Wandering Boy, Careless Sailor, and Result of Inconsideration: A True Narrative*. Skaneateles, NY: L. A. Pratt, 1839.

Lhamon, W. T. *Raising Cain: Blackface Performance from Jim Crow to Hip Hop*. Cambridge, Mass.: Harvard University Press, 1998.

Lott, Eric. *Love and Theft: Blackface Minstrelsy and the American Working Class*. New York: Oxford University Press, 1993.

Nathan, Hans. *Dan Emmett and the Rise of Early Negro Minstrelsy*. Norman: University of Oklahoma Press, 1962.

Olmsted, Frederick Law. *Journey in the Seaboard Slave States*. New York: Dix & Edwards, 1856.

Pleck, Elizabeth H. *Domestic Tyranny: The Making of American Social Policy Against Family Violence from Colonial Times to the Present*. New York: Oxford University Press, 1987.

Rawick, George P. *The American Slave: A Composite Autobiography*. Westport, Conn.: Greenwood Pub. Co., 1972.

Rodgers, Daniel T. *The Work Ethic in Industrial America, 1850–1920*. Chicago: University of Chicago Press, 1978.

Roediger, David R. *The Wages of Whiteness: Race and the Making of the American Working Class*. New York: Verso, 1991.

Rothman, David J. *The Discovery of the Asylum: Social Order and Disorder in the New Republic*. Boston: Little, Brown, 1971.

Stevenson, Brenda E. *Life in Black and White: Family and Community in the Slave South*. New York: Oxford University Press, 1996.

Walters, Ronald G. *The Antislavery Appeal: American Abolitionism After 1830*. Baltimore: Johns Hopkins University Press, 1976.

White, Shane and Graham White. *Stylin': African American Expressive Culture from Its Beginnings to the Zoot Suit*. Ithaca, NY: Cornell University Press, 1998.

Wood, Peter H. "'Gimme de Kneebone Bent': African Body Language and the Evolution of American Dance Forms." In *The Black Tradition in Modern American Dance*, edited by Gerald E. Myers. American Dance Festival, 1988.

★ CHAPTER 3 ★

Billman, Carol. "McGuffey's Readers and Alger's Fiction: The Gospel of Virtue According to Popular Children's Literature." *Journal of Popular Culture* 11 (1977): 614–619.

Brown, H. E. *John Freeman and His Family*. Boston: American Tract Society, 1864.

Burns, Eric. *The Spirits of America: a Social History of Alcohol*. Philadelphia: Temple University Press, 2004.

Douglass, Frederick. *My Bondage and My Freedom*. New York, Miller, Orton & Mulligan: 1855.

DuBois, W. E. Burghardt. *Black Reconstruction: An Essay Toward a History of the Part which Black Folk Played in the Attempt to Reconstruct Democracy in America, 1860–1880*. New York: Harcourt Brace & Co., 1935.

———. *The Gift of Black Folk: The Negroes in the Making of America*. Boston: The Stratford Co., 1924.

Elson, Ruth Miller. *Guardians of Tradition: American Schoolbooks of the Nineteenth Century*. Lincoln: University of Nebraska Press, 1964.

Fisk, Clinton Bowen. *Plain Counsels for Freedmen: In Sixteen Brief Lectures*. Boston: American Tract Society, 1866.

Foner, Eric. *Reconstruction: America's Unfinished Revolution, 1863–1877*. New York: Harper & Row, 1988.

Franke, Katherine. "Becoming a Citizen: Reconstruction Era Regulation of African American Marriages." *Yale Journal of Law and the Humanities* 11 (1999): 251–309.

Gaines, Kevin Kelly. *Uplifting the Race: Black Leadership, Politics, and Culture in the Twentieth Century*. Chapel Hill: University of North Carolina Press, 1996.

Gilfoyle, Timothy J. *City of Eros: New York City, Prostitution, and the Commercialization of Sex, 1790–1920*. New York: W. W. Norton, 1994.

Gutman, Herbert George. *Work, Culture, and Society in Industrializing America: Essays in American Working-Class and Social History*. New York: Knopf, 1976.

Hartman, Saidiya V. *Scenes of Subjection: Terror, Slavery, and Self-Making in Nineteenth-Century America*. New York: Oxford University Press, 1997.

McGarry, Molly. "Spectral Sexualities: Nineteenth-Century Spiritualism, Moral Panics, and the Making of U. S. Obscenity Law." *Journal of Women's History* 12 (2000): 8–29.

Nasaw, David. *Going Out: The Rise and Fall of Public Amusements*. New York: Basic Books, 1993.

Powell, Lawrence N. *New Masters: Northern Planters During the Civil War and Reconstruction*. New York: Fordham University Press, 1998.

Rodgers, Daniel T. *The Work Ethic in Industrial America, 1850–1920*. Chicago: University of Chicago Press, 1978.

———. "Socializing Middle-Class Children: Institutions, Fables, and Work Values in Nineteenth-Century America." In *Growing Up in America: Children in Historical Perspective*, edited by N. Ray Hiner and Joseph M. Hawes, 119–132. Urbana: University of Illinois Press, 1985.

Roediger, David R. and Philip S. Foner. *Our Own Time: A History of American Labor and the Working Day*. New York: Verso, 1989.

Stevens, Thaddeus. Speech delivered in the House of Representatives, March 19, 1867, on the Bill (H.R. No. 20) Relative to Damages to Loyal Men, and for Other Purposes.

⋆ CHAPTER 4 ⋆

Bellocq, E. J. *Storyville Portraits*. New York: Museum of Modern Art, 1970.

Blackburn, George M. and Sherman L. Ricards. "The Prostitutes and Gamblers of Virginia City, Nevada, 1870." *Pacific Historical Review* (1979): 239–258.

Butler, Anne M. *Daughters of Joy, Sisters of Misery: Prostitutes in the American West, 1865–90*. Urbana: University of Illinois Press, 1987.

Chicago Vice Commission. *The Social Evil in Chicago; a Study of Existing Conditions With Recommendations By the Vice Commission of Chicago: A Municipal Body Appointed By the Mayor and the City Council of the City of Chicago, and Submitted as Its Report to the Mayor and City Council of Chicago*. Chicago: Gunthorp-Warren printing company, 1911.

Enss, Chris. *Pistol Packin' Madams: True Stories of Notorious Women of the Old West*. Guilford, Conn.: TwoDot, 2006.

Epstein, Dena J. *Sinful Tunes and Spirituals: Black Folk Music to the Civil War*. Urbana: University of Illinois Press, 1977.

Erenberg, Lewis A. *Steppin' Out: New York City Nightlife and the Transformation of American Culture, 1890–1930*. Chicago: University of Chicago Press, 1984.

———. *Swingin' The Dream: Big Band Jazz and The Rebirth of American Culture*. Chicago: University of Chicago Press, 1998.

Gabbert, Ann R. "Prostitution and Moral Reform in the Borderlands: El Paso, 1890–1920." *Journal of the History of Sexuality* 12 (2003): 575–604.

Gilman, Charlotte Perkins. *Women and Economics: A Study of the Economic Relation Between Men and Women as a Factor in Social Evolution*. Boston: Small, Maynard & Co., 1898.

Goldman, Marion S. *Gold Diggers and Silver Miners: Prostitution and Social Life on the Comstock Lode*. Ann Arbor: University of Michigan Press, 1981.

Hobson, Barbara Meil. *Uneasy Virtue: The Politics of Prostitution and the American Reform Tradition*. New York: Basic Books, 1987.

Kenney, William Howland. *Jazz on the River*. Chicago: University of Chicago Press, 2005.

MacKell, Jan. *Brothels, Bordellos and Bad Girls: Prostitution in Colorado, 1860–1930*. Albuquerque: University of New Mexico Press, 2004.

McGovern, James R. "The American Woman's Pre-World War I Freedom in Manners and Morals." *The Journal of American History* 55 (1968): 315–333.

Mumford , Kevin J. *Interzones: Black/White Sex Districts in Chicago and New York in the Early Twentieth Century*. New York: Columbia University Press, 1997.

Nye, Russel B. "Saturday Night at the Paradise Ballroom: Or, Dance Halls in the Twenties." *The Journal of Popular Culture* 7 (1973): 14–22.

Peiss, Kathy. *Hope in a Jar: The Making of America's Beauty Culture*. New York: Metropolitan Books, 1999.

Petrik, Paula. *No Step Backward: Women and Family on the Rocky Mountain Mining Frontier, Helena Montana, 1865–1900*. Helena: Montana Historical Society Press, 1990.

Rosen, Ruth. *The Lost Sisterhood: Prostitution in America, 1900–1918*. Baltimore: Johns Hopkins University Press, 1983.

Seagraves, Anne. *Soiled Doves: Prostitution in the Early West*. Hayden, Idaho: Wesanne Publications, 1994.

Tone, Andrea. *Devices and Desires: A History of Contraceptives in America*. New York: Hill and Wang, 2002.

West, Elliott. *The Saloon on the Rocky Mountain Mining Frontier*. Lincoln: University of Nebraska Press, 1991.

White, Richard. *"It's your misfortune and none of my own": A New History of the American West*. Norman: University of Oklahoma Press, 1993.

Wild, Mark. *Street Meeting: Multiethnic Neighborhoods in Early Twentieth-Century Los Angeles*. Berkeley: University of California Press, 2005.

★ CHAPTER 5 ★

Bailyn, Bernard. *The Ideological Origins of the American Revolution*. Cambridge: Belknap Press of Harvard University Press, 1967.

Bobrick, Benson. *Angel in the Whirlwind: The Triumph of the American Revolution*. New York, NY: Simon & Schuster, 1997.

Daniels, Bruce C. *Puritans at Play: Leisure and Recreation in Colonial New England*. New York: St. Martin's Griffin, 1996.

Dempsey, Jack, ed. *New English Canaan: Text, Notes, Biography and Criticism*. Scituate, Mass.: Digital Screening, 1999.

Ewing, George. *The Military Journal of George Ewing, 1775–1778*. Yonkers, N.Y.: 1928.

Keller, Kate Van Winkle. *Dance and Its Music in America, 1528–1789*. Hillsdale, NY: Pendragon Press, 2007.

Stearns, Marshall and Jean. *Jazz Dance: The Story Of American Vernacular Dance*. New York: Da Capo Press, 1994.

Stubbes, Phillip. *The Anatomie of Abuses*. 1836.

Wagner, Ann. *Adversaries of Dance: From the Puritans to the Present*. Urbana: University of Illinois Press, 1997.

★ CHAPTER 6 ★

Almeida, Linda Dowling. *Irish Immigrants in New York City, 1945–1995*. Bloomington: Indiana University Press, 2001.

Anbinder, Tyler. *Five Points: The 19th-Century New York City Neighborhood that Invented Tap Dance, Stole Elections, and Became the World's Most Notorious Slum*. New York: Free Press, 2001.

Asbury, Herbert. *The Gangs of New York: An Informal History of the Underworld*. New York: Vintage Books, 2008.

Bayor, Ronald H. and Timothy J. Meagher, eds. *The New York Irish*. Baltimore: Johns Hopkins University Press, 1996.

Beddoe, John. *The Races of Britain: A Contribution to the Anthropology of Western Europe*. Bristol: J. W. Arrowsmith, 1885.

Benshoff, Harry M. and Sean Griffin. *America on Film: Representing Race, Class, Gender, and Sexuality at the Movies*. Malden: Blackwell Publishing, 2004.

Boyer, Paul. *Urban Masses and Moral Order in America, 1820–1920*. Cambridge, Mass.: Harvard University Press, 1978.

Braham, David and Edward Harrigan. *Collected Songs*. Madison: A-R Editions, Inc., 1997.

Brennan, Helen. *The Story of Irish Dance*. Dingle, Ireland: Brandon Books, 1999.

Cassidy, Daniel. *How the Irish Invented Slang: The Secret Language of the Crossroads.* Oakland, Calif.: AK Press, 2007.

Cipolla, Frank J. "Patrick S. Gilmore: The Boston Years." *American Music* 6, no. 3 (1988): 281–292.

Cullen, Frank, Florence Hackman, and Donald McNeilly. *Vaudeville, Old and New: An Encyclopedia of Variety Performers in America.* New York: Routledge, 2007.

Curtis, L. Perry, Jr. *Apes and Angels: The Irishman in Victorian Caricature.* Washington, DC: Smithsonian Institution Press, 1971.

Gorn, Elliott J. "'Good-Bye Boys, I Die a True American': Homicide, Nativism, and Working-Class Culture in Antebellum New York City." *Journal of American History* 74 (1987): 388–410.

Grant, Madison. *The Passing of the Great Race: or, The Racial Basis of European History.* New York: C. Scribner's Sons, 1921.

Harris, Leslie M. *In the Shadow of Slavery: African Americans in New York City, 1626–1863.* Chicago: University of Chicago Press, 2003.

Higham, John. *Strangers in the Land: Patterns of American Nativism, 1860–1925.* New Brunswick, N.J.: Rutgers University Press, 1955.

Horton, James Oliver and Lois E. Horton. *Black Bostonians: Family Life and Community Struggle in the Antebellum North.* New York: Holmes & Meier, 1979.

Ignatiev, Noel. *How the Irish Became White.* New York: Routledge, 1995.

Knobel, Dale T. *Paddy and the Republic: Ethnicity and Nationality in Antebellum America.* Middletown, Conn.: Wesleyan University Press, 1986.

Lee, J. J. and Marion R. Casey, eds. *Making the Irish American: History and Heritage of the Irish in the United States.* New York: New York University Press, 2006.

Lhamon, W. T. *Raising Cain: Blackface Performance from Jim Crow to Hip Hop.* Cambridge: Harvard University Press, 1998.

Linebaugh, Peter and Marcus Rediker. *The Many-Headed Hydra: Sailors, Slaves, Commoners, and the Hidden History of the Revolutionary Atlantic.* Boston: Beacon Press, 2000.

Lott, Eric. *Love and Theft: Blackface Minstrelsy and the American Working Class.* New York: Oxford University Press, 1993.

Miller, Kerby A. *Emigrants and Exiles: Ireland and the Irish Exodus to North America.* New York: Oxford University Press, 1985.

Miller, Wilbur R. *Cops and Bobbies: Police Authority in New York and London, 1830–1870.* Chicago: University of Chicago Press, 1977.

O'Sullivan, Patrick, ed. *The Creative Migrant.* New York: St. Martin's Press, 1994.

Quinlin, Michael P. *Irish Boston.* Guilford, Conn.: Globe Pequot Press, 2004.

Roediger, David R. *The Wages of Whiteness: Race and the Making of the American Working Class.* New York: Verso, 1991.

———. *Towards the Abolition of Whiteness: Essays on Race, Politics, and Working Class History.* New York: Verso, 1994.

———. *Working Toward Whiteness: How America's Immigrants Became White: The Strange Journey from Ellis Island to the Suburbs.* New York: Basic Books, 2005.

Rowland, Thomas J. "Irish American Catholics and the Quest for Respectability in the Coming of the Great War, 1900–1917." *Journal of American Ethnic History* 15 (1996): 3–31.

Schneider, Eric C. *In the Web of Class: Delinquents and Reformers in Boston, 1810s–1930s.* New York: New York University Press, 1992.

Shaw, Richard. *Dagger John: The Unquiet Life and Times of Archbishop John Hughes of New York.* New York: Paulist Press, 1977.

Tomko, Linda J. *Dancing Class: Gender, Ethnicity, and Social Divides in American Dance, 1890–1920.* Bloomington: Indiana University Press, 1999.

Way, Peter. *Common Labour: Workers and the Digging of North American Canals, 1780–1860*. New York: Cambridge University Press, 1993.

Williams, W. H. A. *'Twas Only an Irishman's Dream: The Image of Ireland and the Irish in American Popular Song Lyrics, 1800–1920*. Urbana: University of Illinois Press, 1996.

★ CHAPTER 7 ★

Abernathy, Arthur Talmage. *The Jew a Negro: Being a Study of the Jewish Ancestry from an Impartial Standpoint*. Moravian Falls, N.C.: Dixie Publishing, 1910.

Blady, Ken. *The Jewish Boxers Hall of Fame*. New York: Shapolsky Publishers, 1988.

Blee, Kathleen M. *Women of the Klan: Racism and Gender in the 1920s*. Berkeley: University of California Press, 1991.

Bodner, Allen. *When Boxing Was a Jewish Sport*. Westport, Conn.: Praeger, 1997.

Daniels, Roger and Otis L. Graham. *Debating American Immigration, 1882–Present*. Lanham, Md.: Rowman & Littlefield Publishers, 2001.

Davis, Mac. *From Moses to Einstein: They All Are Jews*. New York: Jordan Publishing Co., 1937.

Diner, Hasia R. *In the Almost Promised Land: American Jews and Blacks, 1915–1935*. Baltimore: Johns Hopkins University Press, 1995.

Dinnerstein, Leonard. *Antisemitism in America*. New York: Oxford University Press, 1994.

Erenberg, Lewis A. *Steppin' Out: New York City Nightlife and the Transformation of American Culture, 1890–1930*. Chicago: University of Chicago Press, 1984.

———. *Swingin' The Dream: Big Band Jazz and The Rebirth of American Culture*. Chicago: University of Chicago Press, 1998.

Ferris, Marcie Cohen and Mark I. Greenberg, eds. *Jewish Roots in Southern Soil: A New History*. Hanover, NH: University Press of New England, 2006.

Ford, Henry. *The International Jew: The World's Foremost Problem, Vol. 1–4*. Dearborn, Mich.: The Dearborn Publishing Co., 1920–1922.

Gabler, Neal. *An Empire of Their Own: How the Jews Invented Hollywood*. New York: Crown Publishers, 1988.

Gerstle, Gary. *American Crucible: Race and Nation in the Twentieth Century*. Princeton: Princeton University Press, 2001.

Gertzman, Jay A. *Bookleggers and Smuthounds: The Trade in Erotica, 1920–1940*. Philadelphia: University of Pennsylvania Press, 1999.

Goldstein, Eric L. *The Price of Whiteness: Jews, Race, and American Identity*. Princeton: Princeton University Press, 2006.

Gurock, Jeffrey S. *Judaism's Encounter with American Sports*. Bloomington: Indiana University Press, 2005.

———. *When Harlem Was Jewish*. New York: Columbia University Press, 1979.

Levine, Peter. *Ellis Island to Ebbets Field: Sport and the American Jewish Experience*. New York: Oxford University Press, 1992.

MacLean, Nancy. *Behind the Mask of Chivalry: The Making of the Second Ku Klux Klan*. New York: Oxford University Press, 1994.

Melnick, Jeffrey Paul. *A Right to Sing the Blues: African Americans, Jews, and American Popular Song*. Cambridge, Mass.: Harvard University Press, 1999.

Mezzrow, Mezz. *Really the Blues*. New York: Random House, 1946.

Riess, Steven A., ed. *Sports and the American Jew*. Syracuse, N.Y.: Syracuse University Press, 1998.

Rogin, Michael Paul. *Blackface, White Noise: Jewish Immigrants in the Hollywood Melting Pot*. Berkeley: University of California Press, 1996.

Rogoff, Leonard. "Is the Jew White?: The Racial Place of the Southern Jew." *American Jewish History* 85, no. 3 (1997): 195–230.

Sachar, Howard Morley. *A History of the Jews in America*. New York: Knopf, 1992.

Saleski, Gdal. *Famous Musicians of a Wandering Race*. New York: Bloch Publishing Company, 1927.

Slobin, Mark. *Tenement Songs: The Popular Music of the Jewish Immigrants*. Urbana: University of Illinois Press, 1982.

Sollors, Werner. *Beyond Ethnicity: Consent and Descent in American Culture*. New York: Oxford University Press, 1986.

Suisman, David. *Selling Sounds: The Commercial Revolution in American Music*. Cambridge, Mass.: Harvard University Press, 2009.

Vaillant, Derek. *Sounds of Reform: Progressivism and Music in Chicago, 1873–1935*. Chapel Hill: University of North Carolina Press, 2003.

Zangwill, Israel. *The Melting-Pot: Drama in Four Acts*. New York: The Macmillan Company, 1909.

Zurawik, David. *The Jews of Prime Time*. Hanover, NH: University Press of New England, 2003.

★ CHAPTER 8 ★

Boulard, Garry. *Just a Gigolo: The Life and Times of Louis Prima*. Lafayette, La.: Center for Louisiana Studies, University of Southwestern Louisiana, 1989.

Brandfon, Robert L. *Cotton Kingdom of the New South: A History of the Yazoo Mississippi Delta from Reconstruction to the Twentieth Century*. Cambridge, Mass.: Harvard University Press, 1967.

Brunn, H. O. *The Story of the Original Dixieland Jazz Band*. New York: Da Capo Press, 1977.

Carr, Ian, Digby Fairweather, and Brian Priestley. *The Rough Guide to Jazz*. New York: Rough Guides, 2004.

D'Acierno, Pellegrino, ed. *The Italian American Heritage: A Companion to Literature and Arts*. New York: Garland Publishing, 1999.

De Stefano, George. *An Offer We Can't Refuse: The Mafia in the Mind of America*. New York: Faber and Faber, 2006.

Erenberg, Lewis A. *Swingin' The Dream: Big Band Jazz and The Rebirth of American Culture*. Chicago: The University of Chicago Press, 1984.

Ewen, David. *Men of Popular Music*. Chicago: Ziff-Davis Publishing Company, 1944.

Fikentscher, Kai. *"You Better Work!": Underground Dance Music in New York City*. Hanover, N.H.: University Press of New England, 2000.

Foerster, Robert F. *The Italian Emigration of Our Times*. Cambridge: Harvard University Press, 1919.

Grant, Madison. *The Passing of the Great Race; or, The Racial Basis of European History*. New York: C. Scribner's Sons, 1921.

Greene, Victor. *A Passion for Polka: Old-Time Ethnic Music in America*. Berkeley: University of California Press, 1992.

Guglielmo, Jennifer and Salvatore Salerno. *Are Italians White? How Race Is Made in America*. New York: Routledge, 2003.

Guglielmo, Thomas A. *White on Arrival: Italians, Race, Color, and Power in Chicago, 1890–1945*. New York: Oxford University Press, 2003.

Higham, John. *Strangers in the Land: Patterns of American Nativism, 1860–1925*. New Brunswick, N.J.: Rutgers University Press, 1955.

LaGumina, Salvatore. *The Humble and the Heroic: Wartime Italian Americans*. Youngstown, OH: Cambria Press, 2006.

———. *WOP: A Documentary History of Anti-Italian Discrimination in the United States*. San Francisco: Straight Arrow Books, 1973.

Light, Alan, ed. *The Vibe History of Hip Hop*. New York: Three Rivers Press, 1999.

Lawrence, Tim. *Love Saves the Day: A History of American Dance Music Culture, 1970–1979*. Durham, N.C.: Duke University Press, 2003.

Luconi, Stefano. *From Paesani to White Ethnics: The Italian Experience in Philadelphia*. Albany: State University of New York Press, 2001.

Martin, Linda and Kerry Segrave. *Anti-rock: The Opposition to Rock 'n' Roll*. Hamden, Conn.: Archon Books, 1988.

McCracken, Allison. "'God's Gift to Us Girls': Crooning, Gender, and the Re-Creation of American Popular Song, 1928–1933." *American Music* 17, no. 4 (1999): 365–395.

Morris, Ronald L. *Wait Until Dark: Jazz and the Underworld, 1880–1940*. Bowling Green, OH: Bowling Green University Popular Press, 1980.

Mustazza, Leonard, ed. *Frank Sinatra and Popular Culture: Essays on an American Icon*. Westport, Conn.: Praeger, 1998.

Nakamura, Julia Volpelletto. "The Italian American Contribution to Jazz." *Italian Americana* 8 (1986): 23.

Orsi, Robert A. *The Madonna of 115th Street: Faith and Community in Italian Harlem, 1880–1950*. New Haven: Yale University Press, 1985.

Pugliese, Stanislao G., ed. *Frank Sinatra: History, Identity, and Italian American Culture*. New York: Palgrave Macmillan, 2004.

Roediger, David R. *Colored White: Transcending the Racial Past*. Berkeley: University of California Press, 2002.

Ross, Edward Alsworth. *The Old World in the New: The Significance of Past and Present Immigration to the American People*. New York: The Century Co., 1914.

Shapiro, Peter. *Turn the Beat Around: The Secret History of Disco*. New York: Faber and Faber, 2005.

Spiro, Jonathan Peter. *Defending the Master Race: Conservation, Eugenics, and the Legacy of Madison Grant*. Hanover, NH: University Press of New England, 2009.

Sudhalter, Richard M. *Lost Chords: White Musicians and Their Contribution to Jazz, 1915–1945*. New York: Oxford University Press, 1999.

Summers, Anthony and Robbyn Swan. *Sinatra: The Life*. New York: Knopf, 2005.

Sweeney, Arthur. "Mental Tests for Immigrants." *The North American Review* 215 (1922): 600–612.

Ward, Brian. *Just My Soul Responding: Rhythm and Blues, Black Consciousness, and Race Relations*. Berkeley: University of California Press, 1998.

Ward, Geoffrey C. *Jazz: A History of America's Music*. New York: Alfred A. Knopf, 2000.

Warne, Frank Julian. *The Tide of Immigration*. New York: D. Appleton, 1916.

★ CHAPTER 9 ★

Beecher, Henry Ward. *Lectures to Young Men on Industry and Idleness*. New York: Fowlers and Wells, 1848.

Blaszczyk, Regina Lee. *Imagining Consumers: Design and Innovation from Wedgwood to Corning*. Baltimore: Johns Hopkins University Press, 2000.

Carnegie, Andrew. "Wealth." *North American Review* 148.39 (1889).

Chapin, Robert Coit. *The Standard of Living Among Workingmen's Families in New York City*. New York: Russell Sage Foundation, 1909.

Chernow, Ron. *Titan: The Life of John D. Rockefeller, Sr.* New York: Random House, 1998.

Converse, Jean M. *Survey Research in the United States: Roots and Emergence 1890–1960*. New Brunswick, NJ: Transaction Publishers, 2009.

Dubofsky, Melvyn and Warren Van Tine, eds., *Labor Leaders in America*. Urbana: University of Illinois Press, 1987.

Enstad, Nan. *Ladies of Labor, Girls of Adventure: Working Women, Popular Culture, and*

Labor Politics at the Turn of the Twentieth Century. New York: Columbia University Press, 1999.

Erenberg, Lewis A. *Steppin' Out: New York City Nightlife and the Transformation of American Culture, 1890–1930.* Chicago: The University of Chicago Press, 1984.

Ewen, Stuart. *Captains of Consciousness: Advertising and the Social Roots of Consumer Culture.* New York: McGraw-Hill, 1976.

Horowitz, Daniel. *The Morality of Spending: Attitudes Toward the Consumer Society in America, 1875–1940.* Baltimore: Johns Hopkins University Press, 1985.

Kann, Mark E. *On the Man Question: Gender and Civic Virtue in America.* Philadelphia: Temple University Press, 1991.

Kasson, John F. *Amusing the Millions: Coney Island at the Turn of the Century.* New York: Hill and Wang, 1976.

LaSelle, Mary A. *The Young Woman Worker.* Boston: Pilgrim Press, 1914.

Lebergott, Stanley. *Pursuing Happiness: American Consumers in the Twentieth Century.* Princeton, NJ: Princeton University Press, 1993.

Nye, David E. *Technology Matters: Questions to Live With.* Cambridge, Mass.: MIT Press, 2006.

Patten, Simon Nelson. *Product and Climax.* New York: B.W. Huebsch, 1909.

Peiss, Kathy. *Cheap Amusements: Working Women and Leisure in Turn-of-the-Century New York.* Philadelphia: Temple University Press, 1986.

Phelan, Rev. J. J. *Motion Pictures as a Phase of Commercial Amusement in Toledo, Ohio.* Toledo: Little Book Press, 1919.

Richardson, Bertha June. *The Woman Who Spends: A Study of Her Economic Function.* Boston: Whitcomb & Barrows, 1904.

Rodgers, Daniel T. *The Work Ethic in Industrial America, 1850–1920.* Chicago: University of Chicago Press, 1978.

Salvatore, Nick. *Eugene V. Debs: Citizen and Socialist.* Urbana: University of Illinois Press, 1982.

Stein, Leon and Philip Taft, eds. *Workers Speak: Self Portraits.* New York: Arno, 1971.

Veblen, Thorstein. *The Theory of the Leisure Class.* New York: Dover Publications, 1994.

Wald, Lillian D. *The House on Henry Street.* New York: H. Holt and Co., 1915.

Wayland, Francis. *The Elements of Political Economy.* New York: Leavitt, Lord & Company, 1837.

Weber, Max. *The Protestant Ethic and the "Spirit" of Capitalism.* New York: Penguin Books, 2002.

★ CHAPTER 10 ★

Bowser, Eileen. *The Transformation of Cinema, 1907–1915.* Berkeley: University of California Press, 1994.

Burbank, Jeff. *License to Steal: Nevada's Gaming Control System in the Megaresort Era.* Reno: University of Nevada Press, 2000.

Carter, David. *Stonewall: The Riots that Sparked the Gay Revolution.* New York: St. Martin's Press, 2004.

Charyn, Jerome. *Gangsters and Gold Diggers: Old New York, The Jazz Age, and the Birth of Broadway.* New York: Thunder's Mouth Press, 2003.

Chilton, John and Max Jones. *Louis: The Louis Armstrong Story, 1900–1971.* New York: Da Capo Press, 1988.

De Stefano, George. *An Offer We Can't Refuse: The Mafia in the Mind of America.* New York: Faber and Faber, 2006.

Doherty, Thomas Patrick. *Pre-code Hollywood: Sex, Immorality, and Insurrection in American Cinema, 1930–1934.* New York: Columbia University Press, 1999.

Duberman, Martin B. *Stonewall.* New York, N.Y.: Dutton, 1993.

Eisenbach, David. *Gay Power: An American Revolution*. New York: Carroll & Graf, 2006.

Fried, Albert. *The Rise and Fall of the Jewish Gangster in America*. New York: Holt, Rinehart, and Winston, 1980.

Gabler, Neal. *An Empire of their Own: How the Jews Invented Hollywood*. New York: Anchor, 1989.

Hampton, Benjamin Bowles. *A History of the Movies*. New York: Covici, Friede, 1931.

Jacobs, Lewis. *The Rise of the American Film: A Critical History*. New York: Harcourt, Brace and Co., 1939.

Joselit, Jenna Weissman. *Our Gang: Jewish Crime and the New York Jewish Community, 1900–1940*. Bloomington: Indiana University Press, 1983.

Keller, Morton. *Regulating a New Society: Public Policy and Social Change in America, 1900–1933*. Cambridge: Harvard University Press, 1994.

Kobler, John. *Capone: The Life and World of Al Capone*. New York: Da Capo Press, 2003.

May, Lary. *The Big Tomorrow: Hollywood and the Politics of the American Way*. Chicago: University of Chicago Press, 2000.

McCracken, Robert D. *Las Vegas: The Great American Playground*. Reno: University of Nevada Press, 1997.

Miller, Nathan. *New World Coming: The 1920s and the Making of Modern America*. New York: Scribner, 2003.

Moehring, Eugene P. *Resort City in the Sunbelt: Las Vegas, 1930–1970*. Reno: University of Nevada Press, 1989.

Morris, Ronald L. *Wait Until Dark: Jazz and the Underworld, 1880–1940*. Bowling Green, OH: Bowling Green University Popular Press, 1980.

Newton, Michael. *Mr. Mob: The Life and Crimes of Moe Dalitz*. Jefferson, N.C.: McFarland & Co., 2009.

Peretti, Burton W. *The Creation of Jazz: Music, Race, and Culture in Urban America*. Urbana: University of Illinois Press, 1994.

Pietrusza, David. *Rothstein: The Life, Times, and Murder of the Criminal Genius who Fixed the 1919 World Series*. New York: Carroll & Graf, 2003.

Raab, Selwyn. *Five Families: The Rise, Decline, and Resurgence of America's Most Powerful Mafia Empires*. New York: Thomas Dunne Books, 2005.

Ramsaye, Terry. *A Million and One Nights: A History of the Motion Picture*. New York: Simon and Schuster, 1926.

Rockaway, Robert A. *But He Was Good to His Mother: The Lives and Crimes of Jewish Gangsters*. Jerusalem: Gefen Publishing House, 2000.

Shapiro, Nat and Nat Hentoff. *Hear Me Talkin' to Ya: The Story of Jazz as Told by the Men who Made It*. New York: Dover Publications, 1966.

Sklar, Robert. *Movie-Made America: A Social History of American Movies*. New York: Random House, 1975.

Slide, Anthony. *Early American Cinema*. Metuchen, NJ: Scarecrow Press, 1994.

★ CHAPTER 11 ★

Cogdell, Christina. *Eugenic Design: Streamlining America in the 1930s*. Philadelphia: University of Pennsylvania Press, 2004.

Diggins, John P. *Mussolini and Italy: The View from America*. Princeton, NJ: Princeton University Press, 1972.

Erens, Patricia. *The Jew in American Cinema*. Bloomington: Indiana University Press, 1984.

Gabler, Neal. *An Empire of Their Own: How the Jews Invented Hollywood*. New York: Crown Publishers, 1988.

Garraty, John A. "The New Deal, National Socialism, and the Great Depression." *The American Historical Review* 78.4 (1973): 907–944.

Jacobs, Lea. *The Wages of Sin: Censorship and the Fallen Woman Film, 1928–1942.*
    Berkeley: University of California Press, 1997.

Johnson, Hugh Samuel. *The Blue Eagle from Egg to Earth.* Garden City, N.Y.: Doubleday,
    Doran & Co., 1935.

Kevles, Daniel J. *In the Name of Eugenics: Genetics and the Uses of Human Heredity.* New
    York: Knopf, 1985.

Kuhl, Stefan. *The Nazi Connection: Eugenics, American Racism, and German National
    Socialism.* New York: Oxford University Press, 1994.

Leuchtenburg, William. "The New Deal and the Analogue of War." In *Change and
    Continuity in Twentieth-Century America.* John Braeman, Robert H. Bremner, and
    Everett Walters, eds. Columbus: Ohio State University Press, 1968.

Munby, Jonathan. *Public Enemies, Public Heroes: Screening the Gangster from Little Caesar
    to Touch of Evil.* Chicago: University of Chicago Press, 1999.

Muscio, Giuliana. *Hollywood's New Deal.* Philadelphia: Temple University Press, 1996.

Namorato, Michael V. *Rexford G. Tugwell: A Biography.* New York: Praeger, 1988.

Ohl, John Kennedy. *Hugh S. Johnson and the New Deal.* Dekalb, Ill.: Northern Illinois
    University Press, 1985.

Patel, Kiran Klaus. *Soldiers of Labor: Labor Service in Nazi Germany and New Deal
    America, 1933–1945.* New York: Cambridge University Press, 2005.

Pickens, Donald K. *Eugenics and the Progressives.* Nashville: Vanderbilt University Press,
    1968.

Richberg, Donald Randall. *The Rainbow.* Garden City, NY: Doubleday, Doran & Co.,
    1936.

Schivelbusch, Wolfgang. *Three New Deals: Reflections on Roosevelt's America, Mussolini's
    Italy, and Hitler's Germany, 1933–1939.* New York: Metropolitan Books, 2006.

Selden, Steven. *Inheriting Shame: The Story of Eugenics and Racism in America.* New York:
    Teachers College Press, 1999.

Steele, Richard W. *Propaganda in an Open Society: The Roosevelt Administration and the
    Media, 1933–1941.* Westport, Conn.: Greenwood Press, 1985.

Suzik, Jeffrey Ryan. "'Building Better Men': The CCC Boy and the Changing Social Ideal
    of Manliness." *Men and Masculinities* 2 (1999): 152–179.

Tugwell, Rexford G. *The Industrial Discipline and the Governmental Arts.* New York:
    Columbia University Press, 1933.

———. *To the Lesser Heights of Morningside: A Memoir.* Philadelphia: University of
    Pennsylvania Press, 1982.

Vadney, Thomas E. *The Wayward Liberal: A Political Biography of Donald Richberg.*
    Lexington: University Press of Kentucky, 1970.

Whitman, James Q. "Of Corporatism, Fascism, and the First New Deal." *The American
    Journal of Comparative Law* 39.4 (1991): 747–778.

★ **CHAPTER 12** ★

Bérubé, Allan. *Coming Out Under Fire: The History of Gay Men and Women in World War
    Two.* New York: Free Press, 1990.

Boyd, Nan Alamilla. *Wide-Open Town: A History of Queer San Francisco to 1965.*
    Berkeley: University of California Press, 2003.

Brecher, Jeremy. *Strike!* San Francisco: Straight Arrow Books, 1972.

Clifford, John Garry. "Grenville Clark and the Origins of Selective Service." *The Review of
    Politics,* 35.1 (1973): 17–40.

Clifford, John Garry and Samuel R. Spencer, Jr. *The First Peacetime Draft.* Lawrence, Kan.:
    University Press of Kansas, 1986.

Gill, Gerald R. "Afro-American Opposition to the United States' Wars of the Twentieth
    Century: Dissent, Discontent and Disinterest." PhD diss., Howard University, 1985.

Glaberman, Martin. *Wartime Strikes: The Struggle Against the No-Strike Pledge in the UAW During World War II*. Detroit: Bewick Editions, 1980.

Kelley, Robin D. G. *Race Rebels: Culture, Politics, and the Black Working Class*. New York: Free Press, 1994.

Malkin, Michelle. *In Defense of Internment: The Case for "Racial Profiling" in World War II and the War on Terror*. Washington, DC: Regnery, 2004.

O'Sullivan, John. *From Voluntarism to Conscription: Congress and Selective Service, 1940–1945*. New York: Garland, 1982.

Pagán, Eduardo Obregón. *Murder at the Sleepy Lagoon: Zoot Suits, Race, and Riots in Wartime L.A.* Chapel Hill: The University of North Carolina Press, 2003.

Pogue, Forrest C. *George C. Marshall*. New York: Viking, 1963.

Sloman, Larry. *Reefer Madness: The History of Marijuana in America*. Indianapolis: Bobbs-Merrill, 1979.

Smith, Page. *Democracy on Trial: The Japanese American Evacuation and Relocation in World War II*. New York: Simon & Schuster, 1995.

Stephan, John J. *Hawaii Under the Rising Sun: Japan's Plans for Conquest After Pearl Harbor*. Honolulu: University of Hawaii Press, 1984.

Stone, Geoffrey R. *Perilous Times: Free Speech in Wartime from the Sedition Act of 1798 to the War on Terrorism*. New York: W. W. Norton & Co., 2004.

★ CHAPTER 13 ★

Cushman, Thomas. *Notes from Underground: Rock Music Counterculture in Russia*. Albany: State University of New York Press, 1995.

Hessler, Julie. "The Birth of a Consumer Society: Consumption and Class in the USSR, 1917–1953." Historians' Seminar, Davis Center for Russian Studies, Harvard University, February 22, 2002.

———. *A Social History of Soviet Trade: Trade Policy, Retail Practices, and Consumption, 1917–1953*. Princeton: Princeton University Press, 2004.

Lytle, Mark H. *America's Uncivil Wars: The Sixties Era from Elvis to the Fall of Richard Nixon*. New York: Oxford University Press, 2006.

Martin, Linda and Kerry Segrave. *Anti-rock: The Opposition to Rock 'n' Roll*. Hamden, Conn.: Archon Books, 1988.

Pecora, Norma, John P. Murray, and Ellen Ann Wartella, eds. *Children and Television: Fifty Years of Research*. Mahwah, N.J.: Lawrence Erlbaum, 2007.

Poiger, Uta G. *Jazz, Rock, and Rebels: Cold War Politics and American Culture in a Divided Germany*. Berkeley: University of California Press, 2000.

Ryback, Timothy W. *Rock Around the Bloc: A History of Rock Music in Eastern Europe and the Soviet Union*. New York: Oxford University Press, 1990.

Starr, Frederick S. *Red and Hot: The Fate of Jazz in the Soviet Union, 1917–1991*. New York: Limelight Editions, 1985.

★ CHAPTER 14 ★

"1 Killed, 7 Hurt When Shotgun Blast Sets Off 7-Hour Battle in Alabama." *Washington Post and Times Herald*, November 18, 1957, A3.

"6 Negroes Are Jailed In Attack On White Man." *Birmingham Post-Herald*, March 7, 1961.

Baldwin, James. "Freaks and the American Ideal of Manhood." In *Collected Essays*. New York: Library of America, 1998.

Belfrage, Sally. *Freedom Summer*. Charlottesville: University Press of Virginia, 1965.

Beron, Kurt J., Helen V. Tauchen, and Ann Dryden Witte. "The Effect of Audits and Socioeconomic Variables on Compliance." In *Why People Pay Taxes: Tax Compliance and Enforcement*, edited by Joel Slemrod. Ann Arbor: University of Michigan Press, 1992.

Bogle, Donald. *Toms, Coons, Mulattoes, Mammies, and Bucks: An Interpretive History of Blacks in American Films*. New York: Viking Press, 1973.

———. *Blacks in American Films and Television: An Illustrated Encyclopedia*. New York: Fireside, 1988.

Cantarow, Ellen, Susan Gushee O'Malley, and Sharon Hartman Strom. *Moving the Mountain: Women Working for Social Change*. New York: McGraw-Hill, 1980.

Carson, Clayborne, ed. *The Papers of Martin Luther King, Jr., Volume IV: Symbol of the Movement: January 1957–December 1958*. Berkeley: University of California Press, 1992.

Chafe, William. "The End of One Struggle, the Beginning of Another." In *The Civil Rights Movement in America*, edited by Charles W. Eagles. Jackson: University Press of Mississippi, 1986.

Chappell, Marisa, Jenny Hutchinson, and Brian Ward. "'Dress modestly, neatly . . . as if you were going to church': Respectability, Class and Gender in the Montgomery Bus Boycott and the Early Civil Rights Movement." In *Gender in the Civil Rights Movement*, edited by Peter J. Ling and Sharon Monteith. New Brunswick: Rutgers University Press, 1999.

Chateauvert, Melinda. *Marching Together: Women of the Brotherhood of Sleeping Car Porters*. Urbana: University of Illinois Press, 1998.

"Citizenship Curriculum." *Radical Teacher* 40 (1991): 9–18.

Clark, Kenneth B. "The Zoot Effect in Personality: A Race Riot Participant." *Journal of Abnormal and Social Psychology* 40 (1945): 142–148.

D'Emilio, John. *Lost Prophet: The Life and Times of Bayard Rustin*. New York: Free Press, 2003.

Dance, Daryl Cumber. *Shuckin' and Jivin': Folklore from Contemporary Black Americans*. Bloomington: Indiana University Press, 1978.

Davis, Lenwood G. *Daddy Grace: An Annotated Bibliography*. New York: Greenwood Press, 1992.

DuBois, W. E. Burghardt. *The Gift of Black Folk: The Negroes in the Making of America*. Boston: The Stratford Co., 1924.

Eskew, Glenn T. *But for Birmingham: The Local and National Movements in the Civil Rights Struggle*. Chapel Hill: University of North Carolina Press, 1997.

Frazier, Edward Franklin. *The Negro Family in the United States*. New York: Citadel Press, 1948.

———. "Negro, Sex Life of the African and American." In *The Encyclopedia of Sexual Behavior*, edited by Albert Ellis and Albert Abarbanel. New York: Hawthorn Books, 1961.

Gill, Gerald Robert. "Afro-American Opposition to the United States' Wars of the Twentieth Century: Dissent, Discontent and Disinterest." PhD. diss., Howard University, 1985.

Ginsberg, Allen. "Howl." In *Howl, and Other Poems*. San Francisco: City Lights Pocket Bookshop, 1956.

Hamilton, Marybeth. "Sexuality, Authenticity and the Making of the Blues Tradition." *Past and Present* 169 (2000): 132–60.

Hughes, Langston. "The Negro Artist and the Racial Mountain." *The Nation* (June 23, 1926).

Hartman, Saidiya V. *Scenes of Subjection: Terror, Slavery, and Self-Making in Nineteenth-Century America*. New York: Oxford University Press, 1997.

Hunter, Tera W. *To 'Joy My Freedom: Southern Black Women's Lives and Labors After the Civil War*. Cambridge, Mass.: Harvard University Press, 1997.

Jackson, Walter A. *Gunnar Myrdal and America's Conscience: Social Engineering and Racial Liberalism, 1938–1987*. Chapel Hill: University of North Carolina Press, 1990.

"Jittery Bessemer Goes On Alert, But Race Riot Rumors Fall Flat." *Birmingham Post-Herald*, February 18, 1956, 1.

Johnson, John H. and Lerone Bennett, Jr. *Succeeding Against the Odds*. New York: Warner Books, 1989.

"Judge Tells Negro Couple City Wants no Race Riot." *Birmingham News*, July 11, 1956.

Kelley, Robin D. G. *Race Rebels: Culture, Politics, and the Black Working Class*. New York: Free Press, 1994.

Kennedy, David M. *Over Here: The First World War and American Society*. New York: Oxford University Press, 1980.

Kerouac, Jack. *On the Road*. New York: Viking Press, 1957.

King, Martin Luther, Jr. "Letter from Birmingham Jail." In *Why We Can't Wait*. New York: Penguin, 1964.

———. *Stride Toward Freedom: The Montgomery Story*. New York: Harper, 1958.

Levine, Lawrence W. *Black Culture and Black Consciousness: Afro-American Folk Thought from Slavery to Freedom*. New York: Oxford University Press, 1977.

Malcolm X. "The Old Negro and the New Negro." *The End of White World Supremacy: Four Speeches by Malcolm X*, edited by Imam Benjamin Karim. New York: Arcade Publishing, 1971.

Martin, Linda and Kerry Segrave. *Anti-rock: The Opposition to Rock 'n' Roll*. Hamden, Conn.: Archon Books, 1988.

Martin, Waldo E., Jr., ed. *Brown v. Board of Education: A Brief History with Documents*. Boston: Bedford/St. Martin's, 1998.

Martinez, Gerald, Diana Martinez, and Andres Chavez. *What It Is, What It Was! The Black Film Explosion of the '70s in Words and Pictures*. New York: Hyperion, 1998.

McAdam, Doug. *Freedom Summer*. New York: Oxford University Press, 1988.

Myrdal, Gunnar. *An American Dilemma: The Negro Problem and Modern Democracy*. New York: Harper, 1944.

"Negro, 70, Freed After Slaying Ala. White Man." *Jet*, January 22, 1953, 11.

"Negroes, Whites Exchange Gunfire." *Birmingham News*, October 29, 1960.

"Negro Group Attacks Youth." *Birmingham Post-Herald*, August 11, 1958.

O'Brien, Gail Williams. *The Color of the Law: Race, Violence, and Justice in the Post–World War II South*. Chapel Hill: University of North Carolina Press, 1999.

Raines, Howell. *My Soul is Rested: Movement Days in the Deep South Remembered*. New York: Putnam, 1977.

Retzloff, Tim. "'Seer or Queer?' Postwar Fascination with Detroit's Prophet Jones." *GLQ: A Journal of Lesbian and Gay Studies* 8: 3 (2002): 271–296.

Roberts, John W. *From Trickster to Badman: The Black Folk Hero in Slavery and Freedom*. Philadelphia: University of Pennsylvania Press, 1989.

Roosevelt, Eleanor. "Freedom: Promise of Fact." *Negro Digest* 1 (1943): 8–9.

———. "Some of My Best Friends Are Negro." *Ebony* 9 (1953): 16–20, 22, 24–26.

Russell, Thaddeus. "The Color of Discipline: Civil Rights and Black Sexuality." *American Quarterly* 60 (2008): 101–128.

Simon, Carl P. and Ann D. Witte. *Beating the System: The Underground Economy*. Boston: Auburn House, 1982.

Theophilus Eugene "Bull" Connor Papers. Birmingham Public Library Archives: Birmingham, Alabama.

    "Number of Females Arrested By Race, 1959–1960," Box 5, Folder 27.

    J. W. Garrison to Jamie Moore, January 28, 1960, Box 5, Folder 23.

    C. D. Guy to Chief Jamie Moore, May 7, 1960, Box 6, Folder 8.

    Sergeant C. D. Milwee to Captain J. W. Garrison, August 3, 1960, Box 5, Folder 23.

    T. E. Sellers to Chief Jamie Moore, August 11, 1960, Box 5, Folder 23.

    Sgt. C. D. Guy to Chief Jamie Moore, April 29, 1962, Box 11, Folder 46.

W. J. Haley to Commissioner Connor, Memorandum, May 25, 1962, Box 11, Folder 46.

L. B. Thompson to Chief Jamie Moore, September 4, 1962, Box 12, Folder 11.

Sgt. C. D. Guy to Chief Jamie Moore, October 3, 1962, Box 12, Folder 11.

George Wall to Chief Jamie Moore, October 4, 1962, Box 11, Folder 24.

"Two farmers in hospital with gunshot wounds after clash with boys, bullets at curb market." *Birmingham News*. August 15, 1955, 21.

Tyson, Timothy B. *Radio Free Dixie: Robert F. Williams and the Roots of Black Power*. Chapel Hill: University of North Carolina Press, 1999.

To Secure These Rights: The Report of the President's Committee on Civil Rights. Washington, DC: U.S. Government Printing Office, 1947.

Van DeBurg, William L. *New Day in Babylon: The Black Power Movement and American Culture, 1965–1975*. Chicago: University of Chicago Press, 1992.

Vincent, Rickey. *Funk: The Music, the People, and the Rhythm of the One*. New York: St. Martin's Griffin, 1996.

Ward, Brian. *Just My Soul Responding: Rhythm and Blues, Black Consciousness, and Race Relations*. Berkeley: University of California Press, 1998.

Watkins, Mel. *On the Real Side: Laughing, Lying, and Signifying: The Underground Tradition of African-American Humor*. New York: Simon & Schuster, 1994.

★ CHAPTER 15 ★

Allyn, David. *Make Love, Not War: The Sexual Revolution, an Unfettered History*. Boston: Little, Brown, 2000.

Bem, Sandra L. "Gender Schema Theory: A Cognitive Account of Sex Typing." *Psychological Review* 88 (1981): 354–64.

D'Emilio, John. *Sexual Politics, Sexual Communities: The Making of a Homosexual Minority in the United States, 1940–1970*. Chicago: University of Chicago Press, 1983.

D'Emilio, John and Estelle B. Freedman. *Intimate Matters: A History of Sexuality in America*. New York: Harper & Row, 1988.

Duberman, Martin B. *Stonewall*. New York: Dutton, 1993.

Eisenbach, David. *Gay Power: An American Revolution*. New York: Carroll and Graf, 2006.

Faderman, Lillian and Stuart Simmons. *Gay L.A.: A History of Sexual Outlaws, Power Politics, and Lipstick Lesbians*. New York: Basic Books, 2006.

Krich, Aron M. *The Sexual Revolution*. New York: Dell Pub. Co., 1964.

Reuben, David R. *Everything You Always Wanted to Know About Sex, but Were Afraid to Ask*. New York: D. McKay Co., 1969.

Stein, Marc. *City of Sisterly and Brotherly Loves: Lesbian and Gay Philadelphia, 1945–1972*. Chicago: University of Chicago Press, 2000.

Stern, Michael and Jane Stern. "Decent Exposure." *New Yorker*, March 19, 1990.

★ CHAPTER 16 ★

Aronowitz, Stanley. *False Promises: The Shaping of American Working Class Consciousness*. New York: McGraw-Hill, 1973.

Carter, Dan T. *The Politics of Rage: George Wallace, the Origins of the New Conservatism, and the Transformation of American Politics*. New York: Simon & Schuster, 1995.

Cutler, Jonathan. *Labor's Time: Shorter Hours, the UAW, and the Struggle for American Unionism*. Philadelphia: Temple University Press, 2004.

Freeman, Joshua B. "Hardhats: Construction Workers, Manliness, and the 1970 Pro-War Demonstrations." *Journal of Social History* 26 (1993): 725–744.

Jerome, Judson. *Families of Eden: Communes and the New Anarchism*. New York: Seabury Press, 1974.

Kazin, Michael. *The Populist Persuasion: An American History*. New York: Basic Books, 1995.

Lemke-Santangelo, Gretchen. *Daughters of Aquarius: Women of the Sixties Counterculture.* Lawrence, Kan.: University Press of Kansas, 2009.

Lichtenstein, Nelson. *The Most Dangerous Man in Detroit: Walter Reuther and the Fate of American Labor.* New York: Basic Books, 1995.

Malone, Bill C. *Country Music U.S.A.: A Fifty-Year History.* Austin: University of Texas Press, 1968.

Melville, Keith. *Communes in the Counter Culture: Origins, Theories, Styles of Life.* New York: Morrow, 1972.

Miller, Timothy. *The 60s Communes: Hippies and Beyond.* Syracuse: Syracuse University Press, 1999.

Owens, Virginia Stem. *Assault on Eden: A Memoir of Communal Life in the Early '70s.* Grand Rapids, Mich.: Baker Books, 1995.

Reich, Charles A. *The Greening of America.* New York: Random House, 1970.

Smith, Daniel A. *Tax Crusaders and the Politics of Direct Democracy.* New York: Routledge, 1998.

Willman, Chris. *Rednecks & Bluenecks: The Politics of Country Music.* New York: New Press, 2005.

Wolfe, Charles K. and James E. Akenson, eds. *Country Music Goes to War.* Lexington, Ken.: University Press of Kentucky, 2005.

Zicklin, Gilbert. *Countercultural Communes: A Sociological Perspective.* Westport, Conn.: Greenwood Press, 1983.

Permissions

★ CHAPTER 13 ★

A portion of this chapter is reprinted from the essay
"Beyonce Knowles, Freedom Fighter," which appeared on Salon.com:
http://www.salon.com/opinion/feature/2006/08/31/beyonce/.

★ CHAPTER 14 ★

A portion of this chapter is reprinted from
"The Color of Discipline: Civil Rights and Black Sexuality," American
Quarterly 60:1 (2008), 101–128. © 2008 American Studies Association.
Reprinted with permission of The Johns Hopkins University Press.

★ CHAPTER 16 ★

A portion of this chapter is reprinted from the essay
"Citizenship and the Problem of Desire in the
Postwar Labor and Civil Rights Movements,"
in *The Columbia History of Post-World War II America,*
Mark C. Carnes, ed. © 2007 Columbia University Press.
Reprinted with permission of the publisher.

★ ART ★

Fig. 02 (p. 117) Permission granted by MacBride Museum of Yukon History

Fig. 05 (p. 255) "You are the front" poster: Courtesy of Randall Bytwerk

Fig. 07 (p. 255) Hitler poster: Courtesy of Randall Bytwerk

Fig. 08 (p. 321) © Charles Moore/Black Star

Index

Page numbers in *italics* refer to illustrations.

★ ★ ★

Thaddeus Russell teaches history and American studies at Occidental College and has taught at Columbia University, Barnard College, Eugene Lang College, and The New School for Social Research. Born and raised in Berkeley, California, he graduated from Antioch College and received a Ph.D. in history from Columbia University. His first book, *Out of the Jungle: Jimmy Hoffa and the Remaking of the American Working Class*, was published by Alfred A. Knopf in 2001. He is a frequent contributor to *The Daily Beast*, and has published articles in *New York* magazine, the *Los Angeles Times*, *The Boston Globe*, *The Christian Science Monitor*, *Salon*, and *The Atlanta Journal-Constitution*, as well as scholarly essays in *American Quarterly* and *The Columbia History of Post–World War II America*. He has also appeared on the History Channel and *The Daily Show with Jon Stewart*.